China's Exchange Rate Regime

The imbalance between China's currency, the RMB, and those of other countries is widely regarded as a major problem for the world economy. There was a reform of China's exchange rate mechanism in 2005, following which the RMB appreciated 17 percent against the US dollar, but many people argue that further reform is still needed. This book reports on a major research project undertaken following the 2005 reform to assess the impact on China's economy. It considers the impact in a number of areas of the economy, including export-oriented companies, the banking industry, international trade, international capital flows, and China's macroeconomic policy. It concludes that the policies pursued so far have been correct, and that further reform, both to the exchange rate, and to the system overall, would be desirable, but that any reform should be gradual and incremental, preserving economic stability, and integrating changes with reform in other parts of the economy.

China Development Research Foundation is one of the leading economic think tanks in China, where many of the details of China's economic reform have been formulated. Its work and publications therefore provide great insights into what the Chinese themselves think about economic reform and how it should develop.

Routledge Studies on the Chinese Economy

Series Editor

Peter Nolan Director, Centre of Development Studies; Chong Hua Professor in Chinese Development; and Director of the Chinese Executive Leadership Programme (CELP), University of Cambridge

Founding Series Editors

Peter Nolan, University of Cambridge and Dong Fureng, Beijing University

The aim of this series is to publish original, high-quality, research-level work by both new and established scholars in the West and the East, on all aspects of the Chinese economy, including studies of business and economic history.

Routledge Studies on the Chinese Economy – Chinese Economists on Economic Reform

China's Exchange Rate Regime

China Development Research Foundation

Routledge
Taylor & Francis Group

LONDON AND NEW YORK

CDRF 中国发展研究基金会
China Development Research
Foundation

First published 2015 by Routledge

2 Park Square, Milton Park, Abingdon, Oxfordshire OX14 4RN
711 Third Avenue, New York, NY 10017

Routledge is an imprint of the Taylor & Francis Group, an informa business

First issued in paperback 2017

British Library Cataloguing in Publication Data
A catalogue record for this book is available from the British Library

Library of Congress Cataloging in Publication Data
China's exchange rate regime/China Development Research Foundation.
pages cm – (Routledge studies on the Chinese economy; 57)
Includes bibliographical references and index.
1. Foreign exchange rates – China. 2. Currency question – China.
3. Renminbi. 4. China – Economic policy – 2000- I. China Development
Research Foundation.
HG3978.C45 2014
332.4'560951—dc23
20140227741

ISBN: 978-1-138-81937-5 (hbk)
ISBN: 978-1-138-48159-6 (pbk)

Typeset in Times New Roman
by Swales & Willis Ltd, Exeter, Devon, UK

Contents

Figures

Tables

Contributors

Members of the research team

Team Leader: Lu Mai, Secretary General of the China Development Research Foundation

Deputy Leader: Tang Min, Deputy Secretary General of the China Development Research Foundation

Heads of individual projects

Zhang Xiaoji, Researcher of the Research Department of Foreign Economic Relations, Development Research Center of the State Council

Li Shantong, Researcher of the Research Department of Strategy and Regional Economy, Development Research Center of the State Council

Zhang Fan, Professor of the National School of Development, Peking University

Huang Yiping, Professor of the National School of Development, Peking University

Lian Ping, Chief Economist, Bank of Communications

Wen Jiandong, Researcher of the Balance of Payments Division, State Administration of Foreign Exchange

Zhang Bin, Researcher of the Institute of World Economics and Politics, Chinese Academy of Social Sciences

Official: Yu Jiantuo, Project Head of China Development Research Foundation

Heads of sub-projects, as well as all participants, took part in this endeavor as private individuals. Statements in this book do not represent the official views of the institutions in which individuals work.

Foreword

The exchange rate of a country represents the 'overall price' of its goods and assets relative to those of another country. Exchange-rate levels and the type of exchange-rate system adopted by a country have an all-encompassing effect on that country's economic development when it is operating under conditions of an open economy. What's more, adjustments to exchange rates are made in the context of highly complex international economic and political gamesmanship. As a 'price', the exchange rate of a country must preserve relative stability while also reflecting the actual situation of market supply and demand. Because of this, implementing a reasonable exchange-rate regime is highly important not only in determining the way resources are allocated, both at home and abroad, but in ensuring a favorable international environment.

In light of the importance of exchange-rate issues, the China Development Research Foundation decided to incorporate the subject into the organization's research plan. We realized that there was a paucity of research on the consequences of the 2005 reform, even though there had been plenty of discussion and writing on RMB exchange rates in general. Between July of 2005 and the end of 2009, the RMB appreciated 17 percent against the dollar, with the real effective exchange rate appreciating close to 16 percent. Theoretical analyses and suppositions had been put forward, but we realized that they should be tested by an actual assessment of policy. We therefore decided to start with an assessment of the impact of the 2005 exchange-rate system reform.

Our concept was supported and encouraged by Wang Mengkui, former Director of the State Council's Development Research Center and concurrently Director General of the China Development Research Foundation. Following on from this, the Office of the Director General approved the plan. In addition, the Deputy Governor of the People's Bank of China and Director of the State Administration of Foreign Exchange, Professor Yi Gang, extended his support and gave full attention to the project.

Our research drew a very positive response from professionals in the field. In January and April, 2010, the Foundation organized two forums for experts, on the basis of which a project team was drawn together. It included authorities and scholars from the Development Research Center of the State Council, Peking University, the Chinese Academy of Social Sciences, the State Administration of Foreign Exchange, and the Bank of Communications. By the end of October, 2010, these various people had completed seven outstanding reports.

The subjects of these reports and their project leaders were as follows: *Analysis of the impact of RMB exchange-rate adjustments on China's economy and national welfare* (Huang Yiping), *The impact of RMB exchange-rate appreciation on China's foreign trade* (Zhang Xiaoji), *The impact of RMB exchange-rate adjustments on enterprises and industries involved in foreign trade* (Zhang Fan), *An analysis of the effect of exchange-rate fluctuations on the banking industry* (Lian Ping), *Evaluating the real equilibrium exchange rate of the RMB* (Li Shantong), *China's strategy for reforming its RMB exchange-rate policy and macroeconomic policies in support of that strategy* (Wen Jiandong), and *An international comparison of exchange-rate policies in countries that have undergone economic transition* (Zhang Bin).

The China Development Research Foundation based its policy recommendations on the above research. It completed its summary report at the end of November, 2010, and submitted that report together with the policy recommendations.

All of the people participating in the research teams are outstanding authorities in their own fields. In the end, they came up with varying conclusions about the degree of exchange-rate imbalance in China, the extent to which it needs adjusting, and the methods for such adjusting. This was due to the ways the various fields of these authorities focused on different aspects of the issue, as well as to the differing perspectives that each brought to the subject and to their differences in methodology and data. After considerable internal discussion and exchange, however, some basic facts emerged relating to exchange-rate reform, and consensus was reached on a fundamental policy orientation.

Research conducted by the various teams made it quite clear that reforms of exchange-rate formation mechanisms undertaken since July, 2005 have had notable success. The negative impact of these reforms on the economy has been minimal, while reforms have moderated China's imbalance in international payments as well as imbalances in the exchange rate itself. Reforms served to clarify the direction in which upgrading of industrial structure must take place, and they provided a window of time for export-oriented industries to undertake such upgrading. This in turn allowed the banking industry to preserve a higher value of loan assets on its books.

Authorities involved in the research ultimately concluded that the policy China has adopted so far has been correct, that is, a policy of incremental change. A dramatic one-time appreciation of the RMB is both impossible and unnecessary. At present, what is needed is a genuine implementation of the system of a 'managed float with reference to a basket of currencies' in order to bring the RMB exchange rate back to equilibrium. This requires taking advantage of strategic timing, in terms of China's own economic situation and the situation internationally. It means employing small but swift adjustments. It also requires setting targets for adjusting the surplus in the current account and for any additional increment of foreign exchange reserves, as part of macroeconomic objectives. In addition, exchange-rate reform cannot charge forward in solitary fashion but must be accompanied by integrated reforms on many fronts. These include reform in the pricing of energy and natural resources, and reform of the systems governing environmental taxes and wages, among others.

During this entire endeavor, including the design process and actual research, a number of people have provided invaluable advice. They include Lu Feng, ZuoXiaolei, Wu Xiaoqiu, Ba Shusong, Ding Zhijie, Shi Jianhuai, Zhai Fan, Zhang Taowei, Gao Jingyi, Xing Ziqiang and Yang Changyong. All of the work of organizing the project was carried out by the China Development Research Foundation. At the Foundation, the head of the project was Yu Jiantuo, who also participated in research as well as the preparation of the final report.

Starting in 2007, the China Development Research Foundation established a fund to be used on policy research, known as the 'Development Research Fund.' Both enterprises and individuals have made contributions to this fund in recognition and support of the overall aims of the Foundation, while the Foundation itself decides on what topics to study. This year, Hang Lung Properties Limited, a Hong Kong company, and China International Capital Corporation Limited have contributed very generously, enabling the smooth completion of this project.

On behalf of the China Development Research Foundation, I would like to extend our sincere appreciation to all individuals and organizations that participated in and supported this endeavor. Thank you!

Lu Mai
Secretary General,
China Development Research Foundation
December 15, 2010

Preface

Assessing the results of reforming China's RMB exchange-rate formation system

Comprehensive reform of China's 'exchange-rate formation mechanism' was launched in 2005. The aim of this current endeavor is to assess the impact of that reform on economic activity in the country. We use a variety of sources to evaluate the subject, including business data at the enterprise level, customs statistics, and statistics from the banking industry. The focus is on measuring the effect of reform on a range of subjects: the production and operations of export-oriented companies, development of the banking industry, import and export trade, international capital flows, macroeconomics, and, finally, the degree to which China can use macroeconomic tools effectively.

In addition, the endeavor seeks to evaluate the 'real equilibrium exchange rate of the RMB' through the use of quantitative models. We integrate the exchange-rate reform experiences of such emerging and industrializing nations and regions as Japan, Germany, Korea, and Taiwan. We propose policy recommendations with respect to short-term exchange-rate adjustments, but also with respect to medium-term and long-term systemic reform.

Our endeavor has the following unique features. First, its evaluation came after the 2005 reform of the exchange-rate regime. Second, it is comprehensive and systematic in the way that it analyzes the impact of exchange-rate reform. From different levels, and on different scales of economic activity, it looks at the impact of reform on enterprises, industries, the banking industry, and macroeconomic performance. Third, the effort has been made to serve the purposes of formulating the *12th Five-Year Plan*, but also to meet the needs of future long-range planning with respect to reforming the national economic system. Fourth, our research has incorporated international comparisons in addition to a perspective on how to change China's overall economic structure.

Speech at the press conference announcing the presentation of this report

Six misconceptions in assessing RMB exchange-rate reform

Lu Mai

Secretary General of the China Development Research Foundation

"Respected Deputy Governor Yi Gang, colleagues, friends in the media:

Thank you very much for attending the press conference this afternoon, held to announce the results of the endeavor we have called, 'Assessing the impact of China's exchange-rate system reform.'

In a certain sense, the exchange rate of a country represents the 'overall price' of its goods and assets relative to those of another country. China's exchange-rate reform is getting considerable attention right now, which can be attributed to our own internal as well as external factors. In terms of our domestic situation, we are currently in the midst of restructuring our economy, changing our mode of economic growth. To do that, we must employ the ability of exchange rates, as a 'price,' to allocate resources. In terms of the international situation, two years ago China surpassed Germany to become the largest exporting nation on the globe. Last year, China surpassed Japan in becoming the world's second largest economy. The exchange rate of the RMB therefore has begun to have a certain impact on global trade and global economic growth. In the process, the RMB exchange rate has also often become the focal point of international economic and political gamesmanship.

In light of the importance of this subject, we decided to incorporate it into the research projects undertaken by the China Development Research Foundation. There has been a wealth of discussion and debate within China about RMB exchange rates. Nevertheless, despite the fact that the RMB appreciated against the dollar by 17 percent between July of 2005 and the end of 2009, with a real effective appreciation of nearly 16 percent, there has been no systematic, comparative, *ex post facto* assessment of China's policy. There has been no attempt to evaluate which theories, hypotheses, and analyses of the situation were correct, and which were not. We therefore decided to initiate our research by looking at the impact of the 2005 exchange-rate reform. We were supported in this by the former President of the State Council's Development Research Center, currently Chairman of the

China Development Research Foundation, Wang Mengkui. The Office of the Chairman later gave the project the stamp of approval.

Authorities in relevant fields were quite positive in their response to the proposal. In January and April of 2010, the Foundation organized two forums on the subject, out of which we organized a research team. I headed the team, with Tang Min serving as deputy. We set up seven supporting teams, researching various aspects of the issue. The heads of these were Researchers Zhang Xiaoji and Li Shantong from the Development Research Center of the State Council, Professors Huang Yiping and Zhang Fan from the National School of Development at Peking University, Chief Economist ProfessorLian Ping from the Bank of Communications, Researcher Wen Jiandong from the State Administration of Foreign Exchange, and Researcher Zhang Bin from the Institute of World Economics and Politics at the Chinese Academy of Social Sciences. Nearly twenty authorities and scholars from other countries also participated in the endeavor.

Team members who participated in the research were all outstanding professionals in their fields. As such, they came up with varying conclusions about the degree of exchange-rate imbalance in China, the extent to which it needed adjusting, and the methods for such adjusting. This was due to the way these authorities focused on different aspects of the issue, as well as to the differing perspectives that each brought to the subject and to their differences in methodology and data. After considerable internal discussion and exchange, however, some basic facts emerged relating to exchange-rate reform, and consensus was reached on a fundamental policy orientation. In addition, the project helped clarify six misconceptions of the subject which I would like to describe here.

> Misconception 1: The appreciation of the RMB is an international conspiracy aimed at limiting the economic competitiveness of China.

For smaller developing countries, there are benefits to maintaining an exchange rate that is slightly under-valued in order to help boost exports and maintain international competitiveness and economic growth. For a country such as China, however, the situation is different. China is a large country and the productivity of its labor force is rising rapidly. Under-valuing the currency over a long period is impossible. So long as China's productivity continues to rise faster than other economies, the appreciation of China's currency is unavoidable. To give an example: let's say that China and America both produce only a certain kind of jeans. At the outset, the price of those jeans in China is RMB 10, while the price in the United States is USD 1. Five years later, China's productivity has risen and jeans are sold in China at only RMB 5, whereas in America the price is still USD 1. By all rights, the RMB–USD exchange rate should have gone from ten to one to five to one. If it does not, then an American can pay one US dollar for two pairs of Chinese jeans. As for China, the country will have been able to dominate the US market for jeans and will have achieved a large export surplus, but the people of China will not have enjoyed the actual benefits of the country's rise in productivity. The example is simplified but relevant. In reality, distorted exchange rates can also lead to an imbalance of resources going into goods that are traded versus goods that are not traded. Distortions can impact the autonomy of the country's monetary policy. (There are many other ramifications) that I won't go into here.

Misconception 2: An appreciating currency will necessarily destroy export industries.

Our research team analyzed a large sample of corporate data on this subject. The actual results turned out to be precisely the opposite. As China's currency appreciated, it is true that some export-oriented enterprises went under, but over the entire period under study, China's net exports maintained a rapid rate of increase. There were several reasons for this. First, although exporting companies earn a relatively small margin on sales, they earn a relatively high margin on their capital. Their ability to withstand currency fluctuations has therefore been higher than many people at first assumed. Second, faced with the likelihood of currency fluctuations, many enterprises adopted risk-mitigation measures which helped reduce their costs. Third, for many companies with 'both ends overseas,' meaning they import materials from overseas markets and then sell finished products to overseas markets, the cost of exchange-rate fluctuations were easily absorbed internally. Fourth, and most fundamentally, (in the face of currency appreciation), export-oriented enterprises took timely measures to adjust the structure of products they were exporting, and regions to which they were selling. They accelerated the process of transforming themselves.

Misconception 3: Exchange-rate adjustments (appreciation of the currency) within China will cause material damage to China's ongoing stable economic growth.

In 2007 and 2008, the RMB appreciated by around 7 percent against the US dollar. According to the results of economic modeling, if this appreciation had not occurred, China's real GDP would have been around 0.28 percentage points higher. However, at the same time, the country's inflation rate would also have been higher, by 0.42 percentage points, and real wages would have declined by 0.07 percentage points. The current account surplus as a percentage of GDP would have risen by 0.28 percentage points. From a long-term perspective, change in the exchange rate improves the country's industrial structure and therefore is in fact beneficial to healthy economic growth in the long run.

Misconception 4: An incremental approach to exchange-rate reform is unworkable. It will lead to monetary policy that is necessarily 'acted upon' or involuntary, to uncontrollable inflation, and to asset bubbles.

In the course of an incremental approach to exchange-rate reform, money supply does in fact increase. Prices of consumer items and assets do indeed increase to a degree and within a certain scope. However, through such means as hedging by issuing notes and monitoring and controlling capital flows, China's central bank has been able to effectively handle these considerations over this past period. Doing these things enabled us to lay a solid foundation for countering the international financial crisis since the second half of 2008. At the same time, the experience made it clear that China can indeed be successful in carrying out an incremental style of exchange-rate reform. Moreover, China's manufacturing industry is at a critical juncture right now as it transforms and upgrades itself. Incremental exchange-rate reform has helped in clarifying the direction of this upgrading. It has provided manufacturing industries with a cushion, a margin of time in which to adjust.

> Misconception 5: Given the enormous quantity of foreign exchange reserves held by China, an appreciating currency will necessarily mean a tremendous loss in the value of those reserves.

Appreciation of the RMB will result in an exchange loss on the books to a degree. If the currency is not actually converted, however, such loss is carried only on the books and is not realized. The critical thing is to use our foreign exchange reserves wisely, in a way that is most beneficial to China's long-term benefit. That means purchasing assets with a high return, and purchasing consumable items that improve the people's welfare. Moreover, it has been our experience throughout the entire process of reform that we must look at the 'increment' and not just the 'overall volume.' In calculating losses, we should not just look at the massive quantity of assets held in foreign currencies, but we should see how the value of our country's tradable assets increases in value when our currency appreciates. What's more, if we maintain our current quantity of foreign-exchange reserve assets, without adding more, such losses as do occur can be offset by expansion of our total economic activity.

> Misconception 6: Exchange-rate reform carried out since 2005 has not had any fundamental effect on eliminating exchange-rate imbalances.

Since exchange-rate reform began in 2005, in fact the deviation of RMB exchange rates from the equilibrium level has seen marked improvement. Theoretically, there are many ways to measure the 'equilibrium' exchange rate and the results of applying different methods are not necessarily the same. In overall terms, however, we all recognize that the RMB is still undervalued relative to equilibrium. The extent of that underestimation, however, is less than 10 percent. Moreover, China's productivity rate is still rising rapidly. If certain things do not change, including the degree to which the country relies on trade, the percent of its investment relative to GDP, and the fact that the relative levels of domestic and foreign prices are not fundamentally different, then we can expect ongoing pressure on the RMB to appreciate, year by year.

(To sum up,) in evaluating all considerations, the team working on this project believes that the reform of China's exchange-rate formation mechanisms that began in 2005 has had a relatively minor negative impact on economic growth. It has in fact been beneficial in controlling inflation. Even more importantly, it has helped increase the percentage of service industries in the economy, helped stimulate the upgrading and restructuring of export industries, increased consumer spending, increased real wages of laborers, and stimulated growth in domestic markets. All of these were priority goals for the period of the *12th Five-Year Plan*, as we sought to accelerate the transformation in our mode of economic growth.

Based on the research described above, we recommend the following policy measures. We recommend these ten items not only with respect to policy in the *12th Five-Year Plan*, but with respect to the country's long-term reform of its exchange-rate system.

First, the long-term policy orientation of exchange-rate reform must be in the direction of a system that enables a freely floating currency. The aim is to achieve unrestricted conversion of the RMB. In the near-term and medium-term, we still must genuinely implement a system of a managed float, then gradually expand the band within which the RMB is allowed to fluctuate. We should gradually reduce the amount of the central bank's direct intervention in the overall level of exchange rates and in exchange-rate movements by fully utilizing the interbank foreign-exchange markets and changes in their RMB–USD rates.

Second, reform should adhere to the principles of being 'voluntary (or self-initiated), incremental, and controllable.' A one-time dramatic appreciation is neither feasible nor necessary.

Third, to genuinely implement a system that references a basket of currencies, we should gradually shift from a focus on the stability of bilateral exchange rates to one that aims for basic stability of multilateral rates (the 'real effective exchange rate'). This should be done to preserve the overall competitiveness of China's exports.

Fourth, adjustments to the exchange rate should ideally be done in a way that is in moderation, incremental, and well timed. Allowing the currency to appreciate should be done when both domestic and international situations are stable, when employment is fairly high and industry shows solid growth. It should take advantage of a time when the regulatory environment has clearly improved and when the international environment is relatively relaxed. If we wait, and then attempt to appreciate the currency when situations have intensified, both at home and abroad, we will not be able to act.

Fifth, (authorities) should set forth specific goals for controlling the surplus in China's current account. We should aim for having the surplus stay within 5 percent of GDP. On average, China's current accounts surplus has been 3.75 percent since 2003, but it exceeded 5 percent in 2006–2008 before falling back to around 5 percent at the end of 2009. With a little effort, the goal of 'within 5 percent' is achievable. In addition, it should be pointed out that it is unnecessary to maintain an excessive surplus in the current account, resulting in even higher foreign-exchange reserves, just for the sake of China's economic growth.

Sixth, we should achieve a basic balance between our current account and our international payments, by employing a variety of means. These would include increasing imports of foreign goods and advanced technology, increasing the purchase of overseas services that are high-quality (such as higher education services), reducing the number of companies allowed to list overseas that do not have a need for foreign exchange, liberalizing policy on allowing individuals to carry out direct investment overseas, expanding the number of qualified institutions within China that are allowed to make overseas financial investments, further relaxing the controls on placing funds abroad by loosening qualifying conditions and restrictions on amounts, loosening restrictions on overseas institutions that want to issue RMB-denominated bonds within China, and allowing the outward remittance of foreign exchange that has been purchased with domestic funds.

Seventh, we should establish objectives for controlling the increase of China's foreign-exchange reserves. By 2015, we should aim for a situation that basically will not allow for another dramatic increase in foreign-exchange reserves. At the same time, with respect to existing foreign-exchange reserves, we should seek to maintain their value. As the value of China's currency gradually appreciates, we want to ensure that the total volume of foreign-exchange-denominated assets does not continue to increase. By applying an incremental approach to RMB appreciation, so long as the aggregate amount of our foreign-exchange reserve assets does not continue to increase, we can absorb foreign-exchange asset losses through ongoing economic growth.

Eighth, we recommend that controls over short-term capital flows be strengthened and that the country curb speculative short-term capital inflows. This should be done in order to buy time for adjusting domestic policies and achieving exchange-rate reform. In the immediate future and over the medium term, we should adopt a system that administers controls over enterprises by categorizing them into different types of business. Those that are in foreign trade should be subject to more rigorous controls that verify the authenticity of their trade-related foreign-exchange settlements. We should strengthen controls over the use of foreign-currency denominated debt, and we should improve the effectiveness of our controls on foreign trade credit.

Ninth, we recommend that China take advantage of the lessons to be learned from other countries, specifically Japan and Germany, with respect to how they handled their exchange-rate policies in the past. We should avoid overly loose monetary policies or excessive financial-stimulus policies as a means of reducing the pressure to appreciate on our currency, since in the end these measures can lead to severe asset bubbles.

Tenth, in the process of economic restructuring during the *12th Five-Year Plan*, it is critical that we include exchange-rate reform in overall price reform measures. In the total 'basket' of policy measures, we must integrate exchange-rate reform with such other aspects as price reform, resource-tax reform, and wage-system reform, so that reform of one area will help propel reform of the others."

February 13, 2011

Summary of research results

Yu Jiantuo[1]

Reforming China's RMB exchange-rate system: substance and process

Introduction to the 2005 reform

On July 21, 2005, the People's Bank of China publicly announced that, from that day onward, it would be implementing a managed-float form of exchange-rate system. This would be based on market supply and demand, with adjustments made with reference to a basket of currencies. This reform complied with the principles of being voluntary or self-initiated, incremental, and controllable. The main objective of the reform was to set up a system that ensured that the RMB exchange rate would remain basically stable at reasonable and balanced levels, by creating a system that was a managed float based on market supply and demand (see Chapter 6 by Wen Jiandong).

First, instituting this system meant that the RMB exchange rate would no longer be solely pegged to the US dollar. Instead, a basket of currencies would be selected that gave an appropriate weighting to each currency included, in accordance with China's actual circumstances with respect to foreign economic relations. The composition of the basket would take into consideration not only foreign trade but would also integrate such things as external debt (interest), foreign direct investment in China (dividends), and so on. It would incorporate the major trading partners of the country, both countries and regions, and their currencies. The selection of currencies to be included in the basket, and the weightings to be given to each, mainly took the following four factors into consideration. First, primary consideration was given to trade in goods and services as the basic determination for selection and weightings of currencies. Second, appropriate consideration was given to the currency composition of foreign debt. Third, appropriate consideration was given to factors relating to foreign direct investment in China. Fourth, among considerations with respect to the weighting, revenues and expenditures from uncompensated transfer items in the current account were also taken into account. Finally, making adjustments to the RMB exchange rate with reference to a basket of currencies was not to be considered the same thing as 'pegging' the RMB to a basket of currencies. Market supply and demand was also relied upon in order to form a 'managed float.'

Second, instituting the system involved a staged process of reforming the benchmark exchange rate, the trading rate, and the quoted rate or nominal rate, as price controls were relaxed. In general, the system works as follows. At the end of each day, once markets are closed, the People's Bank of China announces the closing prices of the US dollar and all other currencies traded against the RMB in the interbank foreign-exchange market. This then becomes the 'central parity rate' for each currency for the start of trading the next day. After July 21, 2005, the exchange rate of the US dollar against the RMB was maintained within a band that was within 0.3 percent above and below the USD–RMB central parity rate, announced by the People's Bank of China, whereas the rates of other currencies were allowed to float in a band that was expanded from 1 percent above and below the central parity rate to 1.5 percent above and below that rate. Banks handled US-dollar exchange transactions of customers in a 'symmetrical way' at a rate of 0.2 percent above and below the USD–RMB central parity rate for cash, and 1 percent for non-cash. They handled non-US dollar exchange transactions by controlling the spread between buying and selling prices around the quoted or nominal rate. Since prices for buying and selling non-USD currencies did not need to maintain a symmetrical relationship to the quoted or nominal rate, banks could now offer flexible pricing of these currencies to their customers. They no longer were bound by the previous system of one fixed price per day.

Third, starting at 7 pm on July 21, 2005, the US dollar rose by 2 percent against the RMB in a 'one-time, small-scale' appreciation. The rate became USD 1 to RMB 8.11. This new rate then became the central parity rate for interbank foreign-exchange transactions among designated 'foreign-exchange banks' the following day. Designated banks could then adjust the rates they quoted to their customers. The extent of this appreciation of the RMB was mainly determined by the degree of China's favorable balance of trade at the time and the need to restructure. At the same time, it took into consideration the adaptability of China's enterprises to such restructuring.

Once the basic framework for this reform was established, in July of 2005, further adjustments to the exchange-rate formation mechanisms of the country were made in September of 2005, January of 2006, and May of 2005, as follows.

In September of 2005, the range within which non-USD currencies could float against the RMB on any given day was broadened. Originally set at 1.5 percent, the band was now expanded to 3 percent. At the same time, the way in which banks handled both cash and non-cash exchange transactions for US dollars with customers was modified. The previous 'symmetrical way' of handling floating limits, set at 0.2 percent around central parity for cash and at 1 percent for non-cash, was now changed to a limit on the spread between buying and selling prices. For cash, the limit was 1 percent and for non-cash it was 4 percent. For bank transactions involving non-USD currencies, limits on quoted-price spreads were eliminated altogether.

In January of 2006, further modifications were made to the price-formation method of deriving the central parity price. On January 4, 2006, the spot foreign-exchange markets introduced a mode of 'inquiry' trading. Authorized members of interbank foreign-exchange markets could, at their own discretion, decide to trade on the basis of an inquiry or on a competitive bid. This increased the flexibility of the market. In addition, a market-making system was officially introduced for RMB trades against foreign currencies in order to increase liquidity. The 'market maker' provided a continuous declared price to both buyers and sellers in the market which ensured that the market was liquid. By regulation, the China Foreign Exchange Trading Center was required to request prices from each market maker in the interbank system every day, prior to the start of trading. All quotations from market makers then were taken into consideration in calculating the RMB–USD central parity rate for the day. This was done by eliminating both the highest and the lowest prices, and then giving a weighted average to the remaining market-maker quotations. The China Foreign Exchange Trading Center determined the weighting of each market maker by considering the volume of trades it conducted, in addition to its price quotations and other indicators. Each designated foreign-exchange bank then formulated its own buying and selling prices for currencies, based on the parity price and in accordance with the regulations on floating limits as set by the People's Bank of China.

In May of 2007, the band within which the RMB exchange rate could float against the US dollar was further expanded. The degree to which the RMB exchange-rate is market-driven was increased by expanding the daily allowed volatility of RMB exchange rates. Starting on May 21, 2007, the band for spot trades in the interbank market went from a limit of 0.3 percent above and below parity to a limit of 0.5 percent. That is, from that day onward, the RMB-USD interbank spot rate could fluctuate by fifty-one-thousandths above and below the price publicly announced by the China Foreign Exchange Trading Center.

In 2008, the subprime-loan crisis in the United States gradually evolved to become a global financial and economic crisis. From July of 2008 until June of 2010, the band within which the RMB was allowed to float was again restricted and the exchange rate returned to a *de facto* pegged-rate system. In June of 2010, as world economic recovery continued and international expectations regarding the RMB exchange rate began to stabilize, and as China's imbalance in international payments declined somewhat, reform of China's exchange-rate formation mechanisms could once again be resumed.

Trends in the RMB exchange rate after initiating reforms

After reforms were initiated in 2005, the rate at which the RMB traded against the US dollar can be divided into three general stages. The first lasted from July of 2005 to June of 2008. During this period, the RMB in overall terms appreciated gradually against the US dollar. The speed of this appreciation was faster between the second half of 2007 and the first half of 2008, during which periods it appreciated by 4.26 per cent and 6.5 per cent (see Chapter 6 by Wen Jiandong). The second stage lasted from July of 2008 until June of 2010. During this period, the range within which the RMB was allowed to fluctuate was restricted and the RMB traded between 6.82 and 6.84 to the dollar, which was a *de facto* return to a peg against the dollar (Wen Jiandong, Chapter 6). The third stage, which lasted from June of 2010 until now, saw the RMB appreciate in general terms as reforms

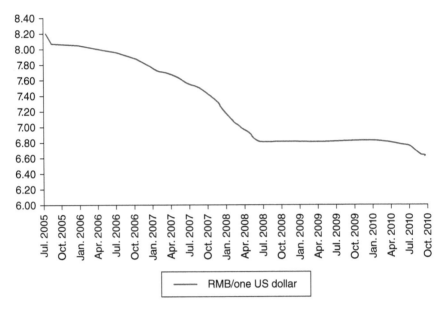

Figure 0.1 Trend line of the RMB–USD exchange rate after the start of the 2005 reform.

Source: State Administration of Foreign Exchange.

were resumed. The speed at which the RMB appreciated was most pronounced between the start of September and the middle of October, 2010. At present, the central parity rate of the RMB against the US dollar is at a general level of 6.6 (see Figure 0.1). By November of 2010, counting from the start of reform in 2005, the RMB had appreciated by 19 percent against the US dollar.

The month of July, 2008, can be seen as a dividing line in terms of the exchange rate between the RMB and the Japanese yen and the Euro. Up until that time, the RMB had gradually and slowly been depreciating against these currencies – with respect to the yen, there was first a stable appreciation and then a slow depreciation. Overall, volatility was low. After July of 2008, the RMB resumed a *de facto* peg against the US dollar given the instability in the international economic situation. With the relatively large volatility of the dollar against other currencies, volatility in the RMB rates vis-à-vis the yen and Euro increased substantially as well. Starting in the second half of 2009, the RMB–yen rate gradually resumed greater stability and tended in the direction of depreciation, while the Euro was different. Given the outbreak of the sovereign debt crisis in the Eurozone at the beginning of 2010, the RMB began appreciating rapidly against the Euro in the second half of 2010 (see Figure 0.2).

The effective exchange rate of the RMB is the weighted rate against various currencies. From the start of reform until March of 2009, both the 'nominal exchange rate' and the 'real effective exchange rate' of the RMB showed an appreciating trend – the nominal rate appreciating by 25 percent and the real effective rate appreciating by 22 percent. This appreciation was most pronounced

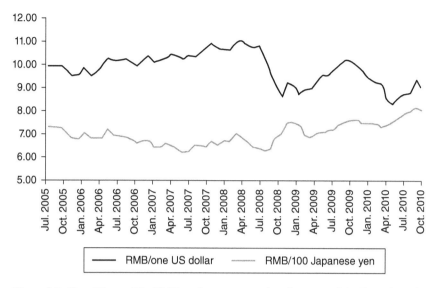

Figure 0.2   Trend lines of the RMB exchange rate against the yen and the Euro since the start of the 2005 reform.

Source: State Administration of Foreign Exchange.

from January of 2008 until January of 2009. Starting in the second quarter of 2009, until January of 2010, both the nominal and the real effective exchange rates dropped back by around 10 percent. In the first half of 2010, the effective exchange rate began a slow appreciation (see Figure 0.3). By the end of September, 2010, the nominal RMB rate had appreciated by 12.75 percent and the effective rate had appreciated by 20.12 percent.

Two points should be noted in looking at the trend of the effective RMB exchange rate. Prior to 2007, the discrepancy between the nominal and real effective rates was relatively small. In the second half of 2007, however, inflationary pressures within China began to be more apparent and the difference between the two rates became quite clear, although price movements in the two moved basically in the same direction. Second, between July and September of 2010, the real effective exchange rate of the RMB appreciated markedly while the nominal rate showed a depreciating trend. This was an indication of worsening inflation in the second half of 2010.

Changes in the RMB exchange rate against a basket of currencies, since the start of reform in 2005.

One important element in the exchange-rate reform of 2005 was creating a mechanism that adjusted the RMB rate with reference to a basket of currencies (although not a peg). Since the People's Bank of China did not reveal the composition of the basket of currencies, however, or the weighting of the currencies, it was difficult for people

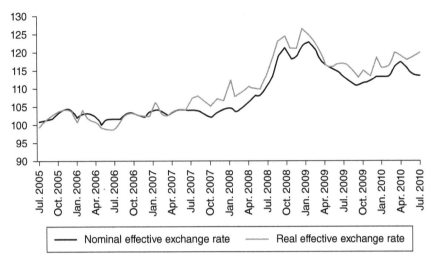

Figure 0.3 Changes in the nominal and real effective exchange rates of the RMB.

Source: BIS.

to use any direct way to judge the actual extent of reform in the RMB exchange-rate formation mechanisms. Nevertheless, some economists were able to use indirect methods to infer the composition of the basket, and the weighting of currencies, by evaluating RMB rates against the currency fluctuations of major currencies.

In a regression analysis done by Frankel (2009), the only currencies considered were the US dollar, the Euro, and the yen. The results of his analysis indicated that the weighting of the US dollar was kept at 93 percent to 100 percent from the start of reform until June of 2006. Between July and September of 2006, the weighting dropped to around 90 percent but then went back up to 93 percent to 100 percent starting in October. From July of 2007 until February of 2008, reform of the RMB exchange-rate formation mechanism was accelerated as the weighting of the US dollar declined to below 80 percent. After March of 2008, however, the dollar again went up to a weighting of over 95 percent. Guo Jin (2009) also evaluated the weighting of currencies in the basket and felt that, while the Euro and the yen were indeed a part of the equation, the US dollar remained dominant. He felt that the dollar could explain 93.5 percent of RMB currency fluctuations, while the Euro and the yen contributed less than 1.2 percent.

Assessing the impact of reforming the RMB exchange-rate system

The effect of currency fluctuations on China's economy

The effects of currency fluctuations on an economy are an issue of general equilibrium. They must be looked at from an overall macroeconomic perspective. We therefore have to adopt an analytical framework that employs general equilibrium in order to evaluate the economic impact of exchange-rate changes. Before discussing such an analytical framework in general, we should confirm consensus on three important conditions. First, exchange rates are a 'price' variable. Second, exchange rates have to be analyzed from a dynamic perspective. Third, China is a major economy, and recognizing this is important in understanding the dynamics between its economy and its exchange rates (see Chapter 1, by Huang Yiping and Tao Kunyu).

Within the framework of a major economy, and a dynamic general equilibrium, the question then becomes, 'What impact do exchange-rate changes have on macroeconomic variables?' Huang Yiping and others looked at this subject by using historical data and the Oxford Economic Forecasting model (OEF). They assumed an appreciation of the RMB against the dollar of 5 percent per year over a period of five years, in analyzing the elasticity of the response of specific economic indicators to exchange rate movements (see Table 0.1).

What their analysis indicates is that an appreciating RMB has only a modest negative impact on China's overall economy. When the RMB appreciates against the US dollar by 5 percent, China's real GDP declines by only 0.2 percentage points over the short term (one year), and it declines by only 0.1 percentage points over the long term. Investment in fixed assets declines by 0.4 percent over the short term and by 0.15 percent over the long term. Industrial productivity declines by 0.2 percent over the short term and by 0.1 percent over the long term. Employment declines by 0.15 percent over the short term and 0.05 percent over the long term. The 'fiscal balance' as a percentage of GDP declines by 0.1 percent over the short term and has no effect at all over the long term. From looking at the elasticity of these economic variables with respect to exchange-rate changes, the negative impact of appreciation is seen to be greater in the short term than it is in the long term.

The results of the simulation analysis described above show that currency appreciation is actually beneficial in stimulating economic restructuring. According

Table 0.1 Short-term and long-term elasticity of macroeconomic indicators with respect to exchange rate movements

	Short-term elasticity (1 year)	*Long-term elasticity (5 year)*
Real GDP	0.04	0.02
Consumer spending	0.02	−0.01
Fixed-asset investment	0.08	0.03
Industrial production	0.04	0.02
Employment	0.03	0.01
Inflation	0.06	0.09
Real wages	−0.01	−0.03
Current account (% of GDP)	0.04	0.06
Fiscal balance (% of GDP)	0.02	0.00

Source: Huang Yiping and Tao Kunyu, Chapter 1.

to the model, if the RMB appreciates against the dollar by 5 percent, consumer spending declines by 0.1 percent in the short run but increases by 0.5 percent in the long run. Real wages of laborers increase by 0.05 percent in the short term and by 0.15 percent in the long term. This is significant, and positive, when it comes to our immediate attempts to lift the wages of workers and increase consumption. In addition, the simulation analysis also makes it clear than an annual appreciation in the RMB of 5 percent helps reduce the current account as a percentage of GDP. In the short term, that figure is reduced by 0.2 percent, and in the long term it goes down by 0.3 percent. Annual appreciation of the RMB by 5 percent reduces inflation by 0.3 percent in the short run and by 0.45 percent in the long run.

The effect of exchange-rate adjustments on international capital flows

Overall, exchange-rate reform has not significantly affected the long-term influx of capital into China. In the short-term, it also has not been able to stem capital inflows by altering the expectation of earnings through both interest-rate differentials and RMB appreciation (see Huang Yiping and Tao Kunyu, Chapter 1).

Adjustments to the RMB exchange rate have had a relatively minor effect on foreign investment coming into China and other kinds of long-term capital.

Raising exchange rate levels (allowing the RMB to appreciate) has not in fact lessened the inflow of such long-term forms of capital as direct foreign investment. This is mainly because of China's strong performance in terms of economic growth, and the fact that input prices are kept low through systemic distortions. These considerations ensure that foreign investment can still make a high return inside China. Meanwhile, ongoing foreign demand for goods ensures a ready market, providing further incentive for foreign businesses to invest (see Figure 0.4).

Short-term capital flows are mainly influenced by interest-rate differentials and the expectation of an appreciating RMB

Monthly cross-border short-term capital inflows can be represented by the difference between China's trade surplus and its foreign-exchange surplus. Every one percentage point in the differential between US and Chinese interest rates can have the effect of increasing monthly short-term capital flows into China of USD 440 million, which means an annual increase of USD 5.28 billion in capital flowing into China.

If the discount for forward NDF contracts of the RMB against the US dollar increases, that means that the RMB is appreciating. For every 1,000 basis points added to the NDF rate, cross-border short-term capital coming into China may increase by USD 650 million per month or USD 7.8 billion a year (see Wen Jiandong, Chapter 6).

(Note to reader: NDF stands for 'Non-deliverable forward.' This type of foreign-currency financial derivative contract is used as a means to hedge exchange-rate risk

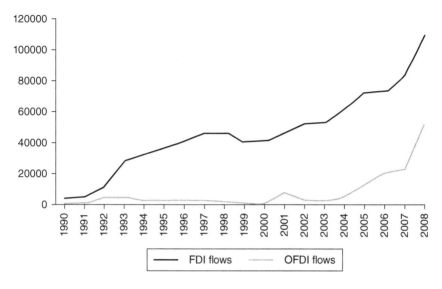

Figure 0.4 Foreign direct investment within China and China's own foreign direct
investment in other countries.
(Unit: USD million)

Source: www.cei.gov.cn database

for non-convertible currencies. There is no physical settlement of the two currencies
at maturity. Instead, a net cash settlement is made by one party to another based on
the movement of the two currencies. (From the Financial Times Lexicon.))

Differentials in returns on stock markets inside China and outside China have
very little effect on cross-border capital flows. This is yet another indication that
China's existing capital controls do have the effect of restricting international
money flowing between domestic and foreign stock markets. International capital
cannot make investment decisions based on the relative yields of markets (Wen
Jiandong, Chapter 6).

The share of capital inflows into China that is held by investments in the more
volatile stock and bond markets, as well as lending by foreign banks, is not in fact
very great. This category includes investments with a maturity of one year or less in
the balance of payments register. It includes money market instruments in the sphere
of financial securities, and it includes both illicit and hidden short-term movements
of international capital (those that are off the balance of payments register). These
things are more driven by the spread between domestic and foreign interest rates and
by the ongoing expectation of an appreciating RMB (Huang Yiping and Tao Kunyu,
Chapter 1). Nevertheless, one cannot exclude the possibility that some short-term
capital comes into China through the avenue of trade credit and through current
accounts (this would include the misreporting or overstating of export quantities).

A strengthening currency helps China expand the scope of its foreign direct
investment abroad. A stronger RMB also helps spur the restructuring of the

domestic economy. Once exchange-rate reform was initiated in 2005, the increase in China's overseas foreign direct investment was quite apparent – on average, overseas investments increased by 70 percent per year. The annual volume of such investment went from USD 5.5 billion in 2008 to USD 52.15 billion in 2008.

The impact of exchange-rate movements on China's import
and export trade

As much as 60 percent of China's economy relies on foreign trade, a figure that is fairly high among major economies. The main reason for this is that China serves as the 'assembly and processing' link in the international supply chain. The country's 'processing trade' business involves a tremendous importing and re-exporting of goods, which often leads to duplicated statistics. This phenomenon also exists in the North American Free Trade Area, with goods going in and out of Canada and Mexico. Since American companies conduct processing trade near the borders of each country, the extent to which these two countries have open trade also exceeds 60 percent. In addition, although China adopted a whole series of measures that would help foreign entities increase imports into the country once China had joined the World Trade Organization, multinational companies did not in fact modify their market strategies to any great extent. They remained dedicated to serving their already established markets. The State Council's Development Research Center conducted a survey of foreign investors on this subject. The scale of China's market might appear to make it the number one choice in terms of where to expand investment, yet the majority of enterprises felt that China's market was already consumed by the intense competition among local companies (Zhang Xiaoji, Chapter 2).

Exchange-rate movements have indeed had a certain effect on China's exporting enterprises and their target markets. Before the financial crisis erupted, the US dollar index was consistently low. The trade-weighted RMB appreciation rate was lower than the appreciation of the RMB against the US dollar alone. Once the RMB began to appreciate in value, the rate at which China's exports to the United States were rising began to slow down. During the same period, the Euro strengthened. As a result, not only are Chinese exports to the Eurozone increasing faster than they are to the United States and Japan, but they are increasing faster than Chinese exports to the rest of the world.

Overall, despite an appreciating RMB, rapid growth in Chinese exports has not experienced any kind of fundamental turnaround. Reasons for that are as follows (see Zhang Xiaoji, Chapter 2).

1 The division of labor in global manufacturing is uneven, which has led to a long-term imbalance or unevenness in the international economic structure.

China's surplus in its balance of trade comes primarily from trade with the United States and Europe. In contrast, China has a huge trade deficit with Japan, Korea, and the ASEAN countries, and it also has long-term trade deficits with such resource-exporting countries as Australia and Brazil. These things reflect the trade relationships of the global supply chain. East Asia is a base for producing and exporting manufactured goods whereas Europe and the United States are importers of those goods. After shifting their own manufacturing production overseas, they have been importing more to the extent that they have become the largest target market for East Asia. In this whole process, China has become the processing center of the supply chain. Much of its trade surplus derives from the surplus that other countries and regions shifted over to the country.

2   The 'WTO-entry effect' has been under-estimated in terms of judging its impact on China's exports.

The production potential of China's export sectors was 'released' once China entered the WTO. Heavy-industry production also expanded to the extent that trade deficits in such things as steel, automobiles, and spare parts turned into surpluses. In addition to these domestic factors, once China had entered the WTO and the trade environment stabilized, multinational corporations began to shift their processing industries to the country, while importers in other countries also began to place orders with Chinese enterprises due to China's relatively high efficiency in supplying goods. In a survey that the United States International Trade Commission conducted on the subject, most respondents declared that they would place orders in China once quota restrictions were ended, despite the possibility that China's costs might be higher than other supplying nations. The reason was that these other nations could not match China's production capacity and production efficiency.

3   China's exporting is dominated by foreign investment, which limits the impact of an appreciating RMB.

Some 55 percent of China's exports actually come from foreign-funded enterprises within China. In addition to this, close to 50 percent of all exports are composed of 'processed' or 'value-added' goods, due to the dominant 'processing-trade mode' of China's export business. China's trade surplus comes primarily from this processing trade (see Figure 0.5). If one takes both of these factors into consideration, namely foreign investment and the country's processing trade, some two-thirds of all exports are dominated or controlled by multinational companies. Given the exporting entity and the exporting model, companies that export out of China are in fact 'cost centers' of multinational companies. In addition, given that China's position in the global supply chain is at the 'assembly' level, the impact of an appreciating RMB is easily absorbed by the internal trade of such multinational companies.

4   The century's first 'commodity-goods boom' erupted during the period under study.

The long period over which this 'boom' has been sustained, the broad range of items that have been included, and the breadth of their prices have meant that one could declare this the 'greatest boom' in the past fifty years. The boom erupted under the influence of a number of factors which have included supply and demand, (positive) financial expectations, and various macroeconomic considerations.

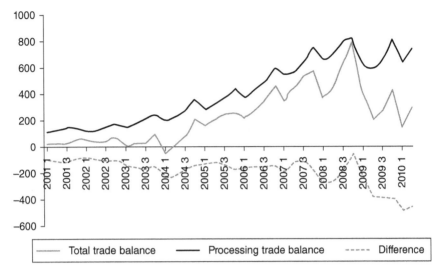

Figure 0.5   The surplus in processing trade items has been greater than the surplus in
trade items overall.
Unit: USD 100 million

Source: China Customs statistics.

5   The influence of China's domestic business (economic) cycle

China's economy entered another round of economic expansion starting in 2003.
At that point, investment began to overheat and credit increased at a somewhat
overly fast rate. Industrialization as characterized by 'oil plus steel,' and urbanization as characterized by 'rebar plus automobiles plus cement' supported rapid
expansion of China's steel, petrochemical, automobile, and building materials
industries. Since macroeconomic controls have not been able to get this expansion
under control, production capacity turns to overseas markets when possible. That
is, when a buying boom ('commodity goods boom') starts overseas, the productive capacity already formed among China's domestic industries begins to shift
toward exports.

6   The pricing of China's natural resources is not rational (it has not been properly straightened out), which leads to the phenomenon of a resource drain as well as the loss of public welfare.

The government plays an improper role in determining input factor prices.
Examples would be under-pricing land in order to attract investment, not charging
(industry) any price at all to use water resources, or just a small water-resource fee.
They would include supplying energy (to industries) at prices that are lower than
the international market price, and they would include the lack of environmental

protection measures that are strong enough to have any effect. They would include extending preferential tax treatment to exporting enterprises, and not enforcing the Labor Law in an adequately rigorous way. Government control over such critical factors as capital, oil, and electricity has already led yet again to the phenomenon of 'upside-down prices' or price inversion between domestic and overseas markets. Under open-economy conditions, relying on such subsidies to ensure low export prices can result in the outflow of a country's resources.

To sum up, an accurate appraisal of the effect of RMB appreciation has to take the overall domestic and international context into account. On the one hand, one should not underestimate the role of exchange rates in regulating China's international balance of payments just because of certain unique factors. On the other hand, one must recognize that exchange rates are only one of many factors affecting trade. Adjustments to the RMB rate that are modest and incremental are insufficient to shift international production in the short run, or the larger trends of supply and demand relationships in domestic and international markets (see Zhang Xiaoji, Chapter 2).

The impact of exchange-rate movements on export-oriented enterprises

Using a large-sample statistical analysis, the project team headed by Zhang Fan evaluated the effect of exchange-rate movements on the exports of and profitability of export-oriented enterprises. The sample included both State-Owned Enterprises and non-State Owned Enterprises whose output value (revenues) exceeded RMB 5 million. Between 2000 and 2008, the team analyzed 110,000 to 350,000 sample enterprises. Looking at the results of quantitative analysis, descriptive analysis, and the classic style of interviews, it was clear that the negative impact of the appreciation of the RMB in 2005 on export-oriented companies was less than had been anticipated (see Zhang Fan and Yu Miaojie, Chapter 3).

The results of the quantitative analysis were as follows. Empirical analysis of 180,000 enterprises over a certain designated size showed that export sales dropped by roughly 0.2 percentage points for every 1 percent rise in the value of the RMB, but the profit margin on the sales rose by 0.01 percent.[2] Currency appreciation therefore had a positive impact both on the terms of trade and on improving industrial structure.

The results of the descriptive analysis were as follows. The export structure of the sample study of enterprises showed that exports as a percentage of sales first rose, then fell. Exports as a percentage of sales peaked in 2004, before beginning a sustained decline. To a degree, this reflected the adjustments made by enterprises as the RMB appreciated, in terms of the amounts they exported versus the amounts they sold domestically. Meanwhile, the percentage of total output value held by export-oriented industries also first rose during this period, then began to fall. This reflected the way China's enterprises adjusted to changes in their operating environments, and restructured their approach to domestic versus international markets. As a natural response, they began to shift from overseas markets in the direction of domestic markets. The shift was unrelated to the way

China's domestic industry turned toward more heavy industries and chemical industries in the first part of the twenty-first century. Looking at specific industries and their changing percentage of total output value: the industries that had the greatest changes among export-oriented businesses were the electric and electronics industries, pharmaceuticals, and textiles. Taking the first three as one category, and textiles as a second category, each category held close to 30 percent of total output in 2000. The percentage of the first category then started to increase, exceeding 50 percent in 2007, while the percentage of the textile category fell to below 15 percent. This demonstrated that there had been a clear restructuring among export-oriented industries.

The results of (interviews conducted during) field surveys showed the following. Although profit margins of many exporting industries were only 3 percent in terms of sale of goods, their return on capital exceeded 10 percent. This gave these industries resilience in the face of an appreciating currency. Moreover, in the period between 2005 and 2008, China's export-oriented enterprises by and large took measures and anticipated the effect of the appreciation on their profitability. Primary measures included renegotiating prices, lowering internal cost structures, changing the percent of inputs that were imported versus those sourced domestically, and so on. Some enterprises also used financial tools to hedge against currency risk and lock in rates, although they are not as yet adept at the procedures.

The effect of currency appreciation on the banking industry

The effect of RMB currency changes on the quality of
assets in bank portfolios.

The project team headed by Lian Ping conducted empirical analysis on fourteen of China's publicly listed banks. They looked at statistics on these banks in the years between 2005 and 2010. Their overall conclusion was that the appreciation of the RMB did not have a notable effect on the quality of loans in the bank's portfolios (see Research Group, Research Center, Bank of Communications, Chapter 4). In their quantitative model, the negative regression coefficient of the exchange-rate variables did indicate the potential for a negative impact of currency appreciation on loan quality, but it was statistically insignificant. During the period under study, the world's economy overall grew at a relatively fast pace prior to the financial crisis; after the crisis, once the global economy sank into recession, foreign demand still remained the primary factor affecting China's exports. Given that the RMB appreciation was not so very large, currency changes did not noticeably affect exporting industries and therefore the quality of loan assets in banks was also not greatly affected.

Among the three variables that have a marked effect on the non-performing loan ratio of banks, the most important is the bank's level of credit supervision, that is, the effort a bank puts into credit supervision. This is most important in terms of the absolute numbers of a bank's balance sheet. For every single unit of change in those efforts, or that level of supervision, there is a corresponding 0.6 percent change in the level of non-performing loans. The total volume of loans being made is secondary in importance when it comes to evaluating non-performing loans. For every single unit of change in the total volume of loans, there is a corresponding change in the level of non-performing loans that has been measured at -7.83×10^{-7} units. The third variable affecting the non-performing loan ratio of banks is real GDP. The impact of this variable is quite clear, but still less than the preceding two variables. For every single unit of change in real GDP, there is a corresponding change in the level of non-performing loans that has been measured at -2.87×10^{-7} units.

The effect of RMB exchange-rate changes on banking-related businesses

Exchange-rate adjustments can have an effect on a variety of banking-related businesses as described below. These include credit, finance, foreign-exchange deposits and lending, international settlements, and the overseas branch businesses of banks (see Research Group, Research Center, Bank of Communications, Chapter 4).

1 **The impact of RMB appreciation on credit.** The impact will be unfavorable on certain industries, including those that rely heavily on exports, that don't have the capacity to set their own prices, and that are in import-substitution type businesses. It will also have an adverse effect on industries that have taken in substantial amounts of speculative overseas capital. On the other hand, it may benefit other industries, including those that sell more on the domestic market, those that rely heavily on imported materials, those with large foreign-exchange liabilities, and some consumer-type industries such as tourism and retail.

2 **The impact of RMB appreciation on finance.** On the one hand, an appreciating RMB, and also the expectation of further appreciation, will lead to decisions to change out of foreign currencies back into RMB. This will be unfavorable for those businesses dealing in foreign-exchange-denominated wealth management and other businesses that are derived from foreign exchange. On the other hand, an appreciating RMB will bring the issue of exchange-rate risk into clearer focus for companies that import and export, who will now be more proactive in adopting risk-mitigation measures. All of this will provide tremendous space for business development among commercial banks that act as intermediaries. It will increase the share of their income that is not related to interest rate spreads, and so will accelerate a shift in their mode of operations.

3 **The impact of RMB appreciation on foreign-exchange deposits and lending.** As expectations of an appreciating RMB strengthen, there will also be increasing pressure on the banking industry to deal with liquidity problems. People's willingness to hold foreign exchange will drop. The demand for loans that are denominated in US dollars, and the demand for trade financing denominated in dollars, will sharply increase with the opportunities for arbitraging the dollar. These will exacerbate the shortage of foreign-exchange funding within the country. At the end of July, 2010, the ratio between foreign-exchange loans and foreign-exchange deposits was as high as 190 percent, which put increasing pressure on banks to handle their foreign-exchange

liquidity. In terms of foreign-trade financing, the expectation of an appreciating RMB is leading to increased demand by customers for import financing.

4 **The impact of RMB appreciation on international settlements.** To a certain degree, an appreciating RMB is constraining the amount of China's export of both goods and labor and therefore also constraining the ability of export industries to create foreign-exchange earnings. The decline in foreign-exchange receipts in turn impacts the international settlements business as related to exports. On the other hand, an appreciating RMB also lowers prices on imports which in turn increases demand for imported goods and labor among China's enterprises. This in turn increases foreign-exchange payments by those enterprises and increases the amount of international settlements business related to imports.

The impact of an appreciating RMB on international settlements business varies with the structure of business. At present, world trade is a 'buyer's market.' The ability of customers or buyers to set prices in international markets is increasing, which means they can stretch payment terms out over a longer period. For example, they can open relatively long-term letters of credit which lowers their operating costs. Second, given that expectations of an appreciating RMB are ongoing, customers' demand for NDF (Non-Deliverable Forward contracts) increases, given that there are short-term-loan quota limitations on this type of agency business. This leads to a rapid increase in the growth of the import factoring business. Third, given that profit margins are relatively low for China's exporting enterprises, as well as its overseas contracting businesses, an appreciating RMB has a fairly large impact on profitability and corporate results, with a commensurate negative impact on settlement business for export-type businesses. However, ongoing RMB appreciation can also lead to greater demand for cross-border settlements in RMB. RMB-based import factoring, RMB-denominated import letters of credit, and RMB-denominated settlement financing portfolios, can all help customers hedge against exchange-rate risk and provide them with arbitrage opportunities.

5 **The impact of RMB appreciation on the overseas branch businesses of banks.** Appreciation of the RMB brings new opportunities to the overseas branches of Chinese banks. First, it stimulates greater imports into China, which provides relatively large potential for increasing trade settlement business. Second, it enables China-invested enterprises to increase their overseas investments and to accelerate the pace of their becoming 'international.' It enables their overseas subsidiaries to carry out more financing. Third, given an appreciating RMB, the desire to hold RMB in the Hong Kong region increases which enables China's government to increase the scope of RMB business in Hong Kong.

6 **The degree to which reforming China's exchange-rate system will be able to dissolve the imbalance in exchange rates**

As described above, between 2005, when exchange-rate reform began, and the end of September, 2010, the RMB appreciated by a cumulative total of 18 percent against the US dollar. In nominal terms, it appreciated by 13 percent, while in real effective terms it appreciated by 20 percent. The question remains: was this degree of appreciation sufficient to eliminate the disparity or imbalance in the RMB exchange rate?

The research team led by Li Shantong addressed this question. Using three mainstream methods of evaluation, namely FEER, BEER, and EPPP (see below), the team analyzed levels of RMB exchange-rate equilibrium between the years 1994 and 2009. They then analyzed the discrepancy between equilibrium levels and the actual levels. They discovered that different methods of analysis produced quite different answers to the question. That is, the extent to which theoretical equilibrium levels and actual levels varied was substantial when different analytical methods were applied.

The three methods used were the 'fundamental equilibrium exchange rate' (FEER), the 'behavioral equilibrium exchange rate (BEER), and the 'extended purchasing power parity' method (EPPP). The results of applying each analytical method are summarized below.

First, EPPP: Using this method, and starting the analysis in 1995, the RMB is seen to have been under-valued over a long period – by the time of the 2005 reform, it was still under-valued by about 20 percent. Once the reform was initiated, the RMB appreciated to the point that the under-valuation had been reduced to around 8 percent by 2009 (see Figures 0.6a and 0.6b). Based on analysis using the EPPP method, Wang Zetian and Yao Yang have estimated that the extent of under-valuation of the

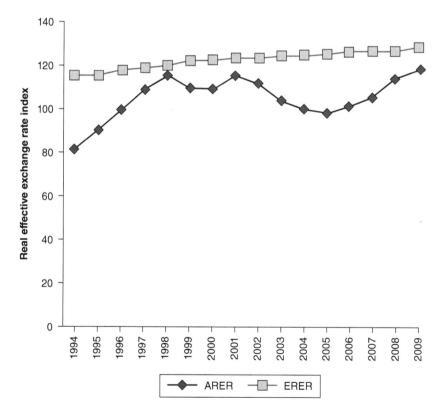

Figure 0.6a   The real RMB exchange rate as estimated using the EPPP method.

Source: Project team headed by Li Shantong, Chapter 5.

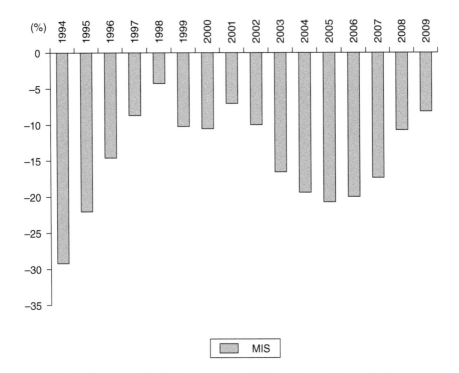

Figure 0.6b The extent of imbalance in the real RMB exchange rate, as calculated using the EPPP method.

Source: Project team headed by Li Shantong, Chapter 5.

RMB was 23 percent in 2005, 20 percent in 2006, and 16 percent in 2007 (see Li Shantong et al., Chapter 5). To a great extent, the conclusions of the Li Shantong research team and Wang Zetian and Yao Yang are similar. Meanwhile, a statistical analysis conducted by the OECD in 2010, using World Bank data from the 2005 ICP program (International Comparison Program), showed a similar result. It found that the RMB was undervalued by around 15 percent in 2007.

Second, FEER: The results of using this method of analysis indicate the following chain of events. First, in 1994 there was a substantial single-event devaluation of the RMB against the US dollar, when the dollar went from 5.762 RMB in 1993 to 8.619 RMB in 1994. Following on this event, China's current account surplus consistently increased between 1995 and 1998, indicating an undervaluation of the effective exchange rate of the RMB. Between 1999 and 2004, however, countries neighboring China were affected by the Asian financial crisis and their currencies depreciated considerably while China's RMB exchange rate remained stable. In relative terms, this lowered the competitiveness of China's exports. The gap between China's actual current account and its theoretical equilibrium in the current account turned negative, meaning that the effective exchange rate was now over-valued. Between 2005 and 2008, the RMB was under-valued slightly while in 2009 it was slightly over-valued, with the difference between the two remaining within 4 percent (see Figures 0.7a and 0.7b). The result of this analysis is quite different from research conducted by Wang Yizhong and Jin Xuejun (2008), in that the extent of imbalance appears much smaller. The research of Wang Yizhong and Jin Xuejun estimated that the target goal of appreciating the effective RMB exchange rate should be set at around 20 percent between the years 2008 and 2010, while the target goal for the RMB–USD rate should be appreciation between 6 percent and 10 percent.

Third, BEER: The 'behavioral equilibrium exchange rate' method for calculating the RMB equilibrium rate led to the following results. After reform of China's

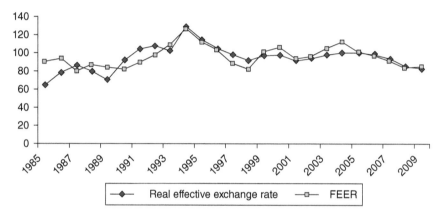

Figure 0.7a The real effective RMB exchange rate index, and the FEER-indicated index.

Source: Li Shantong et al., Chapter 5.

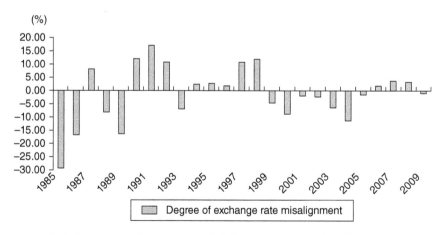

Figure 0.7b The extent of exchange-rate imbalance (greater than 0 indicates under-valuation).

Source: Li Shantong et al., Chapter 5.

exchange-rate formation system in 2005, the RMB realized a certain appreciation, particularly in the second half of 2007 and the first half of 2008. As the appreciation of the RMB against the dollar accelerated, China's real effective exchange rate became slightly over-valued starting in 2008, although only by around 2 percent (see Figures 0.8a and 0.8b).

Summarizing the above, the use of different methods to calculate the extent of imbalance in RMB exchange rates leads to substantially different results. In looking at both domestic and international analyses of the subject, however, the authors are inclined to respect the results of the EPPP method. That is, prior to the initiation of exchange-rate reform in 2005, the RMB exchange rate can be said to have deviated by about 20 percent from the theoretical equilibrium rate, while the

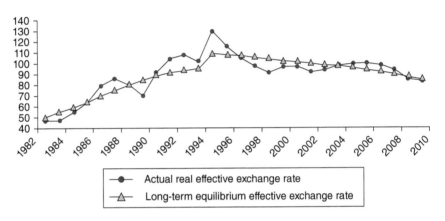

Figure 0.8a The time sequence of changes in the RMB's 'actual real effective exchange rate' and the 'long-term equilibrium effective exchange rate'.

Source: Li Shantong et al., Chapter 5.

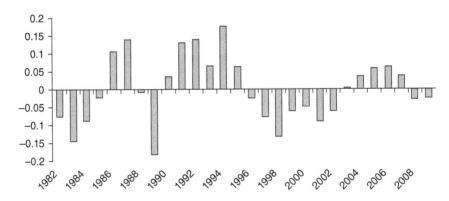

Figure 0.8b The degree of long-term imbalance in the RMB's 'actual real effective exchange rate'.

Source: Li Shantong et al., Chapter 5.

extent of the imbalance is currently around 8 percent. The theoretical underpinning of the EPPP method derives from the Balassa-Samelson hypothesis. Some scholars have questioned how well this theory can be applied to China (e.g., Justin Yifu Lin, 2007; Hu Chuntian and Chen Zhijun, 2009). Their reasoning has been that the fact of long-term massive unemployment or hidden unemployment in China, given the country's dual economic structure, weakens the 'Balassa-Samuelson effect.' Since 2004, however, the persistence of a widespread shortage of manual labor shows that the presumed unlimited supply of labor from former agricultural sectors has already changed to a degree. The Lewisian turning point has occurred (Cai Fang, 2006). The authors feel that this change in China's labor market situation provides a factual basis for applying the Balassa-Samuelson hypothesis.

International examples of adjusting exchange-rate policies

Three different elements operate in an open economy to influence economic growth, namely a rise in productivity, an appreciation of the currency, and an upgrading of economic structure. These three also interact and influence one another (Zhang Bin, Chapter 7). Since the 1960s, both Germany and Japan have experienced pressure on their currencies to appreciate. They faced the need to restructure their economies as they underwent prolonged and fast economic growth. These two countries adopted different methods to deal with the situation, however. The different methods had radically different results on both short-term and long-term economic progress.

Germany's exchange-rate system reform, and lessons to be learned from the experience

Adjusting the exchange rate of the Deutschmark

In the course of rapid economic growth in Germany, the country's currency, the Deutschmark, experienced tremendous appreciation in value. Against the US dollar, it went from 4.17 Marks to the dollar in 1960 to 1.49 Marks to the dollar in 1990, which represented an appreciation of 180 percent. In the thirty years between 1960 and 1990, the trajectory of this appreciation and the pressures on the Mark can be divided into two different stages as demarcated by the dissolution of the Bretton Woods system.

Prior to the end of that system, the Deutschmark was revalued several times against the US dollar. At the time, however, pressures on the Mark, and international debate on monetary issues in general, focused on how to maintain the viability of the Bretton Woods system. The situation was different from the bilateral type of pressure that China is currently facing.

After the dissolution of the Bretton Woods system, there were high market expectations for the Mark to appreciate given Germany's strong trade surplus. If German authorities intervened in foreign-exchange markets, however, there was a possibility that the country would lose control of its domestic money supply, which would aggravate the inflation brought on by the oil crisis. On March 1, 1973, Germany broke all previous records by buying in a total of USD 2.7 billion within the space of one day. The next day, under ongoing market pressure, the government closed foreign exchange markets. Following these actions, however, the government was able to adopt a floating-rate foreign-exchange system and government intervention gave way to the forces of supply and demand. Between 1973 and 1979, the Mark experienced sustained appreciation but then lost value between 1979 and 1984. The currency again appreciated after the Plaza Accord of 1985. Germany's main focus was on the stability of its internal money supply, which meant that the government limited any interventions in the foreign-exchange markets. Since the markets themselves were able to release pressure on the currency to appreciate, the exchange-rate trajectory of the Mark was relatively stable. There was no need to apply coordinated international interventions to stabilize the currency, as per the Plaza Accord (Figure 0.9) (see Zhang Bin, Chapter 7).

The effect of Deutschmark exchange-rate changes on the German economy

Once Germany let go of a system that pegged its currency to the US dollar, the Deutschmark exchange rate was determined primarily by the market. The Mark then appreciated over a long period of time but this did not in fact affect the country's imports and exports in any real way. Instead, it had the noticeable effect of improving Germany's terms of trade. Moreover, Germany's adoption of a floating exchange-rate system actually had the effect of providing stability for economic

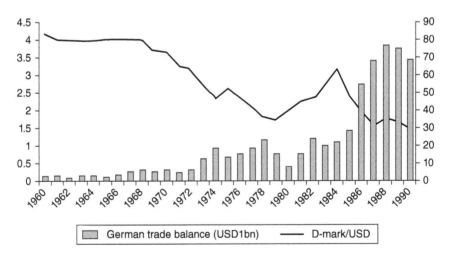

Figure 0.9 Germany's trade surplus between 1960 and 1990, and the Deutschmark exchange rate.

Source: Zhang Bin, Chapter 7.

growth. Real productivity increased steadily, and services as a percentage of the economic structure rose dramatically (Zhang Bin, Chapter 7).

Despite considerable appreciation of the Mark, Germany's real imports and exports did not see any material decline. The Mark underwent two distinct periods of consistent appreciation, from the late 1960s to 1978, and from 1985 to 1990. During these periods, however, both imports and exports displayed stable growth. Excluding price effects, neither fell in any material way.

The role that the appreciation of the Mark played in improving Germany's terms of trade between 1980 and 1995 was extremely apparent. First, in the early 1980s, an appreciating Mark did not bring with it deteriorating terms of trade, while terms of trade improved dramatically from the mid-1980s onward. Between 1985 and 1995, the Mark–USD exchange rate went from 2.46 Marks to the dollar to 1.43 Marks to the dollar. During that same period, Germany's terms of trade went from 93.3 to 107.4 (see Figure 0.10).

An appreciating Mark did not in fact 'shock' the stability of Germany's overall economy. Prior to 1972, the Deutschmark exchange rate was relatively stable. Between 1961 and 1972, inflation averaged 2.8 percent with a standard deviation of 1.07, while the standard deviation of economic growth was 2.11 (that is, the extent to which actual economic growth deviated from what could be regarded as potential economic growth). After 1972, the Mark began to appreciate. Between 1973 and 1990, inflation averaged 3.78 percent with a standard deviation of 2.13. The standard deviation of economic growth was 2.01. In both of these periods, inflation and economic volatility stayed at reasonable levels. The somewhat higher levels in the second period were clearly affected by the two oil crises. Once Germany adopted a floating exchange-rate

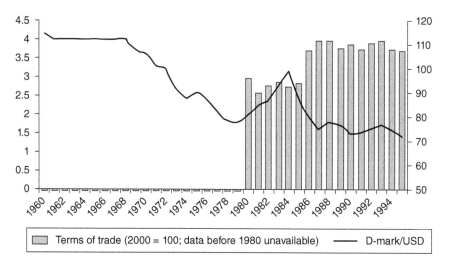

Figure 0.10 The appreciate of the Deutschmark, and improvement in Germany's terms of trade.

Source: WDI.

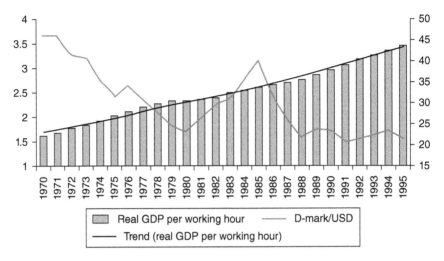

Figure 0.11 Germany's real productivity, plotted against fluctuations of the Deutschmark exchange rate.

Source: WDI. Data on real GDP per working hour from the Penn World Trade 6.3.

system, however, the stability of economic growth actually increased to a certain degree.

Germany's real productivity rate did not display any great volatility as a result of adjustments in the exchange rate of the German currency. By using units of real GDP per hour of work to represent labor productivity, it can be seen that the real productivity rate in the country basically adhered to the trend line with only small fluctuations. Fluctuations in the value of the Mark did not lead to any great increases or declines in productivity (see Figure 0.11).

The appreciation of the Deutschmark had a definite effect on stimulating development of Germany's service industries. Between 1970 and 1980, a period when the Mark was appreciating, the value-added of Germany's services industries as a percentage of GDP sustained ongoing stable growth. The figure rose from 48.2 percent in 1970 to 56.5 percent in 1980, at an average annual rate of increase of 0.75 percent. In the early to mid-1980s, when the Mark fell in value, this figure grew at a much lower rate and averaged an annual rate of increase of only 0.29 percent. Once the Plaza Accord was signed in 1985, the Mark again began a round of appreciation and the figure once again rose accordingly. Between 1986 and 1995, the average annual rate of increase was 0.76 percent. The tight relationship between currency appreciation and service industries as a percentage of GDP indicates, to a degree, that currency changes do have an impact on service industry ratios. At the same time, the exchange rate is only one of a number of factors explaining the growth of service industries – many other economic variables must support a trend of service industries growing as a percentage of GDP.

Japan's exchange-rate system reform and lessons to be learned from the experience

The history of exchange-rate adjustments in Japan

Like Germany, Japan experienced a tremendous appreciation of its currency in the course of rapid economic growth. The Japanese yen went from 360 to the dollar in 1960 to 144 to the dollar in 1990, an appreciation of 150 percent. Compared to Germany, Japan faced even greater pressure to appreciate its currency both domestically and from international forces. Within Japan, however, authorities were reluctant to revalue the currency to the extent that they adopted a variety of measures to slow the pace of appreciation. On the one hand, this put tremendous pressure on monetary policies. On the other, it meant that Japan accomplished its currency appreciation in several abrupt and rapid exchange-rate changes (Zhang Bin, Chapter 7).

From 1960 until the eve of the dissolution of the Bretton Woods system, Japan was able to build up an ongoing trade surplus but both Japanese authorities and the citizens of the country still lacked confidence in the Japanese economy. They feared that an appreciation of the yen would lead to economic recession. The yen–USD rate was therefore kept at a fixed rate of 360 yen to one US dollar. In the face of international pressure, the Japanese administration adopted various other means to mollify trade partners. It passed import incentives and liberalized importing regulations, adopted preferential tariff treatment for less-developed economies, pressed for capital investment both within Japan and outside Japan, lowered non-tariff barriers, increased overseas foreign aid, and so on. Through attempting to lower its trade surplus by these measures, Japan sought to relieve external pressure on the country to modify its exchange rate.

In mid-August, 1971, President Nixon delivered a speech in which he announced the end of the gold standard and therefore the dissolution of the Bretton Woods system. Markets began to sell off US dollars, leading to all major European countries, with the exception of France, closing their markets. Japan, however, continued to buy in dollars at the rate of 360 yen to the dollar. Within the short space of two weeks, the Japanese monetary authorities had bought in USD 4 billion worth of currency. This figure approached one-half of Japan's total foreign exchange reserves at the time. To buy in this quantity of dollars, Japan had spent roughly 1.5 trillion Japanese yen, money that was now launched into public circulation. Japan's total quantity of money supply at the time, as defined by 'M1' money, was 24 trillion. Japanese authorities were therefore facing a very difficult choice: should they accept inflation or should they revalue the currency. They now also began to confront international pressure coming from the direction of the United States. At the end of 1971, Japan appreciated the yen by 16.9 percent upon signing the Smithsonian Agreement. At the time, this was the greatest degree of currency appreciation experienced by any country.

After 1973, the Japanese yen entered a period in which it was allowed to float. Despite a weakening of the yen during the oil crisis, Japan emerged from this crisis earlier than other countries and its trade surplus once again began to increase.

As a result, pressures on the country to appreciate its currency again gathered force. After 1975, within the structure of a floating-rate system, Japanese authorities began frequent interventions in the market. Most of the measures involved buying in US dollars in order to reduce the degree to which the yen appreciated. This aroused widespread criticism in the international community as well as trade sanctions on the part of the United States. At the same time, in order to mitigate ongoing appreciation pressure on the yen, the Japanese government used public-finance stimulus measures to increase domestic demand and to spur imports in order to reduce the country's trade surplus.

The second oil crisis erupted in 1979. Japan did not have appreciable strengthening of its currency between that year and 1984 due to the United States's high interest-rate policies, and due to the purchase of tens of billions of dollars worth of US debt by Japanese insurance companies and pension funds. Nevertheless, the international community generally felt that the US dollar was overvalued, and that the Mark, the yen, and other major currencies in the world would be forced to revalue at some point. In August of 1985, a group of five countries signed the Plaza Accord, the aim of which was to prevent the US dollar from appreciating further. The five were the US, the UK, Germany, Japan, and France. At the same time, the meeting did not press to have the US dollar depreciate in any dramatic way. Japan's finance minister, Noboru Takeshita, stated explicitly that his country could accept an appreciation of the yen of 10 percent to 20 percent. This surpassed the expectations of the United States. This concession on the part of Japan was made in order to ameliorate the trade sanctions on Japan coming from the US Congress. After the Plaza Accord, the yen began to appreciate and continued to appreciate over the next several years, leading to considerable domestic criticism and discontent. During this period, Japanese authorities did intervene in the market but with very modest results. Japan also asked for the United States' help in stemming any further appreciation but this request met with a rejection. In order to reduce pressure on the continued appreciation of the yen after the Plaza Accord, and at the same time in order to stimulate the domestic economy, Japan adopted a low interest-rate policy.

The economic impact of adjustments in the Japanese yen exchange rate

Japan's experience with respect to exchange-rate adjustments between the years 1960 and 1990 indicates that appreciation of the yen after the 1970s did indeed have a certain impact on real imports and exports over the short run. Nevertheless, this did not prevent real imports and exports from experiencing stable growth over the long run. What's more, the appreciation of Japan's currency brought clear benefits in the form of terms of trade. Japan's uncertain approach and its procrastination as its currency appreciated, however, in addition to inappropriate monetary and fiscal policies, laid the foundation for later disaster. This came in the form of an asset bubble and fiscal deficits after the country signed the Plaza Accord (Zhang Bin, Chapter 7).

As noted above, after the 1970s, appreciation of the yen did not prevent real imports and exports from experiencing stable growth but it did play a role in reducing Japan's trade surplus in the short run. Between 1980 and 1985, the yen

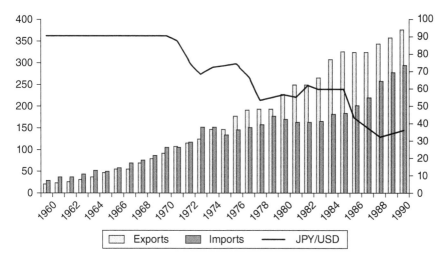

Figure 0.12 Exchange rate adjustments of the Japanese yen and Japan's real imports and exports from 1960 to 1990.

Source: WDI.

stopped appreciating against the dollar, real exports rapidly increased while real imports slowed down, and Japan's trade surplus suddenly grew. In 1985–1986, after the yen appreciated rapidly, real exports went through a brief period of decline while real imports increased very considerably and the real trade surplus of the country declined somewhat (see Figure 0.12).

Appreciation of the yen clearly improved Japan's terms of trade. A look at the changes in terms of trade between 1980 and 1995, and the yen–USD exchange rate for the same period, shows that the yen appreciation brought with it sustained improvement. Between 1980 and 1995, the yen–USD exchange rate went from 226 yen to one US dollar to 94 yen to one US dollar. At the same time, the terms of trade rose from 79.7 to 114.9 (see Figure 0.13). Japanese economists believe that Japanese citizens began to realize the personal benefits of their currency's appreciation after the Plaza Accord (Volcker and Toyoo Gyohten, 1997). At that time, the way appreciation of the yen lowered prices of imported goods was of particular benefit to the welfare of the Japanese people.

Average levels of inflation before and after the appreciation of the yen were not significantly different. The degree of volatility in the real economy was also minor, but the volatility of inflation increased tremendously. Between 1961 and 1972, average levels of inflation in Japan were 5.8, with a standard deviation of 1.3. The standard deviation of the rate of economic growth was 2.82 (this is believed to reflect the difference between the actual rate of economic growth and the theoretical potential rate of growth). Once the yen began to appreciate, after 1972, average levels of inflation in the country were 5.54 between 1973 and 1990, with a standard deviation of 5.55. The standard deviation of the rate of economic growth was 2.24. The primary reason for the relatively large volatility in Japan's

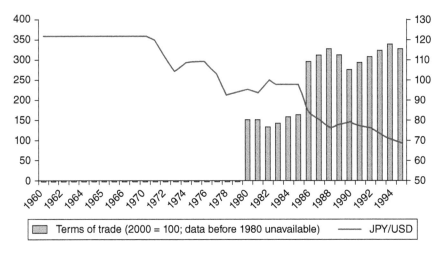

Figure 0.13 Appreciation of the yen and improvement in Japan's terms of trade.
Source: WDI.

rate of inflation can be attributed to mistakes made by Japanese authorities in their conduct of monetary policy. The severe inflation after 1972 is closely connected to the large amounts of money that monetary authorities injected into the economy just prior to that time in order to intervene in exchange-rate markets.

The asset-price bubble experienced by Japan was, in turn, closely related to exchange-rate policy. After 1985, faced with pressure on all sides, authorities in Japan felt that the yen could not be allowed to continue to appreciate. On the one hand, they attempted to intervene in exchange-rate markets to stem the appreciation but found that they were powerless to change expectations of appreciation single-handedly. Even worse, despite indications that the real economy still had sufficient growth momentum, they repeatedly lowered the discount rate. This led to an excess of liquidity in markets which, in turn, helped grow an asset price bubble (Koruda, 2003).

Japan's deteriorating fiscal situation was also closely related to the country's exchange-rate policies. In the mid- to latter part of the 1970s, in order to counter complaints by the international community about Japan's increasing trade surplus, and to reduce pressure to appreciate the yen, the Japanese government adopted expansionary fiscal policies which gradually led to a deterioration of the country's finances. By 1985, the debt of the Japanese government stood at 22 percent of its entire budget. The sum of all public debt reached 42 percent of gross national product, which at the time was the highest among any developed country. In the mid-1980s, the Japanese government made repeated promises to the international community about increasing domestic expenditures and reducing taxes. These promises were similarly aimed at reducing pressure on the country to appreciate its currency and to reduce its trade surplus.

The appreciation of the yen played a considerable role in the restructuring of Japan's economy. Between 1970 and 1980, the yen appreciated notably against the dollar and the value-added of Japan's service industries as a percent of GDP rose every year in that decade by 0.65 percent. Between 1981 and 1985, the yen remained stable relative against the dollar and the value-added of Japan's service industries as a percent of GDP moderated, to 0.38 percent per year. Between 1986 and 1995, the yen again appreciated considerably against the dollar and the value-added of Japan's service industries again rose to an average of 0.67 percent per year. The experience of Japan has shown on several occasions that, while exchange rates are not the sole factor affecting the contribution of service industries to GDP, they are a vitally important factor.

Lessons to be learned from the experiences of Germany and Japan with respect to exchange-rate adjustments

As major trading nations, Germany and Japan hold important positions in the international economic system. The exchange-rate policies of both countries, together with their attendant economic policies, can provide us with important lessons that are well worth consideration (Zhang Bin, Chapter 7).

First, in the process of major, sustained, change in relative economic power between countries, adjustments of exchange rates are unavoidable. Other types of measures aimed at mitigating the pressure to appreciate a country's currency cannot fundamentally eradicate that pressure.

Second, the cost of excessive intervention in foreign exchange markets is prohibitive. The cost includes a high degree of inflation, asset price bubbles, and reactions from the international community in the form of group pressure and trade wars. In the end, such intervention does not result in stable exchange rates.

Third, the sustained appreciation of a country's currency clearly impacts real imports and exports in the short run as well as the total volume of a country's trade. However, within one to two years, real trade quickly returns to the previous medium-term to long-term trend line. Major volatility in exchange rates does not have any noticeable effect on such trend lines.

Fourth, large-scale appreciation of a currency has no appreciable effect on changes in productivity.

Fifth, sustained and large-scale volatility of exchange rates does in fact have an impact on industrial structure. Significant appreciation of a currency can accelerate the percentage of service industries value-added in total GDP. In contrast, a depreciating currency can have the opposite effect by delaying the increase in the services component of GDP.

Sixth, the sustained, large-scale appreciation of a country's currency clearly improves that country's terms of trade and improves the welfare of its citizens. As the currency appreciates, the positive benefits come to be recognized by the people of the country. The attitude of people in all sectors gradually shifts from an initial opposition to understanding and support.

Policy recommendations

1 Reform of China's exchange-rate system should adhere to the principles of being 'voluntary (independently determined), incremental, and controllable.' Adjustments should be in line with macroeconomic conditions and should be modest in size and incremental. A one-off large-scale appreciation of the RMB is neither feasible nor necessary. For the present, we should improve upon the managed float system that is carried out with reference to a basket of currencies. As we undertake adjustments to the exchange rate, we should integrate various other measures such as trade and capital controls, fiscal and monetary policies, and reform of China's markets for natural resources and other input factors. We should push for a greater balance in international payments, and promote economic restructuring and the transformation of our mode of economic development.

2 The long-term orientation of China's reform of its exchange-rate system must be in the direction of a freely floating exchange-rate system. For the immediate future, and over the medium term, we still need to bring about a genuine 'managed float,' then gradually expand the band within which the RMB is allowed to fluctuate. We should fully utilize the interbank foreign exchange markets and the price fluctuations for RMB versus USD on those exchanges. We should reduce the amount of direct intervention by the central bank on general exchange-rate levels as well as more immediate fluctuations.

3 We should genuinely implement the system of referencing the RMB rate to a basket of currencies. Instead of focusing on the stability of the bilateral exchange rate, we should move gradually towards ensuring that the multilateral exchange rate (the 'effective exchange rate') is basically stable in order to preserve the overall competitiveness of China's export commodities.

4 Through small, incremental, but swift moves, we should take opportunities to appreciate the currency in order to eliminate exchange-rate imbalances. Research indicates that the RMB exchange rate still harbors a certain degree of cumulative imbalance. If other circumstances remain unchanged, if China's economic growth rate remains higher than average levels in the rest of the world, and particularly if productivity in the trade sector continues to rise, new pressures to appreciate the currency will emerge each year. Our research team believes that we should use this opportune time, when both domestic and international economies are doing well, to achieve a 4–5 percent appreciation of the real effective exchange rate every year. Within around three years, we should basically return the average level of the exchange rate to a balanced situation, after which we should further broaden the degree to which the RMB is allowed to float.

5 We should establish target objectives for China's current account surplus and aim to have that surplus stay within 5 percent of GDP. Since 2003, the average level of China's current accounts surplus as a percent of GDP has been 3.75 percent, but between 2006 and 2008, it exceeded 5 percent, after which it fell back to around 5 percent at the end of 2009. Keeping the percentage

within 5 percent of GDP should be a goal that is possible if we put some effort into it. In addition, it should be noted that an excessively high surplus, coupled with the resulting (undesirable) increase in our foreign exchange reserves, is unnecessary for China's development.

6 Through a variety of means, we should realize a basic balance in our current account and international payments. Such means would include: increasing imports of foreign goods and advanced technology, increasing the purchase of high-quality foreign services (such as higher education services), reducing the number of companies that list overseas that have no need for foreign exchange, relaxing policy restrictions on overseas foreign direct investment made by individuals within China, expanding the ability of qualified institutional investors within China to carry out financial investments abroad, further relaxing the requirements on qualifications and scale of transactions with respect to overseas investments, further relaxing restrictions on overseas institutions that issue RMB-denominated bonds within China as well as relaxing other restrictions on financing methods, and, finally, allowing the outward remittance of foreign exchange that has been purchased with funds raised in China.

7 We should establish policy objectives for keeping the amount of China's foreign-exchange reserves within certain limits. During the *12th Five-Year Plan* period, we should aim to lower our foreign-exchange reserves every year by RMB 50 billion to RMB 100 billion. By 2015, we should basically realize a situation in which foreign-exchange reserves are unable to increase again in such obvious fashion. At the same time, we should ensure that the value of our existing foreign-exchange reserves is maintained and continues to grow. Under a situation of incremental appreciation of the RMB, as long as foreign-exchange reserve assets do not continue to increase, we should be able to absorb the foreign-exchange losses caused by currency appreciation through economic growth.

8 We should strengthen controls over short-term capital flows, and in particular should curb the inflow of speculative short-term capital, in order to buy time for domestic policy adjustments and for reform of the exchange-rate system. In the near-term and medium-term, we may adopt a system that classifies enterprises by category, and then apply rigorous reviews of the legitimacy of foreign exchange transactions done under the name of trade. We should strengthen controls over the use of foreign-denominated debt, including more efficient monitoring and control of trade credit.

9 We should take to heart the lessons learned from Japan's handling of its foreign-exchange policies – we must avoid excessively loose monetary policies and overly stimulatory fiscal policies on the domestic front, as a way to reduce appreciation pressures on our currency.

10 We should learn from the experience of the 1994 reform. Exchange-rate reform must be done in concert with other reforms, including price reform, natural-resource tax reform, and wage-system reform, among others, integrated in ways that allow these policies to reinforce one another.

Ten. We should take advantage of this moment when there are still strong expectations of an appreciating RMB to push forward greater 'internationalization' of the currency among neighboring countries and regions, in order to ease liquidity pressures in our domestic market.

Notes

1 Yu Jiantuo: China Development Research Foundation.
2 Empirical data as presented here has been estimated by Yu Jiantuo and Huang Wei according to relevant models and data, but not by Zhang Fan and Yu Miaojie in their sub-report.

Bibliography

Balassa, B. "The Purchasing Power Parity Doctrine: A Reappraisal", *Journal of Political Economy*, 72 (6), 1964: 584–596

Frankel, J. A. "New Estimation of China's Exchange Rate Regime", NBER Working Paper 14700, February 2009

Guo Jin. "Examining the Exchange Rate Regime for China", *International Research Journal of Finance and Economics*, 25, 2009: 64–77

Justin Yifu Lin. "Thoughts on the RMB Exchange Rate and Policy Suggestions", CCER Working Paper, No. C2007001

Koruda, H. "The Nixon Shocks and the Plaza Agreement: Lessons from Two Seemingly Failed Cases of Japan Exchange Rate Policy", speech paper to the Institute of World Economics and Politics Chinese Academy of Social Sciences in 2003

Samuelson, P. A. "Theoretical Notes on Trade Problems", *Review of Economics and Statistics*, 46 (2), 1964: 15–154

Volcker, P. and Gyohten, T. "Changing Fortunes", Beijing: China Financial Publishing House, 1996

Wang Yizhong and Jin Xuejun. "Internal and External RMB Equilibrium Exchange Rates: 1982–2010", *Journal of Quantitative & Technical Economics*, 2008 (5)

Wang Zetian and Yao Yang. "RMB Equilibrium Estimates", *Journal of Financial Research*, 2008 (12)

1 Analysis of the impact of RMB exchange-rate adjustments on China's overall economy and national welfare

Huang Yiping and Tao Kunyu[1]

Framework for analysis and issues under consideration

On June 19, 2010, the People's Bank of China said repeatedly that it would be increasing the flexibility of the RMB exchange rate and thereby putting an end to the way in which the RMB had been restricted to a narrow band of trading against the US dollar since 2008. Nevertheless, in subsequent months, the band within which the RMB fluctuated did not in fact widen. If this trend had been allowed to continue, China would have faced a deteriorating international economic environment. From September 10, 2010, however, the pace at which the RMB appreciated began to pick up. By now, the rate has already gone up by 2.5 percent since exchange-rate reform was reinstituted. In general, though, there has been no notable improvement in the extent to which exchange-rate policies are conservative, nor has there been a decline in international pressure as a result.

This situation, declaring that exchange rates will be more flexible and then continuing to keep rates within a conservative band, may indicate that policymakers are facing a dilemma. From the perspective of improving China's domestic economic structure and maintaining a favorable external economic environment in which to do that, the RMB exchange rate should gradually come to be determined by market mechanisms. Right now, however, market indicators are extremely clear in pointing to the need for a more rapid appreciation of the currency. Whether or not China's economy can weather the pressure of rapid appreciation is a matter of opinion. In simple terms, we can summarize the dilemma facing policymakers as follows: long term, the direction of exchange-rate policy reform is quite clear. Short term, there are grave doubts about the consequences.

One fortunate thing is that China can draw on lessons from past experience in increasing the flexibility of its exchange rate. Such experience provides examples of the relationship between RMB exchange-rate changes and China's macroeconomy. In looking at exchange-rate policy during the period of reform, early 1994 was an important line of demarcation. Prior to 1994, the RMB was basically over-valued. In 1978, it was RMB 1.5 to USD 1. Over the next fifteen years, until 1993, the government adopted a series of measures aimed at allowing the exchange rate to reflect market mechanisms in a better way. These included direct depreciation of the currency and the adoption of a dual-track exchange-rate system. The purpose was to force the rate to approach 'equilibrium.'

Then, on January 1, 1994, the central bank of China integrated the 'official rate' and the 'market rate,' and the new exchange rate for the RMB against the dollar became 8.7. It was decided that the rate would increasingly be set with reference to a basket of currencies, as opposed to being set mainly with reference to the US dollar. It was also decided that market mechanisms would be allowed to play a greater role through instituting a 'managed float.' By 1997, the RMB had fallen to RMB 8.3 to USD 1. Once the Asian financial crisis erupted, the Chinese government decided to fix the rate at 8.27 in order to stem the trend of a competitive devaluation of regional currencies. This policy then remained in force for close to eight years.

On July 21, 2005, the central bank of China announced that it would be ending the policy of pegging the RMB exchange rate to the US dollar. The new policy consisted primarily of the following three components. First, it meant that the RMB appreciated by 2.1 percent against the dollar on the evening that the policy was announced. Second, it shifted the exchange rate system from a singular focus on the dollar towards reference to a basket of currencies. Third, it instituted a system of a managed float. In the three years between 2005 and 2008, with respect to the dollar alone, the RMB appreciated by 21 percent. With respect to all currencies, that is, the 'real effective exchange rate,' it appreciated by 16 percent. In mid-2008, the dramatic worsening of the financial crisis in the United States had a severe impact on China's economy. The central bank of China restricted movements of the RMB–USD exchange rate to a very narrow band around the rate 6.84. Finally, on June 19, 2010, once the central bank reinstituted exchange-rate reform, the RMB again began to appreciate in a stable manner.

Despite the above, if we look at changes in the real effective exchange rate over the past sixteen years, we discover that the most notable appreciation of the RMB in fact took place prior to the Asian financial crisis. The index rate was 77 in early 1994, and went to 118 in early 1998. After that time, the index experienced a fairly large reversal, with the RMB depreciating quite notably during the Asian financial crisis. Although the RMB began to appreciate again, in measured steps, after the resumption of exchange-rate reform in 2005, the index at the beginning of 2010 was only approaching the level it had been in 1998, around 120. International experience shows that when a country's per capita income rises at a rate that is 1 percent faster than other countries, its real effective exchange rate will appreciate by roughly 0.4 percent. In light of this, our own exchange-rate policy has clearly been relatively conservative (see Figure 1.1).

Since 1994, therefore, China has consistently been using a 'managed float' with respect to its currency and the trend has clearly been in the direction of RMB appreciation. The managed-float system was temporarily suspended during two periods of financial crisis, but since June 19, 2010, the system has in fact resumed a process that began in 1994. It is fairly easy, therefore, to judge the long-term trend of RMB rates, while it is difficult to identify short-term trends.

The reason for the difficulty in terms of short-term rates relates to two considerations, the market, and policy. Exchange rates are determined by many factors, but if we regard foreign exchange as a kind of 'commodity,' its price

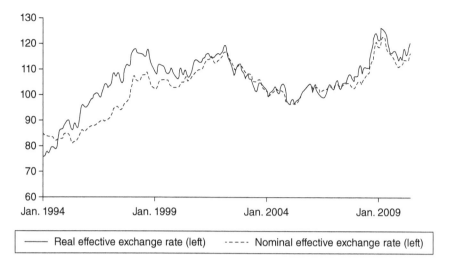

Figure 1.1 Real and nominal effective RMB exchange rate indexes.

Source: WIND database.

is determined by supply and demand just like any commodity. In the simplest terms, the demand for foreign exchange is determined by two factors, namely imports and China's investment overseas. The supply of foreign exchange is similarly determined by two factors, namely exports and the investment of other countries within China. Right now, China has a surplus in its current account, since investment of other countries within China is greater than China's investment overseas. This means that, relatively speaking, the supply of foreign exchange is greater than the demand for it, and this in turn determines the trend of an appreciating RMB.

However, foreign exchange markets also incorporate short-term investment and indeed speculative behavior when seen in their entirety. In deciding what currencies to hold, investors look at returns and they look at risk. Between these two things, risk is the more difficult to predict. For example, the worsening of the European sovereign debt crisis in the second quarter of 2010 affected the confidence of Chinese investors as well. Some international investors also began to discount China in the early part of the year as the result of fears about overheating of the economy and the possibility of an asset bubble. Such things have the ability to affect expectations about exchange-rate trends, and to change the behavior of investors. As a result, they affect supply and demand relationships in foreign-exchange markets.

Nevertheless, with respect to the RMB exchange rate, policy factors trump market expectations. China's central bank intervention in foreign-exchange markets is the most important consideration in determining exchange-rate levels. What then are the actual reasons behind policy-makers' decisions to allow the RMB rate to rise or fall? Given our own incomplete information, we can only provide the following surmise. We assume that the government is probably most worried about the possibility that an appreciating RMB will negatively impact the economy. Considerations would include falling exports, a contraction in the trade surplus, a decline in the rate of economic growth, greater unemployment, and so on. For all levels of government officials in China, the core considerations are probably economic growth and levels of employment. The reason for concern is that these have a direct impact on social stability.

Not allowing adequate change in the exchange rate also brings on its own problems, however. In economics, there is a well-known theory called the 'Mondale impossible trinity,' also known as the 'trilemma.' Basically, this says that a country can at most realize two out of the three main objectives in that country's international economic policy. The three are: maintaining a stable exchange rate, allowing free flow of capital, and maintaining the autonomy of the country's monetary policies. In the past, our policies chose to emphasize the stability of exchange rates and the independence of China's monetary policies. To achieve those things, we relinquished the option of enabling a free flow of currency. We maintained extremely stringent capital controls. More recently, the effectiveness of those controls has declined, and this is beginning to affect the autonomy of China's monetary policies. Given this situation, increasing the flexibility of the exchange rate is in fact necessary as a policy decision.

The aim of this report is to analyze exactly how RMB exchange-rate changes might influence China's overall economy. As with any policy change, decisions to appreciate the RMB will have both positive and negative effects. The key task for policy makers will be to decide how to strike a rational balance between these things in order to set policies that are most beneficial to long-term economic development. We base our analysis on China's actual economic data, set within an existing theoretical framework, and we focus particularly on the impact that RMB appreciation had on China's economy during the years 2005–2008.

At the start of 2010, a particular government department in China conducted a 'stress test' on RMB exchange-rate movements. The test concluded that short-term appreciation of the RMB should not exceed 3 percent. If it did, the resulting appreciation would have a massively negative impact on exports and employment. This conclusion quite obviously deviated from the actual economic experience of other countries as well as China. For example, in the three years after a managed float was instituted in 2005, the RMB appreciated against the US dollar at an average annual rate of 7 percent, yet at the same time both exports and employment remained quite vigorous. In other countries, an exchange rate might vary by as much as 20 percent to 30 percent without striking a fatal blow to the real economy.

The problem with this kind of stress test lies not in the conclusion but in the analytical method. To have government officials going to exporters and conducting surveys of what they think is not, in itself, a bad thing. It is a good thing, but if one only solicits the opinions of exporters, one cannot get objective results. Naturally, exporters do not want the RMB to appreciate, but the views of those who want to invest abroad may be exactly the opposite. More importantly, the economic impact of exchange-rate changes is a matter of general equilibrium and must be evaluated from an overall perspective. It is not very appropriate to frame one's analysis in terms of partial equilibrium of the exporting sector alone.

We therefore need to use a general equilibrium framework in analyzing the impact of exchange rates on the overall economy. Before discussing such a framework in detail, however, we should ensure that there is consensus on three major conditions. First, exchange rates are a price variable. What exchange rates reflect is the price of one currency relative to another – this is not fundamentally different from the concept of the price of rice or the price of steel. Naturally, exchange rates can influence the price variables of all things related to international trade and investment and therefore they represent a special kind of price. For the present time, RMB exchange rates cannot be left completely up to market forces because of this. If we do not agree, however, that exchange rates are a kind of price, then we cannot possibly analyze them within a market framework.

Second, exchange rates should be analyzed from a dynamic perspective. To give an example: under normal conditions, an appreciating currency will lead to a decline in exports, since appreciation will push up the international price of the same goods and make them less competitive. At the same time, however, seen from a dynamic perspective, such decline in competitiveness will also force enterprises to improve their productivity and lower their costs, to make up for lost sales. That is to say, in the long run, an appreciating currency may have less of a long-term than a short-term impact on exporters. Naturally, the situation may also be the opposite. International trade theory includes something called the 'J curve,' for example, which says that the impact of currency appreciation on exports may take months or even several quarters to show any effect.

Finally, China is already an economic power. In terms of international economics, the size of a country's economy has little effect on the extent of its territory or the size of its population, but it does have an effect on international markets. A small economy does not greatly impact international markets, no matter what happens in its internal supply and demand. When a major economy increases supply or demand, however, that can have a direct impact on international market prices. In simple terms, China was a minor economy prior to the Asian financial crisis. By now, it is a major economy in very real terms. This is critical in terms of how we assess RMB exchange rates and their impact on China's economy.

Within a 'general equilibrium framework,' then, how do exchange rates affect an economy? The most direct way is in how exchange-rate changes alter relative prices. An RMB that is appreciating in value makes China's exports more expensive relative to the exports of other countries, while imports into China become cheaper relative to China's own domestic products. Products within China that are not traded rise in price relative to products that are imported. In economics, relative price changes are the most important causal factor leading to structural change in an economy. As China's exports become more expensive relative to the exports of other countries, it may indeed be that China's exports decline. As imports become cheaper relative to domestic products, consumers may indeed increase their demand for imported goods and lower their purchasing of domestically produced goods. As prices of non-traded goods in China rise relative to traded goods, investors will start to put more money into non-traded sectors of the economy.

Put most simply, relative price changes have a direct effect on the behavior of producers, consumers, and investors. To evaluate the extent of that effect, one must look at the results of integrating all factors. For example, an appreciating currency may lead to a decline in the competitiveness of exports and therefore to lower employment in exporting sectors of the economy, but at the same time, it may lead to increased demand for imports and an increase in the employment of importing sectors of the economy. More importantly, an appreciating currency will stimulate the development of non-traded sectors, which means that employment in such sectors, particularly service industries, may see dramatic increase. If one combines all these factors, is the end result increase or a decrease in employment? The answer to that question can only come from a process of empirical analysis.

The appropriateness of changes in exchange-rate systems, or exchange rates themselves, involves more than simply theoretical issues, however. The level of development of a given economy and its institutional environment are critical. For example, Rogoff et al. (2003) studied exchange-rate changes and systemic changes from four different angles: inflation, economic growth, economic volatility, and the likelihood of some kind of crisis. They looked at 158 economic entities, between the years 1970 and 1999, while dividing the countries into three categories, developed, developing, and newly emerging economies. The results of their analysis indicated that there was no clear difference between systems that used two different extremes, a completely free-floating exchange rate and a pegged rate, in terms of the four variables under study. The benefits of one or the other were hard to distinguish. In contrast, the stage of economic development in which a country found itself had a very strong correlation with the pros and cons of exchange-rate changes.

In a developing country, one that lacks well developed financial markets, either a fixed exchange-rate system or one that allows for a limited float can help keep inflation low for a fairly low cost. Either kind of system can stimulate economic growth without generating too much economic volatility. As financial systems are improved within such an economy, and the country is able to penetrate more deeply into global capital markets, the need to have more flexible exchange rates increases. Meanwhile, the increasing credibility of a government's policies, and proven government performance, make it easier for both governments and individuals to use the currency of that country to denominate loans. When this occurs, a floating-rate system can better stimulate economic growth while at the same time keeping inflation low.

The situation for emerging-market economies is somewhat different. Such economies face more frequent international capital flows and therefore greater risk if they try to peg their currencies or keep them at a fixed exchange rate. This increases the likelihood that crises will erupt. The authors (Rogoff et al.) recommend that both developing countries and newly emerging economies should gradually grow out of a 'fear of floating rates' and move towards an awareness that they can use floating rates as a means to improve their economic performance.

Aghion et al. (2009) analyzed this specific issue. This study used data from 83 countries, drawn from the years between 1960 and 2000. It used a technique called the generalized method of moments (GMM) to estimate the nonlinear relationship between exchange-rate volatility and economic output. The model showed that exchange-rate volatility is detrimental to investment by domestic manufacturers when there are strong credit constraints. However, when a country's financial markets are stronger, enabling more access to credit, then the positive effects of exchange-rate volatility are ongoing and beneficial in stimulating economic growth.

An empirical analysis of the effects of exchange rate movements on China's overall economy

Global macroeconomic model analysis

We conducted a simulation analysis on the potential effects of RMB appreciation and to do this we employed the Oxford Economic Forecasting model (OEF).[2] We assumed an appreciation of the RMB against the US dollar of 5 percent per year, totaling 25 percent cumulative appreciation by the fifth year. In the course of the analysis, we evaluated two different scenarios, one in which the RMB exchange rate was unchanged, and the other in which it appreciated by 5 percent per year on average. The difference in results could be seen as the net effect of appreciation on the outcome. We used 'elasticity' as the means of expressing the effect of appreciation on the overall economy, and we divided this into short-term elasticity (one year) and long-term elasticity (five years) (see Table 1.1).

Table 1.1 The impact of RMB exchange-rate movements on key macroeconomic indicators in terms of short-term and long-term elasticity

	Short-term elasticity (1 year)	*Long-term elasticity (5 year)*
Real GDP	0.04	0.02
Consumer spending	0.02	−0.01
Fixed-asset investment	0.08	0.03
Industrial production	0.04	0.02
Employment	0.03	0.01
Inflation	0.06	0.09
Real wages	−0.01	−0.03
Current account (% of GDP)	0.04	0.06
Fiscal balance (% of GDP)	0.02	0.00

Note: The numbers shown in the table represent percentages. They give the change in each indicator as a percentage given a 1 percent appreciation of the RMB. A positive elasticity is an indication that all indicators decline as the exchange rate of the RMB appreciates.

Source: Simulation results as based on the OEF model.

We can see from the results that short-term GDP is lowered by 0.04 percent and employment falls by 0.03 percent for every 1 percent increase in the value of the RMB. If the RMB appreciates by 10 percent, then real GDP is lowered by roughly 0.4 percent and employment is reduced by .3 percent. The long-term effect is somewhat smaller. Meanwhile, in another respect, the impact of exchange-rate appreciation on investment far exceeds that on consumption in the short run. This reflects the greater price elasticity of investment. In the long run, however, the impact of exchange-rate appreciation on both investment and consumption is about the same. We should take note of the fact that real wages increased with an appreciating RMB. This is because, even though economic activity declines to a degree, the decline in nominal wages is less than the decline in inflation, meaning that the real income of wage-earners has actually increased. The ultimate result of an appreciating RMB is an increase in consumption and also an increase in the share that consumption represents in the overall economy.

Superficially, an appreciation of the RMB brings with it some negative consequences for both economic growth and employment over the hypothetical five-year period. These results do not, however, incorporate the benefits to long-term economic growth of structural changes in the economy. In the analysis that follows, we will see the structural changes that an appreciating RMB actually has brought about in China's economy. First, after exchange-rate reform, the share of primary and second industries in the economy underwent a stable decline, while tertiary industries exhibited a stable rise. It is for this reason that we must evaluate the effect of exchange-rate reform on the economy in a dynamic way. In the short run, economic growth is indeed negatively impacted to a degree, but reform has even greater potential to increase long-term economic growth. Looking at actual statistics, in the three-year period following the reforms of both 1994 and 2005, China was in the midst of high-speed economic growth, and appreciation of the RMB actually helped ameliorate the overheating of the economy.

Second, an appreciating RMB has different effects on different industries. (As shown by the research,) real appreciation will reduce employment in the agricultural sector but increase the numbers of those employed in the tertiary sector. It will increase the services component of GDP. In the short term, to a degree, it will negatively impact secondary industries as manifested mainly in employment in industries that compete for imports. Over the long run, however, there will be no appreciable impact on employment numbers in secondary industries. In the long run, therefore, reform of China's exchange-rate system helps bring about the desired structural change in employment patterns. Additionally, average wages of China's citizens will experience a noticeable increase after exchange-rate reform, while a stronger RMB will also enable much greater real purchasing power. These are beneficial in terms of improving the living standards of people in general, and their social welfare.

The impact of exchange rates on inflation is quite apparent (from the modeling). An appreciation of the RMB by 10 percent has the ability to reduce inflation by close to one percentage point. What this indicates is that currency appreciation is an effective means to tighten money supply. Moreover, the results of the modeling make it clear that appreciation of the RMB can lead to a lowering of short-term policy-dictated interest rates, which means that increases in interest rates and appreciation of the currency can be substituted for one another to a certain degree. Finally, results of the modeling show that appreciation of the RMB can lower the surplus in the current account. This is in line with general expectations, but behind this result also stands the 'Marshall-Lener condition,' which states that it is possible for currency appreciation to narrow the current account surplus if the absolute value of the elasticity of all import and export prices is greater than 1.

Finally, we should take note of the fact that some variables have great short-term effects but that these gradually diminish to the extent that they can be cancelled out over the long term. Some of the more prominent of such variables include real GDP, investment in fixed assets, industrial production, and employment. What change in these variables reflects is the ability of an economic entity to self-moderate, and the extent to which such adjustments are flexible. If an economic entity anticipates appreciation, businesses will adjust behavior accordingly so as to mitigate the impact of such appreciation on the real economy. More importantly, though, we should realize that the main impacts of RMB exchange-rate reform come through changes in China's economic structure. Even though the impact may be negative in the short run, the optimization of industrial structure prepares China for economic competitiveness in the long run. In the meantime, exchange rate reform will have effectively mitigated an overheating economy and increased the real income of Chinese citizens, thereby improving their overall level of social welfare.

Appreciation and changes in the rate of economic growth

RMB exchange rates play two major roles in influencing the rate of China's economic growth. The first relates to the impact of appreciation itself, and the second relates to the impact of exchange-rate volatility. Theoretically exchange rates influence economic growth through a number of different channels, while rates are in turn affected by changes in the degree of economic growth. Reform of China's exchange-rate system will first of all affect import and export trade and the country's international capital flows. Secondly, reform will also affect the structure of domestic industries, employment conditions, and price levels, and will thereby have an influence on the overall level of economic growth.

On the one hand, it is not a given that devaluing a currency will automatically have a 'pull effect' on economic growth. In theory, a depreciation of the RMB would increase China's exports and the production of import-substitution goods over a short time. It could also bring on a number of negative effects, however. These include an increase in the cost of imports, an increase in the cost of foreign debt, and more intense inflation. The experience of many countries shows that a depreciation of the currency can actually cause a contraction in that country's economy. Edward (1988) looked at this subject with a study of twelve developing countries between the years 1965 and 1980. Looking at relevant variables, he evaluated the impact of depreciation on the countries' economic growth. The results showed that depreciation had a contracting effect for the first year, but that this was reversed after one year, becoming neutral in the long term. Research on Mexico conducted by Copelman and Werner (1995) shows that depreciation of the Mexican currency actually led to a decline in output.

On the other hand, even though an appreciating currency theoretically has the effect of lowering exports and increasing imports, and can negatively impact countries that rely heavily on exporting, it can also benefit a country. Since importing costs are reduced at the same time, domestic investment and production benefit, so long as demand for overseas goods does not increase too greatly. Meanwhile, an appreciating RMB definitely affects the long-term and short-term flow of international investment capital, both in terms of where it flows and the speed with which it flows. This has a major influence on the accumulation of capital within China. Once the RMB appreciates, not only can this affect the cost of foreign direct international investment in China, thereby changing its dynamics, but it can also affect the quantity of Chinese investment going abroad. The result can involve considerable volatility in short-term capital flows, affecting not only economic stability in the country but China's overall economic development.

Meanwhile, changes in import and export structures, and in international capital flows, in turn affect China's industrial structure and its levels of employment. An appreciating RMB can increase the real wealth of citizens and thereby help expand domestic consumption. At the same time, it can raise wage levels, and stimulate a more rational redistribution of income in the country. Income can thereby be shifted from groups that have an overly high marginal propensity to save toward groups that have a low marginal propensity to save. This in turn helps stimulate the economy from the perspective of both consumption and investment. Finally, such macroeconomic changes can in turn trigger changes in exchange-rate levels, which can then generate yet another round of influence on economic growth.

Empirical studies generally show that an appreciating RMB has a negative impact on China's economic growth, and this is basically consistent with the results of our own OEF modeling analysis. However, each different study comes up with very substantial differences in the degree of influence of RMB appreciation on economic growth. For example, Wei Weixian (2006) studied the impact of RMB appreciation on the Chinese economy by using a 'computable general equilibrium model.' He concluded that RMB appreciation has negative nonlinear effects on China's real GDP growth rate as follows: a 5 percent appreciation lowers real GDP by 0.29 percent, a 10 percent appreciation lowers it by 0.73 percent, and a 20 percent appreciation lowers it by 2.18 percent. This means that the elasticity of economic growth, as relative to currency appreciation, varies between 0.06 and 0.11.

Lu Wanqing and Chen Jianlian (2009) created a model to evaluate the impact of exchange rates on a country's economic growth, in order to investigate the role that exchange rates played on China's domestic output. Using quarterly statistics between the years 1995 and 2005, they estimated the multiplier effect of exchange-rate changes. The results indicated that when the real, effective exchange rate appreciated by 1 percent, exports went down by 2.37 percent and imports by 2.19 percent, while economic growth fell by 0.12 percent. Foreign direct investment in China basically was unchanged. The policy recommendation of these authors was that a small degree of currency appreciation would not affect the economy too much, whereas a large degree of appreciation might lead to crises caused by the inflow of international 'hot money.' They noted that this might destabilize the financial system and severely damage the ability of China's economy to sustain rapid growth.

Shi Jianhuai (2007) used a model called the 'vector autoregressive model' (VAR) to study the effects of RMB exchange-rate changes on China's output. After allowing for factors that might lead to a false relationship between the two, and keeping these at a minimum, he still found that the empirical data showed a decrease in output with an increase in the RMB real exchange rate. This effect was not over-ruling, however. Once the model took into account the ties between China's economy and the international financial system, the effect of exchange-rate 'shocks' on China's output lessened dramatically. The impact of interest-rate changes in the United States, for example, had a greater impact. Furthermore, the model found that appreciation of the RMB affected people in cities differently from people in the countryside, and that it increased the disparity between city and countryside. The policy recommendation coming out of this study was to avoid large-scale appreciation, to increase the band within which the RMB trades, as appropriate, in order to ease pressure to revalue the RMB.

Another important aspect of exchange-rate (policy) adjustments relates to the way exchange-rate volatility in itself can have an impact on economic growth, whether the adjustments relate to increasing the flexibility of exchange rates or broadening the band in which the rate is allowed to float. Ding Jianping (2003) used a model called the 'generalized autoregressive conditional heteroskedastic model' (GARCH) to evaluate this. Using data from the years between 1990 and 2002, he looked at exchange-rate movements in Southeast Asian countries before and after the Asian financial crisis. Before the crisis, essentially all economic entities in the study maintained a growth rate of 7 percent. After the crisis, economic growth dropped to a low level.

Ding Jianping's quantitative analysis further indicated that exchange rates in South Korea and Thailand saw a notably larger variance after the crisis, those in Singapore and China's Taiwan saw some increase, but generally speaking, volatility increased for the great majority of East Asian countries. His policy recommendation was to take advantage of China's sustained high rate of economic growth to implement exchange-rate reform. His reasoning was that exchange-rate variances appear to be relatively small during periods of fast economic growth, and episodes of volatility appear to be shorter. The best time for China to internationalize its currency would be during a period of sustained, fast, growth, since such growth provides a stable economic environment for currency-system reform.

There is in fact no ready-made answer to the question of how economic growth and currency fluctuations affect one another in China. Nevertheless, if

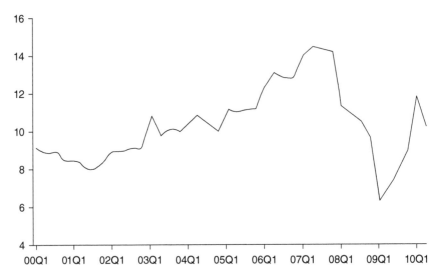

Figure 1.2 GDP growth rates between the first quarter of 2000 and the second quarter of 2010, in percent growth year on year.

Source: WIND database.

we examine the trajectory of economic growth in China since 1994, we discover that two periods of relatively large exchange-rate volatility were also two periods of fast economic growth. Those two were between 1994 and 1997, and between 2005 and 2008 (see Figure 1.2). We cannot infer from this that exchange-rate volatility results in high-speed economic growth, of course, for the cause and effect relationship may be just the opposite – that is, in uncertain economic times, the government may simply be less willing to tolerate high exchange-rate volatility.

International balance of payments and structure of trade

Exchange rates are critical links that serve to tie the economy within a country to the economy outside the country. Changes in the overall level of exchange rates can therefore have a direct impact on the prices of China's imports and exports, the total volume of its trade, and changes in the structure of different business sectors. Exchange-rate reform in 2005 brought with it a certain increase in the flexibility of the RMB rate while the currency also appreciated to a fairly large degree. Seen in overall terms, contrary to what one might assume, this appreciation of the RMB was accompanied by a strong increase in exports and ongoing increase in China's current account surplus. The dramatic increase in the current account reached a peak in 2007, when the surplus totaled some 10.8 percent of GDP. It then dropped somewhat, affected by the international financial crisis (see Figure 1.3).

This does not, however, mean that the appreciation of the RMB is what led to increased exports and China's current account surplus. Trade figures are shaped

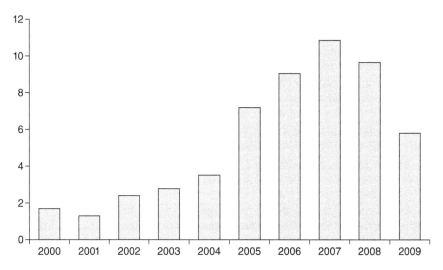

Figure 1.3 China's current account surplus as a percentage of GDP.

Source: WIND database.

by many factors, both domestic and external. For one, the depreciation of the US dollar offset a portion of the appreciation of the RMB. For another, ongoing low interest rates around the world meant that the sound global economy provided strong ongoing demand for China's exports. Combined with somewhat lower costs on imported items, this meant that China's current account saw a dramatic increase.

An analysis of China's imports and exports as divided into categories shows the following. First, imports and exports include the two main categories of primary products and manufactured goods. Some of China's economic sectors benefited more from RMB appreciation than others, specifically those importing raw materials and spare parts. Industries that benefited in particular included the petrochemical industry (because of importing crude oil), the papermaking industry (because of importing pulp and waste paper), the steel industry (due to the import of iron ore), and the chemical fibers and plastic materials industries (due to importing raw materials). Nevertheless, the effect that an appreciating RMB had on changing the structure of China's imports was not in fact very noticeable. The percentages of primary products and manufactured goods that were imported into the country remained fairly steady before and after the exchange-rate reform of 2005. Manufactured goods continued to constitute roughly 80 percent of China's total imports.

The effect that an appreciating RMB had on China's exports was, in contrast, quite apparent. The share of primary products in China's exports consistently fell, from 8 percent of total exports prior to reform to 5 percent after reform. At the same time, certain industries that had been quite competitive prior to reform were now affected by a stronger RMB – these industries were primarily in such labor-intensive businesses as textiles and garments. The share of textile-related products in China's total exports fell from 26.3 percent in 2004 to 23.4 percent in 2008. In contrast, the share of exported machinery in total exports rose from 42.8 percent in 2004 to 47.1 percent in 2008.

These changes in exports were echoed by a change in the composition of China's manufactured-goods production. The manufacture of light-industry goods, textiles, and miscellaneous products continued to grow but at a much slower pace than the rate at which machinery production grew. This was closely related to changes in China's dynamic comparative advantage, given appreciation of the RMB (see Figure 1.4). Meanwhile, many other industries were affected by multiple factors. The automobile industry, for example, benefited from lower prices for imported spare parts but also suffered a competitive impact from lower prices on similar imported cars.

Not only must we take the above complexities into account, but we should also realize the fact that exchange-rate changes have a different effect on different kinds of products given their different price elasticity. According to the theory known as the 'Marshall-Lerner condition,' an appreciation of a country's currency will lower an excessive trade surplus if the sum of the elasticities (in absolute values) of imports and exports, as relative to the exchange rate, is greater than one. After allowing for the influence of economic trends, we can recognize a long-term correlation between China's imports and exports of both primary commodities and manufactured goods and three key variables, namely the real exchange rate, real income, and trade policy. We have carried out calculations on data during

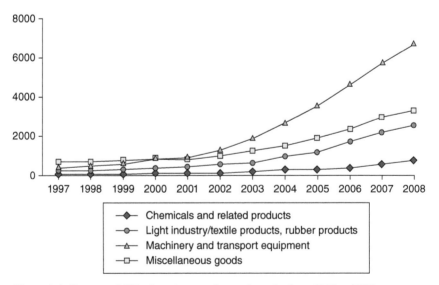

Figure 1.4 Exports of China's main manufactured goods, from 1997 to 2008.
Unit: USD 100 million.

Source: www.cei.gov.cn database.

the period of exchange-rate reform and discovered the following. The elasticity of exported primary commodities against the real exchange rate was −2.48. That of exported manufacture goods was −0.516. In contrast, that of imported primary commodities was 0.668 and that of imported manufactured goods was 0.2.

What this data shows is that the impact of real exchange-rate changes on trade in primary commodities was greater than the impact on trade in manufactured goods. Moreover, the sum of elasticities (in absolute values) of primary-product imports and exports was 3.15, whereas it was only 0.725 for manufactured goods. Primary products therefore meet the 'condition' as proposed by the Marshall-Lerner theory, but manufactured goods do not. This indicates that the appreciation of the RMB has the ability to improve China's trade imbalance by lessening the extent of its trade surplus in primary commodities but not in manufactured goods. Given that manufactured goods currently constitute some 95 percent of China's total imports and exports, it remains to be seen how thoroughly any RMB appreciation can modify the country's foreign trade imbalance.

The effect of an appreciating RMB after the 2005 reform on China's industrial structure was as follows. First, after the reform, the share of both primary and tertiary industries in China's GDP sustained a constant decline. The GDP share of primary industries went from 12 percent in 2005 to 10.6 percent in 2009. The GDP share of secondary industries went from 47.4 percent in 2005 to 46.8 percent in 2009 (see Figure 1.5). In contrast, the GDP share of tertiary industries went up by 2.1 percentage points, to 42.6 percent. The real estate industry is of particular note in this regard. After the exchange-rate reform, the real estate industry and

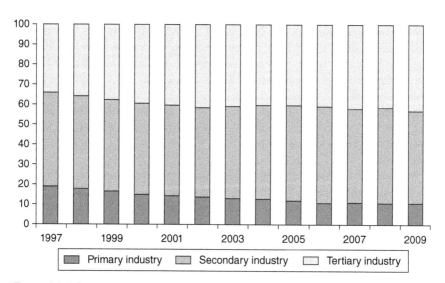

Figure 1.5 Primary, secondary, and tertiary industries in China as a percent of China's GDP, between 1997 and 2008.

Source: ww.cei.gov.cn database

related industries experienced surging growth, driven in part by relatively loose monetary policies. Demand was strong while at the same time asset prices soared. The 'value-added' measurement of China's real estate industry rose steadily as a percentage of all tertiary industries, while the construction industry rose in corresponding fashion. Construction as a percentage of GDP rose by 1.1 percent between 2005 and 2009, to reach 6.7 percent of the economy.

The influence of an appreciating RMB on international capital flows

The impact of RMB exchange rates on China's economy can be measured not only in terms of the trade account, but also of the capital account. Expectations of a higher RMB soared after the exchange-rate reform of 2005. This led to an excessive amount of international short-term capital coming into China, with its potential impact on the economy. The following section analyzes the frequency and direction of short-term and long-term capital flows in China, after the reform.

A number of things can influence international capital flows, including differentials in interest rates, levels of inflation, sophistication of the financial system, exchange-rate expectations, and the state of a domestic economy vis-à-vis the international economy. After the 2005 exchange-rate reform in China, the appreciating RMB and increased flexibility in its rate, together with the resulting differential in interest rates, provided a certain attraction for international capital coming into China. It also, however, created stronger expectations that the RMB would continue to appreciate. This affected short-term capital flows.

Looking at the long-term situation, the amount of 'actually utilized' foreign capital began a clear rise after the unification of the dual-exchange-rate system in 1994. It rose until reaching a stable level of around USD 60 billion. The amount rose again to some extent after the exchange-rate reform of 2005. By 2008, it reached a peak of USD 95.25 billion (see Figure 1.6). Meanwhile, the cumulative sum of foreign direct investment in China reached USD 898.4 billion (in 2008), which constituted 62.5 percent of China's foreign financial liabilities. This figure was an increase of 3.6 percentage points over the amount in 2005. Between 2006 and 2008, the total cumulative inflows of foreign direct investment came to USD 264.5 billion, while outflows came to USD 103.6 billion, for a net influx of USD 160.9 billion.

Meanwhile, China's own direct foreign investment overseas rose swiftly after the exchange-rate reform of 2005. It increased at an average annual rate of 70 percent. The annual sum went from USD 5.5 billion in 2004 to USD 52.15 billion in 2008 (see Figure 1.7). One direct reason for this was the loosening of controls on making foreign direct investments overseas, after the exchange-rate reform. This was in line with the policy goal of reducing or eliminating China's surplus in its international balance of payments.

The rise in the value of the RMB did not in fact lessen the flow of foreign direct investment coming into China, which is a form of long-term capital. A number of ongoing factors continued to provide high returns to foreign investors. These

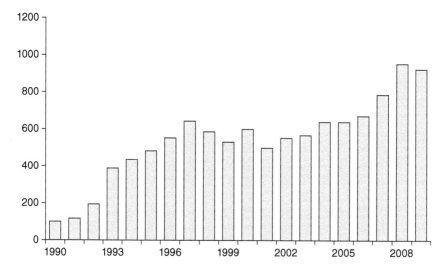

Figure 1.6 'Actually utilized' (realized) foreign capital in China between 1990 and 2009. Unit: USD 100 million

Source: www.cei.gov.cn database.

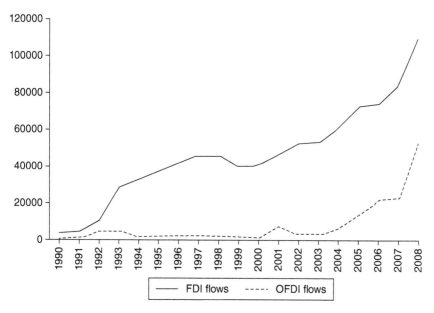

Figure 1.7 China's foreign direct investment overseas and foreign direct investment coming into China, between the years 1990 and 2008. Unit: USD 100 million

Source: www.cei.gov.cn database.

included China's strong rate of real economic growth and its low input-factor prices as the result of price distortions caused by China's systems. Meanwhile, ongoing high levels of demand overseas ensured that the products would sell, which contributed further to incentives to invest. At the same time, though, an appreciating RMB gave China the opportunity to expand its own overseas investments. This in turn helped in transitioning China's domestic economy.

At present, foreign direct investment in China takes up the largest share of China's foreign liabilities. (It is not strongly affected by currency volatility.) The percentage of China's foreign liabilities held in things that *are* strongly affected by currency volatility, such as stocks, bonds, and other forms of financial capital, is fairly small, as is the percentage held by loans made by foreign banks. The category of things that are strongly affected by currency volatility includes investments with a maturity of one year or less that are included in China's balance-of-payments figures ('on-BOP'), it includes money market instruments among securities-type investments, and it includes 'hidden' or 'illegal' short-term international capital movements that are not on balance-of-payment figures ('off-BOP'). These things are more strongly affected by interest-rate spreads between China and other countries, and by expectations of an appreciating RMB.

The volume of China's short-term international capital flows began to surge in 1995. They shifted from net flows out of the country to net inflows in the year 2003. Net inflows were particularly notable in 2004, prior to the exchange-rate reform, when they reached USD 113.954 billion. This figure receded slightly after the exchange-rate reform. Looking at the frequency of fluctuations in the volume of international capital flows, one sees a more apparent rise in two-way flows of short-term international capital after the exchange-rate reform, and also a clear increase in fluctuation of amounts. Wang Shihua and He Fan (2007) conducted a study on the flow of short-term international capital in China – they analyzed the primary factors affecting capital inflows as well as outflows. Their results showed that the primary influences came from interest-rate spreads and expectation of a stronger RMB, but between these two things, the more important was expectations.

Zhang (2009) studied the same issue from a different perspective. He discovered that China's current account surplus grew 'explosively' from 2003 onwards and rose in tandem with the appreciation of the RMB. This is a puzzling phenomenon. Zhang feels that the current account surplus has been artificially over-valued to a certain degree. The reason is that the exchange-rate reform created expectations of a stronger RMB which encouraged more capital to flow into the country. Meanwhile, China's government has continued to implement strict controls over capital accounts, which means that inflowing funds have gone through various alternative channels involving the current account. One example might be the false reporting of export values. According to Zhang's estimates, the volume of 'hot money' flowing into China between the years 2004 and 2007 could represent as much as 2 percent to 3 percent of China's GDP (see Figure 1.8).

Chen Langnan and Chen Yun (2009) looked at China's monthly statistics between the years 1999 and 2008 in order to evaluate the relationship among

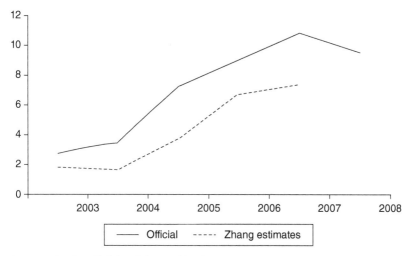

Figure 1.8 The official and the unofficial current account surplus in China, with
'unofficial' being after 'hot money' is deducted from the official figures.
Figures are expressed as a percent of GDP, between the years 2003 and 2008.

Source: www.cei.gov.cn database, and Zhang (2009).

three variables: the RMB exchange rate, asset prices, and China's short-term
international capital flows. They used an 'ARDL-ECM model' to conduct the
research. Their results indicate that certain things have a clear impact on short-
term international capital flows while others do not. Those with a strong long-
term influence include changes in expectations regarding the RMB rate and
interest-rate spreads between China and other countries. Those with little influence include overall RMB exchange-rate levels, the domestic stock market in
China, and the rate of return on real estate. Meanwhile, three variables have an
obviously 'delayed' effect on short-term international capital flows, namely the
RMB exchange rate, interest-rate spreads, and the rate of return on real estate.

Chen Xuebin et al. (2007) evaluated the factors driving long-term and short-
term capital flows in China between 2000 and early 2007 through empirical analysis. His results indicated that high-speed growth of China's economy and a stable
appreciation of its currency contributed to drawing in long-term foreign direct
investment. In contrast, the attractions for short-term capital included the ability
to arbitrage given the development of China's capital markets and the ability to
arbitrage.

Chen's empirical study shows a greater frequency of short-term capital movements after the 2005 exchange-rate reform, with greater capital flows coming as
a result of expectations of a stronger RMB. Nevertheless, our research suggests
that this is not long-term. Our own analysis of the influence of exchange-rate
reform on economic growth includes the evolution of the exchange-rate regime
being used and the different stage of national development that will eventually be
achieved. Results indicate that, once confidence is established regarding China's

exchange-rate policies, and once the domestic economy stabilizes and grows at a sustained pace, movements of short-term international capital will not have any great impact on China's domestic production.

Exchange-rate policies and inflation

Changes in the overall level of RMB exchange rate can have both a direct and an indirect effect on domestic prices. This kind of effect has been given the name 'exchange-rate pass-through effect on prices.' On the one hand, an appreciating RMB means a lower cost of imported goods and raw materials. This lowers domestic prices overall. On the other hand, an appreciating RMB also means higher prices on exported goods, which weakens their competitiveness on international markets. Meanwhile, lower demand among international markets can potentially lower China's domestic production. This in turn can lead to deflation and general price decline. In addition, exchange-rate changes can also have the effect of changing the structure of demand and therefore the price index of China's domestic goods. Added to these things, one must take into account the cost of 'friction' of all kinds, such that exchange-rate changes are not passed through in their entirety to price changes. Finally, a host of other factors also comes into play.

Empirical analysis of the influence of exchange rates on China's domestic prices, before and after the exchange-rate reform, indicates the following. First, exchange rate changes had a lowering effect on both the consumer price index (CPI) and the producer price index (PPI), irrespective of whether the changes were before or after the reform. Appreciation of the RMB had the effect of lowering price indexes. At the same time, the effect of exchange-rate changes was far greater on the PPI than it was on the CPI. This is in line with what should happen in theory, since exchange-rate changes first affect the prices of imported and exported goods, which only then in turn affect the cost structures of enterprises and the ex-factory prices of finished goods. The impact of exchange-rate changes on China's CPI was greater after the reform than before, but the delayed effect was prolonged. The impact of exchange-rate changes on China's PPI was somewhat smaller after the reform than before – going from 18.8 percent down to 16.74 percent. The impact of reform also had a delayed effect, probably by around five months, and the effect was expected to last for around two years (Wu Zhiming and Guo Yukai, 2010).

Figure 1.9 below shows the trend lines of RMB real effective exchange rates after reform of China's exchange rate system in 2005, together with domestic price levels as indicated by the consumer price index and the ex-factory prices of manufactured goods (the producer price index). One can see that the real effective exchange rate of the RMB rose after exchange rate reform. Until mid-2008, the CPI and PPI also exhibited a rising trend. After that, when the real exchange rate rose dramatically, both the CPI and PPI fell back to a great extent.

The three trend lines as shown in this figure indicate several things.

First, the dynamic impact of exchange-rate changes is different for retail prices and producer prices. The PPI is a leading indicator that reflects the direction in

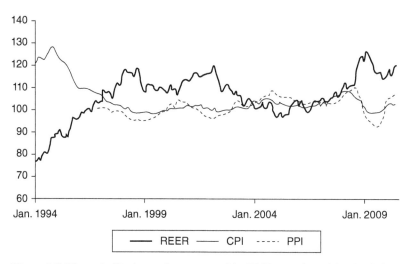

Figure 1.9 The real effective exchange rate of the RMB, together with price indexes, between 1994 and 2010.

Source: WIND database.

which the overall economy is moving. After the exchange-rate reform, the 'pass-through effect' of the RMB on PPI was diminished. This was mainly related to China's imports, particularly energy, due to China's energy-dominated import structure. Since 2005, constant increases in the international price of energy, combined with China's limited capacity to dictate prices in this sector, lowered the role that an appreciating RMB might otherwise have played in lowering costs of imports. This in turn weakened the 'pass-through effect' of exchange rates on the producer price index.

Second, the three trend lines indicate the phenomenon of an appreciation of the RMB that is simultaneous with price inflation within the country, and increased inflationary pressure in general, between 2005 and 2008. This is due to the fact that retail prices are more susceptible to domestic economic factors. Inflation following the exchange-rate reform showed up first in the inflated prices in the real estate market as well as prices in industries related to this market. The next step was an increase in stock-market prices, and finally the price hikes spread to such 'weak links' in the economy as agricultural commodities and food.

An excessive amount of money supply was the main reason such a phenomenon could take place. In addition, other elements played a role, such as the way systemic factors and structural issues distort rational pricing of input factors in China. In recent years, the explosive rise in China's asset prices can to a large extent be attributed to relatively loose or 'easy' money-supply policies. At the same time, distortions in the prices of labor, land, and capital have driven massive amounts of investment into real estate and related enterprises. The resulting increase in demand for this kind of investment has further driven up asset prices.

Meanwhile, since international demand not only has not fallen but in fact continues to increase, China faces a structural shortage in labor supply. The increase in wages that result from this structural shortage are in turn pushing up the cost of production. The rise in international prices for raw materials and energy has offset the appreciation of the RMB to a certain extent, meaning that China does not enjoy the benefits of lower import costs. All of these things have pushed China's prices up to a higher overall level.

In sum, exchange-rate changes are not the determining factor when it comes to China's price-level increase. Exchange-rate appreciation can in fact bring on price declines. From empirical analysis of the exchange-rate pass-through mechanisms at work on CPI and PPI, it is clear that the effect of exchange-rate changes on prices in China has been modest. Instead, China's domestic money-supply exerts a greater influence on price levels, together with other systemic factors. China was implementing a loose money-supply policy as it appreciated its currency. This, in concert with the international economic situation at the time, was the primary reason for the country's price-level increases.

The structure of employment in China and income distribution

In the example of an open economy, exchange-rate changes will lead to changes in the relative competitiveness of products coming from inside and outside the country. This in turn will lead to reallocations of labor and changes in the total labor supply in the respective countries. After the exchange-rate reform in China, the appreciation of the RMB led directly to price changes of both imported and exported goods. (Theoretically) this impacted levels of production and employment among enterprises that were heavily reliant on foreign trade. In addition, the redeployment of various industries also (theoretically) impacted their employment, particularly in such areas as service industries and construction. This affected the structural allocation of employment as well as the overall level of employment.

In the example of China, other factors are at work. China has a 'dual' economic structure, and this unique feature continues to ensure that there is a rich surplus of labor in rural areas. Despite economic growth in the country, and the shift of large numbers of the rural population toward cities, 40 percent of China's population is still employed in traditional agricultural industries. The value of agricultural production in China, however, comes to only 10 percent of GDP. Another unique aspect of China's existing reality is that it has reached the peak of its demographic-dividend period (that is, the period in which baby boomers constitute the majority of the workforce and are productive). This also means that only one dependent person needs to be cared for by every 2.5 people in the working population, a rate that is the lowest in the world. A look at the total employment figures in China (see Figure 1.10) will show that the number of people employed in the country will continue to maintain a slight increase over the next ten years, although there was a slight decline in employment after the exchange-rate reform.

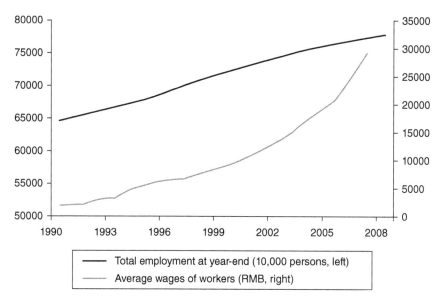

Figure 1.10 Number of people employed in China, and average wages of those who hold
      jobs, 1997–2008.

Source: www.cei.gov.cn database.

At the same time, average wages of those employed rose considerably since 2004.
Between 2007 and 2008, the increase in average wages reached 18 percent. This
increase in wages was an average of 5 percent more than it had been in the three
years prior to the exchange-rate reform.

    Demand for labor can be affected not only by changes in the real exchange
rate, through effects on export prices and import costs, but can also be affected
by future expectations for exchange-rate changes on the part of enterprises. As a
result of expectations, enterprises adjust their investment policies and this in turn
has an impact on employment levels. Fan Yanhui and Song Wang (2005) conducted an analysis of the effect of China's real exchange-rate changes on overall
employment in the years between 1980 and 2002. The results of their statistical
analysis shows that real depreciation stimulates employment in manufacturing
industries while real appreciation constrains employment, but at the same time
the effect of such appreciation or depreciation on real wages is not apparent. The
work of Wan Jieqiu and Xu Tao (2004) indicates that small exchange-rate fluctuations have an insignificant impact on employment when the RMB exchange
rate remains fairly stable. Once the RMB appreciates substantially, the negative
impact on employment in China can be substantial.

    Most research to date focuses on the period before the exchange-rate reform. It
analyzes employment levels given changes in the exchange rate. Since the reform,
however, our own research indicates that overall levels of total employment have

not in fact gone down although the speed at which employment has been increasing has fallen somewhat. Meanwhile, the results of research conducted by Luo Chuanpeng (2009) indicate that RMB appreciation has no adverse substantive effects at all on employment, whether that appreciation is long term or short term. His research employed 'principal components analysis' and 'co-integration tests' to arrive at this conclusion. Over the long term, the elasticity coefficient for employment with respect to exchange rates is 0.022. Over the short term, at most, it does not exceed 25 percent, and it has also been declining every year. There are instead two primary variables affecting domestic levels of employment, namely the domestic level of interest rates and the level of wages. In the short term, interest rates contribute between 28 percent and 30 percent to the determination of levels of employment, while wages contribute between 46 percent and 49 percent.

There are two ways in which exchange-rate movements affect employment. An appreciating RMB means a decline in the prices of imported goods, which curtails the production and employment of industries that compete with such imports. Second, an appreciating RMB means an increase in prices of exports, which curtails or has the potential to curtail the production of companies that rely heavily on such exports. This in turn affects their employment. The reason industries producing such things as textiles and electromechanical devices were not greatly impacted by the exchange-rate reform is that overseas demand remained strong. In contrast, the chemical industry was negatively impacted to a much greater degree, and this could be attributed primarily to a decline in prices among import-competing products.

Using empirical analysis of how exchange-rate changes affect employment, Ba Shusong (2009) studied the effects of an appreciating RMB on employment in the primary, secondary, and tertiary industries in China. His methodology included a 'co-integration test,' 'pulse reaction,' and other forms of measurement. The results of his work were as follows. Long-term effects of an appreciating RMB, that is, a real increase in the exchange rate, will reduce the number of people employed in agriculture, increase employment in tertiary industries, and elevate the percentage of the services component of GDP. An appreciating RMB has no long-term equilibrium effect on the numbers of people employed in secondary industries, but it does have a short-term negative influence on such employment.

Figure 1.11 shows data on the percentages of people employed in each of the primary, secondary, and tertiary industries. Although the share of employment in the primary industries declined somewhat after exchange-rate reform, it still remained as high as nearly 40 percent, guaranteeing an abundant source of rural labor that can eventually be shifted into secondary and tertiary industries. Changes in this primary sector relate almost entirely to the disparity between urban wages and agricultural incomes. The effect of exchange rates on such things as the reform of China's household registration system and the degree to which China's social security system has been improved is minimal. The percentage of employment in secondary and tertiary industries in China is continuing to increase at a stable rate. The increase in secondary-industry employment sustained a rate of 6 percent in the years between 2005 and 2007, after which the rate of increase

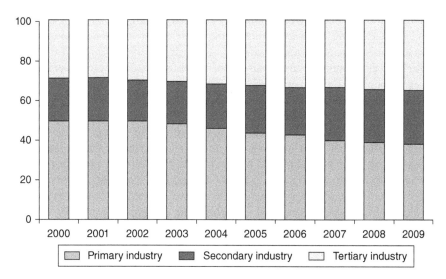

Figure 1.11 Distribution of employment in primary, secondary, and tertiary industries, 2000–2009.
Unit: percentage of total employment.

Source: www.cei.gov.cn database.

dropped to 2 percent. The rate of increase in tertiary industries rose to 3 percent in 2008, and sustained a constant increase after the exchange-rate reform.

The above research results are in agreement with those of Ba Shusong (2009), as well as with Ding Jianping (2006), who used analysis based on the exchange rates and employment situations of eight Asian countries. Even though appreciation of the RMB may have a certain negative impact on employment in manufacturing industries, the stability of overseas demand ensures that this impact on China's manufacturing-related employment is not excessive. Meanwhile, appreciation of the RMB helps facilitate a shift toward service-industry-related employment. This process moves in tandem with the optimization of industrial structure.

The effect of the RMB exchange-rate regime used in China on the country's income distribution can be seen primarily in the way it affects industrial restructuring and changes in general price levels. Changes in the exchange-rate regime initially affect the structure of the country's imports and exports, and then changes in industrial patterns. This eventually affects demand for labor among different kinds of enterprises, as well as compensation for that labor. Another impact of a changing RMB exchange-rate regime is that such change affects commodity prices, which in turn affect the prices of different factors.

Generally speaking, labor is free to move among industries, whereas capital and land are considered to be 'specific factors' in the production process. They are relatively more constrained when it comes to mobility. According to the 'specific factors model' in international trade, the growth of trade is beneficial to increased income of those who own specific factors, but it is unfavorable to owners of mobile factors. Between 2005 and 2008, when foreign demand for Chinese products was strong, the appreciation of the RMB moved in line with an increase in trade. This increase in trade, however, was primarily benefiting, that is, compensating, the owners of capital and land, which was in fact only widening the disparity between their income and those who merely possessed 'labor.'

Zhu Zhongdi and Wang Yunfei (2008) used data from the past thirty years in China to study this particular issue. They found that a growth in trade increases 'total factor productivity,' as well as producer prices in China, and raises the return on all factors but it improves the return on capital more than it improves the return on labor as measured in wages. In industries that rely more heavily on foreign trade, such as the textile industry, the industry that makes goods out of rubber, special-purpose equipment manufacturing, general machinery manufacturing, furniture making and food manufacturing, an appreciating RMB widens this income gap. It returns more to China's owners of capital than it does to owners of labor. As the RMB appreciates, the gap constantly increases.

In 2000, that is, prior to exchange-rate reform, China's national Gini coefficient was already above the warning level of 0.4. This clearly said that China's income disparity was already displaying prodigious levels of inequality. In 2005, the Gini coefficient was 0.46, and in 2007 it worsened on a national basis to 0.48. This meant that, as the RMB was appreciating, the disparity between citizen's income levels was widening. The gap between urban and rural income levels was one part of this. Overall levels of income disparity have in fact already reached what could be considered a line of demarcation, beyond which lies damage to social stability.

Changes in the RMB exchange rate can also change wage disparities among different industries. Supply and demand for labor play a role in determining wage levels in China, but other factors come into play as well. The country imposes severe barriers to entry on such specially designated industries as electric power, post and telecommunications, the financial industries including insurance, real estate development, and so on. Despite an absolute overall growth in average wages in China, and also return on capital, statistics show different degrees of growth for different industries (see Figure 1.12). After the exchange-rate reform in 2005, wage levels were highest in the financial and insurance sector. They also increased at the fastest rate, going up by 19 percent in 2005 to 26 percent in 2007. Second in line in terms of wage increases were such highly monopolized industries as mining, electric power, and gas. The slowest wage increases were seen in such industries as textiles, manufacturing, animal husbandry, agriculture-forestry-and-fisheries, and services. The statistics indicate that wage increases slowed down in China's agricultural sector after the exchange-rate reform of 2005, while increases rose only very slowly in labor-intensive industries such as manufacturing. In contrast, wages rose fairly quickly among general monopolies.

Exchange-rate changes and trade therefore did have some impact on China's general level of wages, but they did not play a key role. For now, wage level changes in various industries are mainly determined by domestic economic

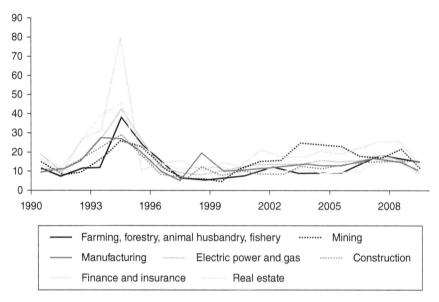

Figure 1.12 Rate of increase in the wages of various industries in China, 1990–2009.
Unit: percentage.

Source: www.cei.gov.cn database.

variables in China. These include the degree of market concentration and the degree to which the industry is a monopoly.

International comparisons in terms of how different countries handled exchange rates and their own macroeconomic policy

Appreciation of the yen was not the primary cause of Japan's economic recession

The value of the yen began a sustained rise relative to the dollar after the Plaza Accord was signed in September of 1985. Within one year of signing the agreement, the rate went from 250 yen to 1 dollar to 152 yen to 1 dollar. It reached a peak of 120 in 1987. Then, between April of 1990 and April of 1995, it appreciated again from 158 yen to 1 dollar to 84 yen to 1 dollar. Many authorities within China feel that this appreciation of the yen was the root cause of Japan's economic stagnation for ten years, or even twenty years. For this reason, they urge the Chinese government to adopt a very cautious stance in how to handle pressures to appreciate the RMB. In fact, their analysis betrays a serious misreading of Japan's economic situation at the time.

First, the ongoing and substantial appreciation of the yen did not negatively impact Japan's domestic economic situation. In reality, the country's economy maintained fairly good growth, given increasing investment and consumption as well as a consistent decline in oil prices. Real GDP rose at an average rate of 3 percent per year prior to the appreciation of the yen, and then between 1985 and 1991, it rose at an average rate of 4.6 percent. Moreover, inflation stayed relatively stable prior to 1989, while imports and exports both declined somewhat but not by much. After the Plaza Accord, imports declined at a faster pace than exports, which meant that Japan's current account surplus increased. Only after the Japanese government instituted policies to stimulate demand in 1988 did that balance start to be reduced.

In fact, the strongest impact of the appreciating yen could be seen in the way it restructured whole industries and the composition of imports and exports. As Japan's terms of trade improved, tertiary industries emerged very quickly, including finance, real estate, and logistical services. Manufacturing, meanwhile, split into areas that benefited and those that did not. The electronic equipment sector continued to play a leading role and machinery developed strongly while such things as textiles and steel were hit very hard. On the export side, such traditional export items as food and textiles declined dramatically while such capital-intensive and technology-intensive products as cars and electronic equipment increased. On the import side, consumer item imports increased tremendously given the rise in real incomes, but the import of such things as raw materials and intermediate products contracted. This was an indication of a shift in the structure of manufacturing industries toward higher value-added goods after the yen appreciated.

The thing that dealt the Japanese economy a devastating blow was not appreciation of the yen after the Plaza Accord, since in reality appreciation in its real sense lasted for only one year. The thing that was in fact most destructive was the way Japanese authorities attempted to counter the appreciation of the yen. In the early 1970s, the yen appreciated by 33 percent and in the 1980s it appreciated by 37 percent. The difference between these two degrees of appreciation was not that great, but appreciation in the 1970s did not result in economic damage. After that time, however, the Japanese government began to resist appreciation which allowed pressures to build up. Once appreciation did take place, the change in exchange rates had to be fairly large.

After the Plaza Accord was signed (in 1985,) Japanese authorities not only did not stop their ongoing efforts to stem appreciation of the yen but they adopted a series of monetary policies in favor of 'easy money.' These included increasing the broad measure of money supply and lowering the central bank's discount rate as a means to release appreciation pressure. After 1987, interest rates within Japan were kept at the low level of 2.5 percent for a long period. The result was that a great bubble in asset-prices was allowed to build within the Japanese economy. Capital flowed into the securities and real estate markets. The government's industrial policies also leaned in the direction of these industries, which encouraged ever greater speculation. As asset prices rose, the intensity of speculative behavior turned into frenzy. In the five years between 1985 and 1990, the price of commercial land in Tokyo went up by a factor of 3.4. The price of residential land went up by 2.5 times. If 1980 prices were regarded as the base price, with a 'real weighted-average asset price index' of 100, then by 1989, Japan's price index had reached 260. In contrast, the same index as applied to such developed countries as the United States, England, and France was below 190.

By 1989–1990, faced with inflationary pressures, the Japanese government took the abrupt and extremely strong measure of tightening the money supply. In a short space of time, authorities increased interest rates from 2.5 percent to 6 percent. This shook investor confidence, and was exacerbated by pressures (on Japanese policymakers) emanating from the United States. As a result, Japan's stock market began a steep decline. Banks, meanwhile, placed stiff restrictions on further real estate loans, which had the effect of 'cutting the financing chain' of real estate developers, that is, drying up their liquidity. Taxes on real estate and consumption taxes, which continued to be levied on the basis of high valuations, now contributed to a drastic decline in land prices. This series of extreme tightening policy measures is what brought on the bursting of Japan's asset price bubble. The process created a massive amount of non-performing loans in the real estate sector. It dealt a severe blow to the confidence of the Japanese people. It threw the economy into chaos and then a long period of stagnation.

Appreciation of the Deutschmark and Germany's relatively stable economic environment

For some time prior to the Plaza Agreement (2005), the Deutschmark experienced a mild and sustained appreciation against the US dollar. After the Plaza Agreement, by 1988, the Mark had appreciated by 61 percent as relative to 1984 levels. By 1995, it had appreciated by 104.4 percent as relative to 1984 levels. As the Mark was appreciating, Germany still maintained a relatively high current account surplus and that surplus continued to increase. Exports increased at a steady rate while imports kept up a steady decline, which added to the broadening trade gap. The primary reason for this was that Germany exported products that were used for investment and that had relatively low price elasticity. At the same time, the appreciating Mark lowered the cost of imported raw materials.

The stable economic environment within which the Mark appreciated was closely related to coordinated policy measures undertaken by the German government. First, the German government guaranteed the absolute autonomy of the central bank through the means of legislation. The central bank's administration, operations, and the formulation as well as enforcing of policy were to be independent by force of law. Such legal assurance made the central bank immune from government interference and enabled it to implement policies to deal with an appreciating currency. Once the central bank's autonomy was confirmed, the bank began to implement prudent monetary policies that provided the foundation for successfully handling a stronger Mark. Through strict control of the money supply, the German central bank stabilized economic growth. Second, slow-paced currency appreciation was a key factor in ensuring that the economy would remain stable, so the central bank also avoided any sharp changes in the value of the Mark that might come from external impacts and that might damage the real economy. This ensured that domestic prices and production in Germany remained steady.

The effect of changes in South Korea's exchange-rate system on the country's economy

South Korea's exchange-rate system progressed through several distinct stages. In the earliest period, exchange rates were strictly controlled. The country adopted a managed-float system in the 1990s. In 1997, as a condition for accepting IMF assistance after the Asian financial crisis, authorities agreed to accelerate the relaxation of restrictions on capital accounts. In December of that same year, South Korea adopted a fully floating exchange-rate regime and then went on to release all controls on capital accounts.

Prior to the transformation of its exchange-rate regime, the country's economic situation did not allow for great optimism. An ill-timed relaxation of capital accounts led to excessive loans to enterprises and a swift expansion of foreign debt. Debt went from USD 43.9 billion in 1993 to USD 154.4 billion in 1997, while short-term debt constituted as much as 44.3 percent of the total. In addition, South Korea's foreign-exchange reserves had essentially gone dry. Its sum total of USD 90 billion was insufficient to pay for one month of the country's import demands. Meanwhile, the central bank of the country lost control over any ability to intervene in foreign-exchange markets. Given these circumstances, under economic pressures both inside and outside the country, South Korea was forced to reform its exchange-rate regime in 1997, when it went to a floating-rate system (see Table 1.2).

For one year following the reform, the Korean won remained highly unstable in part as a result of the Asian financial crisis. Average monthly volatility in the rate reached as much as 8.8 percent, which was 0.64 percent higher than volatility had been before the reform. Later, volatility declined to 1.55 percent between the end of 1998 and 2006. After the reform, the won depreciated slightly for awhile but then appreciated to a modest degree, staying at very nearly the same levels as prior to the reform.

Prior to South Korea's exchange-rate reform, the country's consumer price index rose at an average of 3 percent. In the initial period after reform, inflation reached 0.45 percent but then stabilized at 0.23 percent. The framework for monetary policies was then adjusted and the intermediating target for monetary policy shifted from exchange rates to inflation. Once South Korea changed its exchange-rate regime to a floating system, not only did foreign-exchange reserves not fall but they instead began to increase. Between 1997 and 2007, they went from around USD 45 billion to USD 240 billion. Among the reasons for this was that the country's export-oriented strategy remained the same, resulting in a high level of current account surplus over a long period of time. In addition, intervention by the Korean central bank in foreign-exchange markets also meant that the country accumulated a large amount of foreign-exchange reserves. Capital

Table 1.2 The state of South Korea's economy at the end of 1997, when the country modified its exchange-rate regime

Indicator	Value
Fiscal deficit (% of GDP)	−0.2
Available foreign exchange reserve (USD100 million)	890
Foreign debts (USD100 million)	1,544
Foreign debts (% of GDP)	58.7
Short-term foreign debts (% of total)	44.3
Foreign debts (% of export)	111.4

Source: Qu Fengjie, 'From a managed float to a free-floating exchange-rate system: lessons to be learned from South Korea's experience,' *New Finance*, August 2007.

flowing into South Korea was primarily invested in the stock market, which carried a high degree of risk. In order to cope with the possibilities of short-term flight of capital, the central bank was required to have sufficient foreign-exchange reserves on hand.

The impact on the economy of Taiwan's adjustments to its exchange-rate regime

Taiwan's exchange-rate system went from an early period of fixed rates to a 'flexible' system in the 1980s to the system that is in place now, namely a floating-rate system. Prior to the 1989 reform that established the floating-rate system, there was pressure on the new Taiwan dollar (NT) to appreciate from both internal and external economic factors. As a result, the currency began a sustained appreciation. Between 1986 and 1989, it rose from 39.85 NT to USD 1 to 26.16 NT to USD 1, which represented an appreciation of 33.7 percent. This had a massive impact on Taiwan's economy.

Exports were hit extremely hard, particularly those of labor-intensive industries. The higher value of the NT caused wages to rise and land prices to soar, further increasing the cost of exports. This weakened the price competitiveness of Taiwan's exports and led to the bankruptcy of a large number of small- and medium-sized companies that had produced labor-intensive products for export.

Surging asset prices brought a wave of speculative behavior. Once the NT appreciated, the island was flooded with excess liquidity. A strategy to appreciate the currency that was slow and measured actually triggered higher expectations of appreciation, leading to overheated stock and real estate markets. Asset prices skyrocketed in a crazy manner. The stock market index went from 945 in 1986 to 8616 in 1989, while the price of land in the city of Taipei quadrupled during this period. Meanwhile, the uncontrollable spread of underground lotteries and investment activities, such as '*liuhecai*,' facilitated the speculative craze. ('*Liuhecai*' is the name of a Hong Kong lottery that is based on guessing the bonus number of the Mark Six lottery.) All of this served to threaten the stability of the economy.

The direction of foreign direct investment in Taiwan changed substantially. The appreciation of the NT led to a dramatic increase in overseas investment by Taiwan, concentrated mainly in Southeast Asia and the Chinese mainland. Most of this investment was seeking cheaper production costs. Investment coming into Taiwan from developed countries continued to decline and began to focus now on emerging technology sectors.

Despite the major impact that exchange-rate reform and an appreciating currency had on Taiwan's economy, the economy was able to stay fairly sound. In overall terms, one could say that the exchange-rate reform was relatively successful. Much of this was due to concurrent policy measures adopted by the government that helped play a critical role in guiding the process. First, Taiwan's authorities basically completed the liberalization of interest-rate markets even before the exchange-rate reform began. They gradually expanded the band within which interest rates were allowed to float, and then eventually eliminated controls altogether. This provided a firm foundation for similar liberalization of exchange rates.

Second, as Taiwan's currency appreciated, as foreign exchange reserves increased, and as inflationary pressures mounted, the central bank raised the reserve ratio several times, that is, the percentage of total assets that banks were required to have on hand. It employed credit controls as a way of implementing tighter monetary policies. To a certain degree, this mitigated the severity of the impending economic bubble. In terms of capital controls, Taiwan's authorities had already, since the late 1980s, been stepping up efforts to attract foreign capital to its securities market. As the government opened up access to Taiwan's stock market, however, it also set forth very detailed and stringent regulatory controls and these served to guide foreign investment in a very beneficial way.

As the NT appreciated, and foreign exchange reserves kept growing, Taiwan's authorities also took proactive steps to restructure the composition of these reserves. Between 1987 and 1989, Taiwan purchased a large amount of gold, in the neighborhood of 15 percent of all the world's gold stocks at the time. It also was active in adjusting foreign currencies in its reserves, as the international monetary situation changed. In 1987, the US dollar constituted 80 percent of Taiwan's foreign-exchange reserves but the percentage went down in following years as the dollar exchange-rate declined, until dollar-denominated assets constituted 60 percent.

Finally, in terms of how exchange-rate changes affected various industries: Taiwan's authorities played an active role in upgrading the industrial structure of the economy. They transitioned the economy from reliance on labor-intensive industries to technology-intensive industries. They put high-tech electronic-information industries in a leading position in order to substitute such industries for those that were being affected by lower international competitiveness such as manufacturing industries. They made sure that the value-added component of exported goods was increasing. They elevated the competitive advantage of Taiwan in the international division of labor. They were able to reduce the negative impact of an appreciating currency on exports as a result.

Lessons to be learned from international cases, as China reforms its exchange-rate system

A summary of the three cases described above shows that Japan's experience was a failure, Taiwan's was not highly successful, whereas Korea and Germany maintained fairly sound economic conditions after their exchange-rate reforms. Each country modified its exchange-rate system in the direction of floating exchange rates, but the impact that their actions had on their economies was quite different. Integrating those conclusions with our own currently evolving exchange-rate system, we may be able to draw the following lessons.

1   As a country moves from a managed-float exchange-rate system to a completely floating system, or as its currency appreciates, this will indeed affect the country's economic stability to a degree. A much more important consideration, however, is the degree to which the country selects the correct complementary policy options. It was obvious after the Plaza Accord that the Japanese yen and the Deutschmark would appreciate, but the supporting policy measures that each country took in response had a major effect on the macroeconomic results.

2   In terms of the degree of appreciation, a country should gradually relax controls on exchange rates prior to moving to a completely floating exchange-rate regime. It should allow rates to move at a moderate pace as the currency appreciates, as both Germany and Korea were able to do. If appreciation is held down over a long period of time, it is easy to accumulate incentivized distortions in the economy and thereby sacrifice economic efficiency. In addition, however, as soon as the currency does start to appreciate, movements can be so large and the speed of corrections so swift that they can do serious harm to an economy.

3   Liberalization of interest-rate markets should be undertaken prior to exchange-rate system reform, while adequate regulatory controls should also address capital accounts. To a certain degree, liberalization of domestic interest-rate markets can mitigate the impact that short-term capital influxes might have on an economy, and can thereby preserve domestic economic stability. Meanwhile, as controls on capital accounts are released, appropriate regulatory measures should be implemented to reduce short-term credit movements and to guide the direction of foreign capital flows.

4   As occurred in both Japan and Taiwan, an appreciating currency can bring with it an explosive rise in asset prices. While ensuring that they maintain independence in terms of policy decisions, monetary authorities should implement sound and prudent monetary policies and should strictly control the amount of money that is issued in order to preserve the stability of domestic prices. If authorities instead adopt 'easy' monetary policies as a means to try to combat or lessen appreciation pressures, the consequences can become extremely serious.

5   Authorities should be proactive in adjusting the structure or composition of foreign-exchange reserves. An appreciating currency will not necessarily lead

to a reduction in foreign-exchange reserves, but increasing the band within which that currency is allowed to move means that the country is indeed going to be affected more by changes in international foreign-exchange markets. Because of this, it is necessary to take proactive and voluntary steps to adjust the mix of currencies in one's own portfolio of foreign-exchange reserves as values change. Not only must authorities ensure that the reserves are adequate, but they must ensure their basic stability.

6 Authorities should optimize the industrial structure of their country by providing the appropriate industrial policy guidance. An appreciating currency will necessarily affect the structure of imports and exports and consequently will also affect the general landscape of industries in the country. The experiences of Taiwan and Japan are a case in point. While their respective currencies were appreciating, their governments guided their domestic industries away from traditional labor-intensive industries in the direction of capital- and technology-intensive industries. They repositioned their competitive positions vis-à-vis international markets. As a result, they were able to go further in transitioning their economies and preserving long-term, stable, economic development.

Primary conclusions and policy recommendations

The question of whether or not China's RMB should appreciate has long vexed China's decision makers. Certain things, however, were already decided on January 1 of 1994. They included the sense that the exchange rate should move in the direction of being determined by market mechanisms, in a gradual manner, and that it should fluctuate more and more in line with supply and demand relationships. This policy orientation was confirmed by the central bank on July 21, 2005, and yet again on June 19, 2010. Most recently, several high officials in the central bank have explicitly stated that moving the currency in the direction of a freely floating exchange-rate system and in the direction of being an international currency is China's long-term policy goal.

Nevertheless, over the past several years the government has also adopted an extremely cautious posture with respect to the subject of exchange rates. Since the mid-1980s, the RMB exchange-rate system that is *de facto* used in China is a 'soft peg' to the US dollar. By now, however, there are already at least three considerations that indicate that increasing the flexibility of the RMB exchange rate is an extremely urgent imperative. First, increasing the flexibility of the RMB exchange rate is a necessary precondition for lowering external imbalances and improving the efficiency of China's use of capital. During the global financial crisis, China's external imbalances were already notably declining. The surplus in the current account went from 10.8 percent of GDP in 2007 to 3.5 percent in the first quarter of 2010. Unfortunately, most of this decline is cyclical. Once the crisis passes, the surplus may again rebound and, indeed, the trade surplus is already noticeably rising. At the same time, China's foreign exchange reserves already stand at the high level of USD 2.5 trillion. Other than helping the US government to borrow money in order to get along, these assets contribute very little to the Chinese economy.

Second, increasing the flexibility of the RMB exchange rate is also an essential step if China wants to maintain the autonomy of its monetary policies. In terms of the Mondale Impossible Trinity, China's current policy choice is to maintain relative stability in its exchange rate and an independent monetary policy, while relinquishing the third part of the triangle, allowing the free flow of capital. Research undertaken by Huang Yiping and Wang Xun (2010) indicates, however, that China's control over capital accounts is already notably weakening. The direct consequence of this, namely cross-border capital flows and in particular the free flow of hot money is already directly impacting the autonomy of China's monetary policies. Massive inflows of capital mean that there is a surfeit of liquidity in domestic markets. This interferes with and makes it near impossible for the central bank to achieve its interest-rate policy objectives. As a fast-growing major economic power, China obviously cannot simply abandon the autonomy of its monetary policies, as Hong Kong did.

Finally, an appropriate degree of RMB appreciation is an important link in the process of avoiding trade protectionist policies on the part of other countries. Many 'experts' like to emphasize that exchange-rate policies belong to China alone, and that China has no need for advice from other countries. In principle, this is not incorrect, but it must be recognized that China is already in fact a major economy and anything it does affects global markets. For other countries to have an opinion on what China does is therefore natural. The problem right now is that many newly emerging economies are expressing their views on China's RMB policies, while developed countries are even more vociferous. The US Congress has recently taken numerous actions in this regard, primarily because the United States is approaching two-digit unemployment figures while the US Congress is approaching the mid-term election season. If we cannot respond adequately, there is a very real risk of having a US–China trade war. It should be recognized that taking all steps possible to avoid a trade war is also a policy decision that protects our own interests.

If we do in fact accept that it is necessary to expand the flexibility of the RMB exchange rate, we should then understand exactly what the resulting changes will do to the economy. The critical issue is whether or not such policy will bring about changes that China cannot tolerate – such things might include unemployment to the degree that society is destabilized. Many forms of analysis are available to determine the impact of an appreciating currency on an economy, or the impact of increasing the flexibility of exchange rates on an economy. In simple terms, the frameworks for such analysis can be divided into two major types, namely partial equilibrium and general equilibrium. To answer the relevant questions accurately, we should select an analytical framework that is appropriate and that fulfills the following three conditions. First, it should be able to model general equilibrium; second, it should analyze events from a dynamic perspective; and third, it should be applicable in the context of a major economy. We must avoid those types of exchange-rate analysis that look at only individual variables or only a limited number of pass-through mechanisms.

Our general equilibrium simulation used the OEF model. In this model, a 10 percent appreciation of the RMB can lead to slight declines in GDP, consumption, investment, and employment over the short term and therefore would have an economic impact. At the same time, however, inflation and the current account surplus would also decline so that real wages increase, as well as consumption as a percentage of GDP. The share of non-traded goods in the economy would rise, all of which are changes for the good. Over the long term, the (beneficial) effects of a change of this degree are more apparent. The results of our analysis indicate that the macro-effects of an appropriate degree of appreciation are within a controllable range. Moreover, such a degree of appreciation has positive effects on economic restructuring. Because of this, one of our policy recommendations is that China should continue with the process of appreciating its currency in modest and stable steps.

At the same time, the influence of exchange-rate reform on macroeconomic considerations can be seen more in its effect on economic restructuring. After the reform of 2005, China's primary and secondary industries as a percent of GDP declined while the percentage of tertiary industries in GDP notably increased. This helped optimize our policy goal of restructuring industries. The appreciating RMB also changed the structure of China's exported goods, moving them away from labor-intensive products and more in the direction of capital and technology-intensive products. This helped us reposition the competitive stance of our exports so that we could capture more value-added in our products. In addition, RMB appreciation effectively held down inflationary pressures which, to a degree, moderated the unfortunate effects of an overheated economy.

Finally, RMB appreciation has had the effect of stimulating wage growth and improving real purchasing power, and this, in turn, has improved people's standard of living. It has improved the overall welfare of society at large. Looking out now over a five-year horizon, our research indicates that the negative effects of RMB appreciation on GDP growth and total employment will diminish while the positive effect of RMB appreciation on moderating inflation will increase. At the same time, we believe that, given appreciation of the RMB that remains modest and stable, China can optimize its economy and raise the standard of living of its people over the long term. We believe that this is helpful in maintaining the potential for long-term economic growth as well as for strengthening China's international competitiveness. Past experience shows that the degree of currency appreciation may require some caution, but what needs real attention are areas relating to capital flows and asset prices. These are more likely to be hurt by currency appreciation than the real economy.

The reason the lessons of Japan and Taiwan are so apparent is that these two governments consistently tried to hold down any appreciation of their currencies. In the course of this, their exchange rates and other price variables were able to build up serious distortions so that later adjustments to correct for the distortions were difficult. The steps that had to be taken were intense. Another key consideration is that in the process of appreciating their currencies, these governments maintained extremely loose monetary policies. In doing this, they attempted to relieve the pressures of appreciation. In the end, though, the result was a severe asset bubble that encouraged even more capital to flow in, exacerbating the situation.

How then can the Chinese government satisfy the demands of the market, by allowing the RMB to appreciate to an appropriate degree, while also maintaining macroeconomic stability? Given the analytical results of this report, we propose the following six specific policy recommendations:

First, in order to regain the initiative in the gamesmanship surrounding international economic policy, the RMB should appreciate at an appropriate rate as soon as possible. The ideal time to reinitiate reform of the RMB exchange rate would, in fact, have been the end of 2009. At that time it was already clear that 2010 would be a year of trade protectionism and that the RMB exchange rate would become a focus of international economic policy debates. The direct consequence of procrastination on this issue is that we put ourselves in an involuntary position. If the RMB is still not showing any clear trend to appreciate by the second half of 2010, then we are going to be in a tough position in international markets.

Second, China should change its current excessive reliance on the bilateral RMB–USD exchange rate by instituting a system that genuinely takes a basket of currencies into account. The US dollar is already not, and will not again become, a force for stability in the international currency system. If we continue to allow the RMB to 'chase' the US dollar in such a close way, this will in fact destabilize the exchange-rate system. Excessive focus on the US dollar also makes it easy for RMB exchange-rate policies to become 'bilateralized,' which in fact is an irrational policy approach. To change this situation, not only do we have to move to a genuine 'reference to a basket of currencies,' but we might also take the following action: we could have the central bank announce an 'effective exchange-rate index' every day that gives the RMB rate relative to a basket of currencies, and make this the target rate determining central bank intervention in the markets.

Third, given that we have a 'managed float,' for the time being, the government is still able to control the degree of appreciation. At the same time, however, the government should be putting major effort into developing exchange-rate markets and enabling exchange rates to become a tool for mitigating risk, that is, for hedging. As the RMB exchange rate begins to move in line with market fluctuations, it is still going to be necessary, in the short run, to avoid major volatility in overall levels. We must prevent such volatility from putting too much stress on the economy. As the government increases exchange-rate flexibility, it should also support the development of hedging instruments. When enterprises have mastered the art of using all kinds of financial instruments as an effective way to counter risk, they will be able to withstand market fluctuations in the exchange rate. For the time being, however, it is best to go step by step in increasing the band within which the RMB can fluctuate.

Fourth, we should take active steps to lower China's current account surplus by integrating such measures as currency appreciation and restructuring reforms. We must fundamentally eliminate the risk of getting involved in exchange-rate disputes. In the field of economic research, there is in fact no one single science or standard for judging the proper exchange rate or the degree to which an exchange rate is distorted. The generally accepted practice is simply to look at the current account balance. And in fact one of China's economic policy objectives is to realize a greater balance in its international payments. Naturally, exchange rates are only one means of lowering the external surplus. Other means should also be employed, particularly reducing the extent to which China's domestic economy is distorted by such things as under-valuing factor prices. Not only will this facilitate an increase in domestic consumption and spur the growth of service industries, but ultimately it will also help realize greater balance in international payments, reduce conflict with major trading partners, and benefit China's long-term, sustainable, growth.

Fifth, as we allow the RMB to appreciate, we should be extremely alert to the risk of creating an asset bubble in China. The lesson derived from the experience of both Japan and Taiwan is that attempting to hold down an appreciating currency over a long period not only does not work but it actually inflates an asset bubble. In contrast, currency adjustments made by Germany and South Korea were relatively successful, the reason being that they were able to avoid this very mistake. Given China's own experience between 2005 and 2008, it is clear that the moment the RMB again starts appreciating, increasing amounts of capital will start flowing into the country through both proper and illicit channels. In order to avoid the kind of tragedy that occurred in Japan, China's government should strictly monitor and control any domestic asset bubble. Under normal conditions, appreciating the currency and raising the discount rate in a country are substitutes for one another. We feel, however, that as the RMB appreciates, it would be appropriate for the government to raise interest rates as well, in order to reduce liquidity of the RMB. This will help in preventing an asset price bubble.

Sixth, for the time being, China should consider implementing a combination of macroeconomic policies that include both 'tight monetary policy' and 'loose fiscal policy.' Tight monetary policies are aimed at reducing the risk of inflation and asset bubbles. Loose fiscal policy is aimed at smoothing the transition as the economy restructures. As the RMB appreciates, it is possible that some exporting enterprises will be affected to the extent that workers lose jobs. Relatively relaxed fiscal policies should be in place to provide for unemployment assistance and training for finding new kinds of jobs. Assistance should be available to help both enterprises and workers in the restructuring turbulence that may be brought on by RMB appreciation.

Notes

1 Huang Yiping, Tao Kunyu: National School of Development, Peking University.
2 The OEF model is a global macroeconomic model that incorporates both major economic entities and major economic activities. For more information, please refer to www.oef.com.

Bibliography

Aghion P., Bacchetta, P., Ranciere, R., Rogoff, K. "Exchange Rate Volatility and Productivity Growth: The Role of Financial Development", *Journal of Monetary Economics*, 2009, 56, 494–513

Bordo M.D. "Exchange Rate Regime Choice in Historic Perspective", NBER Working Paper, No. 9654, 2003

Chang R. and Andres Velasco A. "Exchange Rate Policy for Developing Countries", *The American Economic Review*, 2000, 90 (2), 71–75

Chinn, Menzie D. and Shang Iinwei. "A Faith-Based Initiative: Does a Flexible Exchange Rate Regime Really Facilitate Current Account Adjustment?" HKIMR Working Paper No. 12, Hong Kong Monetary Authority, Hong Kong, 2009

Chuanpeng Lu. "Global Economic Imbalance and Trends of RMB Exchange Rate", Wuhan: Wuhan University Press, 2009

Copelman, M. and Werner, A. "The Monetary Transmission Mechanism in Mexico", International Finance Discussion Paper, No. 521, 1995

Edward S. "Real and Monetary Determinants of Real Exchange Rate Behavior, Theory and Evidence from Developing Countries", *Journal of Developing Economics*, 1988, 29, 311–341

Fengjie Qu. "From Managed Floating to Free Floating: South Korean Experience in Exchange Rate Regime Transformation and Lessons", *New Finance*, 2007 (8)

Goldstein, M. "China's Exchange Rate Regime", Peterson Institute for International Economics, Washington D.C., U.S., 2003

Goldstein, M. and Lardy, N.R. "China's Exchange Rate Policy Dilemma", *American Economic Review*, 2006, 96 (2): 422–426

Goldstein, M. and Lardy, N. eds. *Debating China's Exchange Rate Policy*. Peterson Institute for International Economics, Washington D.C., U.S., 2008

Goldstein, M. and Lardy, N.R. "The Future of China's Exchange Rate Policy", Peterson Institute for International Economics, Washington D.C., U.S., 2009

Guolin Li, "Empirical Study on the Relationship between Stability of RMB Exchange Rate Expectations and International Capital Flows", master thesis of Ocean University of China, 2009

Jianhuai Shi. "Is RMB Appreciation Deflationary?", *Economic Research Journal*, 2007 (1)

Jianmin Wang and Zengyin Hu. "Empirical Analysis on the Relationship between Korean Exchange Rate Changes and Trade and Economic Development", *Taiwan Studies*, 1996 (2)

Jianping Ding. "Exchange Rate Volatility and Asian Economic Growth", *World Economy*, 2003 (7)

Jianping Ding and Fei Li. "Effects of Currency Appreciation on Employment by Industry: Empirical Analysis of Relationship between Exchange Rates and Employment in Eight Countries", *Journal of Hebei University of Economics and Trade*, 2006 (7)

Jieqiu Wan and Tao Xu. "Impact of Exchange Rate Adjustments on Employment in China", 2004 (2)

Langnan Chen, Yun Chen. "RMB Exchange Rate, Asset Price and Short-Term International Capital Flows", *Economic Management*, 2009 (1)

Lipschitz, L., Lane, T. and Mourmouras, A. "Capital Flows to Transition Economics: Master or Servant?" IMF Working Paper No. WP/02/11, 2002

McKinoon, R.I. "China's New Exchange Rate Policy: Will China Follow Japan into a Liquidity Trap?" *The Economists' Voice*, 2005, 3 (5), 1–7

Max Corden, W. "Exchange Rate Policies for Developing Countries", *The Economic Journal*, 1993, 103 (416), 198–207

Prasad, E. and Wei, S. "The Chinese Approach to Capital Inflows: Patterns and Possible Explanations," NBER Working Paper, No. 11206, 2005

Reinhart, C.M. and Rogoff, K.S. "The Modern History of Exchange Rate Arrangements: A Reinterpretation," *The Quarterly Journal of Economics*, 2004, 119, 1–48

Rogoff, K.S., Husain, A.M., Mody, A., Robin Brooks, R., and Nienke Oomes, N. "Evolution and Performance of Exchange Rage Regimes", IMF Working Paper, No. WP/03/243, 2003

Shihua Wang and Fan He. "Short-Term International Capital Flows in China: Current Situation, Channels and Drivers", *World Economy*, 2007 (7)

Shusong Ba. "Internal Reform and Restructuring Outweigh Exchange Rate Reform", *Capital Markets*, 2010 (1)

Shusong Ba and Qun Wang. "Empirical Study on the Effects of Real Effective RMB Exchange Rate on Chinese Economy", *Research On Financial and Economic Issues*, 2009 (6)

Sixian Feng and Wei Wu. "Effects of Exchange Rate Changes on Import of Different Goods", *The Journal of Quantitative & Technical Economics*, 2008 (7)

Tahua Zhu. *Study on RMB Exchange Rate Issues*, Beijing: People's Publishing House, 2007

The People's Bank of China. China Monetary Policy Report, 2005–2010

Wanqing Lu and Jianliang Chen. "Empirical Study on Effects of RMB Exchange Rate Movements on Chinese Economic Growth", *Journal of Financial Research*, 2007 (2)

Weixian Wei. "Evaluation of Macroeconomic Effects of RMB Appreciation", *Economic Research Journal*, 2006 (4)

WenbingSha. "Study on RMB Effective Exchange Rate and Internal and External Balance of Macro-economy", Beijing: Economic Science Press, 2007

Xiangqian Lu and Guoqiang Dai. "Effects of Real RMB Exchange Rate Movements on China's Imports and Exports: 1994–2003", *Economic Research Journal*, 2005 (5)

Xingli Fan and Jing Wang. "Plaza Accord, Japan's Long Economic Recession and RMB Appreciation", *World Economy Study*, 2003 (12)

Xuebin Chen, Chenjun Yu and Jingfang Sun. "Empirical Analysis on Factors Affecting International Capital Inflows to China", *Studies of International Finance*, 2007 (12)

Yang Cao. "Effects of Real Exchange Rate Changes on East Asian Economies", doctoral dissertation of East China Normal University, 2007

Yang Yao. "Economic Restructuring and Reform Resumption", *Finance Magazine*, 2010 (3)

Yanhui Fan and Wang Song. "Effects of Real Exchange Rate on Employment: Empirical Analysis of China's Manufacturing Industry", *World Economy*, 2005 (4)

Yiping Huang and Xun Wang. "Analysis on Effectiveness of China's Capital Account Controls", a report under the project entrusted by the Institute of Foreign Economy, NDRC, May 2010

Yu Gu. "Analysis on Effects of RMB Exchange Rate Regime Reform on Chinese Economy", doctoral dissertation of Jilin University, 2008

Yuzheng Lin. "Taiwan Responses to New Taiwan Dollar Appreciation in the 1980s and Lessons for the Chinese Mainland", master thesis of Xiamen University, 2008

Zhiming Wu and Yukai Guo. "Research on the RMB Exchange Rate Pass-Through Effect before the Exchange Rate Regime Reform in July 2005", *Economic Review*, 2010 (2)

Zhiwei Zhang. "Dark Matters in China's Current Account". Paper presented at the China Economist Society Conference on Greater China Economic Integration, March 30–31, 2009, Macau

Zhongdi Zhu and Yunfei Wang. *Theoretical Study and Empirical Test on the Relationship between China's Trade Development and Income Distribution*, Beijing: People's Publishing House, 2008

2 The impact of an appreciating RMB on China's import and export trade

Zhang Xiaoji[1]

The international context for China's import and export trade

Economic globalization as a cause of rapid growth in China's foreign trade

One of the key features of economic globalization is the fact that foreign trade and multinational investment grow at a faster pace than the GDP of any particular country. This is a common phenomenon throughout the world. One of the main reasons for this is that global supply chains greatly increase the amount of international trade in intermediate products. According to World Trade Organization statistics, trade in intermediate products in 2008 represented 40 percent of total trade in finished goods (see Figure 2.1).

The ratio of imports and exports to a country's GDP is on the rise (see Figure 2.2). Within China, this percentage is known as the 'degree of reliance on trade,' or 'trade dependency,' whereas internationally people generally use the

Figure 2.1 Export of goods, worldwide, and global GDP.

Source: WTO report, '2009 Global Trade Statistics'.

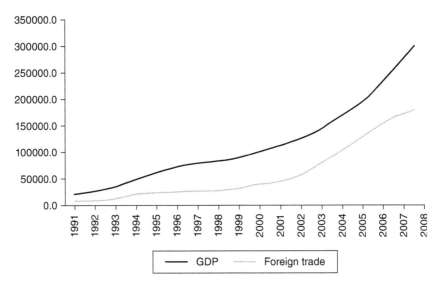

Figure 2.2 The growth in China's foreign trade is notably higher than the country's GDP growth rate.
Unit: RMB 100 million

Source: National Bureau of Statistics of China.

term 'degree of openness in trade.' Despite this use of the term openness, the WTO does not regard this percentage as a figure that can fully represent the openness of a country's trade policy. Generally speaking, economic entities that have a high ratio of service industries, and major economic powers in general, have a trade dependency ratio that is on the low side. For example, the percentage in the United States is lower than 30 percent, while some small countries have a percentage that is higher than 100 percent. In China, for 2008, the figure was 60 percent. This is on the high side for large economies. In the international division of labor with respect to the supply chain, China conducts a great deal of value-added trade that sees products come into the country in quantity and then go out in quantity. This particularly applies to the assembly of telecommunications equipment, office equipment, and so on. The two-way trade has a tendency to duplicate statistics. The phenomenon also exists for Mexico and Canada, within the North American Free Trade Area, since American companies have processing centers along the borders of both countries. Their degree of dependency, or openness, in trade is also, therefore, over 60 percent.

The extent to which trade grows faster than GDP is most pronounced in areas that are tightly integrated into the global economy. International supply chains are often set up in neighboring economic entities. These then become the liveliest centers of global trade and both trade and GDP figures show a rising trend (see Figure 2.3). Intermediary products account for more than 60 percent of exports among east-Asian countries, for example. Of these exports, four

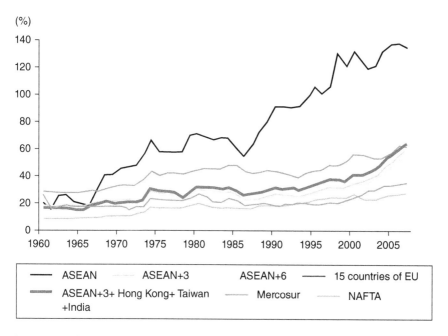

Figure 2.3 The percentage of trade in the GDP figures of major economic regions around the world, from 1960 to 2007.

Source: UN University report, 'A comparative study of regional integration.'

categories of goods constitute more than 80 percent of the total, namely office equipment components (37.5 percent), telecommunications equipment components (27.7 percent), switch apparatus (12.7 percent), and electrical appliance components (6.7 percent).

The trend in the direction of greater global trade imbalances

The 'externalization' of manufacturing industries and services on a regional and also global scale has not only led to international trade growing at a faster pace than economies, but it has led to the creation and intensification of trade imbalances among countries and regions. For quite a long time, it was normal to have net exports constitute less than 5 percent of a country's GDP. Germany and Japan have been major exporters of manufactured goods in the world, and have enjoyed a long-term trade surplus. In contrast, the United States shifted a large portion of its manufacturing overseas and instead relied excessively on consumer demand to drive its economy, so it has seen a long-term trade deficit (see Figure 2.4). Massive changes in the structure of supply and demand on a global basis have brought into focus the cause-and-effect relationships between trade imbalances and economic cycles. When economies are overheated worldwide,

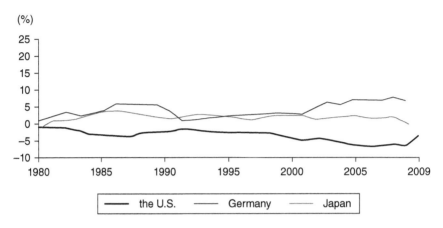

Figure 2.4 Balance of trade in goods as a percentage of GDP, for the United States, Germany, and Japan.

Source: WTO report, '2009 Global Trade Statistics'.

trade accelerates and imbalances become more pronounced. In times of global economic recession, trade imbalances begin to moderate.

Changes in the structure of global supply and demand, coupled with the rise of emerging economies, have led to a trend of rising prices for bulk commodities and also greater volatility in prices. This has been another factor leading to larger trade imbalances between countries that import and countries that export resources. The economies of some countries are closely tied to trade in resources and therefore are far more affected by international price fluctuations. Russia, for example, has derived great benefit from a rise in oil prices. Its trade surplus has actually surpassed 20 percent of GDP. India, in contrast, relies heavily on the import of oil, so when the price of oil soared in 2008, India experienced a huge trade deficit.

One of the primary reasons China's export sector has grown so rapidly has been outsourcing. As developed countries have shifted their manufacturing to China, China has maintained a positive trade balance in goods since the mid-1990s. In the twenty-first century, given the overheating of the global economy, China's trade surplus as a percentage of GDP exceeded 5 percent for three years in a row (see Figure 2.5). With the eruption of the financial crisis in 2008, however, the percentage returned to a more balanced level. The total size of China's economy constitutes a larger and larger share of the global economy. In addition to being influenced by external markets, therefore, China's balance of trade is also to a large extent determined by changes in China's own economic structure.

The patterns by which global trade develops are inherently uneven. In 2008, 85 percent of global trade was generated by North America, Europe, and Asia. Trade is closely related to the vitality of a given country's economy and to the degree to which it has developed manufacturing industries. For example, trade within the Eurozone stayed at around 60 percent of GDP for a long time, while

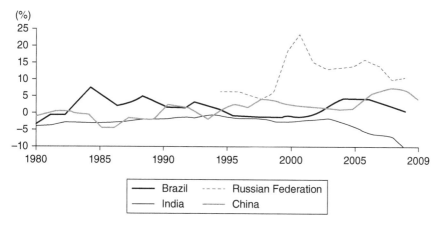

Figure 2.5 The balance of trade in goods as a percentage of GDP, for Brazil, India, Russia, and China.

Source: WTO report, '2009 Global Trade Statistics.'

regional trade within the North America Free Trade Zone stayed above 40 percent of regional GDP. Since the 1980s, the percentage of regional trade within East Asia began to increase as a result of the accelerated transfer of industries to the region and development of supply chain relationships. In recent years, the ratio of trade to GDP has remained above 50 percent (see Table 2.1, and Figure 2.6).

Analysis of the causes for an increase in China's trade surplus

Since the mid-1990s, the speed at which China's trade surplus has been growing has exceeded the speed at which trade has grown on average worldwide. The

Table 2.1 The geographic distribution of global trade in 2008

	North America	Central & South America	Europe	CIS	Africa	Mideast	Asia
World	17.2	3.7	42.9	3.3	2.9	3.9	24.8
North America	49.8	8.1	18.1	0.8	1.7	3	18.4
Central & South America	28.2	26.5	20.2	1.5	2.8	2	16.8
Europe	7.4	1.5	72.8	3.7	2.9	2.9	7.5
CIS	5.1	1.4	57.7	19.2	1.5	3.6	10.9
Africa	21.8	3.3	39.1	0.3	9.6	2.5	20.4
Mideast	11.4	0.7	12.3	0.7	3.6	12	55.7
Asia	17.8	2.9	18.4	2.5	2.8	4.5	50.1

Source: WTO report: '2009 Global Trade Statistics'.

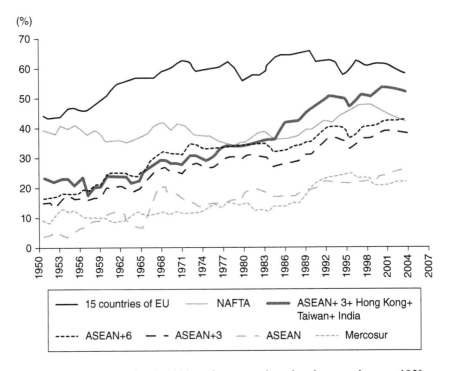

Figure 2.6 Percentage of trade within major economic regions between the years 1950 and 2007.

Source: United National University report: 'Comparative study on regional integration.'

reason for this is the increase in China's exports. China's exports went from 2.5 percent of global trade in 1993 to 9.1 percent in 2008. The pace of China's exports picked up after the second half of 2002, and for the next six years they grew by more than 20 percent per year. Monthly export volume went from USD 20 billion to USD 60 billion, and then on to USD 130 billion, setting new records on the way. According to World Trade Organization statistics, between the years 2000 and 2008, China's exports grew at an average of 15.5 percentage points faster than the average growth of world trade, while imports grew at a pace that was 8.5 percentage points faster. Such astonishing rates have raised doubts among people both inside and outside China, and led to the feeling that thorough analysis should probe the complexities behind this phenomenon.

First, the primary cause of China's sustained growth in international trade has been the transfer of industries, on an international basis, to China. Since the 1980s, the revolution in technologies and the liberalization of global trade and investment have changed the world profoundly. These factors have made it much easier for input factors to flow across borders. Foreign direct investment has been the vehicle for conducting international asset transfers, and this has driven international trade to increase at a fast pace. China was receptive to this wave of international investment. It implemented an open-door policy and took advantage of its own low labor costs, large potential domestic market, and full range of industrial capacities to attract the attentions of multinational corporations. As a result, the country became a key link in the global supply chain, and an important processing base for global manufacturing industries. In 2000, the trade surplus of foreign-invested enterprise trade in China constituted only 9 percent of China's total trade surplus. By 2008, the figure had risen to 57.8 percent (see Figure 2.7).

It is worth noting that China made major changes to its policy of utilizing foreign investment when it joined the World Trade Organization. First, it eliminated the requirement that foreign-invested enterprises buy a certain percentage of goods from within China. Second, it stopped requiring foreign-invested enterprises to maintain a balance in their foreign-exchange receipts and expenditures. Third, in the manufacturing sector, China essentially eliminated all restrictions on wholly owned foreign enterprises. Fourth, it also eliminated preferential tax treatment for export-oriented foreign-funded enterprises. All of these policy changes should have helped foreign enterprises increase their imports into China. In fact, however, multinational corporations did not make major changes in their market strategies and they remained focused on overseas markets. We conducted a survey of multinationals on this issue, and discovered that, although China's market was seen as large enough to justify becoming the first choice in investment decisions, China's market also faced the problem of intense local competition.

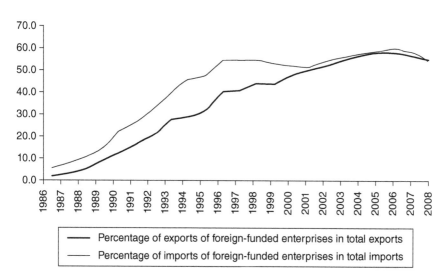

Figure 2.7 Imports and exports of foreign-invested enterprises in China as a percentage of total trade in China.
Unit: percentage

Source: Statistical yearbooks of China.

A second reason behind the astonishing growth rate of China's exports has been the increasing surplus in the processing trade. China's policies in this respect played a critical role. They attracted foreign investment into China for the purpose of carrying on export-oriented manufacturing. The resulting 'processing business' successfully married foreign investment and technology with China's advantages in labor-intensive industries. This form of trade brought goods into bonded warehouses and exempted customs duties, thereby creating a free and convenient business environment along China's coastal regions. The results stimulated a huge expansion in China's foreign trade. Since the start of this century, China's surplus in its processing business has consistently grown faster than its overall trade surplus. In fact, if one subtracted the surplus resulting from the processing trade from China's overall trade, overall trade in goods would actually be running a deficit (see Figures 2.8 and 2.9). China's surplus in exported goods reached its highest point in 2008, which also saw the fastest growth in export trade in general. In 2008, the surplus in processing trade reached USD 296.778 billion. This was still slightly higher than China's trade surplus overall, which came to USD 295.46 billion. The processing trade surplus is a long-term type of surplus, given the patterns by which the trade operates. Marketing and sales of the resulting product are controlled by multinational corporations. Included within the surplus figures are the returns derived from China's labor, land, energy, basic infrastructure, and services. Included also are a portion of the multinational corporation's profits. The expansion of this kind of business is determined in part by an overall expansion of trade, but also by the amount of and pricing of local inputs. For example, since the start of this century there has been a tremendous increase in components procured locally for this kind of trade. Rising labor costs have also contributed significantly to the value-added component of the trade. These things are important factors behind the increasing 'processing trade' surplus (see Figures 2.8 and 2.9).

Third, the unique features of trade imbalances among regions and countries are becoming more and more apparent. China's trade surplus is derived primarily from trade with Europe and the United States. Between 2001 and 2009, China's combined trade surplus vis-à-vis the United States alone came to more than USD 945 billion, which was more than China's entire trade surplus over that same period. China's combined trade surplus vis-à-vis the Eurozone came to USD 422 billion, which was roughly equivalent to half of the total trade surplus for that period. In contrast, during those same years, China had a trade deficit vis-à-vis trade with Japan, South Korea, and the ASEAN countries. That combined deficit amounted to more than USD 580 billion, while China also had bilateral trade deficits on a long-term basis with Australia, Brazil, and other resource-exporting countries. All of these figures reflect the fact that the East Asian region serves as a base for producing and exporting manufactured goods within the global supply chain of trade relationships. Europe and America, in contrast, have increasingly become importers of manufactured goods, having shifted their manufacturing industries overseas. They have become the largest target markets for exports from East Asia. China, meanwhile, is at the epicenter of the processing and assembly

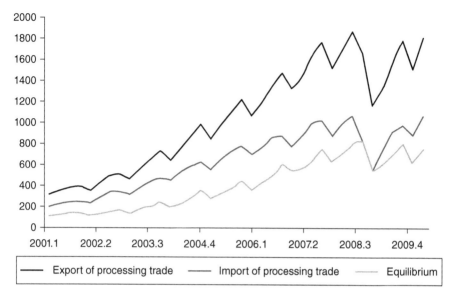

Figure 2.8 Trends in the growth of the processing trade in China, from 2001 to 2010.
Units: USD 100 million

Source: National Customs Administration.

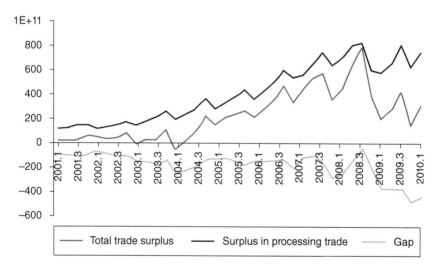

Figure 2.9 Graph showing how the surplus in China's processing trade exceeds the
surplus of overall trade, between 2001 and the first half of 2010.
Units: USD 100 million

Source: National Customs Administration.

trade in the supply chain. A large part of its trade surplus in fact derives from the previous surpluses of other countries and regions that have been shifted over to China.

The above three factors are interrelated and mutually dependent, which determines the fact that China's trade surplus is a long-term issue. China's trade surplus is a direct manifestation of a global trade imbalance (see Figure 2.10).

The fourth consideration relates to the re-import of domestic products, that is, those originally produced inside China. This then creates a fictitious increase in imports and exports. Within Chinese trade statistics, there is an item called 'Re-imported and re-exported national goods,' and the amount of this category of goods is growing. For example, in 2001, Chinese customs determined that USD 8.77 million worth of imports had originally been produced in the People's Republic of China. This figure came to 5.2 percent of total imports in that year. In 2008, the sum of such imports came to USD 92.46 million, which represented 13 percent of total imports in that year. The author will not get into the benefits and defects of the various causes of this category of goods, which relate to such things as China's special export rebate policies, the administrative system that governs the processing trade, special conditions that relate to bonded zones in Hong Kong and coastal regions, the practice of 'exporting for a day,' and 're-importing national goods.' Suffice it to say that the causes as listed do in fact create a fictitious increase in trade statistics.

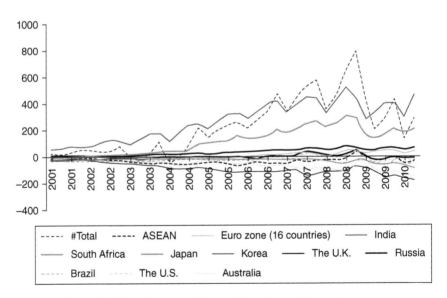

Figure 2.10 Trade balances between China and its major trading partners.
            Units: USD 100 million

Source: National Customs Administration.

Fifth, structural factors have led to the appearance of trade surpluses in China's general trade. The term 'general trade' reflects demand on the part of Chinese companies for things supplied by international markets, as well as Chinese supply capabilities to global markets. Import demand in China has increased with the country's growing industrialization and urbanization and with a rise in the levels of consumption, and resource-intensive products are the fastest growing component of general trade imports. Prior to the eruption of the global financial crisis, both investment and consumption demand maintained fairly high growth rates. At the same time, prices for the world's energy and mineral resources continued to rise. Normally, this would have meant that general trade in China would show a deficit. Since China has instead maintained a surplus, this counter-intuitive phenomenon can be attributed to two factors. The first was China's entry into the WTO. Once China acceded to WTO terms, its trading partners eliminated certain previously discriminatory import restrictions. Most notably, global trade in textiles reverted to being governed by the General Agreement on Trade and Textiles in 2005 which meant that importing countries now eliminated quota restrictions. This released the full potential of China's exports. Between 2001 and 2008, China's surplus in the textiles and garments trade quadrupled, going from USD 29.2 billion to USD 124.8 billion. The deficit in general trade switched to a surplus, largely on the strength of this huge increase in China's textile-trade surplus (see Figure 2.11). The second reason for China's ongoing surplus was increased production in heavy industries. Capacity in such areas as steel, automobiles, space parts all expanded, turning a trade deficit into a trade surplus (see Figures 2.12 and 2.13).

In sum, China's economy is ever more closely tied to international markets given the scale of the country's increased imports and exports and its growing reliance on trade. China imports massive amounts of energy-intensive products and resources that the country itself lacks, while it exports massive amounts of labor-intensive products. This fits the country's realities in terms of comparative advantages and factor endowments. Increased trade has made a significant contribution to increasing China's employment and to growing its economy.

Is there a resource drain associated with China's import and export trade?

One can analyze the degree of 'openness' of China's manufacturing industry through the use of several main indicators. These include the percentage of an industry's total sales that come from exports, the percentage of net fixed assets in a given industry that are held by foreign-invested enterprises, the ratio between capital and labor in an industry, and so on. Looking at such things, China's competitive advantage in exports still lies in industries that are labor-intensive, or in those that may be capital- and technology-intensive but only as related to assembly and processing industries.

One thing worth noting is that returns on capital are not so bad in export-oriented industries, but the profit margins on sales are lower than the average level among manufacturing industries. This means that China's exports rely on

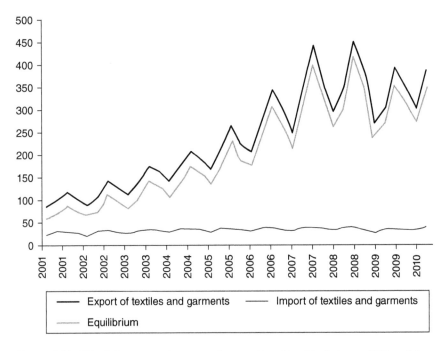

Figure 2.11 China's imports and exports of garments and textiles between 2001 and the first half of 2010.
Units: USD 100 million

Source: Derived from Customs data.

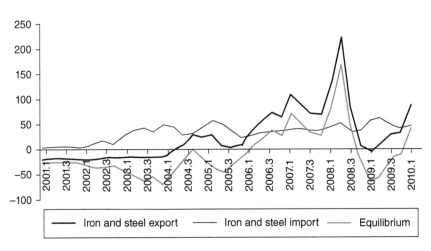

Figure 2.12 China's steel imports and exports between 2001 and the first half of 2010.
Units: USD 100 million

Source: Derived from Customs data; data does not incorporate products manufactured from iron and steel.

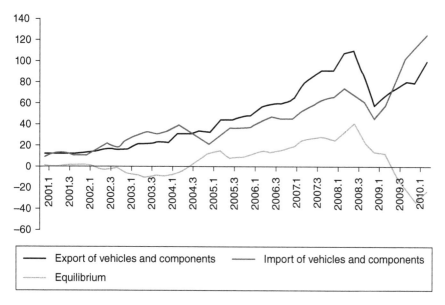

Figure 2.13 China's import and export of vehicles between 2001 and the first half of 2010.
Units: USD 100 million

Source: National Customs Administration.

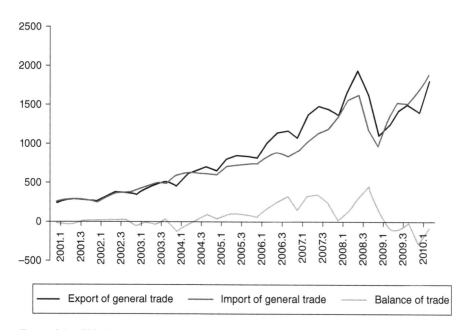

Figure 2.14 China's 'general trade' imports and exports, and trade balance, between
2001 and the first half of 2010.
Units: USD 100 million

Source: National Customs Administration.

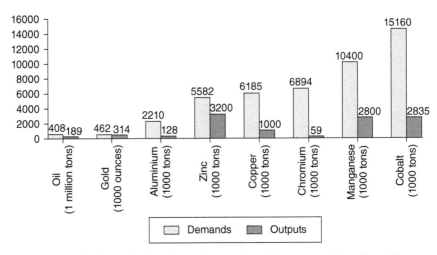

Figure 2.15 China's production of petroleum and non-ferrous metals, together with
demand.

Source: China Analysts, August, 2010.

quantity to be profitable. So far as an enterprise is concerned, if returns on investment are fairly high, the enterprise does not care where it stands in the global
value chain. Anywhere is fine so long as the returns come in. If factor prices are
a true reflection of market supply and demand, and also reflect China's relative
advantage, then China's overall welfare is not hurt by exporting quantities of low
value-added products.

However, factor prices are not a true reflection of market supply and demand
in China. The government plays an inappropriate role in setting the prices of such
things as land, water, and energy. For example, land prices are under-valued in
order to attract investors. Water resources are provided for free to enterprises, or
for minimal fees. Energy prices are lower than international market prices. In addition, China lacks effective and forceful means to ensure environmental protection.
The country gives lower preferential tax treatment to exporting enterprises; it does
not properly enforce the Labor Law, and so on. All of these distort factor prices.
At the same time, China's government controls the pricing of such critical factors
as capital, oil, and electricity. This has already resulted in the phenomena of an
inverted price relationship between domestic and foreign pricing. If such government control continues over the long term, it will create unfair competition among
enterprises and will be detrimental to any efficient use of resources. In the context
of an open system, government subsidies that operate through the means of low
pricing of critical factors will inevitably lead to a drain of resources out of China.

When factor prices are distorted, enterprises that use such factors may well be
profitable, even though returns to the national economy may well be negative.
This then results in the accumulation of a long-term liability. When markets are

sufficiently open, distorted factor prices do indeed create a drain of resources out of the country. The United Nation Trade Organization has analyzed this situation. In 2003 and 2004, the worsening of China's terms of trade led to an economic loss that was estimated at 2 percent of China's GDP. The main things affecting this were (distorted prices for) energy and mineral products.

Another consideration with respect to China's large increase in exports relates to CO_2. Both domestic and foreign scholars have researched the issue of how much carbon dioxide content is incorporated in China's international trade in goods. The results of various studies are essentially in agreement: the carbon dioxide content in traded goods is showing a dramatic increase and the increase in goods exported from China is larger than the increase in goods imported into China. This increase in the intrinsic amount of carbon dioxide in exports may be attributed to two factors. The first is China's trade surplus in terms of total value. The second is that the 'Pollution Terms of Trade' (PTT) of China's exports is greater than one. This means that the strength of carbon dioxide emissions from one unit of exports is greater than it is from one unit of imports. Studies indicate that China's PTT was actually less than one in the years 2000 and 2005. In those years, therefore, the carbon dioxide surplus in net exports from China must be attributed to the former factor, namely the trade surplus. Looked at more specifically, China's PTT was 0.85 in 1995, it was 0.85 in 2000, and it was 0.89 in 2005. This indicates that the strength of carbon-dioxide emissions per unit of exports was smaller than it was per unit of imports in those years, and that international trade was contributing to China's overall energy savings and reduction in emissions. However, if one looks at the longer trends, China's PTT is worsening. This reflects the fact that pollution-intensive types of products are more prevalent in exports and that their ratio in exports relative to imports is increasing. Meanwhile, studies of all industries in China show that the intrinsic carbon dioxide content per unit of China's exports comes increasingly from intermediary products imported into China and not from China's domestic inputs into those products. The percentage of carbon dioxide emissions from domestic inputs is gradually decreasing, while the percentage in imported intermediary products is rising. On an average value basis, the percentage of CO_2 emissions contained in domestic inputs was 83 percent in 1995, 81 percent in 2000, and 72 percent in 2005. In contrast, the percentage of carbon dioxide emissions from imported intermediary products was 17 percent in 1995, 19 percent in 2000, and 28 percent in 2005 (Li Xiaoping, 2006).

Given China's rapid economic growth, the country's comparative advantage is changing. The costs of such production factors as labor, land, water, and environmental carrying capacity are rapidly increasing. Cost advantages enjoyed to date by China's export processing industries are consequently being diluted. On the other hand, other advantages are becoming more apparent. These include sheer market size, capital, technically proficient human resources, labor productivity, full-range manufacturing capacity, and the effect of consolidating industries. In addition, China's logistical foundation is fairly well developed. All of these things allow China to retain relative advantage in the global competition for manufacturing – China remains the most attractive destination when it comes to multinational investment. Over the long term, though, the country's reliance on cost advantages in the international division of labor is going to come under increasing pressure.

Why is it that an appreciating RMB has not yet been able to slow down the rapid rise of China's exports?

Since the exchange-rate reform of 2005, the RMB has appreciated by 21 percent. Statistics indicate, however, that this strengthening of the currency has not in fact spurred imports or held back exports. Reasons may be as follows.

First, prior to the eruption of the financial crisis, the US dollar index was consistently trending lower. As a result, RMB appreciation against the trade-weighted exchange was less than RMB appreciation against the dollar alone. As the RMB began to strengthen, China's exports to the United States began to show a declining rate of growth. By end-2007 and early 2008, this growth rate had fallen back to single-digit figures. During this same period, the Euro was consistently trending higher. The rate at which China increased exports to Europe was consequently higher than the United States, Japan, and also the rest of the world (see Figures 2.16, 2.17 and 2.18). Changes in RMB exchange rates did indeed have an impact on the market orientation of exporting enterprises.

Second, the 'WTO-accession effect' is generally under-estimated in terms of its impact on Chinese exports. In addition to the direct benefits of trade liberalization, as described above, joining the WTO helped stabilize the overall trade environment that motivated multinational companies to shift their processing operations to China. Importers were also more inclined to place orders with Chinese enterprises, given the efficiency of those enterprises in supplying products. As a result, China's share of global markets in such industries as textiles, light industrials,

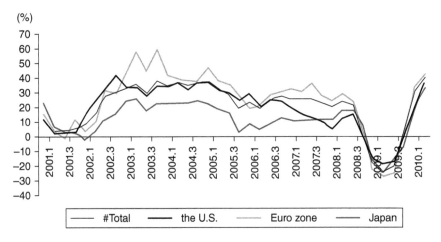

Figure 2.16 Growth rates of China's exports to the United States, the Eurozone, and Japan, between 2001 and the first half of 2010, on a quarterly basis.

Source: National Customs Administration.

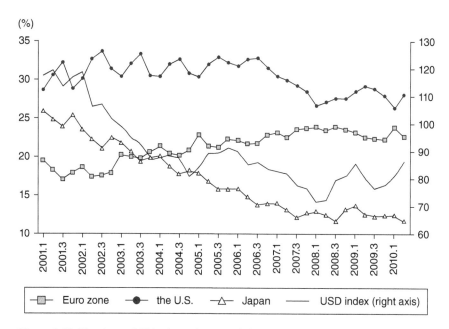

Figure 2.17 The share of China's total exports held by the United States, the Eurozone, and Japan, between 2001 and the first half of 2010.

Source: National Customs Administration.

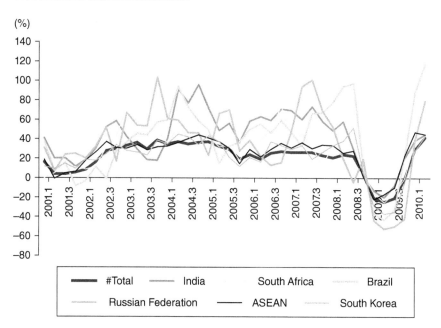

Figure 2.18 Growth rates in China's exports to newly emerging economies, between 2001 and the first half of 2010, on a quarterly basis.

Source: National Customs Administration.

and office equipment rose dramatically. The way in which an appreciating RMB increased costs was not sufficient to change the investing and purchasing behavior of multinationals. For example, under the Multi Fiber Agreement, quota prices had constituted as much as 50 percent of the price of textiles. Once quotas were abolished, import prices fell drastically and importers of textiles from China had plenty of margin to cover increasing costs from an appreciating RMB. The US International Trade Commission conducted a survey on this subject. The response of the majority of enterprises was that they would continue to place orders with China after quotas were abolished, that Chinese costs might well be higher than other countries but those countries could not match China's supply capacities and production efficiencies.

Third, foreign-funded enterprises supply 55 percent of products that China exports. This is because of the 'processing' mode of trade, a kind of trade that contributes nearly 50 percent of all of China's exports. These two percentages do not completely duplicate one another. The processing trade in China is divided into two types, one called '*lai-liao* processing,' which means that materials 'are received in' to be processed, and the other called '*jin-liao* processing,' which means that materials are 'imported in' to be processed. The distinction between these two forms of business relates primarily to whether the capital is provided by domestic enterprises or by foreign-funded enterprises.[2] The similarity between the two is that orders for the resulting products both come from overseas importers. They both generally use the foreign brand, and both employ processing methods and raw materials that are determined by the foreign importer. Both forms of the processing mode of trade limit the ability of Chinese enterprises to be in full control. Some 70 percent of exports from foreign-funded enterprises in China are conducted through this form of processing trade. Foxconn is one example. It is funded by capital from Taiwan and carries out IT processing and exporting through the classic OEM and ODM model. If one adds together exports from foreign-funded exporting enterprises such as Foxconn with processing-industry exports from domestic enterprises, it is estimated that two-thirds of the resulting exports are controlled by multinational companies. The entity conducting the exporting is in fact just a cost center so far as the multinational company is concerned. Given that China is positioned as an 'assembly link' in the global supply chain, the impact of RMB appreciation can easily be absorbed by the internal trade of any given multinational (see Figure 2.19).

All of the above notwithstanding, these things are insufficient to explain why an appreciating RMB has not had an appreciable effect on imports and exports. This is particularly so given the many studies that indicate that the negative impact of appreciation is strongest on those Chinese domestic enterprises that carry on what is known as 'general' trade. Such studies have a heavy influence on policy makers. Here we take a closer look at the statistics. Around the time of the exchange-rate reform of 2005, there was indeed considerable volatility in general export-trade statistics. In the first quarter of 2005, exports rose by 42 percent over the previous quarter, whereas in the fourth quarter they rose by only 18 percent over the previous quarter. This may be a reflection of the way enterprises grabbed

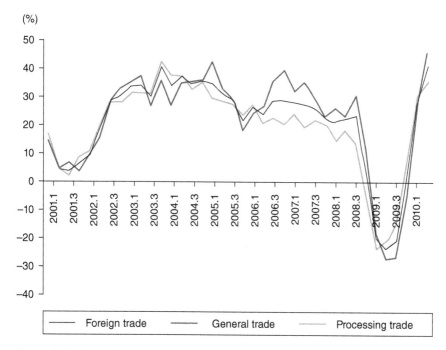

Figure 2.19 Comparison between the growth rates of 'general trade' and 'processing
trade' in China, between the years 2001 and 2010.

Source: National Customs Administration.

their chances before the exchange rates changed, and increased exports accordingly. Nevertheless, looking into this further, after the first quarter of 2006, general-trade exports not only did not slow down but they grew at an accelerating
pace. Indeed, the pace of that growth was notably higher than that of processing-
trade exports. What's more, in 2007, the Chinese government lowered the tax
rebates on export of more than 2000 categories of products. In that same time
period, given the appreciating RMB, the pace of growth in processed-goods
exports began to moderate. The WTO-accession effect and the upgrading of the
composition of exports from domestic enterprises may explain some of this phenomenon. More importantly, reasons may be found in the larger picture, the state
of global markets and major changes in China's domestic market.

First, the twenty-first century's first 'commodity boom' erupted during the
period under study. By commodity boom, we mean a flourishing market for goods
in general. This round of prosperity extended for a long time, involved a broad
range of commodities and saw major price increases for those commodities, all of
which qualified it for superlatives. It was the 'greatest' such 'boom' in fifty years.
Oil is one example. The price for crude oil rose for seventy-three months; prior
to this, the average cycle of price increase had been eighteen months. The price
of crude oil quadrupled relative to the average price in previous years. The price

of metals rose over a fifty-eight-month cycle whereas, before, the cycle had been an average of twenty-two months. Metal prices more than doubled the previous average. The price of food similarly rose over a longer cycle and exceeded previous averages.

This particular 'round' of a commodity boom came in the context of certain financial expectations and a certain macroeconomic environment. In the period between 1997 and 2006, M1 as a measure of money supply rose relative to GDP among the globe's major economies. In the United States it went from 40.6 percent to 53.3 percent, in the European Union from 42.1 percent to 44.6 percent, and in Japan from 29.5 percent to 78.5 percent. Over the past ten years, narrowly defined M1 money supply rose relative to GDP by more than 50 percent on a global basis, while broadly defined M2 money supply rose relative to GDP by more than 30 percent. To a large degree, an excess of liquidity is related to low interest rates. For example, the Federal Reserve in the United States maintained a low interest-rate policy for an extended period of time, filling the market with excess liquidity. The world's major economic entities have implemented low interest-rate policies since 2001 in particular, leading to overflowing global liquidity. Bulk commodities also have financial attributes. Excess liquidity can lead to massively increased investment in them as a result (research from Galaxy Securities).

Another major factor behind this round of commodity boom has been the increase in real demand coming from newly emerging economies and other developing countries. The rise in per capita income among newly emerging economies, the accelerated pace of industrialization and urbanization, and the intensified use of materials in the course of economic growth have led to increased consumption of fuel, electricity, minerals, and food. Some 57 percent of the increase in crude oil consumption between 2001 and 2007, for example, came from the three areas of China, India, and the Middle East. To give another example: 90 percent of the increase in global copper consumption between 2000 and 2006 was due to consumption by China. In similar fashion, statistics indicate that over 50 percent of the increased consumption of aluminum, zinc, steel, and oil was due to consumption by China.

Rapid increase in the price of bulk commodities is highly beneficial to countries that export the commodities, but it is a disaster for countries that have to import them, especially developing countries with net imports. This particular commodity boom has been different from those in the past, however. It has not had a negative impact on the export of finished goods, or what has been called the 'Dutch disease,' since the increase in prices has primarily been driven by demand rather than by price hikes imposed by exporting countries. The intensity with which resources are used in manufacturing in developed countries has already declined substantially, and the core price indexes of these countries have not risen appreciably. On the other hand, countries that export bulk commodities have derived huge incomes from the price hikes. These incomes are then translated into demand for imports of finished goods.[3]

Most of the import and export trade that China conducts with newly emerging economies and developing countries is denominated in US dollars and settlement is done in US dollars. The currencies of these economies are meanwhile either appreciating or depreciating relative to the dollar. If the exchange-rate movements are not too large, then bilateral trade with China is determined by the economic situations and trade structure of the respective trading partners. Meanwhile, the price of bulk commodities is also denominated in US dollars. When demand for commodities is high and there is plenty of liquidity, a weak US dollar will generally be accompanied by rising prices on international commodity markets. Russia, Brazil, and oil-exporting nations are all beneficiaries of rising prices for resources, and the 'wealth effect' then spurs these countries to expand their imports from China. In overall terms, when global economies are expanding, any negative effect of an appreciating RMB (on China's exports) is absolutely offset by rising external market demand. Statistics indicate that China's export of finished goods to developing countries, but particularly those that export natural resources, has outpaced the growth of China's total exports as a whole. This diversification of China's markets can be seen as an advance.

China itself is a net importer of crude oil, metals, and other bulk commodities. The 'contagion effect' of higher international prices for these things has, to a degree, been offset by the benefits of China's appreciating currency. In addition, China's export sectors have felt little impact from the stronger RMB as the result of governmental policies that set prices and that extend subsidies.

Second, during this period of a commodity boom, the Chinese government began to intensify policies intended to curb domestic demand. Starting in 2003, China's economy began a new upswing on the economic cycle. An excessive amount of investment reappeared while credit rose at somewhat too fast a pace. In order to prevent economic overheating, and hold down liquidity, the People's Bank of China raised interest rates on RMB-denominated loans ten times between October of 2004 and December of 2007. It went on to raise the rate from 9 percent to 17.5 percent between January of 2007 and June of 2008, while adjusting the reserve requirement on banks upwards a total of seventeen times. Meanwhile, after 2004, fiscal policy went from being 'proactive' to 'prudent,' and then from 'prudent' to 'tight.' In addition to these actions, the government began to put extremely stiff restrictions on land use, specifically on approvals for non-agricultural use of land. The government put controls on various 'administrative means' that could extend approvals for production of steel, electrolytic aluminum, and property investment. It attempted to achieve sound and rapid economic development through a combination of both carrot and stick, protective and also pressuring policies.

Over the past ten years, urbanization and industrialization have led to extremely fast growth in certain industries in China. Urbanization has meant demand for 'rebar, cement, and cars,' while industrialization has driven demand for 'steel and oil.' Supported by these dual processes, China's steel, oil refining, automobile, and building materials industries have expanded tremendously. Crude steel production has gone from 100 million tons in 2000 to 600 million tons within the space of a decade, for example. Automobile production had just broken through the figure of 2 million cars in the year 2000, but by now annual production comes to over 15 million.

China's macroeconomic measures in fact were unable to contain such explosive increase in production. When the 'commodity boom' hit international markets, therefore, a portion of China's excess production began to shift toward exports. In 2005, for example, positive trade surpluses were seen for the first time in China's steel and automobile industries.

The export of capital-intensive products from China is based on the country's underlying growth of industrial production capacity. It is worth noting, however, that if one analyzes this very closely, one finds that the technological levels and value-added components of China's exports are actually low. Just because certain products are beginning to show a trade surplus does not mean that China's heavy industries and chemical industries, for example, are in a strong competitive position in international markets. One unit of steel material that we export is priced far below what we pay when we import a similar material. The reason for this is the distortion of input prices within China. Some resource-intensive products and capital-intensive products can be exported simply because reform of factor prices within China has been put off. To illustrate this, in 2006–2007, the prices of China's refined oil products were opposite to prices on international markets, severely out of line. This led to a precipitous surge in the export of refined-oil exports to the extent that the government had to adopt administrative measures to control the situation.

What the above analysis shows is that one must evaluate the impact of an appreciating RMB within a larger context. Both the international backdrop and China's overall domestic situation must be taken into account. On the one hand, we should not underestimate the role that exchange-rate adjustments can play in international payments, just because of certain unique factors. On the other hand, we should also recognize that exchange rates are only one among many factors influencing trade. Small-scale, incremental adjustments to the RMB exchange rate are not in themselves sufficient to change an ongoing shift of international industry (in the direction of China,) nor are they sufficient in the short run to change overall trends in international and domestic supply and demand.

China's RMB exchange-rate policies should serve China's medium- and long-term development strategy

In the short run, conditions are not yet appropriate for large-scale appreciation of the RMB

Policy objectives that aim at realizing the 'modernization' of China include 'basically achieving industrialization by 2020,' and 'achieving the modernization of industry by the middle of this century.' Given economic globalization, in order for China to achieve either industrialization or modernization, the country must at the very least develop what could be regarded as a competitive manufacturing industry. At the very least, it must have a group of multinational companies that can organize research and development, carry out production, and realize sales on a global basis. The value-added contained in China's manufacturing industries has already surpassed that of Japan so that China has already become the second manufacturing power in the world. Its export of finished products has also already surpassed Germany so that it is the largest exporter in the world.

At the same time, though, China is a developing country. It has a wealth of labor resources but a scarcity of per capita natural resources. The necessary policy choice for China if it aims to achieve its industrialization objectives is to continue to take in the transfer of the world's industries, to import natural resources and export finished goods. Starting in the 1990s, a 'double surplus' became the common state of affairs in China, meaning a surplus in the capital as well as the current account (see Figure 2.20). Starting in the twenty-first century, China's own production of machinery, automobiles, electronics, and equipment for manufacturing began to enter international markets. The composition of China's exports began to diversify and began to incorporate capital-intensive, technology-intensive, and knowledge-intensive products in addition to labor-intensive products (see Table 2.2). The range of China's industries that are now considered 'export industries' has broadened. This has brought on its own problems. First, China already ranks among the leaders in the world in total volume of greenhouse gas emissions. In per capita terms, the level of the country's emissions has also surpassed the global average. Environmental problems within the country are increasing. Second, China's massive amount of foreign-exchange reserves adds to the difficulty of implementing macroeconomic policy measures (see Figure 2.21). Third, the problem of bilateral trade imbalances has become pronounced (see Figure 2.22).

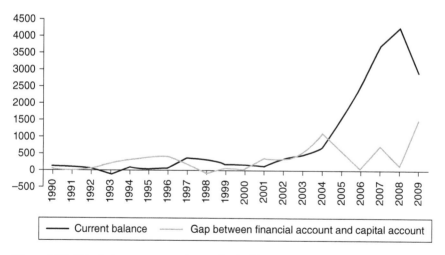

Figure 2.20 China's long-term experience of a double surplus, in the current as well as the capital account.
Unit: USD 100 million

Source: Statistical yearbooks.

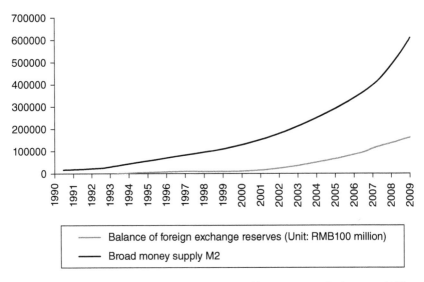

Figure 2.21 China's foreign exchange reserves and its money supply, between 1990 and 2009.

Source: Statistical yearbooks

Table 2.2 A comparison between China's export composition and the export compositions of major industrialized nations in 2005.
Units: percentage

Technical grade	China	Processing trade	US	Germany	Japan	Korea
Primary products	4.4	0.9	8.5	4.8	1.4	2.1
Resource-intensive products	8.5	2.4	14.2	12.3	7.8	11.5
Agricultural products	3.3	1.3	5.2	6.1	2.3	2.6
Other resource-intensive products	5.2	1.1	9.0	6.3	5.5	8.9
Low technical products	31.1	10.9	9.4	11.4	5.9	8.7
Textile, garment, and shoes	17.9	5.5	2.2	3.0	1.0	4.3
Other low technical products	13.2	5.4	7.1	8.3	4.8	4.4
Mid-tech products	22.	11.9	38.4	51.7	60.2	42.3
Automobile	1.9	0.5	9.2	17.8	21.8	13.1
Material industrial products	6.3	2.3	9.5	11.4	11.5	12.4
Mechanical products	14.4	9.1	19.7	22.5	26.8	16.7
High-tech products	33.3	28.3	29.5	19.8	24.6	35.4
Electronic and electrical products	30.6	26.5	17.1	10.9	19.7	31.7
Other high-tech products	2.7	1.8	12.4	8.9	5.0	3.8

Source: Lu Gang (2006): 'Industrial upgrading has to be the foundation for optimizing the structure of China's imports and exports.'

In the economic sphere, China's strategic goal is to transform the country's mode of economic growth. In order to do this, a key part will be raising the competitiveness of China's industries and improving their positioning in the global division of labor. China's import and export trade has long relied on foreign-invested enterprises. The vast majority of our export of high-tech goods is in fact the export of things that multinationals have assembled inside China and then exported. The 'value-added' from inside China relates mainly to the input of labor. The technical content and value-added content of domestically sourced inputs is low. As costs rise, China's export sectors will eventually be damaging their international competitiveness if they do not become more efficient and increase their high-tech content. Moreover, if they themselves are not the ones selling product into international markets then it will be impossible to achieve China's strategy of genuinely diversifying export markets. The role that export sectors play in helping upgrade manufacturing and service industries within China will also be greatly compromised.

At present, 80 percent of high-tech items that are exported fall within the 'processing trade' category. The entities doing the exporting are mainly foreign-invested enterprises. China's domestic industries have made an initial start at producing import substitution items, while items they are manufacturing in their own right are only now beginning to enter international markets, items such as machinery, automobiles, electronics, and equipment for manufacturing. The competitiveness of these industries relies mainly on simply increasing production capacity since they are still relatively weak when it comes to the technology content of their materials, finish-machining, and key components (see Figures 2.22 and 2.23). These are the precisely the areas, however, that reflect a country's competitive edge in manufacturing. If we compare the composition of China's current exports with that of Japan in the 1980s, we see that China's manufacturing industries are situated at a far lower level in the international division of labor than Japan's were at that time. Given these considerations, at this stage in its economic development, China is not ready for a single-event, large-scale, appreciation of the RMB.

Speeding up reform of the way input-factors are priced in China will reduce pressures on the RMB to appreciate

Appreciating the RMB will have the effect of raising China's domestic price levels in general. This in turn will help alleviate the problem of a 'resource drain' that is being caused by the distortion of factor prices in the country. However, relying exclusively on exchange rates to achieve this is insufficient since it does not specifically target the problem and the policy costs are too high. The problem of a resource drain will also not fundamentally be resolved by such things as duties on exports or adjusting our policy of giving tax rebates on exports. The strength of those policy adjustments is simply inadequate to deal with the problem. We absolutely must speed up the process of reforming factor prices, which means the way we price such things as capital, labor, water, land, energy, and minerals.

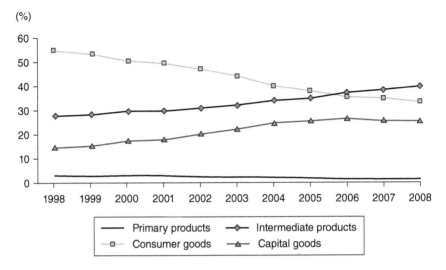

Figure 2.22 Changes in the structure of China's exports, between 1998 and 2008.
Note: For how imports and exports were categorized, please refer to the Appendix.
Source: United Nations COMTRADE.

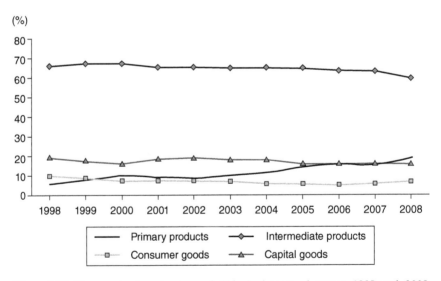

Figure 2.23 Changes in the structure of China's imports, between 1998 and 2008.
Source: United Nations COMTRADE.

Such reform means increasing the extent to which the market determines prices and increasing the strength of tax reform in these sectors. Only through these means will we be able to improve the structural composition of China's imports and exports and thereby address the problem. The problem is that we are enabling a resource drain by under-valuing the cost to the environment in how we produce trade goods and by under-pricing factor inputs.

Achieving a better balance in China's international balance of payments through instituting import incentives and increasing overseas investment, to the proper degree

A long-term policy of import substitution is detrimental to our desire to make China's manufacturing industries more internationally competitive. Moreover, once China joined the WTO and substantially lowered tariffs on imports, our own experience showed that this did not result in a massive increase in the import of finished products. On the contrary, our imports of primary and secondary goods increased as a percentage of the total, while the percentage of consumer items decreased.

China's import tariffs have substantial step increases for different categories of products. Import tariffs on finished products, and particularly on consumer goods, are extremely high. They exceed 20 percent on such things as garments, household electrical appliances, automobiles, and so on. Overall, tariffs on primary goods are low, while intermediate products used in the processing trade are granted tariff exemption. This tariff structure has the effect of encouraging domestic production of basic goods and consumer goods as a kind of import substitution, while it actively stimulates the export of processed and assembled goods. China is already the largest exporter in the world of consumer items. Given the lack of any serious competition in this sphere, its manufacturing industries now have little incentive to improve by doing such things as conserving resources, improving quality, upgrading technologies, and developing overseas marketing abilities. Because of this, the government should now begin to adjust the tariff structure and introduce competition to an appropriate degree by lowering the highest tariffs. This will enable the appreciation of the RMB to have a greater effect on upgrading the structure of our manufacturing industries.

Ongoing increases in China's foreign-exchange reserves are being propelled by the dual forces of a surplus in both the current account and the capital account. Once other East Asian economic entities achieved positive trade surpluses, they adopted policies to encourage their enterprises to invest overseas. This was effective in dampening down pressure to revalue their currencies. China's situation is more difficult. It has a huge domestic market and it has consistently protected that market, while policy measures have also artificially depressed the price structures of input factors. China's enterprises therefore have little incentive to begin investing overseas. Added to that is our system of requiring very stringent 'review and approval' procedures on anyone trying to invest overseas, all of which hinder the growth of such investment.

China's foreign direct investment overseas began to show sustained high-speed growth after 2005. The scale of that investment has constantly reached unprecedented levels. According to UNCTAD statistics, the flow China's overseas investment exceeded USD 10 billion for the first time in 2005, USD 20 billion in 2006, and USD 50 billion in 2008. Between 2005 and 2008, the combined amount of all foreign direct investment flows coming from China totaled USD 108 billion. This sum was equivalent to 2.327 times the total amount in all the years between 1982 and 2004. By the end of 2008, the volume of China's foreign direct investment had reached USD 148 billion, or 3.3 times the amount in 2004. In 2009, an increased flow of foreign direct investment went against the tide at the time and in fact accelerated in the first seven months of 2010. By year-end 2010, foreign direct investments made by China overseas exceeded USD 50 billion (see Figure 2.24).

An appreciating RMB has had a negative impact on some kinds of Chinese investment overseas, specifically overseas engineering-project contractors and exporters of Chinese labor. At the same time, however, appreciation has strengthened the ability of Chinese enterprises to carry out mergers and acquisitions abroad. It has provided the financial backing for Chinese companies to obtain overseas resources, technology, and sales channels via the mechanism of mergers and acquisitions (M&A). Since 2005, more than USD 5 billion every year has gone into such M&A activity. In 2006, M&A investments constituted 70 percent

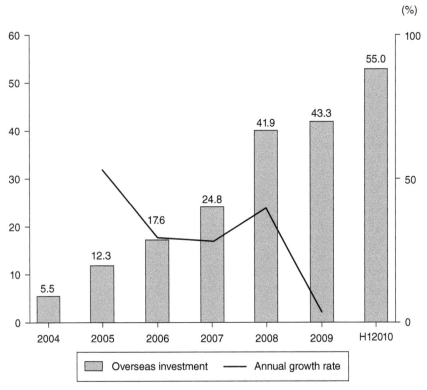

Figure 2.24 Rapid expansion of China's foreign direct investment overseas since 2005.
Source: China Analyst, August, 2010. The figure for 2010 is an estimate.

of all foreign investments made by China; in 2008, the figure was 58 percent. In both years, M&A activity exceeded greenfield investments as a way to acquire overseas assets (see Figure 2.25).

According to a survey conducted by the research group within the Development Research Center of the State Council, breakthrough advances have been made by some Chinese enterprises who have invested overseas. These have used a variety of methods, including mergers and acquisitions and direct investment. They have been able to obtain new technologies, set up R&D centers abroad, and create sales networks and after-sale service networks in such industries as telecommunications, machine tools, engineering machinery, automobiles, and railroad engines. They have been exploring 'shortcut' ways to reduce the gap between the level of China's manufacturing and that of advanced countries.

The response of manufacturers within China to the survey noted above made it clear that the Chinese government's policy objective of 'striding out into the world' still has a long way to go. There is a great deal of room for further policy initiatives. With genuine incentive mechanisms, the government may very well be able to encourage China's enterprises to shift more investment overseas, particularly given excess production capacity within the country as well as increasing costs (see Table 2.3). At the same time, reducing the surplus in China's capital account not only can have the positive effect of mitigating pressure on the RMB to appreciate, but it can help improve the efficiency with which capital is being used. It can help China optimize its economic structure, and it can help China's manufacturing industry become more internationally competitive.

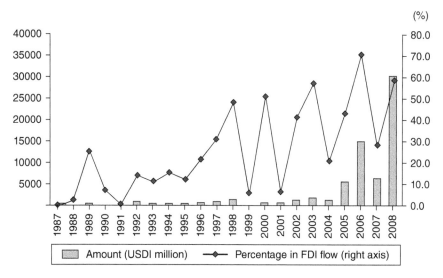

Figure 2.25 Merger and acquisition activity as a percentage of China's foreign direct investment overseas.

Source: UNCTAD statistics: Foreign Direct Investment STAT online. For 2007 and 2008, statistics came from the 2007 and 2008 volumes of *Bulletin of China's foreign direct investment statistics.*

Table 2.3 Types of assistance that would help Chinese enterprises invest overseas: a list of what Chinese enterprises are asking their government to provide

Government function	Percentage of enterprises (%)
Providing financial support	61.51
Improving financing environment	53.96
Providing information support	50.64
Streamlining examination and approval procedures	39.59
Providing more professional training	38.31
Strengthening the protection of their rights and interests overseas	33.89
Providing more support for brand building overseas	29.83
Assisting in solving problems arising from production and operation in the host country	29.10

Source: Research group of the Research Development Center of the State Council, from a report entitled, 'On the Going Global policy and the excess of production capacity in China.'

Policy options with respect to an appreciating RMB

Manufacturing costs in China are going up at an accelerating pace, and labor costs have already surpassed those in many countries of South and Southeast Asia. For the next five to ten years, however, China will still be the main beneficiary as global manufacturing shifts production in its direction. Reasons for this include the size of China's market, the supportive capacity of its range of industries, its basic infrastructure, the quality of its labor force, and so on. During this period, China will also speed up the pace at which it is making investments overseas, including the pace of its mergers and acquisitions. Nevertheless, China's manufacturing industries are not yet sufficiently mature to start manufacturing abroad, through major investments. For this reason, China's double surplus in both the current and the capital account may well continue for some time. There will still, therefore, be ongoing pressure on the RMB to appreciate.

In the mid-1990s, and also in 2005, there were two occasions on which appreciation of the RMB stopped abruptly. These were both due to financial crises, and one should not doubt the ongoing trend of appreciation simply because of these two events. In summing up the lessons of the 2005 exchange-rate reform, we present the following several points. First, the actual effectiveness of the exchange-rate policy of 2005 was compromised by the tentative way in which it was introduced. As a result, the effective trade exchange rate appreciated at only a very slow pace. Second, no decisive measures with respect to domestic pricing reform accompanied the exchange-rate reform. A sole focus on exchange rates cannot resolve structural problems, and in fact only introduces further distortions in the behavior of companies that import and export. Third, it is counterproductive to use the mechanism of lowering export rebates as a way to resolve pricing problems. Not only will domestic prices for resources and resource-intensive products remain the opposite of international prices, but this kind of measure gives inconsistent policy signals and has an unfavorable impact on the international community. It is seen as being a form of export subsidy. Fourth, the exchange-rate reform of 2005 over-emphasized short-term macroeconomic policy objectives. Instead, policy should be set with a view to long-term development strategies.

China's new exchange-rate reform should learn lessons from past experience. First, instead of placing all hopes on RMB appreciation for resolving economic structural problems, we should move as quickly as possible with measures that address price reform and reform of the tax on resources, among others. As a hypothetical example, let us say that prices for such input factors as land, water, and electricity all cost 10 percent more – this would indeed have a very beneficial effect on our current form of wasteful and 'extensive' production. Second, we should increase the flexibility of the RMB exchange rate in order to counter the possibility of another 'commodity cycle,' and volatility among major international currencies. Having said, this, it is not feasible to adopt a one-off substantial appreciation of the RMB, that is, one that is over 10 percent, since this would almost certainly have a damaging effect on newly emerging export industries in China. Third, during this current Doha round of World Trade Organization talks, we might consider adopting a more 'liberal' stance with regard to trade, a stance that would include such things as further lowering of import duties, and further opening up of our services market. Fourth, we should go further in loosening controls over capital accounts. In addition to encouraging enterprises to invest abroad, we could also institute programs whereby foreign governments, or enterprises, issue RMB-denominated bonds, tradable on the Dragon Bond market. We could allow companies based outside of China's borders to list their shares and be traded on China's domestic stock exchanges. Finally, we should be able to export (foreign-exchange-denominated) capital through expanding foreign credit, foreign aid in the form of loans, and a trade surplus backflow.

Notes

1 Zhang Xiaoji: Research Department of Foreign Economic Relations, Development Research Center of the State Council.
2 The form of processing called '*lai-liao*' involves the following: the foreign company supplies both primary and auxiliary materials to the domestic Chinese company, which then processes products in compliance with the foreign company's needs. Such things include compliance with quality standards, compliance with models that are provided, and with packaging specifications. Sometimes the foreign company also provides equipment, instrumentation, and tools in order to ensure the necessary quality of processing. The Chinese government has adopted policies that exempt this form of processing from various taxes, including taxes on imported materials, spare parts, and value-added fees on products that are brought in and then re-exported once processed. In the second form of processing, '*jin-liao* processing,' Chinese domestic entities that have been licensed to conduct this particular kind of foreign-trade business put up the capital. They use foreign exchange to purchase imported materials, components, packaging, and so on. They then process these into finished products and re-export them.
3 Pedro Conceicao and Heloisa Marone, UNDP/ODS Working Paper.

Appendix: BEC commodity classification (COMTRADE)

1	Name: Food and beverages Description: Food and beverages	Data Availability Snapshot
11	Name: Food and beverages, primary Description: Food and beverages, primary	Data Availability Snapshot
111	Name: Food and beverages, primary, mainly for industry Description: Food and beverages, primary mainly for industry	Data Availability Snapshot
112	Name: Food and beverages, primary, mainly for household consumption Description: Food and beverages, primary, mainly for household consumption	Data Availability Snapshot
12	Name: Food and beverages, processed Description: Food and beverages, processed	Data Availability Snapshot
121	Name: Food and beverages, processed, mainly for industry Description: Food and beverages, processed, mainly for industry	Data Availability Snapshot
122	Name: Food and beverages, processed, mainly for household consumption Description: Food and beverages, processed, mainly for household consumption	Data Availability Snapshot
2	Name: Industrial supplies nes Description: Industrial supplies nes	Data Availability Snapshot
21	Name: Industrial supplies nes, primary Description: Industrial supplies nes, primary	Data Availabily Snapshot
22	Name: Industrial supplies nes, processed Description: Industrial supplies nes, processed	Data Availability Snapshot
3	Name: Fuels and lubricants Description: Fuels and lubricants	Data Availability Snapshot
31	Name: Fuels and lubricants, primary Description: Fuels and lubricants, primary	Data Availability Snapshot
32	Name: Fuels and lubricants, processed Description: Fuels and lubricants, processed	Data Availability Snapshot
4	Name: Capital goods (except transport equipment), and parts and accessories thereof Description: Capital goods (except transport equipment), and parts and accessories thereof	Data Availability Snapshot
41	Name: Capital goods (except transport equipment) Description: Capital goods (except transport equipment)	Data Availability Snapshot
42	Name: Parts and accessories of capital goods (except transport equipment) Description: Parts and accessories of capital goods (except transport equipment)	Data Availability Snapshot
5	Name: Transport equipment, and parts and accessories thereof Description: Transport equipment, and parts and accessories thereof	Data Availability Snapshot
51	Name: Transport equipment, passenger motor cars Description: Transport equipment, passenger motor cars	Data Availability Snapshot

52	Name: Transport equipment, other Description: Transport equipment, other	Data Availability Snapshot
521	Name: Transport equipment, other, industrial Description: Transport equipment, other, industrial	Data Availability Snapshot
522	Name: Transport equipment, other, non–industrial Description: Transport equipment, other, non–industrial	Data Availability Snapshot
53	Name: Parts and accessories of transport equipment Description: Parts and accessories of transport equipment	Data Availability Snapshot
6	Name: Consumption goods nes Description: Consumption goods nes	Data Availability Snapshot
7	Name: Goods nes Description: Good s nes	Data Availability Snapshot

Classification

Primary products:

111 (Food and beverage for industrial use, unprocessed)
 21 (Industrial raw materials, unprocessed)
 31 (Fuel and lubricating oil, unprocessed)

Intermediate products:

121 (Food and beverage for industrial use, unprocessed)
 22 (Industrial raw materials, unprocessed)
 32 (Fuel and lubricating oil, unprocessed)
 42 (Components of capital goods)
 53 (Components of transportation equipment)

Consumer goods:

112 (Food and beverage for household use, unprocessed)
122 (Food and beverage for household use, processed)
 51 (Automobile)
522 (Non-industrial transportation equipment, excluding automobile)
 6 (Other consumer goods)

Capital goods:

 41 (Capital goods)
521 (Industrial transportation equipment, excluding automobile)

3 The impact of RMB exchange-rate adjustments on enterprises and industries involved in foreign trade

Zhang Fan and Yu Miaojie[1]

Introduction

The following analysis looks at the impact of exchange-rate changes in China from a microeconomic perspective. It evaluates the impact of RMB appreciation between the years 2005 and 2008 on foreign-trade related enterprises and industries in China. It looks at the impact on their imports and exports, their costs, the interest rates on their debt, their size of overall investment, and their production technologies. It seeks to understand the impact of exchange-rate changes on the restructuring of China's economy and the upgrading of its industries.

On January 1, 1994, China's exchange-rate system moved from a 'two-track' to a 'one-track' system, usually referred to as 'unifying' the exchange rates. The country began implementing a system of 'one rate, that employed a managed float and that was based on market supply and demand.' Prior to this reform, enterprises that engaged in foreign trade were required to deliver up to authorities a certain percentage of the foreign-exchange income derived from their exports. At the same time, they were allowed to retain a percentage of foreign-exchange income, as calculated at a specified rate of exchange to the RMB. This retained amount was known as 'foreign-exchange retentions,' or *waihuiliucheng*. Starting on January 1, 1994, the great majority of China-invested enterprises were now required, on a mandatory basis, to 'settle' their foreign exchange. This meant that they were required, unconditionally, to sell their foreign-exchange income to designated foreign-exchange banks. They received back an amount in RMB that corresponded to their income.

In 1997, the Southeast Asian financial crisis erupted and there was a strong expectation that the RMB would be devalued. China's capital markets were still not completely open at the time, however, which muted the impact of such expectations. The effect of expectations was relatively minor on ongoing economic fundamentals, the trade surplus in China's processing trade, and foreign direct investment. Authorities successfully maintained exchange rates at the general level of 8.27 RMB to one US dollar. China's macroeconomic situation improved after 2002 and expectations of devaluing the RMB then dissipated. Nevertheless, the government still maintained a policy of keeping the RMB rate very stable. Authorities continued to peg the rate against the US dollar.

In 2005, the People's Bank of China announced that it would now be implementing 'an exchange-rate system that involved a managed float, that was based on market supply and demand, and that was carried out with reference to a basket of currencies.' The traded price of the RMB vis-à-vis the US dollar was now adjusted to RMB 8.11 to one US dollar, which meant that the RMB appreciated by around two percentage points. From this time on, the rate at which the RMB traded against the dollar on the interbank market floated within a range of 0.3 percent of the price announced daily by the People's Bank of China, which was the 'central parity rate' of the US dollar. Between 2005 and 2007, the RMB appreciated by close to 20 percent. This period of time provides an invaluable opportunity to evaluate the impact of exchange-rate appreciation on the operations of China's enterprises.

Our analysis was able to use data from a large sample of enterprises, specifically 110,000 to 350,000 enterprises every year in the period between 2000 and 2008. We used that data to analyze the impact of exchange-rate changes on their businesses.

Our basic conclusion was that, overall, the appreciating RMB did indeed have a certain negative impact on the production and operations of enterprises engaged in foreign trade during this period. At the same time, however, the impact was different on various types of enterprises, given their different cost structures and production technologies, so that not only did a strengthening RMB have negative effects, but it also had positive effects. Between 2005 and 2008, China's enterprises took steps to respond to the increased exchange risk caused by appreciation and showed quite some resilience in the face of appreciation. They restructured the composition of their production, exports, and the extent to which they were labor-intensive and capital-intensive, which brought about fundamental changes in China's industrial structure. At the same time, however, our analysis showed that enterprises still need to improve the way they mitigate and prevent risk through technical means, and the government should provide greater services in this regard.

Exchange-rate risk

Exchange-rate risk is the potential for loss due to exchange-rate movements suffered by an economic entity (either an enterprise or an individual) that either holds or uses foreign exchange. Such risk includes transaction risk, operating risk, and translation risk.

Transaction risk is when the price of the accounts receivable or debts payable of an enterprise changes as the result of exchange-rate movements. This price change reflects the impact of exchange-rate changes on the capital flows of the enterprise in the course of doing business. Transaction risk is incurred when an enterprise signs contracts that are denominated in foreign currencies and the exchange rate of that currency changes prior to conclusion of the contract. This affects the cash flow requirements of the enterprise. The types of transaction risk that can affect manufacturing enterprises include the following. First, there is business credit-type transaction risk. This is the primary form of such risk among enterprises that engage in any kind of trade in goods and services. It is incurred when there is a time lag between signing the contract and concluding the business, when the contract is denominated in a foreign currency. Second, we have borrowing or lending-type risk. This occurs when an enterprise either holds or loans foreign currency-denominated funds. The foreign-exchange deposits of a company are an example: when they are invested overseas or loaned out, they incur foreign-exchange risk.

Operating risk refers to risks brought on by changes in future net returns expected by an enterprise that are the result of unexpected movements in exchange rates. This kind of risk can be manifested in changes in the future costs of inputs into a company's products, or by changes in future prices and sales quantities of the products as the result of exchange-rate changes. This kind of risk affects the long-term cash flows of an enterprise. Types of operating risk include the following. First, there is the risk of changing costs. Domestic purchasing costs can be affected by the way exchange-rate changes can lead to overall inflation. Since China's RMB appreciation has had the effect of holding down inflation, over the long run, appreciation can lower the costs of procuring production inputs within the country. Exchange-rate changes can also influence the costs of imports. RMB appreciation has the overall effect of making imports less expensive. If imported materials have a sufficiently high 'substitution elasticity,' then imported materials will be used instead of domestic materials when costs are lowered to a certain point. If, however, RMB appreciation exacerbates inflation overseas, then the price of imported materials will go up over the long run and to a certain extent this will cancel out the lower prices of imported materials in the initial period. Second, there is the income risk of exported products. After the RMB appreciates, the price of exports that are denominated in foreign currencies will increase and the amount of such exports that can be sold will decrease. If a Chinese enterprise in turn adjusts its domestic pricing such that the price of its exports in the overseas market stays at the original level, then the income of the enterprise will decline. In addition, an appreciating RMB can lead to greater competition from imported products, which may in turn reduce an enterprise's sales within China.

Translation risk is also referred to as accounting risk or conversion risk (Li Shuyin, 2009). This is when exchange-rate changes lead to changes in the value of certain foreign-currency-denominated items on the balance sheet. This kind of risk has the biggest impact on the profits and losses of multinational companies. Normally the subsidiary of a multinational will calculate its profits and losses, and its assets and liabilities, in terms of the currency of the country in which it is located. If the exchange rate of that currency changes over a given period, the rate at the end of the financial-statement period is what the subsidiary must use to calculate its profits and losses. The financial statement will accordingly show profits or losses when the results are converted back into the parent-company's books. When the RMB is appreciating, the subsidiaries of Chinese multinationals that are located abroad will show losses on their books if their accounts are denominated in RMB.

The effect of currency appreciation on the operations of China's export-oriented enterprises

Among published statistics in China, there is currently no available data on the business performance of China's export-oriented enterprises, defined as a separate category. The data that this analysis used, therefore, comes from a database of enterprises assembled by the National Statistical Bureau between 2000 and 2008. This database includes all State-Owned Enterprises and any non-State-Owned Enterprises that have more than RMB 5 million in annual output value. The number of enterprises included in the database varies from year to year. The sample size of enterprises ranged between 110,000 to 350,000 in the relevant years, and their observed values are what were used in this study (see Table 3.1). We differentiate between 'export-oriented enterprises' and 'non-export-oriented enterprises' by looking at the percentage of exports in total sales figures as well as in total production value. Based on these figures, we calculate business performance and make comparisons.

After experimenting with varying percentages of exports in total business, our analysis defined an 'export-oriented business' as one that exported more than 40 percent of its production. In the Appendix (see pages 111–112), we also list results that use a lower figure, for example, enterprises that export between ten and twenty, twenty and thirty, and thirty and forty percent of total production. We found that this does not in fact change our basic conclusions.

Business results of all enterprises

As a comparative frame of reference, we first present information on all enterprises in the database, as listed in Table 3.1.

Enterprises included in the database were constantly changing, which meant that increases in profitability might at times be due to increases in output or sales. In order to make valid comparisons of business results across years, in Table 3.2 we set forth both profit margin and exports as a percentage of total output and of total sales.

From the basic statistical data as above, on all enterprises in the database, we can see the following:

1   Between the years 2000 and 2007, including 2005, which was a year in which the RMB appreciated, total output value continued to increase every year for the average enterprise. In 2008, total output value declined due to the economic crisis.
2   The average number of employees in each enterprise declined noticeably, as a general trend.
3   Between 2001 and 2007, the profits of each enterprise on average increased.
4   Between 2001 and 2008, profit margins showed a rising trend on average. In 2008, despite the drop in absolute profits, profit margins continued to rise due to an increase in total output value (and sales revenue).

Table 3.1 Business performance of all enterprises in the database

	Observed value	Number of employees	Total output value (in RMB1000)	Added value per capita (RMB1000)	Profit (in RMB1000)	Export (in RMB1000)
2000	114,131	348	58,296	123	2,234	10,498
2001	126,239	321	60,536	54	2,316	10,668
2002	138,887	313	65,992	71	2,697	12,308
2003	156,046	298	76,202	77	3,253	14,879
2004	158,111	252	80,137	73	3,372	15,789
2005	224,609	254	95,024	114	3,952	18,429
2006	252,327	243	105,965	137	4,702	20,793
2007	284,238	232	121,454	165	5,799	22,297
2008	350,441	200	114,011	–	5,068	19,930

	Profit/ Sales revenue (%)	Profit/ Total output value (%)	Export/ Sales revenue (%)	Export/ Total output value (%)	Fixed asset per capita (in RMB10,000)	National capital fund/capital fund (%)	Foreign capital fund/ capital fund (%)
2000	3.0	2.9	15.8	15.2	6.46	38.1	21.0
2001	2.9	2.9	15.5	15.5	6.37	35.8	21.7
2002	3.1	3.0	16.5	16.0	6.44	33.0	21.5
2003	3.4	3.3	16.9	16.4	7.05	29.7	22.8
2004	3.3	3.3	18.3	18.3	8.50	24.3	23.9
2005	3.6	3.5	16.7	16.3	9.49	19.4	26.5
2006	3.7	3.7	15.8	15.4	9.87	17.1	28.0
2007	4.0	3.9	14.6	14.1	10.68	16.1	28.4
2008	4.2	4.1	12.7	12.4	9.02	–	–

Note: The ±5% abnormal value was eliminated during data processing, and this is why the observed value is less than the primary data.

5   Starting in 2005, exports as a percentage of sales began declining as well as exports as a percentage of total output value.
6   Between 2001 and 2007, per capita fixed assets showed a constant increase.
7   Between 2000 and 2007, the percentage of China's own national capital to total capital in the country declined. Other than exceptional years, foreign capital as a percentage of total capital in China increased.
8   Between 2001 and 2007, the amount of value-added increased, indicating that productivity was increasing.

Business performance of export-oriented enterprises in the database, and the effect of an appreciating RMB on export-oriented enterprises

The situation with respect to all enterprises in the database was described above. We now proceed to look at the situation with respect to export-oriented enterprises (see Table 3.2).

Table 3.2 Operation performance of export-oriented enterprises in the enterprise database

	Observed value (Number of enterprises)	Number of employees	Total output value (in RMB1000)	Added value per capita (in RMB1000)	Profit (in RMB1000)	Export (in RMB1000)
2000	19,295	382	62,202	130	2,231	49,497
2001	21,342	364	63,477	43	2,250	50,660
2002	24,704	363	73,580	58	2,744	57,639
2003	28,378	365	84,027	58	2,983	67,919
2004	31,067	325	81,469	54	2,936	67,679
2005	39,776	364	109,962	78	4,152	87,143
2006	42,349	367	128,346	86	4,846	102,539
2007	44,539	369	148,311	96	5,740	118,487
2008	48,116	358	152,123	–	5,844	121,262

	Profit/ Sales revenue (%)	Profit/ Total output value (%)	Export/ Sales revenue (%)	Export/ Total output value (%)	Fixed asset per capita (in RMB10,000)	National capital fund/capital fund (%)	Foreign capital fund/ capital fund (%)
2000	2.7	2.6	85.9	82.5	6.22	11.2	59.0
2001	2.6	2.6	83.8	83.8	4.90	9.7	61.7
2002	2.9	2.8	85.8	82.9	4.19	9.9	61.5
2003	3.0	3.0	85.9	83.4	5.14	7.0	64.3
2004	2.9	2.9	86.2	86.2	6.66	4.7	66.6
2005	3.1	3.0	86.0	83.7	6.34	3.7	66.8
2006	3.3	3.2	85.6	83.4	6.54	2.9	69.1
2007	3.2	3.1	85.3	82.7	6.56	2.9	69.6
2008	3.1	3.0	84.5	82.2	6.23	–	–

Basic circumstances of export-oriented enterprises

We define 'export-oriented' as an enterprise that exports 40 percent or more of its total sales volume. (We present data in the Appendix on pages 113–114 that covers four different ways of defining 'export-oriented,' in order to make comparisons across enterprises that do not export 40 percent or more – we compare enterprises that export below ten percent of sales, those that export between ten and twenty percent of sales, between twenty and thirty percent, and between thirty and forty percent.)

The similarities between export-oriented enterprises and all enterprises in the database were as follows.

1 Between 2000 and 2008, total output showed an increasing trend, while numbers of people employed showed a decreasing trend.
2 Between 2000 and 2008, profit margins tended to increase.
3 With the exception of 2004, export volume showed a constant increase.
4 Since the year 2005, exports as a percentage of sales volume as well as total output consistently declined.

5   The percentage of national Chinese capital declined, while foreign-invested capital rose.
6   With the exception of 2004, per capital value-added rose between the years 2001 and 2007.

The differences between export-oriented enterprises and all enterprises were as follows.

1   Export-oriented industries showed a declining profit margin from the year 2006.
2   Per capita fixed assets in export-oriented industries reached a peak in 2004 before beginning a sustained decline.

The most apparent thing about export-oriented industries was that their profit margin declined in recent years.

In order to make comparisons across export-oriented industries and all industries, in Table 3.3 we set forth the difference between the two in certain categories.

From the above table of differences, we can note that export-oriented enterprises have a higher value of total output, a greater number of employees, greater exports overall, and more exports as a percentage of both sales and total output value. In addition, export-oriented enterprises have a lower-than-average profit margin, as calculated by both profits per total sales revenue, and profits per total output value. This is calculated by using the average level of enterprises overall. Export-oriented enterprises also have a lower amount of fixed assets per capita, and a smaller percentage of China capital as opposed to foreign capital.

All of this indicates that export-oriented enterprises as a group have higher output value, more employees, and export more. The degree to which they are 'labor intensive' is higher. The degree to which they use national China-invested capital is lower, while they rely more on foreign-invested capital. The average level of their profit margins is lower. This does not exclude the possibility that foreign-invested enterprises shift their profits overseas.

The regional distribution of export-oriented enterprises

More than two-thirds of China's export-oriented enterprises are situated in coastal regions. Our study defines 'coastal' as including Guangdong, Jiangsu, Shanghai, and Zhejiang. In both coastal regions and interior parts of the country, the number of export-oriented enterprises has been constantly increasing. Until 2005, the percentage of all export-oriented enterprises that were located in coastal regions showed an increase, but that number began to decline in 2006. From 2005, the percentage of export-oriented enterprises to all enterprises situated in interior regions also began a sharp decline (see Table 3.4).

We do not exclude the possibility that changes in preferential policies had an effect on the declining percentage of export enterprises. Such policies would include tax treatment – once policies changed, some enterprises no longer had the incentive to register themselves as 'foreign-invested.'

Table 3.3 Difference between export-oriented enterprises and all enterprises

	Number of employees	Total industrial output value (in RMB1000)	Added value per capita (in RMB1000)	Profit (in RMB1000)	Export (in RMB1000)
2000	33	3,906	7	−3	38,999
2001	43	2,941	−10	−66	39,992
2002	49	7,588	−13	47	45,332
2003	66	7,825	−19	−269	53,040
2004	73	1,332	−20	−436	51,890
2005	110	14,938	−36	200	68,714
2006	125	22,381	−51	144	81,746
2007	136	26,857	−68	−59	96,190
2008	157	38,112	–	776	101,331

	Profit/ Sales revenue (%)	Profit/ Total output value (%)	Export/ Sales revenue (%)	Export/ Total output value (%)	Fixed asset per capita (in RMB10,000)	National capital fund/capital fund (%)	Foreign capital fund/ capital fund (%)
2000	−0.003	−0.003	0.701	0.673	−0.24	−0.27	0.38
2001	−0.003	−0.003	0.683	0.683	−1.47	−0.26	0.40
2002	−0.003	−0.003	0.693	0.669	−2.25	−0.23	0.40
2003	−0.003	−0.003	0.690	0.670	−1.91	−0.23	0.42
2004	−0.004	−0.004	0.679	0.679	−1.84	−0.20	0.43
2005	−0.005	−0.005	0.694	0.675	−3.15	−0.16	0.40
2006	−0.005	−0.005	0.698	0.680	−3.34	−0.14	0.41
2007	−0.007	−0.007	0.707	0.686	−4.13	−0.13	0.41
2008	−0.012	−0.012	0.718	0.698	−2.79	–	–

Table 3.4 Geographic distribution of export-oriented enterprises (number of enterprises)

	Coastal			Inland		
	Export-oriented	Non-export-oriented	Percentage of export-oriented enterprises (%)	Export-oriented	Non-export-oriented	Percentage of export-oriented enterprises (%)
2000	48,839	12,585	20.5	65,605	6,016	8.4
2001	56,707	14,530	20.4	70,817	6,423	8.3
2002	63,795	16,873	20.9	76,590	7,487	8.9
2003	72,845	19,226	20.9	83,596	8,767	9.5
2004	82,472	21,184	20.4	72,354	9,079	11.1
2005	106,325	28,096	20.9	118,569	11,529	8.9
2006	117,334	29,703	20.2	133,657	12,400	8.5
2007	131,248	31,323	19.3	150,580	12,750	7.8
2008	166,776	34,825	17.3	182,728	13,277	6.8

Categories of business in which export-oriented industries are engaged

We looked at both the numbers of different enterprises engaged in different industries, and at the total output values of different industries (see Table 3.5 and Figures 3.1a and b). In evaluating enterprises as a whole, we divided 'industrial groups' into (1) food, (2) textiles and garments, (3) materials, (4) chemicals and petroleum, (5) ferrous and non-ferrous metals, (6) machinery, (7) electronics and pharmaceuticals, and (8) a miscellaneous category (for details, refer to Appendix 1 on page 110).

Table 3.5 Basic industry statistics

Category by industry	1 Food				2 Textile and garment			
Sample	All		Export-oriented		All		Export-oriented	
Year	2000	2007	2000	2007	2000	2007	2000	2007
Total profit	1,980	5,390	1,590	3,619	1,542	2,786	1,575	2,526
Total output value	51,561	105,677	44,277	86,883	45,959	64,863	49,604	67,845
Added value per capita	118	223	127	185	106	94	123	67
Cost	38,668	85,740	37,044	71,500	37,617	55,040	41,906	57,775
Number of employees/ practitioners	219	172	235	219	385	259	427	349
Net value of fixed assets	18,024	19,823	12,247	16,270	14,746	13,010	13,667	12,819
Export	3,984	7,899	32,576	65,052	18,320	18,796	40,163	54,881
Profit/sales revenue	0.03	0.04	0.03	0.04	0.03	0.03	0.02	0.03
Profit/total output value	0.02	0.04	0.03	0.03	0.03	0.03	0.02	0.03
Export/sales revenue	0.09	0.09	0.83	0.83	0.38	0.28	0.88	0.88
Export/total output value	0.08	0.08	0.78	0.79	0.36	0.28	0.85	0.86
Fixed asset per capita	11.15	17.61	14.81	11.00	8.73	6.55	5.83	5.46
National capital fund (%)	0.37	0.05	0.14	0.03	0.03	0.03	0.14	0.01
Foreign capital fund (%)	0.27	0.30	0.40	0.44	0.44	0.40	0.47	0.63
Observed value	11,785	23,771	1,127	2,224	16,714	44,601	6,821	13,533

Category by industry	3 Materials				4 Chemicals and petroleum			
Sample	All		Export-oriented		All		Export-oriented	
Year	2000	2007	2000	2007	2000	2007	2000	2007
Total profit	1,577	2,799	1,949	2,366	1,989	5,316	1,822	5,491
Total output value	37,598	58,896	51,363	62,494	74,272	132,128	53,730	112,418
Added value per capita	108	110	161	72	154	196	171	134
Cost	30,287	49,007	42,728	52,416	61,801	113,639	43,322	93,692
Number of employees/ practitioners	250	189	357	306	311	180	276	277

Net value of fixed assets	15,006	14,472	11,113	11,712	35,809	32,563	19,525	31,533
Export	10,164	15,229	44,221	52,199	7,573	12,444	38,644	75,951
Profit/sales revenue	0.03	0.04	0.03	0.03	0.03	0.04	0.03	0.03
Profit/total output value	0.03	0.04	0.03	0.03	0.03	0.04	0.03	0.03
Export/sales revenue	0.20	0.25	0.89	0.90	0.11	0.10	0.81	0.80
Export/total output value	0.19	0.24	0.85	0.87	0.11	0.10	0.78	0.78
Fixed asset per capita	7.10	8.73	4.66	6.41	7.51	12.97	10.34	4.13
National capital fund (%)	0.19	0.04	0.05	0.00	0.33	0.17	0.07	0.04
Foreign capital fund (%)	0.39	0.44	0.73	0.70	0.21	0.26	0.65	0.67
Observed value		9,145	26,555	1,947	6,951	17,656	43,587	2,147	4,620

Category by industry	5 Metal and non-metal				6 Machinery			
Sample	All		Export-oriented		All		Export-oriented	
Year	2000	2007	2000	2007	2000	2007	2000	2007
Total profit	1,992	8,020	1,722	4,377	2,169	6,118	2,612	7,146
Total output value	54,061	147,510	49,824	100,770	54,941	109,138	70,685	132,792
Added value per capita	132	194	137	113	107	152	97	106
Cost	44,707	130,368	40,498	84,186	42,099	89,306	57,171	110,592
Number of employees/ practitioners	346	209	305	257	477	256	422	279
Net value of fixed assets	31,665	37,400	15,207	20,029	26,857	24,831	31,153	29,263
Export	6,183	14,062	39,136	74,286	6,114	13,314	53,491	99,807
Profit/sales revenue	0.03	0.04	0.03	0.04	0.03	0.04	0.03	0.04
Profit/total output value	0.03	0.04	0.03	0.03	0.03	0.04	0.03	0.04
Export/sales revenue	0.09	0.10	0.84	0.84	0.08	0.09	.79	0.79
Export/total output value	0.09	0.09	0.80	0.81	0.07	0.08	.76	0.77
Fixed asset per capita	6.27	12.09	9.23	7.79	6.92	13.48	.67	19.92
National capital fund (%)	0.46	0.19	0.11	0.03	0.43	0.22	0.25	0.10
Foreign capital fund (%)	0.14	0.20	0.53	0.62	0.16	0.25	0.38	0.60
Observed value	20,619	48,233	2,099	5,070	17,557	52,497	1,391	4,799

Category by industry	7 Electric, electronics, medicine and others			
Sample	All		Export-oriented	
Year	2000	2007	2000	2007
Total profit	4,582	7,505	6,639	15,817
Total output value	95,275	186,504	162,844	465,966
Increment per capita	127	150	118	105
Cost	76,719	161,658	139,089	414,477

(continued)

Table 3.5 (continued)

Category by industry	7 Electric, electronics, medicine and others			
Sample	All		Export-oriented	
Year	2000	2007	2000	2007
Number of employees/ practitioners	335	314	543	708
Net value of fixed assets	25,524	28,610	34,147	59,353
Export	29,045	87,168	130,920	387,597
Profit/sales revenue	0.03	0.04	0.0314	0.0325
Profit/total output value	0.03	0.04	0.0303	0.0317
Export/sales revenue	0.17	0.20	0.857	0.8431
Export/total output value	0.16	0.19	0.8267	0.8181
Fixed asset per capita	7.95	9.62	5.8858152	7.1326676
National capital fund (%)	0.22	0.05	0.069158	0.0149093
Foreign capital fund (%)	0.38	0.49	0.7840975	0.8043786
Observed value	11,589	34,169	2,097	7,265

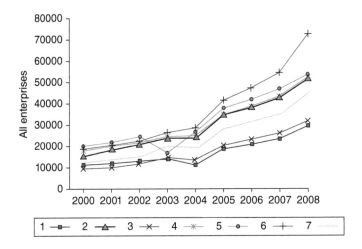

Figure 3.1a Distribution of the number of all enterprises as a whole in various industries.

In contrast to the distribution of all enterprises as a whole, the greatest number of export-oriented enterprises was concentrated in category 2, namely textiles and garments. Export-oriented enterprises also tended to concentrate in category 7, electronics and pharmaceuticals, and in 3, materials, while the fewest number were in category 1, food.

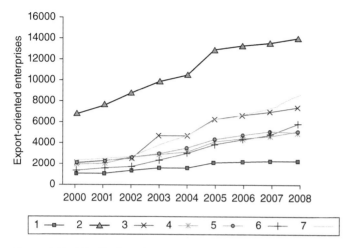

Figure 3.1b   Distribution of export-oriented enterprises in various industries.
Units: number of enterprises

In terms of output value, the distribution shown in Figures 3.2a and b was in evidence.

When we evaluate the data according to output value, we see a distinct difference between export-oriented enterprises and all enterprises as a whole. The two categories of electronics and pharmaceuticals (7) and textiles and garments

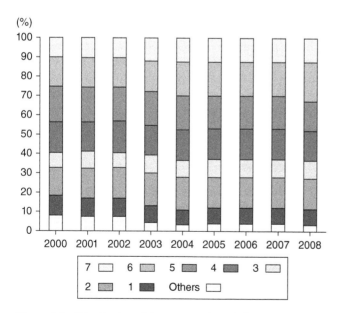

Figure 3.2a   Distribution of the output value of all enterprises as a whole in various industries.

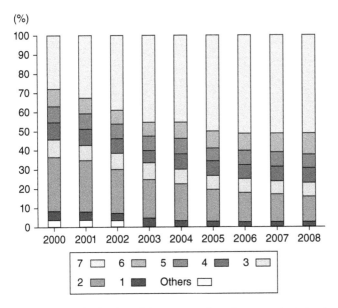

Figure 3.2b Distribution of the output value of export-oriented enterprises in various
industries.
Units: Percentage of total output value of each industry

Note: The value for category 8 after the year 2003 is zero, which may be due to a change in the way
statistics were measured.

(2) show the largest change in percentages. In 2000, both of these categories held
close to 30 percent of the total. Electronics and pharmaceuticals then began a
steady increase until the category held over 50 percent in 2007. In contrast, the
percentage held by textiles and garments began to decline until it represented less
than 15 percent. This demonstrates that there was clearly a major restructuring
within export-oriented enterprises.

The 'survival rate' of enterprises

Every year, the statistics within the large-sample database showed enterprises
being added while some were eliminated. The disappearance of some enterprises
could be attributed to a number of factors, including bankrupcy, decrease in size
to below the RMB 5 million limit of what was included in the database, or other
reasons such as statistical error. In Table 3.6, we set forth the 'survival rate' of
enterprises as supplementary evidence for the possibility of the first two factors, namely bankruptcy and a decrease in size. We caution that any conclusions
derived from these figures should be tentative.

In these two tables (Tables 3.6 and 3.7), one can see how many enterprises
were started up in each year and how many managed to survive in each year.

Table 3.6 Survival rate among all enterprises as a whole

		Year of survival							
	Inception year	2000	2001	2002	2003	2004	2005	2006	2007
Number	2000	114,131	76,846	67,239	58,343	31,768	42,101	39,176	36,167
	2001	0	49,393	37,497	31,441	17,150	22,584	21,067	19,499
	2002	0	0	34,151	24,952	13,703	17,920	16,677	15,554
	2003	0	0	0	41,310	20,095	26,180	24,215	22,730
	2004	0	0	0	0	75,395	54,630	51,482	48,760
	2005	0	0	0	0	0	61,194	50,384	45,615
	2006	0	0	0	0	0	0	49,326	41,765
	2007	0	0	0	0	0	0	0	54,148
	Total	116,131	128,240	140,889	158,049	160,115	226614	254333	286,245
%	2000	100	67	59	51	28	37	34	32
	2001		100	76	64	35	46	43	39
	2002			100	73	40	52	49	46
	2003				100	49	63	59	55
	2004					100	72	68	65
	2005						100	82	75
	2006							—	85
	2007								100

Table 3.7 Survival rate among export-oriented enterprises

| | Year of survival | | | | | | | |
	Inception year	2000	2001	2002	2003	2004	2005	2006	2007
Number	2000	19,295	11,832	10,470	9,260	5,496	7,130	6,472	5,917
	2001	0	9,510	6,035	5,116	3,041	3,878	3,536	3,148
	2002	0	0	8,199	5,113	2,995	3,677	3,326	3,018
	2003	0	0	0	8,889	3,676	4,689	4,212	3,807
	2004	0	0	0	0	15,859	8,416	7,780	7,136
	2005	0	0	0	0	0	11,986	8,015	6,855
	2006	0	0	0	0	0	0	9,008	5,755
	2007	0	0	0	0	0	0	0	8,903
	Total	19,295	21,342	24,704	28,378	31,067	39,776	42,349	44,539
%	2000	100	61	54	48	28	37	34	31
	2001		100	63	54	32	41	37	33
	2002			100	62	37	45	41	37
	2003				100	41	53	47	43
	2004					100	53	49	45
	2005						100	67	57
	2006							–	64
	2007								100

A comparison of Tables 3.6 and 3.7 above shows that the survival rate of export-oriented enterprises is fairly low.

For example, 114,131 enterprises first appeared in the year 2000. By 2001, 76,846 of them still survived. In 2002, 67,239 still survived, and so on. The line at the bottom, giving the 'Total,' shows how many enterprises in all were in existence in each year. The second half of the table shows the figures for each year as a percentage of the year in which enterprises started. For example, among all enterprises that started operations in 2000, only 32 percent were still in existence in 2007.

We may derive the following initial conclusions from the analysis of both 'all enterprises as a whole' and 'export-oriented enterprises' as represented by the basic statistics in the database.

1   Export-oriented enterprises that export more than 40 percent of their total sales volume are in a minority. They constitute less than 20 percent of the total number of all enterprises.
2   Export-oriented industries have a larger number of employees, higher output value, and they export more, but their total profits and their profit margins are relatively low.
3   Export-oriented industries are concentrated in coastal areas in the eastern part of China.
4   The greatest concentration of export-oriented industries, in terms of numbers of companies, is in garments and textiles. In terms of output value, it is in electronics and pharmaceuticals.
5   Profit margins of export-oriented industries have been going down dramatically since 2006.
6   Exports as a percentage of all sales volume, as well as all output value, have been declining for all industries as a whole, as well as export-oriented industries, since 2005.
7   A relatively large number of export-oriented enterprises have been eliminated from the database. One of the reasons for this may be that they ran into business problems and had to shut down.

The impact of an appreciating RMB on business operations between the years 2005 and 2008: a general analysis

For quite a long time, Chinese enterprises faced very little exchange-rate risk as a result of the long-term *de facto* peg of the Chinese currency against the US dollar. It may well be that enterprises were therefore not well adapted to RMB appreciation and to a business environment that was becoming more international. In the general analysis that we describe below, we also employ surveys and other research materials to support our points.

The foreign-exchange risk confronting all kinds of export-oriented enterprises

Given that different enterprises have a variety of products and different invest-ment structures, the types of foreign-exchange risk that they have to face vary depending on situation. We describe different types of enterprises below.

Enterprises that deal in general trade

The foreign-exchange risk faced by this kind of enterprise includes transaction risk and operating risk. Transaction risk is short term whereas operating risk is long term.

Transaction risk comes about when transactions are settled in a foreign cur-rency. If the exchange rate changes against the enterprise, then loss of income may result. If the settlement is in a currency that loses value against the RMB, then the exporter's income is reduced when that foreign currency is translated into RMB. For enterprises that are engaged in both importing and exporting, the foreign-exchange risk relates only to the differential between imports and exports. If an enterprise is engaged in only exporting or only importing, then its exposure to foreign-exchange risk is on the total amount.

In addition to transaction risk, enterprises engaged in general trade also confront 'operating risk.' Exchange-rate changes create changes in the relative prices of goods, which can then influence sales and the income of an enterprise. Operating risk has different kinds of effects on different kinds of businesses. Those involved in products with relatively high price elasticity face a relatively larger amount of operating risk. The reason is that large price swings will lead to relatively large changes in demand. Those that procure materials from within China and then sell products abroad will have a relatively larger amount of operating risk if the RMB appreciates. Those that buy materials from abroad and that sell in the Chinese domestic market will gain from an appreciating RMB. Those that buy materials from abroad and then export products will be able to offset additional costs with additional earnings to a degree that depends on relative amounts.

Processing-trade enterprises

The influence of an appreciating RMB on processing-trade enterprises in China is different from the influence on general-trade enterprises. General export-type companies source their materials from inside China, and an appreciating RMB means higher costs of materials as well as labor, so the impact on them is larger. Processing-trade enterprises source their materials from outside China, so the impact on them is smaller.

Meanwhile, processing-trade enterprises come in two types, those that are provided with materials by a foreign-funded entity (the *lai-liao* type of enter-prise, which 'receives materials,') and those that import materials themselves (the *jin-liao* type of enterprise, which 'imports materials.') The first type, *lai-liao* processing, utilizes materials provided from outside China. It takes in components and assembles them into complete units, for example, and receives a processing fee. It uses no foreign exchange to purchase the materials. The second type, *jin-liao* processing, *does* use foreign exchange to import materials. It 'adds value,' or processes the materials and then re-exports finished goods. The transaction risk faced by both types of processing-trade enterprise is the same as it is for a general-trade enterprise. This risk is represented by the potential lost income due to the weakening of the currency in which the contract is denominated. In contrast, the economic risk for the two different kinds of processing-trade enterprises is different. *Lai-liao* processing gets its materials from a foreign-funded entity and takes no foreign-exchange risk itself in this regard, but the processing fees that it derives from the business do have a foreign-exchange risk associated with them. If the RMB appreciates but the processing fees stay the same as denominated in the foreign currency, then the enterprise earns less income. *Jin-liao* processing uses foreign exchange to purchase materials so this kind of processing does have foreign-exchange risk, while exchange-rate fluctuations can also change its cost structures and income. Nevertheless, when the RMB appreciates, imports for a *jin-liao* processing enterprise are cheaper, which to a degree can offset lower RMB income derived from exported products. Overall, *lai-liao* processing is more affected by an appreciating RMB than *jin-liao* processing.

In terms of the dominance of one type of trade over another, in 2008, China's general-trade and processing-trade each had roughly half the total volume of trade (see Table 3.8). Within the sub-category of processing-trade, *jin-liao* processing predominated. That is, enterprises involved in processing mainly took in goods that were supplied by foreign entities, processed them, and re-exported them. As noted above, the impact of exchange-rate changes on this type of enterprise is relatively low.

Table 3.8 China's total volume of foreign trade in 2008, by type of trade

	Export		Import	
	USD1bn	*(%)*	*USD1bn*	*(%)*
General trade	6,629	46	5,721	51
Processing of materials supplied by foreign enterprises	1,106	8	902	8
Processing with imported materials	5,646	39	2,882	25
Contracting foreign project	110	1		0
Inbound and outbound goods in bonded warehouses	285	2	574	5
Others	533	4	1,247	11
Total	14,307	100	11,326	100

Source: China's Statistical Yearbook of Trade and Foreign Economic Relations 2009, page 671, by Trade and Foreign Economic Relations, Administration of National Bureau of Statistics

Case study 1 A limited liability company located along China's eastern coast

Product: tennis balls. Annual value of output: RMB 100 million. Number of employees: 500. Profit margin: over 10 percent.

This company produces tennis balls in three grades, high, medium, and low. It imports large quantities of raw materials such as rubber. Its medium and low-grade product is sold mainly within China; its high-grade product and part of the medium-grade product is exported.

Cost of labor: Including overtime, each worker receives a monthly compensation of over RMB 2,000.

Impact of RMB appreciation: The head of the company feels that RMB appreciation has been beneficial since it lowers the cost of imported materials. Recently, the cost of necessary materials has skyrocketed. Since this company has a large inventory of raw materials relative to smaller companies that can keep less in stock, the RMB appreciation has been good for this company.

Labor-intensive industries

China's export-oriented enterprises include large numbers of labor-intensive companies. The profit margin among these companies has been declining to the point that it is quite modest now, due to the increased cost of labor in recent years. In addition, most of the materials for such companies come from inside China. It is possible that RMB appreciation is, therefore, reducing already-slim profit margins even further.

Case study 2: A limited liability company that produces shoes, along China's eastern coast

This enterprise was set up in 1980. Its ownership transitioned from a 'collective' to a 'joint venture' to a 'domestically-funded company.' The factory has a total floor space of 80,000 square meters; registered capital totals RMB 50 million, assets are valued at RMB 1 billion, and the company has 3,000 employees. The company produces shoes of a well-known brand within China, and it exports over 95 percent of its production. Its primary markets are Russia, the United States, and Germany. Men's leather shoes are the primary product; the company ranks among China's Top Ten exporters of footwear.

More than 95 percent of workers in this enterprise come from elsewhere, that is, are migrant laborers. Labor costs have been rising consistently. In the 1980s, labor costs made up between 10 percent and 13 percent of total costs of a pair of shoes; the figure now is between 17 percent and 20 percent on average. The total annual payroll for the company is RMB 70 million; minimum monthly wages rose from RMB 1,350 in 2010 to RMB 1,600 at present. Technicians receive between RMB 3,000 and 4,000. Most workers are paid on a piecework basis.

The enterprise imports less than 10 percent of its materials. Due to the rising cost of materials, between January and March, 2010, the company has had to pay RMB 1 million more for its materials than it did in 2009. By now, each pair of shoes costs an additional RMB 1.

Senior management of the enterprise estimates that for every 1 percent appreciation of the RMB, profit margins for the enterprise go down by between 1 percent and 1.5 percent.

This enterprise deals with the above in the following ways. First, 'Dollar in, dollar out.' That is, it pays costs in US dollars and takes in proceeds in US dollars. It is increasing the percentage of its imported materials. Second, it 'locks up' the exchange rate for bank settlement. Third, it buys raw materials on a spot basis as opposed to long-term contracts. Fourth, the moment the exchange rate changes, it initiates price renegotiations with foreign merchants.

Multinational companies

In recent years, some Chinese companies have begun to set up branches abroad. The main foreign-exchange risk that these Chinese multinationals are encountering relates to the way exchange-rate changes lead to different values on the balance sheet of the parent company when the subsidiary's assets and liabilities are incorporated into the parent-company balance sheet. The same is true of incorporating the profit and loss statements of subsidiary companies into the RMB-denominated statements of the parent company.

As the RMB appreciates, the returns to the parent company of a subsidiary's income decline by the amount of appreciation. (That is, if the subsidiary's income stays constant.)

Case study 3: A 'Group' or consolidated company making automobile components in eastern China

This company was founded in 1985, and makes universal coupling devices and tire units for the automobile industry. In 2008, the enterprise was converted to a shareholding company with the intent of eventually going public. At the time of writing, the company had annual sales of RMB 700 million and a net profit margin of between 5 percent and 10 percent. More than 95 percent of its products are exported, with 30 percent of exports going to the United States and another 30 percent going to Europe. The company applies its own brand to its products and is a member of the AAP sales network of chains in the United States. Although its products can fit all types of cars, on a global scale, to date the company has only been a supplier to maintenance facilities; it does not yet supply to assembly plants. It employs 1,000 workers.

(continued)

(continued)

> The company has one manufacturing plant and two branch offices in the United States and one branch office in Germany. In 2007, it acquired a plant in South Carolina that employs 100 people. It hired a Taiwan-born American citizen to manage the facility; technicians were sent out from the China headquarters and are native Chinese from the Mainland.
>
> Labor costs (within China): In 2010, labor costs rose by 20 percent over the previous year. Wages are paid on a piecework basis. General unskilled labor is paid at below RMB 3,000 (for example, transporting goods). Skilled labor is paid at over RMB 3,000. There is considerable mobility within the labor force – for example, for every 290 workers who are recruited, some 200 leave. The loss of experienced staff is also severe. Reasons include the preferential policies of China's government (that is, preferential to urban residents as opposed to rural migrant laborers). Children of rural parents must return to their home towns in order to go to school. In addition, a number of employees are graduates of college and technical schools and, being of the 1990s generation, they are more inclined to high mobility.
>
> Senior officials of the enterprise estimate that for every 1 percent appreciation of the RMB, the company loses 1 percent in profits. Solutions: (1) push the loss onto customers by raising prices, although this requires some finesse; (2) lower costs and raise efficiency; (3) use financial instruments to hedge against currency losses. In other words, lock in exchange rates; use zero-interest rate loans denominated in US dollars; settle accounts in advance using forward exchange markets.

The impact of exchange-rate changes on other major exporting industries: the results of other types of research

The impact of exchange-rate changes has varied depending on the type of industry, given the specifics of each industry's products and cost structures. Three key industry sectors are described below.

Textiles

Research conducted by GuRen and Wu Haibin (2007) has indicated that change in the 'real effective exchange rate' of the RMB has had the greatest impact on the export of goods from China's garments and textiles industry. Within this category, the impact on cotton yarn textiles has been less than on other sectors. The 'transferral' coefficient for the impact of exchange-rate changes is greater than 1 for both categories of goods, indicating a complete carryover effect. Appreciation of the RMB therefore has the potential to weaken the competitiveness of these two types of goods. The transferral coefficient for woven textiles made of cotton has been somewhat less, so the impact of exchange-rate changes has also been less.

Electromechanical products

Research conducted by Hu Xiaoqun (2007) has indicated that China's exports of this type of product have not been as affected by RMB appreciation as they have by changes in the real income of overseas purchasers. China's electromechanical imports have been more sensitive to changes in the real effective exchange rate than they have to changes in China's domestic real incomes. That is to say, both imports and exports of electromechanical goods have been affected by changes in the real effective exchange rate of the RMB, but the impact has been greater on imports. The authors of this study feel that the reason behind this may be the greater value-added content and technology content of China's own products, which has been strengthening China's competitiveness in this area.

Agricultural products

Research conducted by Song Haiying (2005) has looked into the impact of exchange-rate changes on China's agricultural industry. The research discovered that changes in RMB rates do have an impact on exports of Chinese agricultural goods. Exports are negatively correlated to the real effective exchange rate of a given year. The official nominal rate of the RMB has a noticeably delayed impact on China's exports of agricultural goods.

Risk mitigation measures that are customarily used by Chinese enterprises

At present, Chinese enterprises have a limited capacity for dealing with foreign-exchange risk. Knowledge about how to prevent such risk is inadequate, but the measures that enterprises might potentially learn how to take are also limited. Risk-mitigation procedures that are actually used right now include the following.

1   Enterprises retain as little foreign exchange as possible. They do their best to settle accounts into RMB at banks as soon as possible.
2   Enterprises reopen price negotiations with their foreign customers once exchange rates change. This is a very short-term measure.
3   Enterprises use such financial tools as credit, cash trade (spot transactions), and investment. A combined form of these methods, the so-called BSI, or 'borrow-spot-invest' procedure works as follows:

After signing an import contract, the Chinese enterprise borrows RMB from a bank. The term of the borrowing corresponds to when it will need to have the foreign exchange to pay for the imports. The amount of the foreign exchange it will need to pay out in the future is calculated at the current spot rate. Then, the enterprise takes the RMB that it has borrowed and converts it into the foreign exchange it will need in the future. It invests that in the money markets of the foreign country, with a term that is equivalent to when it will need to pay out the money. On the day of settlement, it takes the foreign exchange that has come to maturity, converts it into RMB, and uses it to pay the bank from whom it took the loan.

Similarly, after signing an export contract, the Chinese enterprise borrows foreign exchange from a bank. The term of the loan is the same as the term of when the enterprise expects the income from the exported products. The exchange rate is set at the spot rate, for the amount of income that has been contracted for once the sale goes through. Then, the enterprise takes the foreign exchange it has borrowed and changes it into the RMB income it expects to receive. It invests that in the money markets of China, with a maturity that is equivalent to when the transaction comes due. On the day of settlement, it takes the RMB to repay the loan from the bank.

4 Mitigating exchange-rate risk through the use of forward contracts for purchase and sale of foreign exchange. 'Forward exchange purchase and sale' means that entities outside China's borders sign contracts with China's designated foreign-exchange banks. These contracts specify the currency, amount, rate, and term of the foreign exchange. The completion of the sale or purchase of foreign exchange is then conducted according to the contract. By fixing or 'locking in' the future exchange rate, Chinese enterprises can attempt to prevent losses due to the appreciation of the RMB (Li Shuyin et al., 2009).

The response of Chinese enterprises to appreciation of the RMB

By and large, China's enterprises did respond and take action to the appreciation of the RMB between the years 2005 and 2008. The evidence for this comes from our surveys and from statistical analysis.

From our surveys, we can see that enterprises had a clear idea of how exchange-rate appreciation would be affecting their profitability.

Many of the enterprises then adopted the method noted above of 'renegotiating prices' with foreign merchants. (One example would be the shoe company.) Many of these, moreover, received a positive response from the foreign buyers.

Some companies attempted the method of lowering costs and improving efficiencies, and thereby attempting to realize the potential inherent in their own companies (an example would be the automobile components company).

Some companies began to evaluate whether or not to restructure the amount of materials they imported versus those they purchased domestically. (One example would again be the shoe company.)

Some companies adopted risk-mitigation procedures through financial measures, such as locking in an exchange rate. (An example would be the tennis ball company.)

Despite the fact that most companies did in fact adopt some measure or other, they were insufficiently experienced at this practice to be effective. This problem applied particularly to the use of complex financial instruments.

Statistics show that large enterprises were already beginning to modify their businesses in the first decade of this century, given changes in their operating environments, including a changing RMB exchange rate.

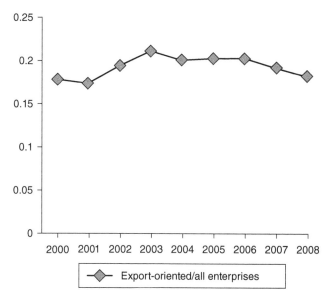

Figure 3.3 Percentage of export-oriented enterprises to all enterprises, as expressed by their output value.

1   Exporting enterprises as a percentage of all enterprises in China first rose and then declined in the first eight years of the century (see Figure 3.3). This eflected decisions that Chinese enterprises were making about aiming at foreign markets as opposed to domestic markets, given the changing operating environment. The balance began to shift in favor of domestic markets. This is not unrelated to the heavy industrialization of China's industries at the start of the twenty-first century.

Figure 3.3 demonstrates that the product composition of China's export-oriented enterprises has already undergone a fundamental change since the year 2000. There has been a tremendous increase in the output value of such things as electronics and pharmaceuticals, while there has been a tremendous decline in the output value of garments and textiles.

2 Since 2000, the export component of enterprises in China displayed first an increase and then a decrease (see Table 3.1). The ratio of exports to sales reached its peak in the year 2004. One cannot exclude the possibility that the appreciation of the RMB in 2005 had something to do with this. One could interpret this as reflecting decisions on the part of enterprises to adjust the composition of their sales given the appreciating RMB, that is, fewer exports versus more domestic sales (see Figure 3.4).

By dividing exported goods into different industry types, one can analyze how change affected different industries (see Figure 3.5).

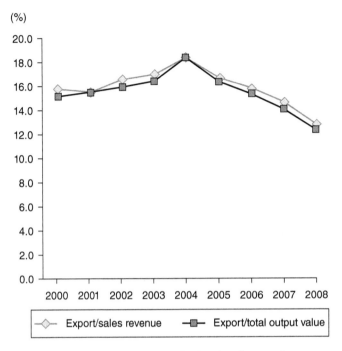

Figure 3.4 The ratio of exports to all sales, for all enterprises.

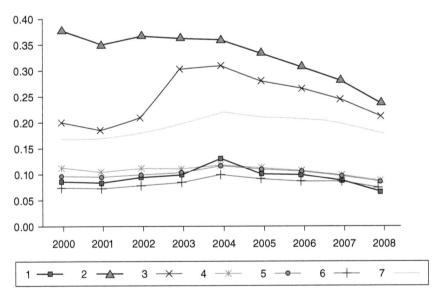

Figure 3.5 The ratio of exports to all sales, for all enterprises but divided into different kinds of industries.

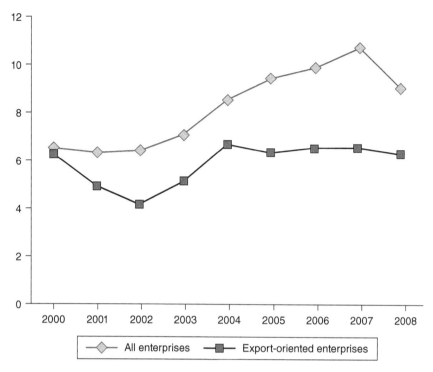

Figure 3.6 Per capita fixed assets.
Units: RMB 10,000 per person

Within the category of 'export-oriented enterprises,' exports as a percentage of all sales did not show a clear change. Within the category of 'all industries,' however, there was a clear decline in exports as a percentage of sales. This phenomenon was most apparent in the textiles and materials sectors, although it was clear in all major categories of goods.

3 There was an increase in the degree to which China's industries are capital intensive. This is apparent from analysis of enterprises of a certain large size, and from analysis of industry-specific figures (see Table 3.2).

An increase in the capital-intensive degree of export-oriented industries was slower than in industry as a whole. The world economic recession in 2008 had a marked influence on the degree to which China's enterprises are moving in a capital-intensive direction.

4 Changes in the structure or composition of inputs. (With an appreciating RMB), China began to import a higher percentage and higher total value of raw materials and equipment. According to publicly released statistics, imports of non-food raw materials and mined fossil fuels increased by around seven times between the years 2000 and 2008 (see Table 3.9). This was higher than the growth rate of GDP, which demonstrated that enterprises were changing the composition of what they imported to use in producing China's products.

Table 3.9 Dollar value of China's imports of certain types of goods

Unit: USD 100 million

	1980	1990	2000	2008
Total	200.17	53,345	2,250.94	11,325.62
Primary commodity	69.59	98.53	467.39	3,623.95
Manufactured goods	35.54	41.07	200.03	1,666.95
Of which, non-edible raw materials	2.03	12.72	206.37	1,692.42
Fossil fuel	130.58	434.92	1,783.55	7,701.67
Of which, chemicals	29.09	66.48	302.13	1,191.88
Mechanical and transportation equipment	51.19	168.45	919.31	4,417.65

Source: Statistical yearbook of China's Foreign Trade and Economic Relations Department, 2009, page 676.

The impact of RMB appreciation between 2005 and 2008 on China's enterprises: an econometric analysis

While controlling for the influence of other variables, we attempted to isolate the impact of exchange-rate changes on China's enterprises through the use of a regression analysis. The three tables below express the results of this analysis. They present exports as a percentage of sales, profitability, and export volume as the three 'explained variables' in the regression analysis. Line Number Three in the tables shows the 'explained variable.' Line Number One in the tables shows the variable that acts upon the other two, or the 'explaining variable.' In different models, we distinguished between and utilized the 'effective exchange rate' and the 'real effective exchange rate' as the primary 'explaining variable.' Other variables were then added in as a control for the effect of these variables.

Table 3.10 uses the percentage of exports to sales as the 'explained variable.' We used the entire sample of enterprises in this regression analysis, including export-oriented enterprises and non-export-oriented enterprises. Rows 1, 3, and 5 use the 'real effective exchange rate' as the primary explaining variable. Rows 2, 4, and 6 use the 'weighted real effective exchange rate' as the primary explaining variable. The exchange rate in 2005 is taken to be 100. An increase in the value of the exchange rate indicates an appreciation of the exchange rate. The 'dummy variable' of exchange-rate government policy is '0' between 2000 and 2004, and in other years is '1.'

The regression conducted on 'exports as a percentage of sales' demonstrates the clear impact of changes in the 'effective exchange rate.' This holds with respect to the entire sample of enterprises, as well as the export-oriented and non-export-oriented enterprises within that sample. The real effective exchange rate also had a demonstrable impact on the entire sample as well as the non-export-oriented enterprises but the correlation was wrong. Its impact on export-oriented enterprises in the sample was positive but not notably so. The influence of the

Table 3.10 Regression result 1: exports as a percentage of sales revenue

Independent/dependent variable	(1)	(2)	(3)	(4)	(5)	(6)
	All samples		Export-oriented		Non-export-oriented	
	Export/Sales revenue	Export/Sales revenue	Export/Sales revenue	Export/Sales revenue	Export/Sales revenue	Export/Sales revenue
Effective exchange rate	-0.00151*** (0.000386)		-0.00102*** (9.95e-05)	-0.000388 (0.000576)	-0.000174*** (3.62e-05)	
Real effective exchange rate		0.00894*** (0.0022)				0.00109*** (0.000361)
Profit	-3.67e-09 (2.59e-08)	-4.34e-09 (2.6e-08)	-4.6e-08** (1.95e-08)	-4.6e-08** (1.96e-08)	1.95e-08** (7.33e-09)	1.95e-08** (7.31e-09)
Fixed asset	-9.67e-09* (5.15e-09)	-9.58e-09* (5.13e-09)	-3.56e-08 (2.22e-08)	-3.58e-08 (2.24e-08)	-1.49e-09 (1.02e-09)	-1.48e-09 (1.02e-09)
Number of employees	1.24e-05* (6.33e-06)	1.24e-05* (6.31e-06)	9.46e-07 (1.47e-06)	9.80e-07 (1.46e-06)	2.66e-06* (1.42e-06)	2.66e-06* (1.42e-06)
GDP of the US	-2.94e-06 (3.63e-06)	-6.53e-06** (3.16e-06)	1.80e-06 (1.24e-06)	1.81e-06 (1.30e-06)	-7.48e-07* (3.77e-07)	-1.20e-06*** (2.83e-07)
Capital fund as controlled variable						
2. stock–control	0.00575 (0.00733)	0.00551 (0.00732)	0.0613*** (0.00728)	0.0601*** (0.00729)	-0.0050*** (0.00128)	-0.00503*** (0.00128)
3. stock–control	-0.00270 (0.00697)	-0.00600 (0.00714)	0.0807*** (0.00925)	0.0772*** (0.00910)	-0.00796*** (0.00150)	-0.00831*** (0.00149)
4. stock–control	0.215*** (0.0144)	0.211*** (0.0142)	0.0959*** (0.00897)	0.0927*** (0.00909)	0.0196*** (0.00178)	0.0193*** (0.00149)
5. stock–control	0.260*** (0.0145)	0.255*** (0.0139)	0.104*** (0.0105)	0.100*** (0.0106)	0.0296*** (0.00205)	0.0291*** (0.00211)

(continued)

Table 3.10 (continued)

Independent/dependent variable	(1)	(2)	(3)	(4)	(5)	(6)
	All samples		Export-oriented		Non-export-oriented	
	Export/Sales revenue	Export/Sales revenue	Export/Sales revenue	Export/Sales revenue	Export/Sales revenue	Export/Sales revenue
9. stock–control	0.0506***	0.0553***	0.0925***	0.0955***	-0.00331**	-0.00277**
	(0.00827)	(0.00883)	(0.00954)	(0.00963)	(0.00132)	(0.00133)
99. stock–control	0.0521***	0.0521***	0.0688**	0.0698**	0.00132	0.00132
	(0.0153)	(0.0150)	(0.0321)	(0.0321)	(0.00288)	(0.00289)
Dummy variables of exchange rate policy	-0. 0086*	0.00462**	-0.00523***	0.00150	0.0016***	0.00320***
	(0.00470)	(0.00196)	(0.00140)	(0.00159)	(0.000489)	(0.000450)
Constant term	0.238***	0.107**	0. 808***	0.696***	0.0392***	0.0246***
	(0.0343)	(0.0399)	(0.0222)	(0.0243)	(0.00396)	(0.00421)
Provincial dummy variable	Yes	Yes	Yes	Yes	Yes	Yes
2-digit code industrial dummy variable	Yes	Yes	Yes	Yes	Yes	Yes
Observed value	1,805,015	1,805,015	299,566	299,566	1,505,449	1,505,449
R-square	0. 099	0.099	0. 044	0. 044	0. 029	0. 029
Number of industries	40	40	38	38	40	40

Note: Data in brackets are Robust standard deviations.

*** $p < 0.01$, ** $p < 0.05$, * $p < 0_0$

Controlled variables of capital fund: 1. National capital 2. Collective capital 3. Corporate capital 4. Individual capital 5. Hong Kong, Macau and Taiwan capital 9. Foreign capital 99. Others.

control variable of capital was apparent in most cases. The 'dummy variable of exchange-rate policy' also had a distinctly positive correlation with respect to the total sample and to export-oriented enterprises (rows 1, 3) when the 'effective exchange rate' was used as the explaining variable.

Table 3.11 shows the results of a regression using profit as a percentage of sales as the 'explained variable.' This was meant to explore the effects of exchange-rate changes on profitability. Dummy variables were used for all years in Rows 6 and 8, while dummy variables for exchange-rate policies were used in the other rows. (We split policy changes into two time periods.)

This regression indicated that exchange-rate movements had only a limited impact on the profitability of 'all enterprises as a whole.' This can be explained by the fact that non-export-oriented enterprises export very little and so their overall profitability is less affected by exchange rates in general. In contrast, changes in both the 'effective exchange rate' and the 'real effective exchange rate' had a pronounced impact on the profitability of export-oriented enterprises. The coefficients are positive in Rows 3, 4, 7, and 8, showing that the impact of real effective exchange rates is positively correlated and significant. The coefficients in Rows 3 and 7 and in Rows 7 and 8 are quite similar. They indicate that a 1 percent appreciation of the effective exchange rate results in a decline in profitability of export-oriented industries of between 0.014 and 0.015 percent. Meanwhile, a 1 percent appreciation in the real effective exchange rate results in a decline in profitability of these industries of 0.035 percent. The impact of 'exchange-rate policy dummy variables' on export-oriented enterprises is generally quite apparent. In addition, US GDP as an explaining variable to reflect overseas demand also shows that the impact of this variable is generally significant.

We also used export volumes as the explained variable in conducting a regression analysis (see Table 3.12).

Using export volumes as the explained variable, the coefficient of 'effective exchange rate' and 'real effective exchange rate' was not significant in most cases. When the coefficient was indeed significant (Rows 2 and 4), the symbol was wrong. The reason was that exports (and output value) kept rising even as the exchange rate appreciated, indicating positive correlation. Since output values rose at a relatively faster rate (than exports increased), the ratio of exports to output value declined.

Overall, our regression analysis indicates the following three points:

- For enterprises as a whole, an appreciating RMB will lower the ratio of exports to sales, that is, exports will decline as a percentage of total sales.
- For both 'all enterprises' and 'non-export-oriented enterprises,' the impact of exchange-rate changes on profitability is not dramatic.
- For 'export-oriented enterprises,' the impact of exchange-rate changes (an appreciating RMB) on profitability is significant, and the impact on exports as a percentage of sales is also very clear in most cases.

Table 3.11 Regression result 2: using profit as a percentage of sales as the explained variable

Independent/ dependent variable	(1) All samples	(2)	(3) Export-oriented	(4)	(5) All samples	(6)	(7) Non-export-oriented	(8)
	Profit/Sales revenue	Profit/Sales revenue	Profit/Sales revenue	Profit/Sales revenue	Profit/Sales revenue	Profit/Sales revenue	Profit/Sales revenue	Profit/Sales revenue
Real effective exchange rate	1.40e − 05 (2.42e − 05)		−0.000153*** (4.31e − 05)		2.07e − 05 (2.04e − 05)		−0.000139*** (4.28e − 05)	
Weighted real effective exchange rate		−0.00027 (0.000207)		−0.000345** (0.000150)		−0.000346 (0.000224)		−0.000353** (0.000138)
Fixed asset	1.90e − 09** (7.81e − 10)	1.89e − 09** (7.79e − 10)	1.503 − 08*** (3.68e − 09)	1.50e − 08*** (3.67e − 09)	1.90e − 09** (7.81e − 10)	1.89e − 09** (7.74e − 10)	1.50e − 08*** (3.68e − 09)	1.49e − 08*** (3.65e − 09)
Number of employees	1.80e − 07 (3.05e − 07)	1.81e − 07 (3.05e − 07)	8.32e − 07 (6.17e − 07)	8.38e − 07 (6.18e − 07)	1.80e − 07 (3.05e − 07)	1.81e − 07 (3.05e − 07)	8.34e − 07 (6.17e − 07)	8.38e − 07 (6.16e − 07)
Foreign capital	1.51e − 08*** (3.30e − 09)	1.51e − 08*** (3.29e − 09)	−3.78e − 09 (3.52e − 09)	−3.66e − 09 (3.53e − 09)	1.51e − 08*** (3.30e − 09)	1.51e − 08*** (3.28e − 09)	−3.75e − 09 (3.53e − 09)	−3.65e − 09 (3.52e − 09)
GDP of the US	2.20e − 06*** (4.68e − 07)	2.18e − 06*** (4.85e − 07)	1.43e − 07 (2.43e − 07)	8.86e − 07*** (3.12e − 07)	1.47e − 06* (8.62e − 07)	2.25e − 06*** (4.48e − 07)	−8.82e − 07 (9.51e − 07)	1.39e − 06*** (2.95e − 07)
Export	2.69e − 10 (8.72e − 10)	2.86e − 10 (8.78e − 10)	−7.32e − 10 (6.61e − 10)	−7.21e − 10 (6.65e − 10)	2.69e − 10 (8.72e − 10)	2.89e − 10 (8.79e − 10)	−7.73e − 10 (6.61e − 10)	−7.22e − 10 (6.63e − 10)
Export /Sales revenue	−0.00587*** (0.000801)	−0.00586*** (0.000804)	−0.0115*** (0.00198)	−0.0114*** (0.00198)	−0.00587*** (0.000801)	−0.00586*** (0.000806)	−0.0115*** (0.00198)	−0.0116*** (0.00199)

Capital fund as controlled variable

2. stock_control	0.0144*** (0.00101)	0.0145*** (0.00101)	0.0138*** (0.00172)	0.0133*** (0.00170)	0.0145*** (0.000974)	0.0140*** (0.00110)	0.0139*** (0.00175)	0.0123*** (0.00184)
3. stock_control	0.0145*** (0.00116)	0.0145*** (0.00116)	0.0141*** (0.00135)	0.0132*** (0.00132)	0.0146*** (0.00107)	0.0138*** (0.00125)	0.0143*** (0.00141)	0.0118*** (0.00165)
4. stock_control	0.0151*** (0.00105)	0.0152*** (0.00107)	0.0138*** (0.00151)	0.0129*** (0.00159)	0.0152*** (0.00100)	0.0145*** (0.00115)	0.0139*** (0.00146)	0.0114*** (0.00156)
5. stock_control	0.0186*** (0.00124)	0.0188*** (0.00124)	0.0162*** (0.00153)	0.0154*** (0.00154)	0.0187*** (0.00121)	0.0180*** (0.00136)	0.0163*** (0.00154)	0.0139*** (0.00174)
9. stock_control	0.0151*** (0.00104)	0.0151*** (0.00102)	0.0133*** (0.00137)	0.0136*** (0.00138)	0.0151*** (0.00107)	0.0154*** (0.00109)	0.0132*** (0.00135)	0.0140*** (0.00132)
99. stock_control	0.0202*** (0.00337)	0.0202*** (0.00336)	0.0267*** (0.00614)	0.0273*** (0.00608)	0.0203*** (0.00335)	0.0198*** (0.00333)	0.0272*** (0.00616)	0.0273*** (0.00610)
Dummy variable of 2001						-0.00206*** (0.000237)		-0.00263*** (0.000446)
Dummy variable of 2002						-0.000496		7.37e − 05
Dummy variable of 2003						0.000374 (0.000537)		0.000765 (0.000688)
Dummy variable of 2004						-0.00200*** (0.000563)		-0.00190** (0.000854)
Dummy variable of 2005						-0.00149** (0.000552)		-0.000719 (0.000954)
Dummy variable of 2006						-0.000734** (0.000329)		0.00133*** (0.000404)

(continued)

Table 3.11 (continued)

Independent/ dependent variable	(1) All samples	(2)	(3) Export-oriented	(4)	(5) All samples	(6)	(7) Non-export-oriented	(8)
	Profit/Sales revenue	Profit/Sales revenue	Profit/Sales revenue	Profit/Sales revenue	Profit/Sales revenue	Profit/Sales revenue	Profit/Sales revenue	Profit/Sales revenue
Dummy variables of exchange rate policy	-0.000395	-0.000386	0.00100**	0.000945**	0.000359		0.000812	
	(0.000614)	(0.000610)	(0.000434)	(0.000431)	(0.000459)		(0.000614)	
Constant term	-0.00722	-0.00544	0.0392***	0.0146***	-0.720	-0.00549	-1.576	0.00974*
	(0.00687)	(0.00555)	(0.00778)	(0.00489)	(0.910)	(0.00543)	(1.218)	(0.00540)
Provincial dummy variable	Yes	Yes	Yes	Yes	Yes	Yes	Yes	Yes
2-digit code industrial dummy variable	Yes	Yes	Yes	Yes	Yes	Yes	Yes	Yes
Observed value	1454574	1454574	251450	251450	1454574	1454574	251450	251450
R-square	0.046	0.046	0.026	0.026	0.046	0.046	0.026	0.026
Number of industries	40	40	38	38	40	40	38	38

Data in the bracket are Robust standard deviations.

*** p<0.01, ** p<0.05, * p<0.1.

Table 3.12 Regression result 3: using export volumes as the explained variable

Independent/ dependent variable	(1)	(2)	(3)	(4)	(17)	(18)
	All samples		Export-oriented		Non-export-oriented	
	Export	Export	Export	Export	Export	Export
Effectiv exchange rate	−182.8 (223.2)		112.7 (463.7)		−1.294 (5.539)	
Real effective exchange rate		21474*** (2319)		37432*** (9123)		22.90 (84.00)
Export /Sales revenue			119476** (47308)	119082** (47371)		
Profit	1.912* (1.122)	1. 910* (1.121)	4 338* (2.221)	4 334* (2.220)	0.145*** (0.0532)	0.145*** (0.0532)
Fixed assets	−0.115 (0.103)	−0.115 (0.103)	−0.599 (0. 364)	−0.598 (0.364)	0.00332 (0.00853)	0 00332 (0. 00853)
Number of employees	68.08 (56.58)	67.91 (56 45)	246.5* (136 5)	246.0* (136 3)	3.482 (2.284)	3.482 (2.284)
GDP of the US	2.763 (2.472)	−1. 898 (1.411)	17.48** (7.448)	8.663* (5.038)	0.100 (0.117)	0.0939 (0.124)
Controlled variables of capital fund						
2. stock–control	24,113 (22,196)	25,788 (23,618)	102,150 (74,147)	105,117 (76,597)	−464.0 (574 5)	−462.9 (575. 8)
3. stock–control	24,826 (26,995)	25,305 (28,057)	90,567 (98,626)	93,049 (101,091)	−721.0 (733.5)	−723.1 (736.1)
4. stock–control	41,448* (22,830)	38,404* (21,042)	76,343 (82,898)	72,531 (80,954)	−907.4 (569.0)	−911.3 (568.8)
5. stock–control	96,245* (56,356)	91,664* (53,486)	156,239 (124,397)	150,307 (121,524)	−389.7 (434.9)	−394.9 (434.2)
9. stock–control	32,178 (28,168)	34,494 (29,012)	113242 (100,036)	116,139 (101,850)	−306.4 (766.0)	−301.1 (761.1)
99. stock–control	37,543 (27,544)	35,900 (26,459)	160,158 (116,643)	150,580 (11,156)	64.32 (828.8)	63.72 (827.1)
Dummy variables of exchange rate policy	−474.4 (2,298)	2,370*** (790.4)	−4,171 (7202)	−3560 (4540)	189.1** (87.56)	202.2** (83.44)
Constant term	−42,358 (41,205)	−20,096 (39,689)	−363,442** (161010)	−275,155* (161,058)	−1,100 (2,148)	−1,182 (1,830)
Provincial dummy variable	Yes	Yes	Yes	Yes	Yes	Yes
2-digit code industrial dummy variable	Yes	Yes	Yes	Yes	Yes	Yes
Observed value	1,805,015	1,805,015	385,377	385,377	1,419,638	1,419,638
R-square	0.136	0.137	0. 325	0.326	0. 217	0. 217
Number of industries	40	40	40	40	40	40

Note: Data in brackets are Robust standard deviations.
*** p <0.01, ** p <0.05, * p<0.1

Conclusion, and policy recommendations

Between 2005 and 2008, the appreciation of the RMB had a certain negative impact on the growth of China's export-oriented enterprises. All forms of the analysis described above make this clear, including the classic interviews, analysis of the large-sample database of enterprises, and the regression analysis.

At the same time, however, the impact was different on different types of enterprises. Those engaged in 'general trade' and labor-intensive types of business were more negatively affected. Those engaged in 'processing-type' trade, and particularly of the '*jin-liao*' type, that imports materials for value-added processing, were less affected. Meanwhile, there was a positive impact on enterprises that import their materials.

Faced with a changing competitive environment, China's enterprises did in fact respond with specific actions to the appreciating RMB between the years 2005 and 2008. In immediate terms, they began to learn about and then use various risk-mitigating measures to deal with foreign-exchange-risk. Over the longer term, enterprises have begun adjusting their product mix and their operating methods. This has been one positive result of the RMB appreciation. A very quiet change has therefore been taking place within China's industrial structure. First, export-oriented industries are changing their product composition. Second, China's enterprises are shifting away from exporting and toward domestic sales in terms of their sales structure. More and more enterprises are transferring their focus from external markets to domestic markets.

Policy recommendations

In the short term, banks should provide enterprises with a greater range of financial services, so as to help them deal with foreign-exchange risk. Enterprises have already begun to use financial tools in handling such risk, but they lack sufficient knowledge and experience to use them well. Banks should therefore provide more information, including training.

Over the long term, the government itself must help enterprises modify their mode of operations and the composition of their product offerings. Given an operating environment that is more international by the day, enterprises must be able to respond to constantly changing new challenges. They must continually adapt by readjusting business policies, product composition, and technological 'path.' The government should be fully aware of what is happening and should provide the necessary financing, information, and services. It should help enterprises shift their products and policies to adapt to the internationalization of the business environment.

Note

1 Zhang Fan, Yu Miaojie: National School of Development at Peking University.

We are indebted to the funds provided by the China Development Research Foundation, the guidance provided by Secretary General Lu Mai, Deputy Secretary General Tang Min and Yu Jiantuo, Project Manager. Our thanks also go to Huang Wei from National School of Development of Peking University, who conducted data processing and econometric analysis. Thanks also to Tao Hui, Chairman of Yameixin Corporate Consulting Co., Ltd. in Wenzhou, Chen Huanquan, Department Head of Economic and Trade Commission of Wenzhou, Pan Pingping, Deputy Director General of Foreign Trade and Economics Bureau of Wenzhou, Pan Zhongqiang, Deputy Director of Politics Research Office of Wenzhou Municipal Party Committee, Zhou Yaohua, Deputy General Manager of Dongyi Footwear Co., Ltd., Mr. Pan, Department Head of Economic and Trade Commission, Ni Zhenzhen, Head of President Office of Guansheng Auto Component Group, Lin Xian, Manager of Accounting Dept of Dongfang Light Industry Co., Ltd., Chen Xu, General Manager of Tianlong (Group) Co., Ltd., and Quan Ning, General Manager of Kaiqi (Group) Co., Ltd..

Bibliography

Haiying Song, "Empirical Study on Impact of RMB Exchange Rate Movements on Export Trade of China's Agricultural Products", *Issues in Agricultural Economy*, 2005 (3)

Ren Gu and Haibin Wu, "Exchange Rate Movements, Market Share and Export Competitiveness of China-Made Textile and Garment", *World Economy*, 2007 (3)

Shuyin Li and Zhengping Zhang, *Theory and Empirical Analysis of Exchange Rate Risk Management*, Beijing: Intellectual Property Publishing House, 2009

Trade and Foreign Economic Relations Administration, National Bureau of Statistics, Statistical Yearbook of China's Trade and Foreign Economic Relations, Beijing: China Statistics Press, 2009

Xiaoqun Hu, "Empirical Analysis of Impact of RMB Real Effective Exchange Rate Movements on China's Import and Export of Mechanical and Electrical Products", *Mathematics in Practice and Theory*, 2007 (3)

Appendix

1   Industrial classification

Annexed table 3.1 Industrial classification

Broad categories defined in the report	2-digit industries included
1 Food	13 Agricultural and sideline food processing 14 Food production 15 Beverage production 16 Tobacco production
2 Textile and garment	17 Textile 18 Textile, garment, shoes and caps 19 Leather, coat, feather and such products
3 Materials	20 Wood processing 21 Furniture making 22 Papermaking and paper products 24 Cultural and sports products 42 Artwork
4 Chemicals and petroleum	25 Oil processing, coking and nuclear fuel processing 26 Chemical materials and products 28 Chemical fiber 29 Rubber products 30 Plastic products
5 Metal and non-metal minerals	31 Non-metal mineral products 32 Black metal smelting and rolling 33 Non-ferrous metal metallurgy and rolling 34 Metal products
6 Machinery	35 Universal equipment 36 Special-purpose equipment 37 Transportation equipment
7 Electric, electronics and medicine	39 Electrical, mechanical equipment and materials 40 Communication equipment, computer and other electronic equipment 41 Instrument, apparatus and cultural and office machine 23 Printing and duplication of recording media. 27 Pharmaceutical industry
8 Others	

2   Basic statistical information of export-oriented enterprises under various definitions

'Export-oriented enterprise' herein refers to enterprise with export accounting for over 10%, 10%–20%, 20%–30%, and 30%–40% of sales revenue. 'Export-oriented enterprises' in this report refer to enterprises with export making up over 40% of sales revenue.

Annexed table 3.2 Information on other export-oriented enterprise in the enterprise database

		Observed value	Number of employees	Total output value (RMB1000)	Added value per capita	Profit (RMB1000)	Export (RMB1000)
Export rate < 0.1	2000	89,428	312	51,279	119	1,879	50,154
	2001	98,569	291	54,080	55	2,007	54,080
	2002	107,703	281	58,016	74	2,393	56,829
	2003	120,178	262	66,597	81	2,969	65,297
	2004	118,853	217	73,384	78	3,109	73,384
	2005	173,112	213	83,196	123	3,401	81,679
	2006	197,174	196	89,773	148	3,984	88,151
	2007	227,001	189	104,553	179	5,104	102,626
	2008	287,631	161	97,472	–	4,356	95,383
Export rate >= 0. 1 But < 0. 2	2000	2,250	1,031	172,079	199	7,469	168,140
	2001	2,550	783	180,758	63	8,712	180,758
	2002	2,660	805	221,718	77	10,758	218,194
	2003	3,096	702	248,034	91	9,993	242,123
	2004	3,408	465	200,052	81	10,531	200,052
	2005	5,509	520	258,502	122	14,540	254,080
	2006	5,685	626	342,731	151	19,543	337,250
	2007	5,090	612	419,535	169	23,771	414,707
	2008	5,958	515	422,522	–	21,420	414,558

(continued)

Annexed table 3.2 (continued)

		Observed value	Number of employees	Total output value (RMB1000)	Added value per capita	Profit (RMB1000)	Export (RMB1000)
Export rate >= 0.2 But < 0.3	2000	1,693	662	166,225	146	10,934	162,074
	2001	2,064	572	129,442	56	5,010	129,442
	2002	1,999	562	138,676	71	5,306	135,685
	2003	2,303	601	173,687	85	8,496	168,732
	2004	2,537	546	176,269	75	8,889	176,269
	2005	3,249	498	199,407	108	9,417	195,441
	2006	3,787	489	242,628	133	13,497	239,451
	2007	4,084	492	311,726	153	18,858	306,118
	2008	4,652	412	257,895	–	14,619	252,432
Export rate >= 0.3 But < 0.4	2000	1,465	730	135,676	135	5,850	132,986
	2001	1,714	542	133,339	59	8,141	133,339
	2002	1,821	544	127,519	74	5,413	125,102
	2003	2,091	556	160,225	80	7,438	155,967
	2004	2,246	389	128,539	69	6,262	128,539
	2005	2,963	422	167,110	103	7,805	163,006
	2006	3,332	469	220,371	124	10,046	217,328
	2007	3,524	434	219,657	142	10,228	213,194
	2008	4,084	367	215,845	–	11,352	212,136

Annexed table 3.3 Operating indicators of other export-oriented enterprises

		Profit/slaes revenue	Profit/total value of output	Export / sales revenue	Export/total value of output	Fixed asset per capita (RMB10,000)	Percentage of national capital fund in capital fund (%)	Percentage of foreign capital fund in capital fund (%)
Export rate < 0. 1	2000	0. 030	0.029	0.002	0.002	0. 85	0. 42	0. 14
	2001	0.029	0.029	0.002	0.002	1.07	0.40	0.13
	2002	0.032	0.031	0.002	0.002	1.12	0.38	0.13
	2003	0.034	0.033	0.002	0.002	1.08	0.35	0.14
	2004	0.034	0.034	0.003	0.003	2.54	0.30	0.13
	2005	0.037	0.036	0.004	0.003	2.03	0.23	0.16
	2006	0.038	0.037	0.003	0.003	2.55	0.19	0.17
	2007	0.041	0.040	0.002	0.002	2.73	0.19	0.17
	2008	0.044	0.043	0.002	0.002	1.93	–	–
Export rate >= 0. 1 But < 0. 2	2000	0.031	0.029	0. 146	0.142	1.83	0.47	0.17
	2001	0.032	0.032	0. 148	0.148	1.97	0.45	0.23
	2002	0.036	0.035	0.145	0.142	2.13	0.37	0.21
	2003	0.038	0.037	0.146	0.143	2.28	0.27	0.22
	2004	0.038	0.038	0.146	0.146	2.73	0.18	0.28
	2005	0.044	0.043	0.146	0.143	2.84	0.28	0.27
	2006	0.044	0.043	0.144	0. 141	3.09	0.33	0.23
	2007	0.042	0.041	0.147	0. 144	3.34	0.24	0.30
	2008	0.041	0.040	0.146	0. 144	3.29	#VALUE!	#VALUE!

(continued)

Annexed table 3.3 (continued)

		Profit/slaes revenue	Profit/total value of output	Export / sales revenue	Export/total value of output	Fixed asset per capita (RMB10,000)	Percentage of national capital fund in capital fund (%)	Percentage of foreign capital fund in capital fund (%)
Export rate > = 0.2 But < 0. 3	2000	0.030	0.029	0.248	0.240	1.97	0.43	0.26
	2001	0.030	0.030	0.247	0.247	2.19	0.30	0.33
	2002	0.034	0.033	0.249	0.242	2.10	0.28	0.28
	2003	0.037	0.036	0.249	0.244	2.41	0.25	0.32
	2004	0.037	0.037	0.249	0.249	2.79	0.20	0.30
	2005	0.038	0.037	0.249	0.243	2.95	0.17	0.34
	2006	0.041	0.040	0.249	0.244	3.14	0.20	0.35
	2007	0.041	0.040	0.249	0.243	3.52	0.16	0.37
	2008	0.040	0.039	0.248	0.242	3.36	–	–
Export rate >=0. 3 But < 0.4	2000	0.028	0.028	0.348	0.337	1.96	0.44	0.23
	2001	0.030	0.030	0.350	0.350	2.39	0.23	0.43
	2002	0.034	0.033	0.350	0.340	2.28	0.24	0.35
	2003	0.036	0.035	0.349	0.342	2.93	0.25	0.29
	2004	0.036	0.036	0.348	0.348	2.90	0.11	0.42
	2005	0.039	0.038	0.350	0.342	3.14	0.12	0.43
	2006	0.037	0.037	0.349	0.342	3.32	0.15	0.39
	2007	0.039	0.039	0.350	0.343	3.45	0.18	0.39
	2008	0.039	0.038	0.349	0.342	3.41	–	–

4 An analysis of the effect of exchange-rate fluctuations on the banking industry

Research Group, Financial Research Center, Bank of Communications[1]

China initiated reform of its exchange-rate regime in July of 2005. At that time, the country adopted a system of a 'managed float, based on market supply and demand but also regulated with reference to a basket of currencies.' This signified that China was taking a major step in the direction of instituting a genuinely flexible, floating, exchange rate. Since that time, the RMB has appreciated by over 20 percent against the US dollar. In nominal effective terms, it has appreciated by over 15 percent. This appreciation happened most quickly in the years between 2005 and 2008, when the RMB appreciated at an average annual rate of over 6 percent; during the financial crisis, the RMB maintained a fairly stable level against the US dollar.

Meanwhile, the elasticity of the trading range has also expanded since the start of reform, that is, the band within which the RMB is allowed to float. In May of 2007, China's central bank announced that it was expanding this range, against the US dollar and in the interbank spot market, from three one-thousandths to five one-thousandths. On June 19, 2010, the central bank made it clear that it would be going further in reforming the exchange-rate formation mechanism of the RMB and that it would be further increasing the elasticity of the exchange rate. It indicated that, as China's economy regained stability and began a new cycle of growth, the expedient measure of pegging the RMB to the dollar would gradually be phased out. This meant that a new cycle of exchange-rate reform was already being initiated. Within the short space of just over three months, the RMB appreciated by 1.7 percent against the US dollar while also, for a short time, trading in both directions. Looking to the future, the degree to which the RMB rate relies on the US dollar will gradually diminish, while the elasticity of the rate will increase. The hope is that the RMB will appreciate in an incremental and modest fashion. Given the close relationship between exchange rates and the operations of commercial banks, it is imperative that we understand how exchange-rate reform and RMB exchange-rate movements have impacted commercial banks to date. This can provide invaluable lessons for the next stage of reforms.

The influence that reform of the RMB exchange-rate formation mechanism has had on commercial banks, including the impact of exchange-rate changes

The rate of the most practical significance to commercial banks is the 'nominal' exchange rate. Other concepts, including the 'real exchange rate,' the 'effective exchange rate,' and the 'real effective exchange rate,' are used primarily in theoretical studies and macroeconomic analysis. In discussing the impact of exchange-rate changes on commercial banks, therefore, we primarily use the 'nominal' exchange rate in this chapter.

Whether one uses theoretical concepts or looks at practical experience, however, it is clear that the impact of exchange-rate changes on China's commercial banks has been comprehensive and profound. The impact incorporates features that are direct and indirect, short term and long term, and domestic and international. In light of this, in what follows, we divide the various business components of commercial banking into different categories in order to carry out analysis that is thorough and clear. Specifically, we look at the effect of exchange-rate changes on commercial banks' credit business, funds business, business of foreign-exchange deposits and loans, business of foreign-trade settlement, and the business of their overseas branches. In addition, we look at the impact of exchange-rate changes on such related aspects as the reserve requirements for banks (the 'capital adequacy ratio,') and the raising of capital overseas.

Credit business: handling both challenges and opportunities

A general analysis of the impact of exchange-rate changes on all business sectors

The appreciating RMB has affected the prosperity of different industries and enterprises in different ways. This in turn affects the banking industry by impacting the quality of loan assets held by banks, leading to greater credit risk in some areas. From the banking perspective, a distinctly unfavorable impact can be seen with respect to three specific industries. The first includes businesses that rely heavily on exports and are not able to set their own prices. An appreciating RMB lowers the price competitiveness of their exported products, which are primarily denominated in US dollars. The second includes businesses that produce import-substitution type products within China. A stronger RMB means that imports of the same products into China become more competitive. The third includes businesses that are heavily engaged in speculative capital outside China's borders. An appreciating RMB can lead to profit-taking by the overseas speculative capital, leading in turn to lower prospects for the industry in the future.

On the other hand, a favorable impact can also be seen with respect to three different industries in the banking sector. The first relates to businesses that sell mostly within China and that rely heavily on imported materials. An appreciating RMB lowers their costs and therefore raises their profits. The second involves industries with a large amount of foreign-exchange denominated debt. As the RMB appreciates, companies that hold US dollar-denominated debt in particular can enjoy a single-event exchange-rate return on the currency, giving them a short-term boost to profits. The third relates to businesses that are in such lines as tourism and the retailing of certain consumer goods. An appreciating RMB provides greater purchasing power to Chinese citizens, which in turn raises the returns to such companies.

An analysis of the impact of exchange-rate changes on specific industry sectors

TEXTILE INDUSTRY: THE NEGATIVE IMPACTS OUTWEIGH
THE POSITIVE

The degree to which China's textile industry relies on exports is high (it exceeds 30 percent). Most exported goods, moreover, are priced in US dollars and the ability of the industry to set its own prices is low, which makes the industry vulnerable to exchange-rate changes. In evaluating the extent of this vulnerability, it is estimated that the cost of exported textiles and garments goes up by 4 percent for every 5 percent appreciation of the RMB, when those exports are denominated in US dollars. Meanwhile, in comparison to other industries, much of the textile industry's exported products are 'made within China.' This means that the industry as a whole benefits very little from an appreciating RMB. Overall, the textile industry has been hard hit by a stronger RMB. Within this industry, garment exports have an export-dependency ratio of around 60 percent and also have little clear advantage with respect to such things as branding and design. It is estimated, therefore, that for every 1 percent appreciation of the RMB, the garment industry sees its profits drop by 6.18 percent. In recent years, the textile industry has held a declining share in total loan portfolios of commercial banks. By the end of June, 2010, loans made to the textile industry came to at most 1.5 percent of the total (see Figure 4.1). What this indicates is that commercial banks were already making adjustments to their credit strategies as the RMB appreciated. They were already viewing the textile industry as a 'sunset industry.'

THE IRON AND STEEL INDUSTRY: THE OVERALL IMPACT IS
SOMEWHAT NEGATIVE

The benefit of an appreciating RMB to this industry lies in the way it lowers procurement costs. At present, some 40 percent of iron ore used by the industry is imported. Moreover, the costs of iron ore constitute between 30 percent and 40 percent of all materials costs and are the primary component in the industry. Nevertheless, the negative impacts of an appreciating RMB are also extremely apparent. First, the 'export dependency' of the iron and steel industry is relatively high. As much as 20 percent of all iron and steel products are exported, whether through direct exports of the material itself or indirect export through processed

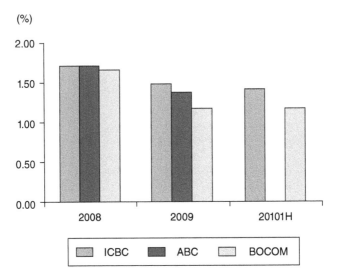

Figure 4.1 Percentage of total loans made to the textile industry by three
publicly listed banks.

Source: The annual reports of the listed banks.

goods. An appreciating RMB lowers the price competitiveness of these products.
Second, an appreciating RMB lowers the price of imported iron and steel products, which negatively impacts domestic producers of the same products. Third,
industries that are 'downstream' from the iron and steel industry, such as automobiles, shipbuilding, home appliances, and so on, are clearly being hurt by an
appreciating RMB and this in turn affects domestic producers of iron and steel.

In overall terms, the general impact of an appreciating RMB on the iron and
steel industry is on the negative side. In more specific terms, the impact varies since
each enterprise in the industry has a different set of circumstances. Companies
that are major importers of iron ore, the primary raw material, are the beneficiaries of a rising RMB. These include Baogang (the Baosteel Group Corporation,]
Wugang (the Wuhan Iron and Steel Co., Ltd.,] Magang (the Magang (Group)
Holding Co., Ltd.,] Jigang (the Jigang Group Co., Ltd.,] and Nangang (Nanjing
Iron & Steel Co., Ltd.] Other companies, which have their own mining operations,
are hurt by a rising RMB. These include Angang (Angang Steel Company, Ltd.,]
and Xingang (Xinyu Iron & Steel Group Co., Ltd.].

Iron and steel is considered a 'key industry' within China's national economy.
It is therefore also the recipient of a key amount of bank credit. Loans made by the
Industrial and Commercial Bank of China (ICBC] and the Bank of Communications
(BOCOM] will serve as examples. As of the end of June, 2010, loans made by the
ICBC to the iron and steel industry came to RMB 87.8 billion and constituted 1.38
percent of that bank's total loan portfolio. Loans made by BOCOM came to RMB
43.9 billion and constituted 2.12 percent of the total loan portfolio (see Figure 4.2).

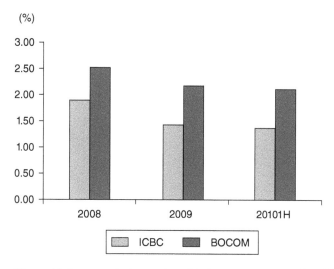

Figure 4.2 Loans to the iron and steel industry as a percent of total loans, for two
      publicly listed banks.

Source: Annual reports of the banks.

THE REAL ESTATE AND HOUSING INDUSTRY: THE POTENTIAL RISK
IS RATHER LARGE.

Expectations of an appreciating RMB have led an influx of foreign capital, a large
percentage of which has then been invested in the real estate market. This has
increased the demand in this sector, pushing up housing prices. The experience of
both Japan and Korea shows that housing prices have a positive correlation with
exchange-rate movements. An empirical analysis of China's situation between
the years 2006 and 2009 indicates that every 1 percent appreciation of the RMB
against the US dollar resulted in USD 5 billion per month flowing into the country. By now, the cumulative amount of foreign capital within China is massive –
current estimates put the amount of 'hot money' at roughly USD 500 billion.
There is zero doubt that a large percentage of this money has been invested in
China's real estate market. Meanwhile, the rising price of housing has led to a
boom in demand for mortgage loans. The increasing amount of each individual
loan has benefited the banking industry (see Figure 4.3).

The booming demand for mortgage loans also has a downside, however. If
prices are inflated to the extent that a bubble is the result, mortgage loans in
China may decline in quality. In that case, an appreciating RMB will have led
to a negative impact on banks. Housing prices in China's 'first-tier' cities are
already in bubble territory. As a result, frequent policy adjustments have been
applied recently, to some effect, and housing prices are already showing signs
of falling back. If the large amount of 'hot money' that is embedded in the housing industry suddenly decides to cut risk levels and take out its profits, however,

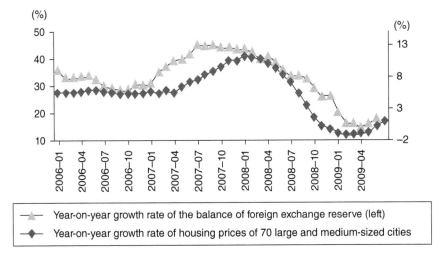

Figure 4.3 Housing prices and foreign exchange reserves move in a fairly synchronized
manner.

Source: WIND.

the results can be devastating to the housing industry. A large number of empty
units will be flung onto the market. This will potentially lead to cascading prices,
which in turn will lead to declines in the value of collateral that is used to under-
pin mortgage loans.

Loans related to the housing industry in China include those for real estate
developers and those for mortgages. Together, these constitute more than 20 percent of all loan portfolios of commercial banks. Because of this, an appreciating
RMB carries substantial potential risk for banks, even though the situation at present may not be that apparent (see Figure 4.4).

THE ELECTRIC POWER INDUSTRY: THE IMPACT IS
RELATIVELY POSITIVE

Most of the business of China's electric-power generating companies is domestic. It is denominated in RMB, and it relies very little on export of power, which
means that an appreciating RMB has little impact on the income of these companies. What's more, these companies use little in the way of foreign capital. Some
debt is denominated in foreign currencies, mainly in US dollars and Japanese yen,
but since the loans are mainly long term, exchange-rate fluctuations do not greatly
impact profits and losses. Meanwhile, an appreciating RMB has lowered the procurement costs of some key items in an industry that is fairly import-reliant. These
include large fuel and gas turbine generators, and high-capacity, high-parameter
supercritical units. Our understanding also is that many other items rely heavily on imports, including materials for electric power equipment such as extra-
thick plates, large-diameter pipes, axles, silicon sheets, copper, electronic devices,

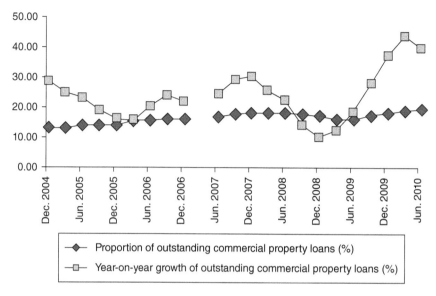

Figure 4.4 Loans made for commercial property (including real estate development and housing purchase): percentages and rate of increase.
Units: percentages

Source: WIND.

and various components. An appreciating RMB reduces the cost of all of these, including manufacturing costs but also the importation of technology and technical consultation fees. Some equipment used in the industry relies fairly heavily on the import of materials from elsewhere. This kind of equipment includes pressure transformers, electric wires, electric cables, and so on. Industries producing such equipment have benefited notably from as stronger RMB.

Overall, an appreciating RMB has had a relatively positive impact on the electric power-generation industry. It is estimated that the industry enjoys a 1 percent increase in net profits for every 5 percent appreciation of the RMB. This in turn benefits the commercial banking industry. By the end of June, 2010, loans to the electric power industry constituted between 6 percent and 9 percent of all bank loans. The electric-power industry is a major recipient of credit from China's commercial banking industry (see Figure 4.5).

THE AIRLINE INDUSTRY: THE POSITIVE IMPACT OF AN
APPRECIATING RMB IS QUITE APPARENT

China's airline industry is a classic example of an industry that relies heavily on foreign debt. The debt is primarily denominated in US dollars, so that RMB appreciation presents the industry with a one-off chance to earn income from currency exchange. At present, the industry as a whole has foreign-currency

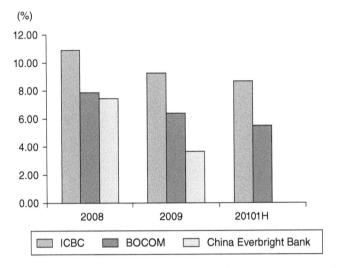

(%)

Figure 4.5 Loans made to the electric-power industry as a percent of all loans made by three publicly listed banks in China.

Source: The annual reports of the three banks.

liabilities in the range of RMB 230 billion, when translated into RMB. When the RMB appreciates 1 percent against the US dollar, China's airline industry therefore reduces its debt by RMB 2.3 billion (see Table 4.1). Within this total figure, China's three main airline companies reduce their debt by RMB 1.3 billion. Meanwhile, an appreciating RMB also lowers the cost of imported fuel, and fuel costs constitute around thirty percent of the total costs of airline companies. Another increase in profitability comes from greater outbound tourism given the strength of the Chinese currency. Publicly listed companies have disclosed figures that indicate that these three companies have earned a net income from currency exchange alone of RMB 20.5 billion since July of 2005.

Table 4.1 The effect of a 1% appreciation of the RMB on three large airline companies in China.

Unit: RMB 100 million

Impacts of 1% appreciation of RMB on the three biggest airlines in China		*Unit: 100 million*	
	China Southern	*China Eastern*	*Air China*
Increase in exchange earnings	4.69	3.57	4.03
Decline in operating expenditures	0.38	0.38	0.56
Increase in pre-tax profits	5.07	3.95	4.59

THE PETROCHEMICAL INDUSTRY: THE IMPACT OF AN APPRECIATING
RMB VARIES, DEPENDING ON SUBSIDIARY INDUSTRIES

The importing and exporting patterns of China's petrochemical industry involve an exchange of resources in return for technology and capital. In terms of the composition of exports, the petrochemical industry mainly exports low value-added chemicals and materials. These include such things as carbamide, sodium carbonate, sodium hydroxide, phosphate fertilizers, magnesium sulfate, and so on. The industry mainly imports such things as technology and capital-intensive products. An appreciating RMB makes highly processed imported petrochemical products more competitive within China, while it hurts the competitive price advantage of low value-added chemical goods that China exports.

The impacts of an appreciating RMB on specific segments of the petrochemical industry are as follows.

Crude oil extraction: At present, China's reliance on imported oil is growing. Given that the price of crude is set in US dollars in three international locations (Brent, Dubai, and Sinta,] an appreciating RMB is beneficial in lowering the cost of imported oil. At the same time, however, the selling price of oil produced within China suffers a corresponding decline. The impact on oil development within China is therefore negative.

Oil refining: The unique feature of this industry is that the price of the chief raw material, namely crude oil, is determined on the international market, whereas the prices of products made from crude oil are set by government policy. If the RMB appreciates by 5 percent, therefore, the direct consequence is a lowering of crude oil costs by 5 percent. Profits rise accordingly.

Petrochemicals: The unique feature of this industry is that the price of the raw material, namely petroleum, is controlled by the government while the prices of products (all kinds of petrochemical products) are internationalized. As a result, RMB appreciation has precisely the opposite impact on this industry to what it has on the oil refining industry. The price of its raw material does not change, whereas the price of its products declines. Profits are squeezed accordingly.

Nitrogenous fertilizers: In overall terms, the extent to which this domestic industry is 'internationalized' in China is low. Both raw materials and products are sourced and sold within the country. An appreciating RMB therefore has little impact.

Loans to the petrochemical industry make up a substantial portion of the loan portfolios of Chinese banks (see Figure 4.6). For example, by the end of June, 2010, the percentage of such loans within the Bank of Communications portfolio stood at 4.15 percent. We should therefore pay close attention to the impact of an appreciating RMB on the industries described above.

THE MACHINERY INDUSTRY: THE IMPACT OF AN APPRECIATING
RMB IS GENERALLY POSITIVE.

China's machinery industry relies on exports for only around 10 percent of its sales. At the same time, the price of the same products within China is

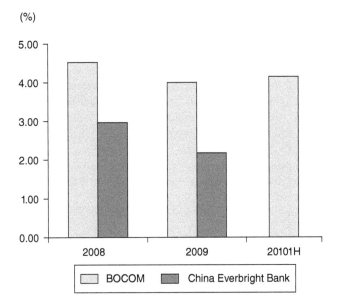

Figure 4.6 Loans made to the petrochemical industry as a percent of all loans made by two publicly listed banks.

Source: Annual reports of the two banks.

roughly one-third higher than it is outside of China. As a result, an appreciating RMB may indeed lead to somewhat lower exports but the impact on the industry as a whole is not that great. In terms of the cost effect of RMB appreciation, this too is not apparent: the overall technological level of China's equipment manufacturing industries is not high, which means that highly processed components still have to be imported. An appreciating RMB helps lower costs of such imports as marine crankshafts and electrical control equipment.

This industry is also a major customer for bank credit. By the end of June, 2010, ICBC had loaned the industry a sum of RMB 120.9 billion, and such loans constituted 1.9 percent of its total loan portfolio. BOCOM had loaned the industry RMB 87.7 billion, and such loans constituted 4.23 percent of the bank's total (see Figure 4.7).

AUTOMOTIVE INDUSTRY: THE IMPACT OF AN APPRECIATING
RMB IS ON THE NEGATIVE SIDE

On the one hand, an appreciating RMB lowers the cost of parts that must be imported from abroad. At the same time, however, it lowers the price of imported automobiles, which presents a challenge to domestic manufacturers. In over-all terms, the impact of lowered prices on imported cars more than offsets the

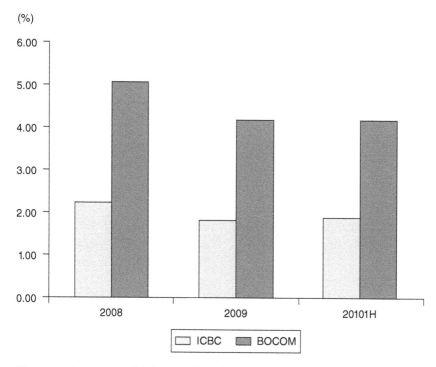

Figure 4.7 Percentage of all loans made to the machinery industry, by two publicly listed banks.

Source: Annual reports of the listed banks.

benefits of lowered costs for imported components, the reason being that most components used in domestic production of cars are now also produced domestically. The result is a net negative impact on China's automotive industry. If the RMB appreciates by 5 percent, data indicates that the price of an imported car will decline by 5 percent – if one assumes that other factors do not change. The impact of this on China's domestic car industry is somewhat greater on sedans than it is on trucks or passenger cars. Meanwhile, costs of producing some of China's cars are lowered, such as the Mazda 6 and the Mondeo, since components are not yet produced within China. This benefits the makers of those cars. Some exporters of automobile components are hurt, however, such as the Fuyao Group and the Wanxiang Qianchao Co., Ltd.

China's commercial banks have extended a certain amount of credit to this industry but the percentage of total loans is still relatively small. By end-June, 2010, ICBC had extended RMB 47 billion in loans, which constituted 1 percent of its total (see Figure 4.8).

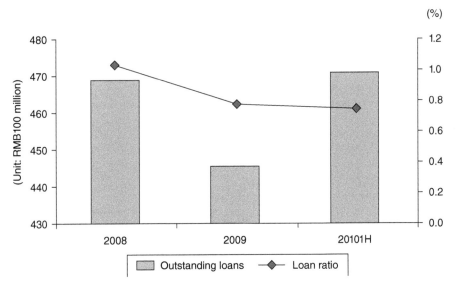

Figure 4.8 Volume of outstanding loans to the automotive industry, and that industry's
percent of total loans.

Source: Annual report of publicly listed banks.

THE PAPER-MAKING INDUSTRY: THE IMPACT OF AN APPRECIATING
RMB IS CLEARLY FAVORABLE

The papermaking industry in China is a classic case of 'importing raw materials and then selling to a domestic market.' This industry enjoys clear benefits
as the RMB appreciates. A stronger RMB lowers the cost of imported pulp and
wastepaper, which benefits companies involved in those businesses. Pulp is the
primary raw material in the cost structure of paper production, requiring as much
as 65 percent to 75 percent of total production costs. If the RMB appreciates by 5
percent, the direct cost savings to the papermaking industry can come to RMB 1.1
billion. If one adds in such factors as value-added tax, the cost savings can climb
to nearly RMB 1.4 billion. Moreover, most of China's large-scale papermaking
companies rely on imported equipment, so that a stronger RMB lowers the cost
of that equipment as well. Around 60 percent of fixed assets in the industry are
invested in equipment, most of which is imported. A stronger RMB has the corresponding effect of lowering prices of imported equipment, and therefore the
equipment procurement costs of paper producers. Estimates are that the industry's
profits are actually increased by 15 percent for every 5 percent of RMB appreciation. An appreciating RMB is extremely beneficial to this industry.

   Since this industry is also known as a 'double-high' industry, however,
meaning it is both highly polluting and highly energy consuming, the government has applied restrictive regulations to its ongoing development. In recent

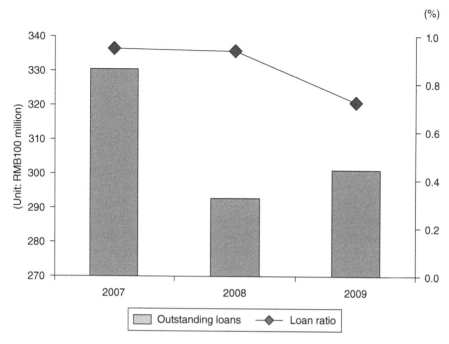

Figure 4.9 Volume of loans made by the Agricultural Bank of China to the papermaking
industry, and the percent of such loans to all loans made by the bank.

Source: Annual reports of publicly listed banks.

years, the commercial banking industry has begun to lower its loan exposure as
a result. For example, by end-June, 2010, the Agricultural Bank of China was
loaning only 0.73 percent of its total loans to the papermaking industry. This
figure was already down by 0.22 percentage points from the end of 2007 (see
Figure 4.9).

THE SHIPBUILDING INDUSTRY: THE IMPACT OF AN APPRECIATING
RMB IS EXTREMELY NEGATIVE

From the beginning, China's shipbuilding industry has been export-oriented,
with a high degree of 'internationalization.' Products have mainly been exported
into a unified, single, global market. The global percentage of exported ships
has continued to climb in recent years – at the beginning of the 1990s, roughly
60 percent of all ships sold internationally were exported, while today, that
figure has grown to between 75 percent and 80 percent. China's own shipbuilding industry is now exporting some 80 percent of all new orders for ships,
and most of these sales are denominated in US dollars. Moreover, unlike most
exports, shipbuilding requires a long production cycle. The time between signing a contract and delivering finished ships generally runs between eighteen

and twenty-four months. Some ships can take as long as thirty months to build. What this means is that all contracts for ships are signed on a futures basis – they are all 'forward contracts.' Exchange-rate risk is higher in this industry, since an appreciating RMB has the direct effect of lowering income and the profitability of the shipbuilder. Estimates show that appreciation of the RMB by 5 percent can lead to a situation where the entire industry is beginning to show a loss.

THE RETAIL INDUSTRY: THE IMPACT OF AN APPRECIATING RMB IS FAVORABLE OVER
THE LONG TERM

Actual figures since 2005 show that an appreciating RMB has not had an apparent impact on the credit standing of the retail industry in China. Over the medium-term and the long-term, however, RMB appreciation is expected to be positive for the industry. For one thing, an appreciating RMB brings with it a 'wealth creation effect.' The real purchasing power of consumers increases, stimulating sales growth in consumer items, and both banks and retailers benefit. Second, an appreciating RMB leads to declining prices of imported goods, creating an income multiplier effect and stimulating further increases in consumption. Some of the most obvious beneficiaries of this process are department stores that import a fairly large percentage of their goods. Third, with appreciation of the RMB, export prices rise and companies that previously had produced for export markets now turn their attention to the domestic market. They look to domestic retail channels as a substitute measure. The retail industry thereby benefits not only from lowered import prices but also from increased supply of goods. Moreover, as the end-point in the sales process, retailers have a much stronger negotiating position vis-à-vis suppliers. The largest beneficiaries in this process are those chain stores that have massive 'channel' advantages. These would include, for example, Bailian Group Co., Ltd., New World Department Stores, the Dashang Group, Beijing Hualian Hypermarket Co., Ltd., and the Suning Corporation.

Looking at actual data from banks, loans made to the retail sector are far below loans made to the manufacturing industry, in terms of percentage of total loans (see Figure 4.10). What this means is that there is a great deal of room into which bank's lending business can grow.

Summing up the above, an appreciating RMB has had a negative impact to varying degrees on China's iron and steel industries, its automotive, textile, shipbuilding, and petrochemical industries, and on its real estate lending and personal mortgage businesses. The degree to which the appreciation of China's currency has increased credit risk to China's commercial banks must not be taken lightly. At the same time, however, an appreciating RMB has had a positive impact on certain industries in China, including the airline industry, papermaking, electric power generation, and machinery industries. As the RMB appreciates, opportunities for growth open up to banks that are extending credit to these industries (see Table 4.2).

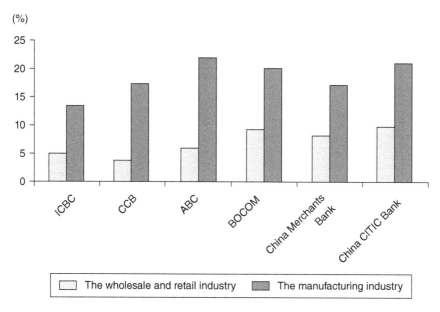

Figure 4.10 Loans made to the wholesale and retail industries in China, as contrasted to loans made to China's manufacturing industry, as represented by percentage of total loans in a bank's portfolio.

Source: Annual reports of publicly listed banks.

The impact of an appreciating RMB is greater in eastern China, and less in central and western China

RMB appreciation has a greater impact on the economies of eastern China because eastern China and the coastal regions are more dependent on exports, and also because their export-oriented economy is a greater percentage of their total economy. The 'export dependency ratio' of Guangdong, for example, is extremely high. The trade volume of the province in 2009 was USD 611.12 billion. Total production output came to RMB 3.908159 trillion that year, and the area's dependency on foreign trade overall reached 106.88 percent. Changes in foreign trade volume directly affect tax revenues of the province. They affect employment, logistics, service industries, and many other aspects of the economy. In contrast, China's central and western regions are much less affected by appreciation of China's currency. The export-oriented component of their economy is fairly small.

The experience since 2005 has made it clear that labor-intensive industries are indeed shifting westward, under the impact of several new considerations. These include the appreciating RMB, the rising cost of labor along the coast, and increased efforts on the part of the Chinese government to achieve 'coordinated development' among different parts of the country. The combined effect of

Table 4.2 The impact of a 5% appreciation of the RMB on select industries in China

Industry	Impacts on net profits (%)	Industry	Impacts on net profits (%)
Aircraft	Exceptionally evident	Automobile	−1.5
Papermaking	15	Textile	−6
Electric power	1	Shipbuilding	Loss
Machinery	0.8	Petrochemicals	Impacts differ among sub-industries, being negative on crude oil mining and petrochemical industries, positive on oil refining industry and neutral on nitrogenous fertilizer industry. Impacts on the whole industry is slightly negative
Retail	Favorable in the medium and long term	Real estate and personal mortgage loans	Foreign capital may retreat from China, constituting looming risks
Iron and steel	−1		Relatively large

Notes
a Supposing that there are RMB 230 billion USD-denominated debts of the aircraft industry, a 5 percent appreciation of RMB will bring RMB 11.5 billion exchange gain or loss. The net profit of the whole industry was RMB 12.2 billion in 2009, which indicated that the appreciation of RMB may change its net profit by over 100 percent.
b Since the impacts of the appreciation of RMB is favorable in the medium and long term, changes in net profit of the retail industry are hard to estimate accurately.

these things has led to a gradual shift of labor-intensive industries from the east coast towards the central and western regions. In the future, these regions will be the beneficiaries of development opportunities, while the east coast is still in the midst of reconfiguring and upgrading its industries.

Meanwhile, China's banking industry clearly continues to discriminate in favor of loans to the eastern seaboard. The percentage of its loans to central and western areas is low. The Bank of Communications can serve as an example: loans to the eastern areas constitute more than 70 percent of the total, while those to central and western region are not even 30 percent. This means that there is room for considerable opportunities in central and western regions in the future (see Figure 4.11).

Potential new credit business: growth opportunities that have come about as the result of an appreciating RMB

The appreciation of China's own currency has strengthened the 'capital power' of the country's enterprises. This has in turn propelled them to expand overseas. A similar event happened in the 1980s, when appreciation of the Japanese yen was accompanied by a massive and swift wave of overseas mergers and

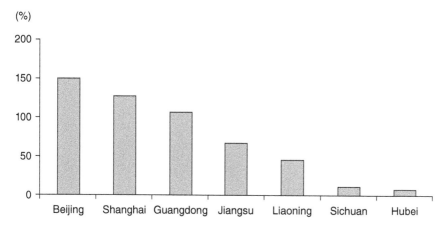

Figure 4.11 The degree of foreign trade dependency of select provinces in China.

Note: This figure is derived by dividing the sum of total imports and exports by China's GDP.

Source: WIND.

acquisitions. From 1985 to 1990, more than twenty individual M&A transactions were for sums in excess of 50 billion Japanese yen. China's current situation is much the same. Between the exchange-rate reform of July, 2005, and 2008, during a period of rapid appreciation of the RMB, Chinese enterprises went on a buying spree abroad. Such companies as the Haier Group, China National Petroleum Corporation, China Offshore Oil Co. Ltd., BOE Co. Ltd., and TCL Corporation, all 'strode out of China's front gate, into the world.'

Commercial lending for merger and acquisition activity benefited from the growth opportunities, while such intermediary banking services as consulting benefited as well. At the end of 2008, the China Banking Regulatory Commission issued the 'Guidelines on the risk management of merger-and-acquisition loans made by commercial banks.' This officially deregulated the M&A loan business. In 2009, the volume of loans granted for M&A purposes came to a total of around RMB 20 billion. At this time, it is estimated that the total for 2010 will reach a scale of some RMB 50 billion. Business in this arena is growing at a pace of over 100 percent per year. Given the backdrop of an appreciating RMB, which is encouraging domestic companies to 'stride out' into the world, cross-border merger and acquisition loan business is also making dramatic advances.

Meanwhile, under the impetus of an appreciating RMB and various government policies aimed at stimulating consumption, China's increasing consumption is also providing opportunities for growth in the lending business. This includes housing mortgages, but also loans for such personal consumption items as automobiles. Since 2005, consumption in China has been increasing at a steady pace. In the first six months of 2010, the volume of domestic spending on retail items in China grew by 18.2 percent over the same period the previous year. In 2005,

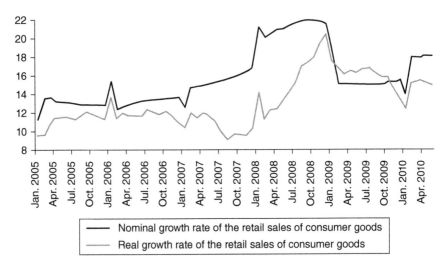

Figure 4.12 The nominal and real rates of growth in retail sales of consumer goods in
China.
Units: percentage

Source: WIND.

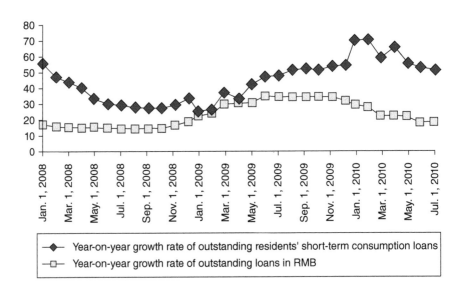

Figure 4.13 The pace at which short-term consumer loans to Chinese citizens are
growing has exceeded the growth rate of loans overall.
Units: percentage

Source: WIND.

the growth rate for the entire year had been less than 13 percent. Currently, short-term personal loans are growing at a relatively fast pace – most consumer loans are short term, with the exception of housing mortgages. In recent years, the pace at which short-term consumer loans to Chinese citizens are growing has exceeded the growth rate of loans overall (see Figures 4.12 and 4.13).

An empirical analysis of the ways in which RMB exchange-rate changes are affecting the quality of banks' assets

As everyone knows, credit loans constitute the main asset of China's banking system – such loans make up more than 50 percent of all bank assets. As described above, changes in the RMB exchange rate affect different industries in different ways. Similarly, the credit business of different regions faces different opportunities, such as merger-and-acquisition loans, and consumer-type loans. We conducted the following empirical analysis in order to identify the impact of RMB appreciation on China's banking industry in a more accurate way. The analysis looks at the impact of RMB appreciation since 2005 on the asset quality of the loan portfolios of commercial banks in China.

The RMB has appreciated by more than 20 percent against the US dollar since 2005. During this same period, in overall terms, the operating results of China's banks improved considerably after banks undertook share-holding system reform. Banks' assets expanded quickly, while non-performing loan ratios continued to decline. By the end of June, 2010, non-performing loan ratios among China's commercial banks were 1.3 percent, a figure that was 7.6 percentage points lower than it had been at the end of 2005. Looking at the nature of this improvement, the lowering of non-performing loan ratios was intimately connected to ongoing economic prosperity in recent years, to the rapid expansion of loan portfolios, and to improvements in levels of risk management by commercial banks. Because of this, we used all the above variables as control variables in attempting to analyze the impact of exchange-rate changes.

In more specific terms, in our empirical analysis, we took the non-performing loan ratio of commercial banks as the 'explained variable' (using the common logarithm, NPL). For 'explaining variables,' apart from the nominal exchange rate of the RMB against the USD (LNFX), we used changes in total loans of banks(ΔTL), net return on equity (ROE), changes in loan/interest-bearing assets ratio (ΔLPA), real gross domestic product (season-adjusted, RGDP), inflation rate (INF), provided reserve for overall loans (PROL) and the capital adequacy ratio (CA). For financial data, we selected fourteen publicly listed banks. Our sample period went from the third quarter of 2005 to the second quarter of 2010. We adopted a 'panel data analysis method' for the analysis. The results are presented in Table 4.3.

The results of Table 4.3 indicate that regression coefficients of three variables were indeed significant. Those three variables were: change in total loan amount of banks (ΔTL), real gross domestic product (RGDP), and provided reserve for

Table 4.3 Regression results of the impact of exchange-rate changes on the
non-performing loan ratio of banks in China

Estimation model	Fixed-effect model
Explained variable	NPL
Explanatory variable	
ΔTL	−7.82E-07*
	(4.12E-07)
	[0.0603]
ROE	−0.020344
	(0.022294)
	[0.3631]
ΔLPA	−0.003217
	(0.015000)
	[0.8305]
RGDP	−2.87E-07***
	(7.22E-08)
	[0.0001]
LNFX	−0.009339
	(0.017404)
	[0.5924]
INF	0.031665
	(0.058157)
	[0.5870]
PROL	0.599961***
	(0.136189)
	[0.0000]
CA	−0.007682
	(0.017480)
	[0.6610]
C(constant term)	0.051537
	(0.040527)
	[0.2057]
F-statistic[P-value]	22.11174
	[0.0000]
R^2	0.773464

Note: These results were obtained with the use of Eviews 6.0 software. Numerical values in
parentheses represent standard deviations. Those in square brackets represent P-values. One asterisk
indicates that the correlation is significant below the level of 10%, two means it is significant below
5%, and three means it is significant below 1%. Only our results are displayed in this table; for the
actual process of how we derived the results, please refer to the Appendix.

overall loans (PROL). Looking at the coefficients of the variables, we can see that
an increase in loan amount and in real GDP led to a decline in the ratio of non-
performing loans. This is in line with our expectations. The positive correlation
between the reserve fund for loans, or 'provided reserve for overall loans,' and the
ratio of non-performing loans, was also in line with economic laws. An increase
in the ratio of non-performing loans would tend to increase an expectation of

losses from loans. Banks would then tend to set aside greater reserves against those bad loans, increasing the size of the provided reserve. In addition, although the regression coefficient was not clear with respect to return on equity and the capital adequacy ratio, the overall coefficient was negative. This indicated that those banks with better profit levels and higher capital adequacy ratios would also have lower non-performing loan ratios. This too was in line with our expectations.

Finally, we look at exchange rates. Given that the regression coefficient is insufficiently clear, it appears as though the impact of a changing RMB exchange rate on non-performing loans is not in fact very dramatic. We attribute this to the overall context of the time period of our sample. Prior to the financial crisis, the world's economic growth rate was relatively fast. Whether you add in this fact, or the fact that the world's economy slumped after the crisis, external demand factors were paramount in determining China's exports. When the RMB was appreciating at a modest pace, exchange-rate changes did not greatly affect exporting industries and, in turn, the asset quality of banks. Moreover, as analyzed above, the impact of RMB exchange-rate changes on bank credit is, in its very nature, a highly complex process. Exchange-rate changes can be both detrimental and beneficial, sometimes cancelling each other out and thereby leading to highly indeterminate results. Nevertheless, given the negative sign of the regression coefficient, it can be said that an appreciating RMB has indeed had the effect of increasing the non-performing loan ratio. (That is, when the LNFX decreases, the NPL value increases.)

What all of this indicates is that an appreciating RMB should be the signal for banks to apply alert attention to the quality of their assets. Just because an appreciating RMB over the past five years has not yet led to a tremendous increase in bad loans, that does not mean that we can overlook the possibility of an increase in non-performing loans in the future.

The funds business: pleasures and disappointments in equal measure

While an appreciating RMB has had a negative effect on the overall funds business of commercial banks, it has also brought new growth opportunities.

On the one hand, RMB appreciation and the expectation of further appreciation can lead to a decision on the part of foreign-exchange-denominated funds to get out of the foreign exchange position. This can then have a negative effect on the development of the foreign-exchange-denominated wealth management business and other foreign-exchange derivative businesses. This brings pressure to bear on commercial banks to create innovative responses.

For example, expectations for an appreciating RMB have been in force and growing since 2010. On January 1 of that year, until June 22, sales of RMB-denominated wealth management products nearly doubled over the same period the previous year. Meanwhile, the number of foreign-exchange-denominated wealth management products that were sold in the market contracted by nearly two-thirds. Adding to the complexities, expansion of the band within which the exchange rate is allowed to trade also led to greater daily volatility, increased market activity, and, to a degree, greater market risk. When the RMB gradually moves from being pegged to the dollar to being pegged against a basket of currencies, this means that banks will have to look at the distribution of currencies in their balance sheets and make appropriate adjustments.

On the other hand, the awareness of exchange-rate risk on the part of enterprises engaged in trade has clearly improved. In the future, enterprises will be taking the initiative in adopting risk-mitigation procedures. For example, foreign trade enterprises will more aggressively participate in forward currency transactions as a way to offset their exchange-rate risk. Companies with large amounts of foreign-exchange-denominated assets, and with a mandate to preserve and increase the value of those assets, will become more urgently engaged in asset management. This will in turn create a massive market for the intermediary services of commercial banks and a way to increase intermediary fee-based revenue. It will spur banks to increase their percentage of non-interest-type income by increasing fee-type income. It will accelerate the desire on the part of banks to transform their mode of operations.

Since 2005, the non-interest income of banks in China has been on the rise (see Figure 4.14). It has gone from around 10 percent in 2005, to the current 20 percent or even 30 percent among some banks. The appreciation of the RMB has been an important incentive in this process, in addition to such factors as rapidly developing capital markets and the way in which banks themselves have tried to change their business models. The increase in volatility of exchange rates has also provided greater trading opportunities by widening out the spread in which one can make a profit. At the same time, however, it has placed ever higher demands on banks' foreign-exchange traders, who must be more sensitive to market changes and more adept at seizing market opportunities.

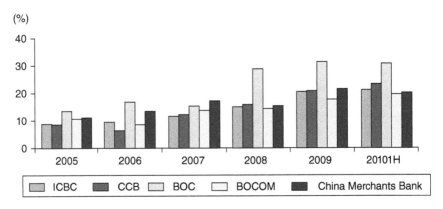

Figure 4.14 Non-interest income as a percent of total income among select publicly traded banks: showing a constant increase of the percentage of non-interest income since 2005.

Source: Annual reports of the publicly listed banks.

RMB-denominated funds business shows promise, although
banks should be alert to potential risks

The ongoing strong expectation for the RMB to appreciate may well lead to even more capital flowing into China. In order to take excess liquidity out of the market, China's central bank needs to buy in ever more US dollars – this then puts ever more of China's own currency in the system. Given more money supply, money-market interest rates may hover at a low level. In terms of the bond markets, prices may rise as interest rates fall, while the yield curve flattens out due to expectations of a strengthening RMB, the resulting inflow of capital, and the huge amount of foreign money-holding RMB accounts. On the other hand, if that foreign money were suddenly to exit after taking a profit, then liquidity in the interbank market would suddenly dry up. Money-market interest rates would soar and bond prices would plummet. The risk of this happening is fairly large.

The business of managing foreign-exchange deposits and
foreign-exchange loans: the impact of an appreciating RMB
in this area is pronounced, meaning that there is substantial
pressure on banks to manage liquidity properly

The willingness to hold foreign exchange in China continues to decline with the ongoing expectation that the RMB will appreciate and that foreign exchange will thereby lose value. This being the case, there is a sharply increasing demand for loans denominated in foreign currencies, given the opportunities for arbitraging the US dollar. Trade finance in particular is using dollar-denominated debt instruments, which is exacerbating the shortage of foreign-exchange funds within China. From 2007 to the first half of 2008 and from the second half of 2009 until now, expectations of an appreciating RMB have been relatively strong and there has been an accelerated demand for foreign-exchange denominated loans. As a result, foreign-exchange deposits have dropped precipitously while the loan-to-deposit ratio of foreign exchange has risen.

Since 2010, loans denominated in foreign currencies that are made by financial institutions increased by over 70 percent as compared to the previous year. In contrast, foreign-exchange balances increased by less than 10 percent. By the end of July, 2010, the loan-to-deposit ratio of foreign exchange had reached 190 percent. Foreign-exchange liquidity issues are putting ever greater pressure on banks.

In terms of trade financing, the ongoing expectation that the RMB will appreciate further is leading to ever greater demand for import trade financing. First, an importer can apply for standard trade financing in order to pay for imports. On the maturity of the term of the financing, the importer purchases the foreign exchange and repays the bank, meanwhile also gaining a return off the appreciation of the RMB during the financing period. Second, however, another method of benefiting from RMB appreciation is being employed by importers. This involves what is known as 'structured trade financing.' The importing enterprise provides a certain amount of RMB as a security deposit. The bank then issues trade financing to the

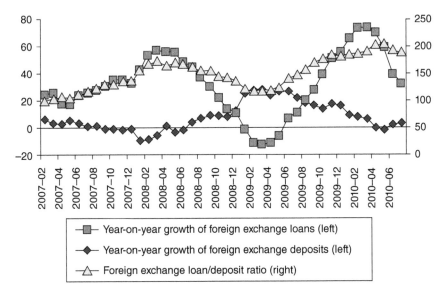

Figure 4.15 Loans denominated in foreign exchange, foreign-exchange deposits, and the ratio of loans-to-deposits.
Units: percentage

Source: WIND.

enterprise for a term of one year, at the same time providing long-term currency settlement for the enterprise. At the end of the term, the enterprise purchases foreign exchange from the bank at the agreed-upon exchange rate and repays the bank loan in RMB (see Figure 4.15).

The appreciation of the RMB is having a structural impact on the business of international trade settlement

Business in the area of export settlement is declining, while settlement for imports is increasing

Appreciation of the RMB will tend to have a structural impact on the business of international trade settlements. On the one hand, RMB appreciation has a certain constraining effect on the export of China's products and its labor force. This in turn reduces the foreign-exchange earning capacity of China's exporters and reduces the rate at which foreign exchange is coming in to China's exporters, which affects the banking business of export settlements. On the other hand, RMB appreciation has the effect of lowering the prices of imports, which raises demand within China for imported goods and labor. This increases import payments made by Chinese enterprises and leads to growth of the settlements business of banks for trade imports.

At the same time, an appreciating RMB will have an asymmetrical relationship on the two sides of the equation, given structural differences among customers and their businesses. In more specific terms, the following considerations apply. First, right now world trade markets are a 'buyers' market,' since buyers have stronger negotiating power and are increasingly able to set prices. This means that they prefer settlement products with a longer term in order to lower their costs (for example, letters of credit are being opened for longer periods of time). Second, since expectations of an appreciating RMB are continuing, customers' preference for 'non-deliverable forwards' continues to rise. There are quota restrictions in China on short-term unsecured debt, however. This is leading to a swift rise in the import factoring business (that is, third parties or 'factors' accept responsibility for accounts receivable from the exporter, and advance a line of credit and associated services to the importer). Third, profit margins for export-type businesses in China, as well as China's overseas contractors, are fairly low. An appreciating RMB has a fairly large impact on this type of company, given higher costs and lower profits, and this may in turn have a negative impact on the settlements business of banks. For example, the quantity of letters of credit for exporters is declining while the quantity of letters of guarantee for overseas contractors is also declining (the latter includes such things as guarantees for bidding, advance payment, and quality).

Demand for cross-border trade settlements that are denominated in RMB is increasing

A pilot project that allows for the use of RMB in cross-border trade settlements was begun in July of 2009. Since that time, after an exploratory period, the trajectory for this kind of trade settlement has begun to rise quickly. In the early period, various considerations led to an unexpected cold shoulder for the business. These included imperfect policy approaches, the limited scope of the trial, and a wait-and-see attitude on the part of enterprises. In 2009, the cumulative amount of RMB settlements came to a mere RMB 3.585 billion. Nevertheless, China had made the major step of allowing this kind of settlement, as opposed to not allowing it. As various other policy measures were adjusted, including tax rebates on exports and changes in customs duties, the business has begun to pick up. By the end of June, 2010, on a nationwide basis, cross-border settlements denominated in RMB had reached RMB 70.6 billion (see Figure 4.16). In the context of a strengthening RMB, it is reasonable for customers to use a combination of financing scenarios for trade settlement, including RMB import factoring, RMB letters of credit, and RMB cross-border settlement. This not only helps reduce exchange-rate risk, but it provides customers with arbitrage opportunities. The use of RMB to carry out cross-border settlement should see further increases.

As one example: a bank within China provides a long-term RMB-denominated letter of credit to an enterprise within China. A bank outside of China provides US-dollar-denominated financing to an enterprise outside of China. When the outside-China financing comes to maturity, the enterprise outside of China uses

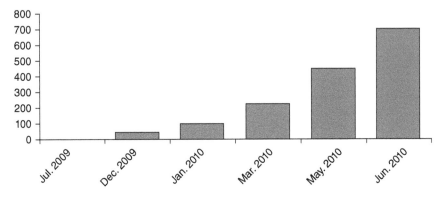

Figure 4.16 Total volume of cross-border trade settlements conducted in RMB,
          nationwide.
          Units: RMB 100 million

Source: China's central bank, assembled from publicly disclosed statistics.

the RMB that it receives under the letter of credit to pay back the loan from the
overseas bank. In this way, it is able to take in the additional income gained by
appreciation of the RMB.

Overseas branches of Chinese banks: an appreciating RMB brings new opportunities

An appreciating RMB is distinctly beneficial to the overseas branches of Chinese
banks (see Figure 4.17). First, it stimulates importing into China, and there is
a fairly large potential for growth in the trade settlement business. Second, it
increases investment by Chinese enterprises overseas, picks up the pace of 'inter-
nationalizing' Chinese companies, and therefore increases the financing needs of
Chinese-funded overseas subsidiaries. All of this applies to Hong Kong in particular. Chinese enterprises generally use Hong Kong as a base for setting up
subsidiaries – they then use this platform for expanding their business operations
and making further overseas acquisitions. Often these Hong Kong subsidiaries
need local financing for various reasons. Sometimes they are set up only briefly,
sometimes funding does not come in a timely manner from the parent company.
There is particular growth potential (for the banking business] in the arena of having overseas subsidiaries take advantage of what is known as 'enjoying domestic
guarantees for overseas loans.'

Third, there is considerable potential for more RMB-denominated business of
the branches of Chinese banks in Hong Kong. As the RMB continues to appreciate, the inclination to hold RMB in Hong Kong strengthens and is further enabled
by the way the Chinese government is relaxing restrictions on the scope of RMB
business in Hong Kong. (For example, China's central bank recently announced
that it would be allowing three types of institutions to invest in the domestic

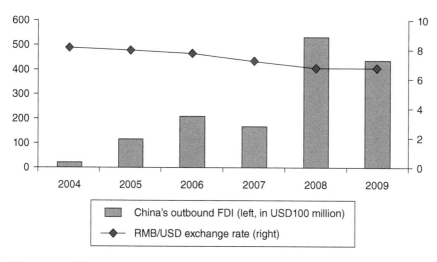

Figure 4.17 China's foreign direct investment abroad in recent years, and the exchange rate of the RMB.

Source: WIND.

interbank bond market. The three include overseas RMB clearing banks.) In point of fact, in recent years Chinese banks have already been hard at work expanding their international business, given the backdrop of an appreciating RMB. Their overseas business has grown fairly fast. The Communications Bank can serve as one example since its overseas assets have grown tremendously, as well as the profits derived from overseas branches. The profit contribution that branches made to the Group was 4.35 percent more in 2009 than it had been in 2008. Assets held by branches increased by 13 percent in just the first half of 2010.

Other impacts of an appreciating RMB should not be overlooked

The appreciation of the RMB is leading to a fall in banks' capital adequacy ratio, albeit to a limited extent

RMB appreciation affects the capital adequacy ratio of commercial banks through two separate channels. First, appreciation has a negative effect on banks' net profits. This arises because of the impact of exchange-rate changes on the 'fair value' of monetary and non-monetary assets, the 'net liability position' of banks, and the value of RMB-related monetary derivatives. For the net liability position and spot foreign-exchange exposure of banks, please see Table 4.4.

Second, appreciation has an effect on the capital adequacy ratio of banks: when foreign-currency capital is translated into RMB, the value of reserves goes down. This is primarily the result of a) currency-conversion differences in the foreign-currency-denominated statements of overseas operating institutions, b) foreign-currency assets which consist of overseas investments, c) non-monetary

Table 4.4 The foreign currency exposure of publicly listed banks, when the RMB
appreciates by 3%
Units: RMB 100 million

	Net liability position of foreign currency assets[2]	*Changes in fair values caused by RMB appreciation*
ICBC	2141.95	−64.26
BOC	3564.92	−106.95
CCB	555.01	−16.65
BOCOM	328.04	−9.84
China Merchants Bank	399.19	−11.98

Note: This assumes that the RMB appreciates by an even 3% against all foreign currencies.

Source: Annual reports of publicly listed banks as of the end of 2009.

foreign-currency items that are available for sale, such as stocks, and, d) it is the
result of other book balances of monetary assets available for sale after deducting
the amortized cost. An appreciating RMB reduces the relevant foreign-exchange
capital stock, capital reserves, and foreign exchange operating capital of commercial banks' overseas branches in the course of translating financial statements.
This reduces shareholders' equity.

*The appreciation of the RMB is increasing exchange-rate risk to
publicly listed Chinese banks, when those banks raise funds
on the capital markets*

The major commercial banks have all begun plans for increasing their capitali-
zation, given the relatively fast increase in demand for loans and also given the
impact of higher standards required by the Chinese government's regulatory bodies. However, plans to raise funds on overseas markets are at present facing a
number of restrictions that were put in place by those regulatory bodies. In order
to avoid tremendous volatility in cross-border flows of capital, regulations have
been instituted that prevent publicly listed Chinese banks from immediately transferring money that they have raised on international markets on into China. At a
minimum, banks must wait for several quarters or even one year before transferring such funds. The funds that banks raise in the H-market and the A-market
are denominated in different currencies. Moreover, the transition time between
determining how to raise funds and actually raising the funds and being able to
use them is rather long. During this period, exchange rates change. Banks must
bear the risk of exchange-rate losses if they are not able to convert currencies in a
timely manner or if they do not adopt risk-mitigation measures.

*The appreciation of the RMB also impacts the growth of banking
business indirectly through changes in asset prices.*

Given expectations for RMB appreciation, capital inflows into China have the
potential to exacerbate price inflation to the extent that they may cause a bubble.

On the one hand, rising prices enable banks to earn more income as individuals take out loans, and as banks serve as agents for selling funds. Even though the growth in savings deposits may also be curtailed, overall, this is beneficial to banks. On the other hand, an exorbitant increase in prices may also lead to government action and strict controls. Such actions might lead to a swift decline in prices. This then is detrimental to banks – it reduces the quality of a bank's individual loans as well as its business of serving as agent for selling funds. Recently, government policy is taking more frequent action with respect to real estate markets. Housing prices are falling back somewhat as a result, while the stock market has experienced a major correction. The impact of these things on bank business should not be ignored.

Recommendations for measures that banks might take in countering the above risks

We learn from the above analysis that the various business lines of commercial banks in China are being subjected to different kinds and degrees of forces as the RMB exchange rate changes. Reform of China's exchange-rate regime has led to the following complex mix of effects. The credit business of commercial banks has, by and large, been negatively affected. The funds business has experienced the dual effect of positives and negatives. The impact on foreign-exchange deposits and loans has been most pronounced with tremendous pressure on banks

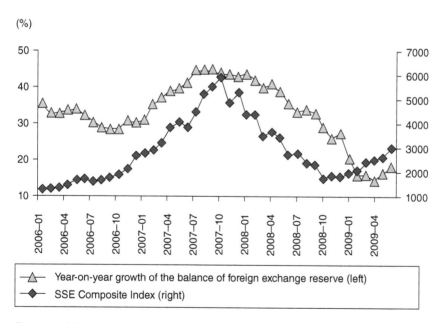

Figure 4.18 Foreign exchange reserves are generally trending in line with the Shanghai Stock Exchange composite index.

Source: WIND.

to manage liquidity properly. The international settlements business has experienced a structural effect. Overseas branches of Chinese banks have seen growth opportunities. Meanwhile, the effects of an appreciating RMB on such things as capital adequacy ratios should not be ignored. China's commercial banks must therefore evaluate their own situations in a rigorous and thorough way and must make adequate preparation for all contingencies. They must adhere to reform and innovation and should simultaneously adopt various measures to deal with issues. They should meet the challenges with a positive attitude and should seize opportunities, but in a realistic manner.

Optimize credit structures

Given the different ways in which RMB appreciation affects different industries and regions, banks should take steps to optimize their credit policies. Their general policies should be quite cautious with respect to industries that are negatively impacted. Such industries include the petrochemical, shipbuilding, textile, automobile, iron and steel, and real estate industries. Banks should intensify the way they have been lowering the volume of their loans to these sectors. They should adopt quota controls and closely track the financial situations of existing customers. They should look into the measures that enterprises are taking to reduce exchange-rate risk. Emphasis should be placed on assessing the technological and innovative capacities of the enterprise. If capacities are strong, products are being marketed well, and pricing can be kept at a fairly firm level, then a degree of support can be extended to these companies.

With respect to industries that directly stand to benefit from RMB appreciation, banks may offer a greater degree of support. Examples of such industries would be aviation, papermaking, machinery, and electric power. Industries that stand to benefit over the long term from a stronger RMB, such as retail, should be actively pursued.

Nevertheless, banks should also integrate these considerations with national industrial policies and the growth situation within the industries themselves. For example, the papermaking industry actually contains two industries, one of which the government is actively restricting through various policies. Even though this industry might benefit in the short run from an RMB appreciation, in the long run, its prospects are not good. Banks should approach it with caution.

In terms of how banks allocate credit on a regional basis, banks should increase their degree of support to central and western parts of the country. They should allocate more resources in order for these areas to be ready to receive the industrial shift (from the east coast]. They should gradually expand the market share of these areas. The priority for banks in the developed economies of China's eastern seaboard should be to adjust credit structures and strengthen risk management and controls (see Table 4.5).

Table 4.5 Recommendations on improving the allocation of credit for various industries

Industry	Main strategies
Aircraft	Appropriately give more credit support to expand the sectoral market share, mainly support the business development of the biggest three state-owned airline companies, and preferentially support quality private airline companies which benefit from the appreciation of RMB considerably.
Papermaking	Treat different enterprises on a differentiated basis. More efforts should be made with regard to large papermaking groups which greatly benefit from the appreciation and enjoy resource, technology and scale advantages. But a prudent attitude shall be adopted to develop poorly performing enterprises which fail in meeting the requirements of the national industry and environmental protection policies.
Electric power	More unsecured loans shall be appropriately made, particularly to sub-industries that enjoy a noticeable drop of import costs as a result of RMB appreciation such as the transformer and electric wire and cable industries.
Machinery	Preferentially support core and highly competitive leading equipment makers, while making prudent lending to the traditional equipment manufacturing industry. Appropriately provide more support to industries that greatly benefit from the appreciation such as the marine crankshaft and electric control equipment industries.
Retail	Under the context of RMB appreciation, seize the opportunities in the promising retail industry, provide preferential support to important regions and customers, and develop large premium group customers.
Iron and steel	Pay close attention to industrial risks, manage the unsecured loan delivery on a limit basis to control the growth of unsecured loans, and provide preferential support to leading enterprise groups.
Automobile	Taking the exchange rate fluctuations and the laws of industry development into consideration, extend lending to the industry moderately, mainly provide support to leading automobile enterprises such as FAW Group and SAIC Motor Corporation Limited to optimize the customer structure.
Textile	Comprehensively considering the fact that it is a sunset industry under great impacts of the appreciation of RMB, a restrictive entry policy shall be adopted for credit extension, trying best to increase guarantees and accelerate the recovery and reduction of unsecured loans to enterprises in the industry.
Shipbuilding	Enterprises in the industry face big business risks in the short term. Therefore, more efforts should be made to strengthen the guarantee and accelerate the recovery of unsecured loans to small and medium-sized enterprises with great potential risks. In the long term, in light of the national development of the shipping financial industry, regional leading premium shipbuilding groups could be supported.

(continued)

Table 4.5 (continued)

Industry	Main strategies
Petrochemical	Treat different enterprises on a differentiated basis. Active lending can be made to the oil refining industry which is under positive impacts of RMB appreciation and supported by the national industrial revitalization planning. However, a prudent and selective policy should be adopted in lending to a petrochemical industry that is heavily stricken by the appreciation.
Property loans and personal loans	Close attention should be paid to the development trend of real estate industry. More forward-looking studies shall be made. Under the name list-basis management and classified authorization, property-related loans shall be granted in an orderly way, focusing on collateral mortgage and customer credit review to strengthen risk resistance capacity.

Strengthen business ties within banks so as to achieve better use of foreign-currency assets and liabilities

First, banks should seek to increase deposits of foreign exchange through a variety of means. Bank's product lines, logistical systems, and quality of service should all be improved upon and upgraded, in order to draw in customers who deposit foreign exchange. To an appropriate degree, banks may increase interest rates on their foreign-currency deposits. Second, banks should improve ties between their domestic and foreign branches. Banks should seek to transfer foreign-exchange funds within their own systems in an efficient way through reasonable transfer pricing. Third, banks should structure their foreign-currency assets in a way that reduces investments in foreign-currency bonds, and that raises the percentage of high-yield returns on foreign-exchange loans. The aim should be to raise the overall yield rate on foreign-currency assets. Fourth, banks should seek to improve the composition of customers to whom they make foreign-currency loans. They should tighten up their systems for approving foreign-currency loans, and they should control the pace at which they extend foreign-exchange loans. They should put their limited foreign-exchange funds into projects and with customers that have the highest returns, the greatest overall efficiency, and the highest strategic effect.

Take advantage of an appreciating RMB to expand different lines of business

In a proactive but also prudent way, banks should promote the business of making loans for mergers and acquisitions, and they should seek to expand their fee-based intermediary business. They should pay close attention to trends in overseas M&A activity in such key sectors as energy and mining. Once careful and detailed assessments have been made, they should select outstanding industries for making M&A-related loans. In a steady way, they should then grow this line of business. At the same time, banks should increase their ability to extend consulting services that are related to the M&A business, including consulting on investments, restructuring, and funds settlement. To do this, they should cultivate human resources that are familiar with the investment banking side of the business. They should actively transition from a focus on raising funds to a focus on services in terms of how they conduct their intermediary business.

Second, given the backdrop of national policies that favor expanding personal consumption, as well as the fact of an appreciating RMB, banks should seek to expand the business of extending personal-consumption loans. The emphasis should be on loans for automobile purchases and on unsecured small loans. Third, banks should seize the opportunities provided by increased demand for trade financing. On the condition that they maintain effective control over possible risks, they should actively try to build up their trade-financing business. They should help exporters lock in profits by offering such products as forward settlement in different currencies, and note financing.

Grow the international settlement business

An appreciating RMB brings benefits but also disadvantages to China's foreign trade. It has a negative impact on exports but a positive impact on imports. At the same time, its impact is quite different on different industries and enterprises – banks should take this into account as they seek to expand their international settlement business. They should optimize the composition of their customers, industries, and mix of imports and exports. They should seek to explore all potential through cultivating and maintaining a core group of customers, via close domestic and international ties among all their lines of business. They should seek to offer customers an entire range of services so as to achieve rapid, comprehensive, and organic growth of the business.

Promote cross-border RMB settlement business

On June 22, 2010, the People's Bank of China and five other governmental departments and commissions jointly issued a notice allowing expanded use of RMB in cross-border trade settlement. The notice was called, 'Notice on considerations relating to expanding the pilot program allowing cross-border trade settlement in RMB.' In addition to the ongoing appreciation of the RMB, this action will lead to an unprecedented demand for RMB settlement services. It will continue to encourage cross-border trade and will facilitate cross-border investing. This should provide new growth opportunities for the international business of participating banks. In addition, the demand for risk-mitigation products (hedging products] will grow as volatility of the RMB exchange rate is allowed to increase. The cross-border RMB settlement business should serve as a means to enable importers and exporters to manage exchange-rate risk. Commercial banks should seize the opportunity of expanding this pilot program by developing their cross-border settlement business, particularly in the area of RMB payment and settlement for imports.

First, banks should readdress their own policy considerations so as to be ready to modify their approach to customers and products. Second, banks should be innovative in the way they provide targeted professional services to specific types of customers. They should intensify their marketing and promotion efforts and try to differentiate themselves. Third, banks should undertake a thorough analysis of where the greatest demand is and where to place their efforts in growing their RMB cross-border settlement business. We recommend that they consider the Asia-Pacific region, Latin America, and Europe as three areas of potential growth in demand. Fourth, banks should strengthen their marketing and the sales push behind introducing new products. They should focus on key customers both inside and outside China and should go on 'road shows' to introduce their products and services. Fifth, banks should go further in improving their incentive mechanisms and performance evaluation processes. They should put more resources, including bonuses, into rewarding business that has resulted from cooperative ties between branches inside and outside China.

Expand product mix: encourage innovation in both foreign-exchange and RMB products and cultivate human talent so as to meet the demand for new products

The nature of the business of foreign-exchange deposits and foreign-exchange wealth management dictates the nature of bank responsibilities in serving customers. This business requires a greater degree of product innovation on the part of banks and a greater degree of market participation, since banks are serving as agents for customers in managing their accounts. In order to diversify sources of foreign-exchange funds and to increase fee income from intermediary services, banks must interact with a broader range of customers. They should therefore upgrade the design, portfolios, and marketing of the foreign-exchange products that they trade, for different targeted customers. First, banks should design more short-term products that help clients avoid exchange-rate risks. Second, they should make every effort to assess, in accurate ways, the expected returns from products with longer-term maturities. They should attempt to increase earnings on these products in order to offset the increased risk of RMB appreciation.

Banks should play close attention to how the process of pegging the RMB exchange rate to a basket of currencies actually takes place. They should observe and analyze the types and weighting of the currencies and then use this information to readjust the currency composition of their own assets and liabilities. They should enhance their capacity to service customers by providing for the availability of different currencies. Banks should study the trading opportunities provided by the broader band within which the RMB is allowed to float and should increase the frequency of participating in the market. Depending on the specific supply and demand conditions of different markets, they should enhance their own ability to make price quotations.

Meanwhile, the management of commercial banks should feel a great sense of urgency about developing adequate talent to handle new responsibilities. Management should adopt effective incentives, including reform of compensation mechanisms, so as to cultivate a group of professionals who can handle foreign-exchange fund trading, risk management, and product design. Banks should seek to create a team of professionals who both understand China's situation and are familiar with international standards and technologies. They should put massive effort into raising the overall level of human resources that handle their foreign-currency funds business. As soon as possible, they should be able to handle the increased challenges that come with a broader range of volatility in exchange rates, as well as the new business opportunities.

As the expectations for an appreciating RMB grow ever stronger, and as foreign funds flow into the country and increase liquidity in the interbank market, the business of RMB fund management is facing a relatively favorable situation. First, banks should continue to optimize the composition of their funds business and their spot trading. Secondly, they should take into full consideration such factors as the effect of exchange-rate adjustments and China's overall economic situation on the trend line of interest rates, in order to handle the market risk of their RMB funds business effectively. Third, banks should stay highly alert to the possibility of an abrupt withdrawal from the market once profits start to be taken. They should take measures to guard against and mitigate potential risk.

Increase international business through mergers and acquisitions and establishment of overseas branches

An appreciating RMB will necessarily spur the growth of direct investment overseas by Chinese enterprises. China's commercial banks should follow in their footsteps in a timely manner and at an appropriate pace. They should expand overseas in order to provide financing services to China-invested businesses. At the same time, since an appreciating RMB lowers the cost of currency conversion for China, it is conducive to general expansion of the business of Chinese commercial banks overseas. Commercial banks should take into consideration the long-term trajectories of trends as described above. According to their own growth strategies, they should develop human resources, people who are familiar with overseas markets and international standards, by both hiring new people and cultivating talent from within their ranks. They should integrate their plans with the key growth areas of Asia, Latin America, and other emerging markets. They should increase their overseas presence in a stable but proactive way through the means of both newly established entities and mergers and acquisitions. They should constantly increase their international operating capacities. At the same time, they should keep a very close eye on Chinese policy changes with respect to RMB business in Hong Kong and Macao. They should be fully prepared to capitalize on opportunities for RMB business and the business of their branches in these regions.

Avoid exchange-rate risks when refinancing

The Bank of Communications has at present completed its refinancing process. The refinancing plans of the Construction Bank of China and the Industry and

Commerce Bank of China may also be completed within this year. In order to avoid exchange-rate risk due to extreme volatility of the RMB vis-à-vis the Hong Kong dollar, during the period when refinancing has not yet been completed we recommend that banks undertake a comprehensive evaluation of their overseas development needs in tandem with their exchange-rate risks. They should figure out how long they need to retain foreign exchange, and what percentage it should constitute, while at the same time taking measures to minimize exchange-rate risk.

Note

1 This research was undertaken by the Financial Research Center of the Bank of Communications. The research team was led by Lian Ping; the report was written by E Yongjian and Ni Zhiling.

Appendix

An empirical study of the impact of RMB exchange-rate changes on the non-performing loan ratios of commercial banks in China

1 Specification of variables

(a) Explained variable: risk level of bank loans

Here, we take non-performing loan ratio (NPL) as the representative variable to measure risk level of bank loans.

(b) Variables

i   ΔTL refers to the variation of the total amount of bank loans (TL) which is not a stable variable. To avoid spurious regression, we adopted the first-order difference of TL, which means that the variation in TL was taken as an explanatory variable. Under the condition that the total amount of NPL remained stable, the faster TL grows, the more apparently NPL declines. Therefore, it is expected that variation of TL has a negative impact on NPL.

ii   Rate of return on equity (ROE). A higher value of ROE indicates the higher profitability of a bank that can make up losses incurred by NPLs. It is therefore expected that ROE has a negative impact on NPL.

iii   Variation of loan/interest-bearing assets (ΔLPA). LPA represents the ratio of loans to interest-bearing assets. According to results of the panel-data unit-root test, the ratio is not stable. To avoid spurious regression, we used the first-order difference of the loan/interest-bearing assets ratio, that is, the variation of LPA as an explanatory variable. According to results of the panel-data unit-root test, ΔLPA is stable. A positive ratio indicates an increase in the proportion of loans in interest-bearing assets, while a negative one means a decline. The more commercial banks rely on loans to make profits, the greater chances for the NPL ratio to go up. Therefore ΔLPA is expected to have a positive impact on NPL.

iv   Season-adjusted real gross domestic product (RGDP). We obtained the nominal GDP and CPI data on a quarter-on-quarter basis during the third quarter of 2005 and the second quarter of 2010 from Wind Information Co., Ltd. Because of the lack of GDP deflator, we adopted CPI instead and converted the quarterly nominal GDP into real GDP (taking the second quarter of 2005 as the base period). The real quarterly GDP shows a quarterly trend, so we made quarterly adjustments to the real quarterly GDP by the X11 seasonal adjustment method and got the real GDP after deducting seasonal variation factors. Upon examination, the data of season-adjusted real GDP is found to be stable. The better the economic situation is, the lower NPL is. Therefore, GDP is expected to have negative impacts on NPL.

v   The logarithm of the USD/RMB nominal exchange rate (LNFX). It is the nominal exchange rate of USD against RMB, whose original data are not stable. To meet the requirements of the empirical test for stable data, we usually adopt its logarithm in literature. The logarithm turned out to be stable in the test. Here, LNFX refers to the logarithm of the USD/RMB nominal exchange rate.

vi   Rate of inflation (INF). INF here refers to the inflation rate of the current quarter compared with the previous one. We calculated the inflation rate with CPI data on a quarterly basis, or INF. It is expected that INF's impact on NPL is not evident.

vii Efforts level of banking credit supervision (PROL). We took the total loan reserve ratio as the representative variable of PROL. Total loan reserve ratio=loans impairment reserve/TL. Yunus (2005) argued that total loan reserve ratio could reflect a bank's credit supervision capacity. However, since credit supervision capacity usually doesn't vary significantly from quarter to quarter, we think that total reserve ratio can be adopted to measure the changes of PROL.

Suppose a bank's credit supervision capacity remains the same, a significant increase of total loan reserve ratio, which means an increase in its expected loan impairment losses, indicates a decrease in PROL of the bank. If PROL declines, then the bank's NPL will increase accordingly. Therefore, it is expected that the regression coefficient of the PROL value (a larger value means a lower PROL) to NPL is positive.

viii Capital adequacy ratio (CA). A bank with a higher capital adequacy ratio has a stronger capacity of risk resistance. Since CA has some impacts on NPL, we adopted it as an explanatory variable.

2 Regression equations

Referring to the general idea of the panel data analysis, we respectively established the random effect model, fixed effect model and ordinary least square estimation model of pooled data to study the impacts of a bank's risk tolerance and PROL on its risks. Regression equations of the three methods are as follows.

Random effect model:

$$NPL_{it} = \beta_1 \Delta TL_{it} + \beta_2 ROE_{it} + \beta_3 \Delta LPA_{it} + \beta_4 RGDP_{it} + \beta_5 LNFX_{it} + \beta_6 INF_{it} + \beta_7 PROL_{it} + \beta_8 CA_{it} + b + \mu_i + u_{it}$$

Fixed effect model:

$$NPL_{it} = \beta_1 \Delta TL_{it} + \beta_2 ROE_{it} + \beta_3 \Delta LPA_{it} + \beta_4 RGDP_{it} + \beta_5 LNFX_{it} + \beta_6 INF_{it} + \beta_7 PROL_{it} + \beta_8 CA_{it} + c_i + u_{it}$$

Pooled regression model:

$$NPL_{it} = \beta_1 \Delta TL_{it} + \beta_2 ROE_{it} + \beta_3 \Delta LPA_{it} + \beta_4 RGDP_{it} + \beta_5 LNFX_{it} + \beta_6 INF_{it} + \beta_7 PROL_{it} + \beta_8 CA_{it} + b + u_{it}$$

The subscript 'i' represents different banks, and 't' represents quarters. In the random effect model and the fixed effect model, 'u_i' and 'c_i' refer to impacts of unobserved banking factors, of which 'u_i' is a random variable, 'c_i' is merely a constant relating to banks, and 'u_{it}' is a residual term.

3 Data sources and descriptive statistics of variables

Since China's exchange rate reform was started from the third quarter of 2005, we chose quarterly financial data during the third quarter of 2005 and the second quarter of 2010 of almost all listed banks, including ICBC, CCB, BOC, BOCOM, China Merchants Bank, China CITIC Bank, China Minsheng Banking Corporation, Industrial Bank, Shanghai Pudong Development Bank, Hua Xia Bank, Shenzhen Development Bank, Bank of Beijing, Bank of Nanjing, and Bank of Ningbo. As ABC and China Everbright Bank went public not long ago and the public information is limited, our study didn't cover these two banks.

Most of our data came from Wind Information, while part of the data came from calculations with listed banks' public information. Since banks went public at different times, and their frequency of data disclosure was not consistent (as for some indicators, some listed banks published every 6 months, while some others disclosed quarterly, some banks' data in several quarters were inaccessible. The software Eviews 6.0 we used can properly handle missing panel data set, and will not affect the final empirical results. Therefore, we left blank for inaccessible data rather than using estimated values.

4 Data sources and descriptive statistics of variables

(a) Stationary test of data

To avoid spurious regression, we first made a panel-data unit-root test on the data. The commonly practiced unit-root tests include LLU test (Levin, Lin & Chu test), IPS test (Im, Pesaran& Shin W test), ADF test (ADF-Fisher Chi-square test) and PPF test (PP-Fisher Chi-square test). Annexed table 4.2 displays the results of the unit root-test of the overall sample data.

Annexed table 4.1 Descriptive statistic results of full sample variables

	Variable	Mean value	Median	Maximum	Minimum	Standard deviation	Sample group number	The Total number of samples
Explained variable	NPL	0.0340	0.0148	2.4000	0.0033	0.1710	16	211
	ΔTL	608.2267	221.3496	6,364.350	-886.6000	995.5454	16	218
	ROE	0.0487	0.0478	0.1079	-0.1555	0.0221	16	226
	ΔLPA	-0.0019	-0.0003	0.1050	-0.0919	0.0261	16	218
Explanatory variables	RGDP	69,529.99	71,001.97	93,074.21	44,430.57	14,749.74	16	280
	LNFX	1.9895	1.9684	2.0909	1.9193	0.0695	16	280
	INF	0.0006	-0.0010	0.0140	-0.0090	0.0064	16	280
	PROL	0.0229	0.0233	0.0430	0.0000	0.0071	16	218
	CA	0.1130	0.1117	0.3067	0.0343	0.0337	16	196

Annexed table 4.2 Results of unit-root test of the overall sample data

Variable	LLU	IPS	ADF	PPF
NPL	−8.15269	–	88.0933	193.632
	(0.0000)		(0.0000)	(0.0000)
ΔTL	−6.36697	−2.32977	51.2810	79.7000
	(0.0000)	(0.0099)	(0.0046)	(0.0000)
ROE	−8.44358	−6.69791	95.9357	103.719
	(0.0000)	(0.0000)	(0.0000)	(0.0000)
ΔLPA	−13.9035	–	187.454	190.727
	(0.0000)		(0.0000)	(0.0000)
RGDP	−6.16274	−2.98162	48.3265	106.446
	(0.0000)	(0.0014)	(0.0099)	(0.0000)
LNFX	−4.07044	–	39.4791	114.892
	(0.0000)		(0.0735)	(0.0000)
INF	−16.3303	–	235.127	244.305
	(0.0000)	–	(0.0000)	(0.0000)
PROL	−7.5494	−2.7196	45.7768	84.8608
	(0.0000)	(0.0033)	(0.0184)	(0.0000)
CA	−4.21647	−0.34916	29.3156	24.7323
	(0.0000)	(0.3635)	(0.2085)	(0.4204)

Note: When making the stationary test on the panel data with Eviews 6.0, we had to select items of 'test equations include (1) intercept, (2) intercept and trend, (3) none (including neither intercept nor trend) according to the features of the data. If item '(3) none' was selected according to the characteristics of the data, then the panel data stationary test can produce the results of LLU, ADF, PPF, except IPS. The mark '−' in the table means that Eviews6.0 provide no results. The values in brackets are P-values of test.

According to the results of the unit-root test on the overall sample, the test results of variables, namely NPL, ΔTL, ROE, ΔLPA, RGDP, LNFX, INF and PROL, disproved the hypothesis that variables have unit roots at the confidence level of 1 percent. The LLC test appropriate for the same unit roots disproved the hypothesis that variable CA had a unit root at the confidence level of 1 percent, while the IPS, ADF and PPF tests for different unit roots did not disprove the hypothesis. CA represents capital adequacy ratio, and capital adequacy ratios of different banks vary around the regulatory requirements on capital adequacy ratio. Therefore, the test method appropriate for the same unit roots is more reasonable; we thus adopted the results of LLC test, which disproved the hypothesis that variables have unit roots at the confidence level of 1 percent. Variable CA was believed to have no unit root and remain stable during the sample period.

(b) Analysis on the results of empirical tests

We used the 'Redundant Fixed Effect' test and 'Hausman' test provided by Eviews 6.0 in Annexed Table 4.3 to select the model. The null hypothesis of the 'Redundant Fixed Effect' is that the pooled regression model is more appropriate,

Annexed table 4.3 Regression results of the factors affecting the NPL of commercial banks

Explained variable	NPL		
Estimation model	Random effect model	Fixed effect model	Pooled regression model
ΔTL	−3.77E-06	−7.82E-07*	2.14E-07
	(4.18E-06)	(4.12E-07)	(3.81E-07)
	[0.3684]	[0.0603]	[0.5752]
ROE	0.089572	−0.020344	−0.050880
	(0.172553)	(0.022294)	(0.026637)
	[0.6045]	[0.3631]	[0.0580]
ΔLPA	0.146880	-0.003217	0.008204
	(0.169272)	(0.015000)	(0.020192)
	[0.3869]	[0.8305]	[0.6851]
RGDP	3.77E-08	−2.87E-07***	−2.55E-07***
	(8.52E-07)	(7.22E-08)	(8.61E-08)
	[0.9647]	[0.0001]	[0.0036]
LNFX	0.060038	-0.009339	−0.000850
	(0.209206)	(0.017404)	(0.022469)
	[0.7745]	[0.5924]	[0.9699]
INF	0.313310	0.031665	0.064013
	(0.734999)	(0.058157)	(0.077918)
	[0.6705]	[0.5870]	[0.4127]
PROL	2.129069***	0.599961***	0.838694***
	(0.669808)	(0.136189)	(0.081014)
	[0.0018]	[0.0000]	[0.0000]
CA	−0.338185**	−0.007682	−0.001317
	(0.132310)	(0.017480)	(0.019869)
	[0.016]	[0.6610]	[0.9473]
C (Constant)	−0.08748	0.051537	0.02359
	(0.472303)	(0.040527)	(0.050474)
	[0.882]	[0.2057]	[0.6728]
F-statistic [P-value]	3.622898	22.11174	31.58725
	[0.000705]	[0.0000]	[0.0000]
R²	0.162842	0.773464	0.629075

Explained variable	NPL		
Test results of selected models	Redundant fixed effect test [P-value]	Chi2(13,136) = 6.460148 [0.0000]	
	Hausman random efect test [P-value]	Chi2(8) = 16.117990 [0.0407]	
Sample group number	14	14	14
The total number of samples	158	158	158

Note: The results were calculated by Eviews 6.0. The numerical values in parentheses are standard deviations, while those in square brackets are P-values; *, ** and *** respectively indicate that NPL are significant below the significance level of 10 percent, 5 percent and 1 percent.

with the alternative hypothesis that the fixed effect model is preferable; the null hypothesis of the 'Hausman' test is that the random effect test is more appropriate with the alternative hypothesis that the fixed effect model is preferable.

The redundant fixed effect test showed that the fixed effect model is more appropriate than the pooled regression model (P-value is 0.0407), and the Hausman random effect test also indicated that the fixed effect model is more appropriate than the random effect model (P-value is 0.0000). Our discussion therefore mainly focused on the results of the fixed effect model. R^2, regression of the fixed effect model is 0.77, indicating that the regression results are very significant.

Regression coefficients of three variables are significant in the regression results of the panel data of the fixed effect model. The coefficient of ΔTL is -7.83×10^{-7}, significant at the level of 10 percent. The regression coefficient of RGDP is -2.87×10^{-7}, significant at the level of 1 percent. And the regression coefficient of PROL is 0.599961, significant at the level of 1 percent.

According to absolute values, among three variables which have significant impacts on the NPL of commercial banks, PROL has the most impacts on it. NPL changes about 0.6 of a unit when the credit supervision efforts change by 1 unit; ΔTL takes the second place with NPL changing -7.83×10^{-7} unit when ΔTL changes by 1 unit; RGDP's impacts on NPL, though not comparable with the above-mentioned two ones, are also significant with NPL changing -2.87×10^{-7} unit when RGDP changes by 1 unit.

Viewing from symbols of the variable, among three variables that have significant impacts on NPL, the regression coefficient of PROL to NPL is positive, indicating that the lower effort level of banking credit supervision (the larger the value of PROL), the higher non-performing loans ratio (the larger the value of NPL); the regression coefficient of ΔTL to NPL is negative, indicating that the faster the size of bank loans expands (the larger the value of ΔTL), the lower the non-performing loans ratio (the smaller the value of NPL). The regression coefficient of RGDP to NPL is negative, indicating that the better economic situation (the larger the value of RGDP), the lower non-performing loans ratio (the smaller the value of NPL).

Though the regression coefficients of ROE and CA to NPL are not significant, they are both negative, indicating that the better profitability or higher capital adequacy ratio of a bank, the lower its non-performing loans ratio, which conforms to our expectations.

The impact of LNFX on NPL is not significant. Nevertheless, since its regression coefficient is negative, an appreciation of RMB (the smaller the value of LNFX) will result in an increase in non-performing loans ratio (the larger the value of NPL). Therefore, an excessively rapid appreciation of RMB is unfavorable to the sound operation and management of commercial banks.

5 Evaluating the 'real equilibrium exchange rate' of the RMB

Li Shantong[1]

Introduction

In an open economy, exchange rates represent the 'overall price' of one country's goods, services, and assets, relative to the overall price of another country's goods, services, and assets. The degree to which a country's overall price is in 'equilibrium' provides a fundamental basis for economic policy. Determinations of exchange-rate equilibrium, and the degree to which exchange rates are out of line, enable the formulation of domestic policy as well as coordinated international adjustments. Given the globalization of economies, determinations of what equilibrium really is, or should be, also involve a complex kind of economic gamesmanship. Both international economics and politics are involved. As China's position has gradually risen amid the world's economies, a determination of the 'real, equilibrium exchange-rate level' is highly significant. A realistic determination not only benefits China, by creating an international environment that is beneficial to its own development, but it helps promote world economic development as well.

In July, 2005, China began to implement an exchange-rate system that was described as a 'managed float, based on market supply and demand, with adjustments made in reference to a basket of currencies.' Despite the international financial crisis which erupted in the second half of 2008, the RMB to US dollar exchange rate fluctuated within a narrow band, while the 'real, effective exchange rate' first rose, and then fell. Between July of 2005, when exchange-rate reform was initiated, and September of 2010, the RMB had appreciated against the US dollar by 23 percent, while the real effective exchange rate had appreciated by 19 percent. Now, given the current global situation, we should begin to address several questions. In the five years since exchange-rate reform, has the RMB reached levels that are reasonable and appropriate? Is the RMB exchange-rate in balance, or not? If misaligned, what is the degree of that misalignment? Finally, for the near term, from 2010 to 2015, what range of exchange rates for the RMB would be reasonable? The primary purpose of this chapter is to address these questions.

The substance of our chapter is divided into five main sections. The first presents a literature review of the methodology, as applied to the subject of determining real equilibrium exchange rates. The second section presents the results of our own measurements, using a method called the 'Fundamental Equilibrium

Exchange-rate Theory,' or FEER. This section also suggests a reasonable scenario for a 'targeted equilibrium effective exchange rate,' as well as nominal bilateral exchange rates for the RMB vis-à-vis the US dollar, and the RMB vis-à-vis the Euro.

The third section presents our results in deriving a real equilibrium effective exchange rate through the use of a second method called the 'Behavioral Equilibrium Exchange-rate Theory,' or BEER. The fourth section presents our results through the use of a method called the 'Extended Purchasing Power Parity Theory,' or EPPP.

In the last section, we summarize our evaluation of the real equilibrium exchange rate of the RMB, and we present specific policy recommendations.

Literature review

Recent literature on the subject, from both inside and outside China, includes three main methods of assessing the real equilibrium exchange rate of the RMB.

The first is the Extended Purchasing Power Parity Theory, or EPPP. An example of using this method would be the work of Wang Zetian and Yao Yang (2008). They calculated the rate by evaluating data from 184 countries and regions in the period between 1974 and 2007. Their conclusion was that the RMB had been undervalued since 1985. In 2005, it was undervalued by 23 percent, in 2006 by 20 percent, and in 2007 by 16 percent.

The second is the Fundamental Equilibrium Exchange-rate Theory, or FEER. Examples would be, first, the work of the Peterson Institute for International Economics, a well-known think-tank in the United States, which looked at the subject in 2008, 2009, and 2010; second, the work of Wang Yizhong and Jin Xuejun (2008); and third, the work of Hu Chuntian and Chen Zhijun (2009). All of these used the FEER, but the conclusions of their research were quite different. The Peterson Institute concluded that China's real effective equilibrium exchange rate should appreciate to a substantial degree. Wang Yizhong and Jin Xuejun concluded that the RMB real effective equilibrium rate should have appreciated by about 20 percent between 2006 and 2008. Hu Chuntian and Chen Zhijun concluded that the RMB had already appreciated by too much by the end of 2008.

The third is the Behavioral Equilibrium Exchange-rate Theory, or BEER. An example would be the work of Qin Duo and He Xinhua (2010). Their analysis included the latest quarterly data in looking at the degree of misalignment of the RMB. Their conclusion was that the RMB is basically not misaligned at present in terms of the real effective exchange rate. They felt that research conclusions in the past were credible but generally over-estimated the degree of RMB imbalance.

The Extended Purchasing-power Parity Theory (EPPP) uses purchasing-power parity as the underlying methodology, but adds in certain explanatory variables in attempting to measure real equilibrium exchange rates. The commonality between these two is that such explanatory variables incorporate the relative productivity of sectors producing non-trade items and those producing trade items. These are used to illustrate the Balassa-Samuelson Effect. One drawback of this method is the fact that China has long had a large amount of hidden unemployment, which weakens the Balassa-Samuelson Effect (Hu Chuntian and Chen Zhijun, 2009). The Fundamental Equilibrium Exchange-rate Theory (FEER) is more trustworthy as a reliable indicator since it concentrates on fundamental economic factors in calculating a rate, but at the same time it excludes short-term cyclical considerations and contingent factors. It also may not reflect actual economic realities to a degree since it may be overly idealized – this comes from using fundamental economic variables and conditions that prevail over the medium term, which might not correspond to the actual situation. The advantage of the Behavioral Equilibrium Exchange-rate Theory (BEER) is that it is simply and easily applied. It sets up a single-equation model to measure the direct effect of economic fundamentals on the equilibrium real exchange rate. However, the definition of 'economic fundamentals' as variables can be subjective. The model therefore places demands on the choice of the sample data that is being analyzed.

The whole issue of the RMB's real equilibrium exchange rate is not just a theoretical issue, with its questions of methodology, but a very key economic and policy issue. As mentioned above, many scholars have researched the issue, both inside and outside China. One primary aim of this particular study is to arrive at policy recommendations that are based on a common discussion of results. We have done our best, therefore, to make our methodology and framework for analysis consistent with those of researchers in other institutions so that discussion can proceed within the same framework. At the same time, we have used various methodologies in our calculations, in order to facilitate comparisons and cross-verifications.

To determine a 'reasonable level' for China's RMB exchange rate, and to estimate the degree to which it is out of alignment, our study used three different methods for calculating the 'real equilibrium exchange rate level.' Then, on the basis of interactive comparisons and cross-verification, we came to a determination of what we do in fact believe to be a 'reasonable level' for the RMB exchange rate, and how far we feel it is out of alignment.

Calculations using the FEER (Fundamental Equilibrium Exchange-rate Model)

Principles underlying the methodology

Cline and Williamson (William R. Cline and John Williamson) first proposed the concept of a fundamental equilibrium exchange rate in 1985. By keeping the real effective exchange rate consistent with macroeconomic equilibrium, the theory attempted to arrive at what the real effective exchange rate level should be. In this process, 'macroeconomic equilibrium' refers to an economy that is at full employment, has low inflation, and whose current account balance reflects ongoing net capital flows that are sustainable. In other words, both internal and external elements of the economy are in equilibrium – this is taken as the ideal economic situation. One key element in the FEER methodology is the assumption of a constant equivalence between the current account and the capital account:

$$CA = -KA \tag{1}$$

Several main factors are generally felt to determine the current account. These include total domestic output (or total demand) [Y], total overseas output (or total demand), real effective interest rates [q] and so on. A determination of the medium-term capital account equilibrium can be derived by relying on relevant economic factors. Therefore, formula (1) as above can be converted into an equation that reflects the equivalency between the current account and the capital account. For purposes of clarity, it is best to express the current account as a linear function, determined by factors as described above including full employment. Equation (1) then becomes:

$$C4 = b0 + b1R + b2Y + b3Yw = -KA \tag{2}$$

In the equation above, [R] represents the real effective exchange rate. [Y] refers to domestic income of the country and [ ] refers to total income of all other countries in the world, with both being in a state of full employment. In the left-hand side of Equation (2), the real effective exchange rate [R] represents the rate that is compatible with macroeconomic equilibrium. Changes in [R] allow for an equivalency between the current account balance and the normal, internally sustainable, capital account balance. In deriving a solution to Equation (2), we arrive at the following:

$$FEER = \frac{-K\bar{A} - b_0 - b_2 Y - b_3 Y_w}{b_1} \tag{3}$$

What Equation (3) means is that FEER is a kind of exchange rate that is compatible with medium-term macroeconomic equilibrium. Moreover, FEER can be derived by fixing the various parameters of the current account model and then looking at the exogenous factor of sustainable net capital flows.

Borowski and Couharde (2003), Coudert and Couharrde (2005), and Isard and Faruqee (1998)[2] further developed the FEER model as follows. First, they assumed trade formulas as described below in Equations (4), (5), and (6):

$$X = X_0 Y_w^{\eta_x} R^{\varepsilon_x} \qquad x = \frac{dX}{X} = \eta_x y_w + \varepsilon_x r \tag{4}$$

$$M = M_0 Y^{\eta_m} R^{-\varepsilon_m} \qquad m = \frac{dM}{M} \eta_m y - \varepsilon_m r \tag{5}$$

$$B = PX - PRM \tag{6}$$

In the above equations, [R] indicates the real effective exchange rate and a rise in [R] indicates depreciation. $r = \dfrac{R - \overline{R}}{\overline{R}}$. That is, the degree to which the real effective exchange rate is misaligned out departs from equilibrium. When r is less than 0, the exchange-rate is over-valued.

X, M and Y respectively refer to the exports, imports, and the total outputs at home and abroad.

X refers to the export volume; x refers to the deviation of the export volume from the equilibrium, and ε_x is the elasticity of exports to exchange rate.

Yw refers to the total overseas outputs, $y_w = \dfrac{Y_w - \overline{Y}_w}{\overline{Y}_w}$ is the deviation of the total overseas outputs from the potential outputs, and η_x refers to the elasticity of export trade.

M refers to the import volume; m refers to the deviation of the import volumefrom the equilibrium and ε_m is the elasticity of imports to exchange rate.

Y refers to the total domestic outputs, $y = \dfrac{Y - \overline{Y}}{\overline{Y}}$ is the degree of total domestic outputs deviating from the potential outputs, and η_m refers to the elasticity of import trade.

B refers to the nominal trade balance. The current account balance (CA) is the sum of the trade balance (B), the net income (IPD) and the net transfer income (NT).

Leaving out NT, IPD is considered to be irrelative to the real effective exchange rate. Therefore, the relationship between the real effective exchange rate and the current account balance is represented by the trade volume of goods and services, or dCA=dB.

Suppose $ca^* = \dfrac{CA^*}{p_y Y}$, $\tau = \dfrac{PX}{PRM}$ represents the export-import ratio and $\mu = \dfrac{PRM}{PY}$ is the proportion of imports to the gross domestic product (GDP), differencing the trade balance equation (6) yields equation (7):

$$\frac{1}{\mu}\left(\frac{CA - CA^*}{P_y Y}\right) = \frac{dCA}{PRM} = \frac{dB}{PRM} = \tau x - r - m \tag{7}$$

Substituting equations (4) and (5) into (7) yields:

$$r = \frac{1/\mu}{\tau \varepsilon_x + \varepsilon_m - 1}\left[(ca - ca^*) + \mu(\eta_m y - \tau \eta_x y_w)\right]$$

$$= \frac{1/\mu}{\tau \varepsilon_x + \varepsilon_m - 1}\left[(ca + ROG) - ca^*\right]$$

$$= \beta(\overline{ca} - ca^*) \tag{8}$$

Equation (8) represents the relationship of the real effective exchange rate with the potential current account (ca which has been adjusted for the relative output gap) and the equilibrium current account (ca*). In Equation (8), ROG stands for the relative output gap, and ß refers to the elasticity of the current account ratio to the real effective exchange rate (or the growth rate of the real effective exchange rate with every percentage point of decline in the current account).

From the above elaboration, we can conclude that FEER and the degree of exchange rate misalignment can be calculated by firstly estimating the elastic coefficients in trade equations (4) and (5), and then setting the equilibrium current account ca* in equation (8).

Estimates of trade elasticity

In estimating China's trade elasticity, we used a sample of seventeen countries and regions, and data from the period between 1985 and 2009. During this period, imports and exports between China and the sample of trading partners exceeded 77 percent of China's total trade on average. We included the following China trade partners: the USA, Canada, Australia, Japan, Germany, France, Italy, the Netherlands, the UK, Hong Kong (China), Taiwan (China), Indonesia, South Korea, Malaysia, Singapore, Thailand, and India.

We calculated the real effective exchange rate through the following equation (9):[3]

$$R = \sum_{i=1}^{17} \omega_i [E_{d/i} (P_i^* / P_d)] \tag{9}$$

In this equation, R refers to the real effective exchange rate. When R increases, the RMB is depreciating, and when R decreases, the RMB is appreciating. The symbol w_i stands for the weight of a country' trade i; $E_{d/i}$ refers to the nominal bilateral exchange rate under the direct quotation; P_i^* and P_i respectively refer to the consumer price index (CPI) of country i and of China.

Using the trade equations (4) and (5), as given above, the estimated results of the elasticities of import and export volume, exchange-rate index, and domestic and foreign output are given in Table 5.1, expressed as the corresponding natural logarithms and elasticity coefficients.

Assumptions involved in determining the equilibrium current account

One key element of the FEER model is the assumption about medium-term capital flows as a way to establish the trend or equilibrium of the current account. There is no single agreed-upon method at present of establishing an 'equilibrium' current account. We used the following 'explained variables' to conduct a regression analysis: the dependent elderly population (DEP), government fiscal

Table 5.1 Estimated results of the elasticity coefficients of the trade equations

Elastic coefficient	Estimated value	Standard deviation	T value	P
	0.961126	0.16336	5.883478	0
	4.135089	0.580811	7.119502	0
	1.072	0.223351	4.799622	0.0001
	1.269866	0.239947	5.292276	0

Note: Our estimated trade elasticity result differs slightly from that of Hu Chuntian and Chen Zhiyan (2009). Our elasticity of exchange rates with respect to exports is less than 1 while that of Hu and Chen is larger than 1; and our elasticity of exchange rates with respect to imports is larger than 1, while that of Hu and Chen is less than 1. The discrepancy may be attributable to the choice of different time sequences.

surplus-to-GDP ratio (BA), net foreign assets-to-GDP ratio (NFA)[4], and current account-to-GDP ratio (CA). Our equation was as follows (10):

$$CA = -30.273 + 3.694 * DEP + 1.586 * BA - 0.096 * NFA \qquad (10)$$
$$\;\;\;(0.771)\quad 1.24 \qquad\quad 0.534 \qquad\quad 0.099$$

From the above equation, we note that several elements move in the same direction, namely government fiscal surplus, degree of age disparity, and current account. Moreover, we see that they move in an opposite direction to net foreign assets. In recent years, the rapid rise of China's net foreign assets has put increasing pressure on the RMB to appreciate. This means that the current account surplus must decline (if we don't take other things into account). When one takes into consideration the aging of China's population, however, and the intensified demand for pensions for the elderly, we feel there is a need for the country to preserve a certain level of reserves. This in turn takes up a certain amount of the increase in the current account (again, not taking other things into account). By substituting the HP-filtered data as an independent variable into Equation (10), we are able to arrive at a calculation of the equilibrium current account (see Figure 5.1).

Our calculation of the Fundamental Equilibrium Exchange-rate (FEER), and resulting analysis

By using Equations (2) and (3), we calculated the trade elasticity coefficient and equilibrium current account level, then derived the output discrepancy between domestic and foreign GDP (post-HP-filtering). Based on the FEER model, and using Equation (8), we derived a 'real equilibrium exchange rate' for the RMB, as well as the degree to which the effective exchange rate of the RMB was out of line (see Figures 5.2 and 5.3).

It can be seen from Figure 5.3 that the degree to which China's real effective exchange rate has been misaligned stayed within 20 percent since 1986. Since 1994, when the two different exchange rates were unified, the degree of misalignment

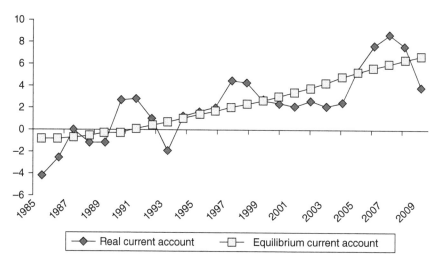

Figure 5.1 The 'actual' and the 'equilibrium' level of the current account between the years 1985 and 2009.

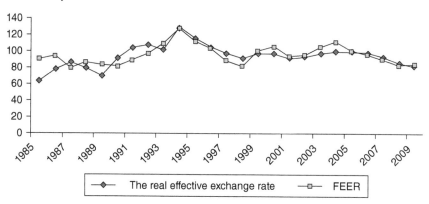

Figure 5.2 The index of the 'real effective exchange rate' versus the FEER index, from 1985 to 2009.

has remained within 13 percent. Since the exchange-rate reform of 2005, during the period that is the focus of our attention here, the degree of misalignment has been kept within 4 percent. With respect to these results, it can be said that the reform was relatively successful.

In 1994, the RMB underwent a large, single-event, depreciation against the US dollar (from RMB 5.762 per dollar in 1993 to RMB 8.169 per dollar in 1994). Following that event, China's current account balance rose between the years 1995 and 1998, leading to an undervalued effective rate of the RMB. Between 1999 and 2004, however, the currencies of China's neighboring countries depreciated substantially under the impact of the East Asian financial crisis. China's RMB exchange-rate in contrast remained stable, which had the effect of lowering the

(%)

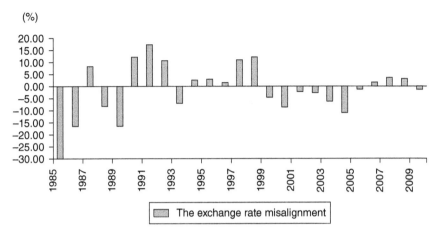

Figure 5.3 The degree to which the RMB was misaligned, between 1985 and 2009 (when greater than 0, the RMB is undervalued).

competitiveness of the country's exports. The disparity between China's real current account and its equilibrium current account was negative, resulting in an effective RMB exchange rate that was then over-valued. Between 2005 and 2008, it was again slightly under-valued, whereas in 2009 it was slightly over-valued. Since the misalignment remained within 4 percent, the effective exchange rate during this period could be viewed as reasonable. Compared to the results derived by Wang Yizhong and Jin Xuejun (2008), our results for the RMB exchange rate as calculated above show a much lower degree of misalignment.

A potential predetermination of the (proper) equilibrium exchange rate for the period between 2010 and 2015

The basic thinking behind coming up with a 'predetermined equilibrium exchange rate' is to derive an equilibrium exchange rate that corresponds to an equilibrium in domestic and foreign economies, as defined by the equilibrium current account of the future and the total domestic and overseas output.

Or, it is to find an exchange rate level that is compatible with the actual current account of the future and domestic and overseas levels of output. This idea stands in contrast to the already-existing idea of an *ex post facto* derivation of the equilibrium exchange rate. The concept involves deriving an exchange rate (an equilibrium exchange rate) that conforms to the trajectory of future economic changes as a way to ensure that the exchange rate is appropriate for those changes. This is in contrast to an *ex post facto* derivation of equilibrium exchange rates as a way to adjust existing economic realities.

Using equation (8), and taking 2009 as the base year, we first calculated the beta-value, which was 4.03 (ß was 4.03, meaning the real effective exchange rate will rise by 4.03 percentage points if the current account (CA) drops by one percentage point). We then made assumptions about the percentage of equilibrium current account between the years 2010 and 2015, and the potential output of China's GDP as well as that of other countries. With the results, we were able to calculate the FEER of the RMB for the years between 2010 and 2015.

Our assumptions about domestic and overseas GDP output for the relevant years were generated by an auto-regression model. The specific results had a high 'fit' and passed relevant residual tests. Our assumptions about the current account balance were stated in terms of their percentage of China's predetermined policy goals for the years 2010 to 2015. Using Equation (7), we then calculated the predetermined 'Fundamental Equilibrium Effective exchange-rate' and its degree of bias with respect to the actual real effective exchange rate of 2009. In what follows, we analyze five different scenarios (see Table 5.2).

First, the target percentage of the equilibrium current account for 2015 was set at 3.0 percent as per the work of Cline & Williamson (2010). Between 2010 and 2014, the percentage was estimated by interpolating between the years 2009 (when it was 6.68 percent) and 2015.

Second, given the fact that China's current account as a percentage of GDP was an average 2.3 percent between the years 1985 and 2009, we hypothesized a situation where the percentage was 2.5 percent in the year 2015. For the intervening years, we interpolated as well.

Third, we assumed that the current account balance in 2015 was level, and then interpolated the data for the intervening years.

Fourth, given that China's exports already constitute an extremely large share of GDP, we lowered the elasticity of exports between 2010 and 2015 by one standard deviation. At the same time, we made the assumption that China's current account goal for 2015 would be 3.0 percent of GDP. We calculated the figures from 2010 to 2014 by interpolation.

Fifth, we lowered the elasticity of exports by one standard deviation, kept the current account balance even in 2015, and used the interpolation method for the years 2010–2014.

For details on the extent to which the real effective exchange rate of the RMB would need to appreciate in 2010, 2011, 2012, 2013, 2014, and 2015, see Table 5.3.

Integrating the above five scenarios, we feel that a reasonable degree of RMB appreciation would lie somewhere between the results of Scenario 1 and Scenario 5. For this realistic appraisal of the real effective exchange rate for the

Table 5.2 Policy targets for the current account under different scenarios, for the years between 2011 and 2015

Scenario	2011	2012	2013	2014	2015
CA at 3%	5.45%	4.84%	4.23%	3.61%	3%
CA at 2.5%	5.28%	4.59%	3.89%	3.19%	2.5%
CA at 0	4.45%	3.34%	2.23%	1.11%	0%

Table 5.3 Extent to which the real effective exchange rate of the RMB would need to appreciate under different scenarios, 2010 to 2015

Scenario	2010	2011	2012	2013	2014	2015
CA at 3%	2.68%	3.09%	4.42%	6.57%	9.52%	13.26%
CA at 2.5%	3.15%	4.03%	5.83%	8.45%	11.87%	16.08%
CA at 0	4.69%	7.12%	10.5%	14.63%	19.59%	25.34%
CA at 3%, and n declined by one standard deviation	0.23%	-0.1%	0.45%	1.71%	3.62%	6.19%
CA at 0, and n declined by one standard deviation	2.25%	3.95%	6.49%	9.76%	13.69%	18.27%

RMB, see Figure 5.4. In 2010, the real effective exchange rate of RMB fluctuated between 81.07 and 81.42, and the RMB needed to appreciate by 2.25 percent–2.68 percent. In 2015, the rate may decline to 70.39–73.51, which means it should appreciate by 13.26 percent–18.27 percent. According to the effective exchange rate index released by the Bank for International Settlements (BIS), China's real effective exchange rate index in October 2010 was 114.12, meaning that it had appreciated by 1.74 compared with the end of 2009. Between now and the end of the 12th Five-Year Plan, China's real effective exchange rate index should appreciate by about 11.52 percent~16.53 percent. The sequence of appreciation for each year between 2011 and 2015 would be as follows: 0.4 percent–1.64 percent, 1.26 percent–2.39 percent, 2.03 percent–2.97 percent, 2.69 percent–3.45 percent and 3.3 percent–3.88 percent.

Based on a 'predetermined equilibrium exchange rate,'
an analysis of the extent of bilateral RMB appreciation
against select currencies

The real effective exchange rate as described above was derived from the weighted nominal exchange rates and inflation rates of 17 countries. As such, it indicates a desired appreciation of the RMB by some 11.52 percent to 16.53 percent by the year 2015. This is not the same as saying that the RMB should appreciate against the US dollar or other individual currencies to the same degree. Individual bilateral exchange rates can be set, however, in a way that has the result of an overall effective exchange rate of that amount. Since the 'predetermined equilibrium exchange rate' is determined under the assumption of domestic and foreign economic equilibrium, for the purpose of simplification, the appreciation of the nominal exchange rate of the RMB against other currencies can be determined using the degree to which trade with those countries is imbalanced.

Table 5.4 gives China's trade imbalances with major trading partners as a percentage of total trade imbalances. The percentages are listed from the largest

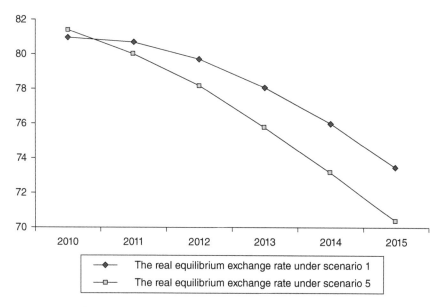

Figure 5.4 A forecast of appreciation of the real equilibrium exchange rate of the RMB
between 2010 and 2015, using Scenario 1 and Scenario 5 as described above.

down to the smallest, so one can quickly see that the highest bilateral imbalances
are with Hong Kong and the United States. After that come Taiwan and South
Korea.

In what follows, we begin to consider different scenarios for bilateral exchange-
rate changes of the RMB against various individual currencies. We first present
our assumptions.

First, we assume that the trade weighting remains the same. Second, we do not
take into consideration the depreciation of the RMB exchange rates induced by
China's trade deficits with Japan, South Korea, Taiwan (China), and so on. We
only take into consideration the factors of exchange-rate appreciation of the RMB
vis-à-vis the US dollar, the Hong Kong dollar, the Euro and the pound. Third, we
assume that the rate at which prices rise inside China will exceed the weighted
average of price increases in other countries. We put China's average inflation rate
at 3 percent. We put that of the United States, England, and other such countries
and regions at an average 2 percent. Given these assumptions, we come up with
the following trajectory of RMB appreciation for three different policy scenarios.

The first allows for RMB exchanges rates against the US dollar, the Hong
Kong dollar, the Euro, and the pound to appreciate to the same degree. The
second allows for nominal RMB appreciation against a given currency as the
degree of trade imbalance with that country increases. The third allows for RMB
appreciation against a given currency as the degree of trade imbalance with that
country declines.

Table 5.4 Bilateral trade imbalances as a percentage of total trade imbalances
Units: percentages

	Sino- Hong Kong	Sino- US	Sino- Netherlands	Sino- Britain	Sino- Italy	Sino- France	Sino- Taiwan	Sino- South Korea	Sino- Japan
2005	27.1	27.6	5.5	3.2	1.2	0.6	14*	10.1*	4*
2006	27.6	27.6	5.2	3.3	1.4	0.5	12.7*	8.6*	4.6*
2007	27.1	25.8	5.8	3.8	1.7	1.1	12.2*	7.5*	5*
2008	26.8	25.8	6.1	4	2.3	1.2	11.7*	5.8*	5.2*
2009	26.1	23.7	5.2	3.9	1.5	1.4	10.8*	8.1*	5.5*
2010+	12.3	19.8	2.8	2.5	2	2.1	7.9	10.5	15.8

Note: The total trade imbalance represents the sum of bilateral trade imbalances with this specific sample of countries. If the imbalance showed the trading partner having a trade deficit, then the absolute values of the imbalances were added. Items with an asterisk refer to trade deficits of China with respect to those countries. Item 2010+ indicates the percentage of China's total foreign trade in goods that is taken up by each sample country for the years 2005 to 2009.

Specific policy scenarios are represented in Tables 5.5 and 5.6. The foreign exchange rates quoted on September 21, 2010, were taken as the benchmark figures. In 2010, the nominal exchange rate of the RMB against the US dollar ranged from 6.6080 to 6.6292, which should have appreciated by 0.56 percent to 1.37 percent; and the nominal exchange rate of the RMB against the Euro ranged from 9.1622 to 9.2345, which should have depreciated by 4.68 percent to 6.61 percent. In 2015, the nominal exchange rate of the RMB against the US dollar will range from about 5.4153 to 5.7575, which should appreciate by 14.06 percent to 19.17 percent; and that of the RMB against Euro will range from about 7.2723 to 8.0374, which should appreciate by 8.17 percent to 16.91 percent.

Analysis of RMB exchange rates using the BEER model, or the 'Behavioral Equilibrium Exchange-rate Theory'

The original theory behind this model

In 1995, Brad McDonald of the International Monetary Fund proposed the BEER theory, with an underlying equation as follows:

$$q_t = \alpha_1 L_t + \alpha_2 M_1 + \beta S_t + \mu_t \tag{11}$$

Table 5.5 Appreciation of the RMB against specific currencies by the year 2010, under scenarios 1, 2, and 3

	RMB/USD	RMB/HKD	RMB/GBP	RMB/EUR
The exchange rates quoted on 21 Sept.2010	6.6997	0.8629	10.42	8.7522
Plan 1: Appreciation of the bilateral exchange rates (%)	1.05	0.89	0.42	−5.5
The bilateral exchange rates which should be reached in 2010	6.6292	0.8552	10.376	9.2345
The real effective exchange rate of 2010		81.07		
Plan 2: Appreciation of the bilateral exchange rates (%)	1.37	1.21	−0.93	−6.61
The bilateral exchange rates which should be reached in 2010	6.6080	0.8525	10.5171	9.2830
The real effective exchange rate of 2010		81.07		
Plan 3: Appreciation of the bilateral exchange rates (%)	0.56	0.40	2.47	−4.68
The bilateral exchange rates which should be reached in 2010	6.6620	0.8594	10.1621	9.1622
The real effective exchange rate of 2010		81.07		

Table 5.6 Appreciation of the RMB against specific currencies by the year 2015, under scenarios 1, 2, and 3

	RMB/USD	RMB/HKD	RMB/GBP	RMB/EUR
Exchange rate quoted on 21 Sept. 2010	6.6997	0.8629	10.42	8.7522
Plan 1: Appreciation of the bilateral exchange rates (%)	17.14	17.01	16.62	11.65
The bilateral exchange rates which should be reached in 2015	5.5512	0.7161z	8.6887	7.7328
The real effective exchange rates of 2015		71.25		
Plan 2: Appreciation of the bilateral exchange rates (%)	19. 17	19.04	8. 03	8. 17
The bilateral exchange rates which should be reached in 2015	5.4153	0. 6986	9. 5837	8. 0374
The real effective exchange rate of 2015		71.26		
Plan 3: Appreciation of the bilateral exchange rates (%)	14.06	13. 93	29. 65	16.91
The bilateral exchange rates which should be reached in 2015	5. 7575	0. 7427	7. 3308	7. 2723
The real effective exchange rate of 2015		71.24		

In this equation, L refers to the vector of basic economic factors that influence the exchange rate over the long term. M refers to medium-term influences, and S refers to short-term as well as ad hoc influences. μ refers to random disturbance terms.

Referring to Equation (4), we can see that the real exchange can be interpreted in its entirety by these four factors. We can therefore define the 'current real equilibrium exchange rate' as q'.

$$q_t^{'} = \alpha_{L_t} + \alpha_2 M_t \qquad (12)$$

The current misalignment of the real effective exchange rate (cm_t) can be defined as the disparity between the actually observed exchange rate and the current real equilibrium exchange rate. This can be expressed as:

$$cm_t = q_t - q_t^{'} \qquad (13)$$

Since basic economic factors tend to deviate from their own long-term level of equilibrium, the long-term real equilibrium exchange can be defined as:

$$q_t^{*} = \alpha_1 L^{*} + \alpha_2 M^{*} \qquad (14)$$

The definition of real, long-term, effective exchange-rate imbalance can be defined as pm, expressed as follows:

$$pm = a_t - q_t^*$$

(15)

A quantitative model and selection of appropriate variables

In selecting the right economic variables to represent 'fundamentals' in order to derive an equilibrium exchange rate for the RMB, Shi Jianhuai and Yu Haifeng (2005) felt that three specific factors should be taken into account. The first was the BEER theoretical model, and the variables that it required as described in the literature. The second was the accessibility of actual data. The third was the specific set of circumstances in China. We selected fundamental variables by integrating the methods proposed by Qin Duo and He Xinhua (2010) and by Shi Jianhuai and Haifeng (2005). Our variables were: relative per capita income (RY), share of net foreign assets (NFA), and degree of openness (OPEN).

In order to facilitate comparison of results with FEER, we used the same method of determining the real effective exchange rate. Please see Equation (9) and its explanation.

Relative per capita income (RY): this is a relatively direct indicator for measuring the disparity between domestic and foreign productivity growth, which is quoted to illustrate the Balassa-Samuelson Effect.

$$RY = \ln (Y) - \Sigma_{i=1}^{17} \omega_t \ln (Y_i)$$

(16)

Net foreign assets (NFA): this is an indicator for capturing external environmental factors, which we defined as the net foreign assets-to-GDP ratio. For specific equations in this calculation, please refer to the above explanation.

Openness (OPEN): this is an indicator for capturing trade policy factors, which we adopt to describe the opening-up (or liberalizing) policies of a country. This measures the total value of foreign trade as a percentage of GDP.

We used a sample size of twenty-eight items, and looked at these over the period from 1982 to 2009.

The process of applying the BEER model, and its results

The process of applying the model and coming up with projections included the following: (1) a 'unit root test,' (2) a co-integration test, and (3) an error correction. Part (2) of this process utilized the Johansen co-integration method when we estimated the number of co-integration relationships, but it used the Engle-Granger two-step method for other processes.

(1) Unit root test

From Table 5.7, we can learn that REER, TNT, NFA and OPEN are all integrated of order; therefore they can be tested by the co-integration test.

(2) Co-integration test

We first calculated an unrestricted vector auto-regression (VAR for short). Table 5.8 lists the diagnostics of system VAR (2) which stood the heteroskedasticity test, the autocorrelation tests from 1 to 4, and the normal test.

Then we conducted a co-integration test of VAR (2). Please refer to Table 5.9. From Table 5.9, we can see either the trace statistics or the maximum eigenvalue statistics indicated the existence of one and the only co-integration equation. Therefore, we could go on to conduct a static regression.

Lastly, we conducted a static regression, using the ordinary least squares method. We tested the residual sequence of the regression results by using an ADF unit root test. For the test results, please refer to Table 5.10 (Results of the ADF test on the residuals of the regression equation). The residual sequence remained stable. For the auto-regression equation, please refer to Equation (17). From this, we see that the real equilibrium exchange rate of the RMB is determined by three major long-term factors, including RY (relative income), NFA (net foreign assets-to-GDP ratio) and OPEN (degree of openness). Their correlations with the RMB real equilibrium exchange rate are as follows: an increase in NFA and OPEN

Table 5.7 Unit root tests of the REER, RY, NFA, and OPEN

	Intercept	Time trend	Lag order	ADF statistics	10% critical value
REER	Y	Y	2	−1.735923	−3.22923
RY	Y	Y	2	−1.005451	−3.229230
NFA	Y	Y	2	−0.410055	−3.22923
OPEN	N	N	2	−0.203894	−1.609329
D (REER)	Y	Y	2	−4.970380	−4.356068
D (RY)	Y	Y	2	−5.267479	−4.374307
D (NFA)	Y	Y	2	−4.422499	−4.356068
D (OPEN)	N	N	2	−2.685617	−2.656915

Table 5.8 VAR (2) Model evaluation diagnostics

Multivariate diagnostic test				
Auto-correlation LM test	LM (1)	LM (2)	LM (3)	LM (4)
20.51245	22.3342	17.30768	21.13283	20.51245
	(0.1328)[①]	(0.3660)	(0.1735)	(0.198)
Heteroskedasticity test	$X^2 (160) = 182.2031$ (0.1103)			
Jarque–Bera normal test	$X^2 (8) = 11.15512$ (0.1931)			

Note: Numbers in brackets refer to P values.

Table 5.9 Results of the co-integration test of VAR (2)

Co-integration rank	Trace statistic	5% Critical value	Prob.
None *	60.80873	47.85613	0.0019
At most 1	26.41610	29.79707	0.1168
At most 2	8.301526	15.49471	0.4337
At most 3	0.217135	3.841466	0.6412
Co-integration rank No. of CE (s)	Maximum eigenvalue statistic	5% Critical value	Prob. **
None *	34.39263	27.58434	0.0057
At most 1	18.11457	21.13162	0.1256
At most 2	8.084391	14.26460	0.3702
At most 3	0.217135	3.841466	0.6412

Table 5.10 Results of the ADF tests of the residuals of the regression equation

		t - Statistic	Prob.*
Augmented Dickey – Fuller test statistic		−4.205807	0.0002
Test critical values:	1% level	−2.656915	
	5% level	−1.954414	
	10% level	−1.609329	

leads to a decline in the RMB real equilibrium exchange rate, while an increase in RY results in a rise in the RMB real equilibrium exchange rate.

$$REER = -0.904 * RF + 0.023 * NFA + 0.009 * OPEN + 0.133 * TD + 0.955$$
$$(0.067) \quad (0.003) \quad (0.002) \quad (0.036) \quad (0.221)$$
$$R^2 = 0.951. \tag{17}$$

(3) Error correction

For the error correction equation, please refer to Equation (18) below. In this Equation, the ECM actually is the first-order lag of the residuals of the regression equation (17), which is called error correction term whose coefficient is −0.319 (with the absolute value less than 1). The coefficient reflects the dynamic self-correcting mechanism of the error correction model. If the equilibrium exchange rate is lower than the real effective exchange rate (ECM <0) in the previous year, which means the exchange rate is undervalued, then the long-term REER will depreciate in the following year, for the coefficient of the error correction term is positive. It is evident that the larger the coefficient of the error correction term, the stronger the ability of the system to correct itself. When the coefficient reaches 1, the exchange rate misalignment of the year can be completely straightened out.

$$D(REER) = -0.319ECM(-1) - 0.845D\ (RY) + 0.007D\ (NFA)$$
$$+0.003D(OPEN) + 0.039 \tag{18}$$

Calculating and analyzing the degree to which the real exchange rate is out of alignment

Measuring long-term misalignment of the real exchange rate

In order to derive a long-term equilibrium rate for the RMB, it is necessary to understand the lasting effect of economic fundamentals on the real equilibrium rate. The long-term equilibrium value of economic fundamentals therefore needs to be calculated, and to do that, we used HP-filters to extract the long-term equilibrium value of three specific economic-fundamentals variables, namely capita income (RY), degree of openness of the economy (OPEN), and net foreign assets (NFA). We substituted the filtered economic-fundamentals variables into Equation 15 in order to derive the long-term RMB real equilibrium exchange rate.

Figure 5.5 presents the results: the actual real effective exchange rate, as contrasted to the long-term equilibrium real effective exchange rate, over a certain period of time. The formula for calculating the degree of long-term misalignment is: Long-term misalignment of the actual real effective exchange rate = (actual real effective exchange rate − long-term real equilibrium exchange rate)/long-term real equilibrium exchange rate × 100 percent.

Figure 5.6 illustrates the long-term misalignment of the actual real effective exchange rate.

Analysis of the degree of misalignment of the actual real effective exchange rate, (that is, the degree of deviation of the 'actual' from a long-term hypothetical equilibrium)

From Figures 5.5 and 5.6, we can see that China's actual real effective exchange rate fluctuated around the long-term equilibrium effective exchange rate with a deviation of less than 20 percent. In 1994, China unified its two exchange rates, whereupon the RMB depreciated sharply against the US dollar, leading to an undervaluation of the actual real effective exchange rate for that year of 17.4 percent. In 1997, the Asian financial crisis led to a promise by China in 1998 that China would not devalue its currency, which led to an overvaluation of the actual real effective exchange rate of 13.1 percent. After these events, the actual real effective exchange rate of the RMB remained within a 10 percent deviation from the long-term equilibrium effective rate. Notably, after the exchange-rate reform of 2005, the deviation remained within 6.2 percent.

The RMB did exhibit a certain degree of appreciation after the exchange-rate reform of 2005, and this accelerated in the second half of 2007 and the first half of 2008. Corresponding to this, the actual real effective exchange rate of the RMB went from a previous undervaluation to a slight overvaluation, starting in 2008. The overvaluation was modest, however, only around 2 percent. In overall terms, the exchange-rate reform of 2005 was successful.

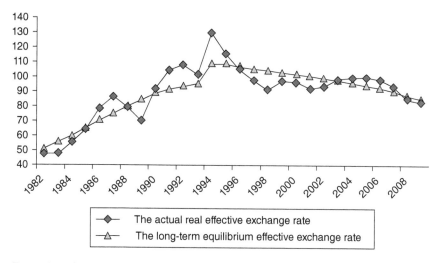

Figure 5.5 The actual real effective exchange rate, as contrasted to the long-term equilibrium effective exchange rate, between 1982 and 2010.

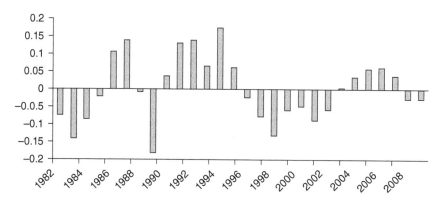

Figure 5.6 The degree of long-term 'misalignment' of the actual real effective exchange rate.

The Enhanced Purchasing Power Parity method

The model itself

The theoretical basis for the Enhanced Purchasing Power Parity approach to evaluating exchange rates comes from the Balassa-Samuelson Effect. This Effect says that if a country's productivity grows faster than other countries, then its currency will appreciate against those of other countries, when productivity is measured by the productivity ratio of traded sectors to non-traded sectors in a country's economy. The productivity of traded sectors generally grows faster than that of non-traded sectors. According to this theoretical Effect, the process of 'overtaking' other economies will be accompanied by an appreciation of that country's real exchange rate. Because of this, the Extended Purchasing Power Parity method generally uses 'cross-section data' or 'panel data' in regressing per-capita income (demonstrating the Balassa-Samuelson Effect) in order to calculate the real exchange rate. The result of the regression is the real equilibrium exchange rate. Some scholars have integrated other variables into the model, in addition to per-capita income. These have been demonstrated either by theory or experience to influence real exchange rates and they include net foreign assets (NFA), the degree of openness (OPEN), and a country's terms of trade.

With respect to the Balassa-Samuelson Effect, our research mainly took into consideration the effective exchange-rate indexes of 58 countries and regions as verified by the Bank for International Settlements (BIS). These are comprehensive exchange-rate indexes of a given country's currency against a basket of currencies, and so differ from the normal bilateral rates.

Our model relied primarily on the models of Bergin et al. (2004) and Rogoff (1996), as represented by the following equation:

$$\ln RER_{i,t} = \beta_0 + \beta_1 \ln RY_{i,t} + z_{i,t} \Gamma + \alpha_i + \mu_t + \varepsilon_{i,t}$$

In this equation, $RER_{i,t}$ is the effective exchange rate index of Country i of Issue t; $RY_{i,t}$ refers to the RY of Country i of Issue t; Z refers to other explanatory variables; a_i refers to specific effects of Country i.; μ_t refers to the time effect; and ε refers to the residuals.

Apart from RY, some explanatory variables that are thought to have great impact on the medium- and long-term real exchange rate were also taken into consideration. They are openness (trade), government expenditure (govern) and investments (invest). Generally speaking, the freer the trade, the lower the real exchange rate, for trade restrictions (mainly on imports) will result in a rise in prices of imports and non-tradable products. In contrast with private investments, government spending is more likely to go to non-tradable products. Therefore, the higher the level of government spending, the higher the actual exchange rate is. As for investments, the higher the ratio of capital to labor, the higher the resulting productivity and salaries, and the higher the real exchange rate.

Explanation of data

We collected the annual panel data of the effective exchange rate indexes of 57 countries and regions as released by the Bank of International Settlements. (Since data from countries in the Eurozone was already included, we excluded the data of the European Union as a single unit.) We used that to calculate the equilibrium effective exchange rates of RMB against other currencies in the period between 1994 and 2009. The total number of recorded samples was 771.

'Relative per-capita income,' or RP, is the ratio of per capita income of Country i to the weighted per capita income of other countries of the same year. This is calculated by multiplying one country's trade weight (the ratio of the total foreign trade volume of each country to that of all sample countries) by its per capita income. As with other research studies, trade is represented by the percentage of the total foreign trade volume to the GDP; govern is illustrated by the percentage of the government expenditure to the GDP; and invest by the percentage of investments to the GDP.

The empirical results

First, the regression results were calculated by using the following equation:

$$\text{In}RER_{i.t} = -3.587221 + 0.0282626\text{In}RY_{i.t} + 0.0160483 \text{ govern}$$
$$+ 0.007251\text{invest} - 0.0023561 \text{ trade}$$

Estimated coefficients are evident when below 1 percent, R2 is 0.1463, and the regression coefficient symbols of all indexes accord with the expected economic meaning. According to the regression results, the RMB real equilibrium exchange rate and the misalignment can be calculated. Since the fundamental factors which determine the real exchange rate are not necessarily at the equilibrium point, to calculate the long-term real equilibrium exchange rate, we have to calculate the equilibrium values of these fundamental factors. We smoothed these fundamental factors with the commonly used HP filter to get their equilibrium values. In this case, in Figure 5.7, the ERER curve illustrates the estimated values of the indexes

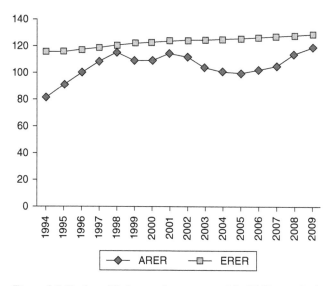

Figure 5.7 Real equilibrium exchange rates of the RMB as calculated by the EPPP.

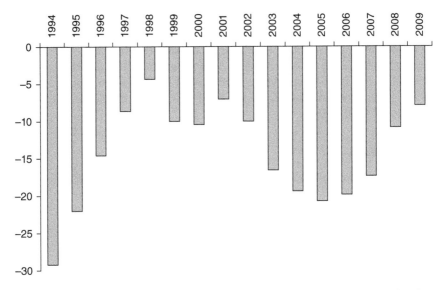

Figure 5.8 The misalignment of the RMB real equilibrium exchange rate as calculated
by the EPPP.

of the RMB real equilibrium exchange rates and the ARER indicates the indexes
of the RMB real effective exchange rates.

Having calculated the estimated real equilibrium exchange rate, the
misalignment of the real exchange rate can be measured by the following equation:

$$MIS = (ARER - ERER)/ERER \times 100$$

The real exchange rate is undervalued when the MIS is negative and is overvalued
when the MIS is positive. The misalignment of RMB real exchange rate is
illustrated by Figure 5.8. It can be seen that, although the RMB was undervalued
by some extent, the degree of undervaluation has been considerably reduced since
2005.

Determining the equilibrium level of the RMB exchange rate, and some policy recommendations with respect to that rate

This study used three different methods to calculate the 'actual equilibrium
exchange rate' of the RMB, namely the FEER, the BEER and the EPPP. The
three methods result in some discrepancies, with results of the FEER and BEER
being somewhat closer in value. These two indicate that China's actual real
effective exchange rate had periods when it was over-valued and periods when
it was under-valued, and that the degree of misalignment in either direction was
within 10 percent in most years. Both these methods indicate that the RMB has

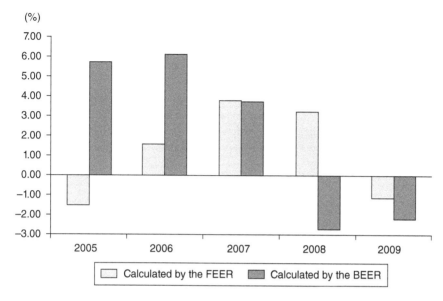

Figure 5.9 Comparison of the degree of misalignment of the RMB equilibrium rate, as calculated by the FEER method and the BEER method.

already now appreciated to an appropriate level. It is even slightly over-valued (but within 3 percent). Both methods indicate that the exchange-rate reform of 2005 was a success (see Figure 5.9). In contrast, the EPPP method indicates that the actual real effective exchange rate of the RMB has been consistently under-valued. Nevertheless, since the 2005 reform, the extent of this under-valuation has declined considerably (it went from 20.63 percent in 2005 to 7.93 percent in 2009). Integrating these three methods, we conclude that the actual effective exchange rate of the RMB right now lies within a relatively appropriate range. The rate requires neither a great appreciation nor a great depreciation.

Policy recommendations

First, by 2010 (the time of this writing), the equilibrium effective exchange rate of the RMB had appreciated slightly over the rate of 2009, by between 2.25 per-cent and 2.68 percent. By the end of the 12th Five-Year Plan period, the actual effective exchange-rate index will appreciate by between 11.52 percent and 16.53 percent. Within this period, it will appreciate by the following ranges in the fol-lowing years: 0.4 percent to 1.64 percent in 2011, 1.26 percent to 2.39 percent in 2012, 2.03 percent to 2.97 percent in 2013, 2.69 percent to 3.45 percent in 2014, and 3.3 percent to 3.88 percent in 2015.

Second, in 2010, the nominal exchange rate of the RMB vis-à-vis the US dollar was roughly between 6.6080 and 6.6292. The nominal exchange rate of the RMB vis-à-vis the Euro was roughly between 9.1622 and 9.2345. If we take the officially declared foreign exchange rate as quoted on September 21, 2010 as the baseline, by 2015 the nominal exchange rate of the RMB vis-à-vis the US dollar will have appreciated by between 14.06 percent and 19.17 percent. It will then be roughly between 5.4153 and 5.7575 to the US dollar. It will have appreciated against the Euro by between 8.17 percent and 16.91 percent, and will then be roughly between 7.2723 and 8.0374 to the Euro.

Third, (we recommend that) the government put out an 'effective exchange-rate index' of the RMB, and that it make this public on a regular basis. This should be done to inform the public, and ensure that people know that the effective exchange rate is reasonable, in order to reduce appreciation pressures on the RMB.

Notes

1 This chapter was co-authored by Liu Yunzhong, Hu Zhiguo, Li Huan, and He Jianwu.
2 This is a single-nation model. The model as developed in 2003 (Borowski and Couharde) and 2005 (Coudert and Couharde) involved three countries.
3 For explanations of the methodology behind this real effective exchange rate, please refer to Borowski and Couharde (2003).
4 Method of calculating the NFA: Statistics disclosed by the State Administration of Foreign Exchange (SAFE) during 2004 and 2009 was quoted. Since SAFE had not disclosed statistics before 2004, the NFA of the previous year was calculated by deducting the current account balance from the NFA of the year.

Bibliography

Bin Zhang. The Equilibrium Exchange Rate of RMB: Single-Equation Model Research of Simplified General Equilibrium, *World Economy*, 2003 (11)

Boqiang Lin. Estimate of RMB Real Equilibrium Exchange Rates and Measurement of Real Exchange Rate Misalignment, *Economic Studies*, 2002 (12)

Borowski, D. and Couharde, C. The Exchange Rate Macroeconomic Balance Approach: New Methodology and Results for the Euro, the Dollar, the Yen and the Pound Sterling, *Open Economics Review*, 2003, 14, 169–190.

Chuntian Hu and Zhijun Chen. Is RMB Over Appreciated? An Empirical International Study on Fundamental Equilibrium Exchange Rates (1994–2008), 2009 (11)

Clark, P. B. and MacDonald, R. Exchange Rates and Economic Fundamentals: A Methodological Comparison of BEERs and FEERs, in MacDonald, R. and Stein, J. (eds), *Equilibrium Exchange Rates*, Kluwer Academic Publishers, 1999.

Cline, W. R. and Williamson, J. Estimate of the Equilibrium Exchange of the Renminbi: Is There a Consensus and if Not, Why Not? in Goldstein, M. and Lardy, N. R. (eds), *Debating China's Exchange Rate Policy*, IIE, 2008, pp. 131–168.

Cline, W. R. and Williamson, J. Estimates of Fundamental Equilibrium Exchange Rates Policy Brief 09–10, Peterson Institute for International Economics, 2009.

Cline, W. R. and Williamson, J. Estimates of Fundamental Equilibrium Exchange Rates Policy Brief 10–15, Peterson Institute for International Economics, 2010.

Duo Qin and Xinhua He. On Measurement of the Disequilibrium of RMB: Definition of Indicators, Calculating Methods and Empirical Analysis, Work Paper of the Statistics Research Laboratory of the Institute of World Economics and Politics of the Chinese Academy of Social Sciences, 2010

Edwards, S. and Savastano, M. Exchange Rates in Emerging Economies: What Do We Know? What Do We Need To Know?, NBER Working Paper No. 7228, 1999.

Jianhuai Shi and Haifeng Yu. The Equilibrium Exchange Rate and the Misalignment of RMB: 1991–2004, *Economic Studies*, 2005 (4)

Xiaopu Zhang. *Theories of RMB Equilibrium Exchange Rates and Model Economic Study*, 1999 (12)

Yizhong Wang and Xuejun Jin. Internal and External RMB Equilibrium Exchange Rates: 1982-2010, *The Journal of Quantitative & Technical Economics*, 2008 (5)

Zetian Wang and Yang Yao. RMB Equilibrium Estimates, *Journal of Financial Research*, 2008 (12)

Appendix

Definition of variables and data sources

1 Variables and data sources of the FEER

The real effective exchange rate is the weighted average of the real bilateral effective exchange rates of a currency against a basket of currencies, which is generally represented in the exponential form. It was 100 in 2005. The increase of the exponent indicates depreciation of the currency, while the decrease indicates appreciation. It is represented by the following equation:

$$R = \sum_{i=1}^{17} \omega_i [E_{d/i} (P_i^* / Pd)]$$

Wi refers to the proportion of China's foreign trade volume with Country i to its total foreign trade volume with all sample countries. Statistics of China's total foreign trade volume with each country are from the Economic Databases for Emerging and Developed Markets (CEIC Data); CPI of China is from the databases of the National Bureau of Statistics of China, recalculated with that of 2005 as the benchmark of 100; and the nominal bilateral exchange rate and the foreign CPIs are from the Bureau Van Dijk – Economist Intelligence Unit Country Data (BVD-EIU Country Data).

X, M, Y, and Y_w respectively refer to the exports, imports, domestic and overseas outputs, respectively. The year 2005 is taken as the base year for X, M, Y, and Y_w. The overseas outputs refer to the total outputs of 17 sample countries. Specific statistics are from the BVD-EIU Country Data.

Current account-GDP ratio (CA): The balance of current account is represented by the net exports of goods and services. Statistics of the net exports of goods and services and the annual GDP of China are from the CEIC Data.

Dependent elderly population (DEP): refers to the proportion of the dependent elderly population to the working population. Statistics of DEP during 1985 and 2008 are from the World Bank database and DEP of 2009 is from an auto-regression calculation.

Fiscal surplus-GDP ratio (BA): Statistics of BA are from the BVD-EIU Country Data.

Net foreign assets-GDP ratio (NFA): Statistics of NFA during 2004 and 2009 are from the statistics released by the National Bureau of Statistics of China. Since NFA data are not available before 2004, NFA of the previous years was calculated by deducting the balance of current account from the NFA of the year.

2 Variables and data sources of the BEER

The real effective exchange rate is the same as above.

Relative per capita income (RY): a relatively direct indicator for measuring the difference between the domestic and foreign productivity growth, which is quoted to illustrate the Balassa-Samuelson Effect.

$$RY = \ln(Y) - \Sigma_{i=1}^{17} \omega_i \ln(Y_i)$$

For the definition of $_i$ and the data sources, please refer to the above mentioned real effective exchange rate; statistics of W_i and per capita income (Y and Y_i) are quoted from the BVD-EIU Country Data.

Net foreign assets-GDP ratio (NFA): please refer to the variables and data sources of the FEER.

Openness (OPEN): an indicator for capturing the trade policy factors, which represents the opening up policies of a country as the ratio of the total foreign trade volume to its GDP. Statistics of China's total foreign trade volume and the GDP are from the CEIC Data.

3 Variables and data sources of the EPP

The basic equation is as follows:

$$\ln RER_{i,t} = \beta_0 + \beta_1 \ln RY_{i,t} + Z_{i,t} \Gamma + \alpha_i + \mu_t + \omega_{i,t}$$

$RER_{i,t}$ refers to the effective exchange rate index of Country i of Issue t. Statistics of $RER_{i,t}$ are quoted form the website of the Bank of International Settlement.

RY refers to the relative per capita income of Country i of Issue t. It is the ratio of the per capita income of Country i to the weighted per capita income of other sample countries. The weighted per capita income is calculated by timing one country's trade weight (the ratio of the total volume of imports and exports of the country to the total foreign trade volume of all sample countries) with its per capita income. Per capita income and the total foreign trade volume are quoted from the EIU Country Data.

Z refers to other explanatory variables of the openness (trade), government expenditure (govern) and investments (invest).Trade is represented by the percentage of the total foreign trade volume to the GDP; govern is by the percentage of the government expenditure to the GDP; and invest by the percentage of investments to the GDP. Statistics of the 'trade,''govern' and 'invest' are from the BVD-EIU Country Data.

6 China's strategy for reforming its RMB exchange-rate policy and macroeconomic policies in support of that strategy

Wen Jiandong[1]

In July, 2005, China began to improve the mechanisms by which the RMB exchange rate is derived. Guided by the overall principles of 'retaining the initiative, proceeding incrementally, and staying under control,' the policy aimed at a gradual increase in the degree to which market forces set the rate. Since that time, the country's domestic economy and its financial situation have essentially remained stable, which indicates that the 2005 policy reform was generally successful.

When the global financial crisis worsened in 2008, China narrowed the band within which the RMB was allowed to trade. Between June of 2008 and June of 2010, the exchange rate of the RMB vis-à-vis the US dollar was kept in a tighter range that fluctuated between 6.82 and 6.84. Once the crisis had calmed down, the People's Bank of China decided to resume the process of reforming RMB exchange-rate formation mechanisms. On June 19, 2010, it made a determination to increase the elasticity of the rate by broadening the band within which it can trade.

Nevertheless, there has been much discussion about how far this process of reforming the RMB exchange rate should go. It is now necessary to re-evaluate our policies, given financial and economic circumstances both at home and abroad, and think of how to handle the RMB exchange rate in the future.

Main factors affecting the general trend of the RMB exchange rate

The RMB has appreciated by a total of 21 percent against the US dollar since the start of the 2005 exchange-rate reform. According to data provided by the Bank for International Settlements (BIS), the 'real effective exchange rate' of the RMB in May of 2010 was 120, which was 23 percent higher than it had been in June of 2005. From the fourth quarter of 2008 to May of 2010, the 'average exchange rate' was 119. This was the longest period of time that the rate was sustained at this high level since 1994. During this period, the RMB exchange rate was closer to equilibrium than at any time in the past. The evidence for this comes from the fact that China's current account surplus relative to the country's first quarter GDP in 2010 declined to the equilibrium level of 3.5 percent.

Fluctuations in the RMB rate fundamentally relate to the performance of China's real economy

The strength of a country's currency depends on the fundamentals of that country's economy. How the Chinese economy is performing is therefore a key determinant in the trend of the RMB exchange rate. Since the start of Reform and Opening Up, China's economy has grown rapidly in all sectors, but the manufacturing sector has shown a particularly fast rise in productivity. The speed at which this sector's labor productivity has risen has been notably faster than the average in the rest of the world, including in other newly emerging market economies. Studies made by international organizations show that China's productivity rose by 63.4 percent between 2000 and 2005. This was much faster than India's productivity increase over the same period, 26.9 percent, and also faster than ASEAN's, which was 15.5 percent. There is no doubt that the strong growth of China's economy has provided the underlying economic support for appreciation of China's currency. This also is in line with the theory propounded by the Balassa-Samuelson Effect.

China experienced capital outflows and depreciation of the RMB during both the Asian financial crisis and the global financial crisis of 2008. The reason for this was that the domestic economy at the time was harboring a certain risk of slow-down and deflation. Publicly released economic indicators since October, 2008, for example, demonstrate declining growth to the extent that the trend line is toward negative growth. These indicators include exports, industrial value-added, and fiscal revenue. They show increasing downward pressure on China's economy.

After the third quarter of 2008, the rate at which China's GDP was growing dropped precipitously. It went from an average of 10 percent over the previous three years to 9.6 percent in the third quarter, and then to 6.8 percent in the fourth quarter. Meanwhile, urban unemployment reached 4.2 percent at the end of 2008, which was 0.2 percentage points higher than it had been the previous year. In January of 2009, the growth rate of the Consumer Price Index (CPI) declined drastically to 1.0 percent. The Producer Price Index (PPI) dropped to 3.3 percent.

Given these indicators, in early 2009 the markets feared that a situation similar to that of 1998 might arise if the economy encountered more serious trouble. In 1998, China had a large foreign trade surplus and at the same time experienced massive outflows of capital. The expectation that the RMB would devalue reached 3 percent for a certain period. Beginning in the second quarter of 2009, therefore, the Chinese government adopted a series of policies aimed at stimulating domestic demand. In addition, it adopted an incremental and proactive program of fiscal, tax, and foreign trade measures. Given these measures, markets began to feel that China's economy could return to sound development after all. The RMB exchange rate vis-à-vis the US dollar then returned to its normal path of appreciation.

One direct cause of RMB appreciation has been China's large and ongoing surplus in its balance of international payments

Since 1994, the savings of China's citizens have been growing at a rate that is consistently higher than the rate of domestic investment. Between the years 1982 and 2007, the national savings rate of individuals rose from 36 percent to 50 percent, while the investment rate rose from 34 percent only to 42 percent. The equivalency equation of national income states that [Savings minus Investments = (Current account income such as exports) minus (Current account payments such as imports)]. This can be restated as [Net savings (savings minus investments) = Net exports (the current account surplus)].

Given economic globalization, the transfer of international industries and the restructuring of internal trade within multinationals have been major contributors to China's expanding trade surplus. Statistics indicate that the largest part of China's trade surplus can be attributed to the surplus in processing industries. In the period between 2000 and 2008, the 'contribution rate' of processing trade to the overall trade surplus was 125 percent. Meanwhile, 80 percent of all processing-trade exports were exported out of China by foreign-funded enterprises.

The 'value chain' of multinational companies has therefore been shifting, as well as the international division of labor, in ways that show that China is ever more important as a factory to the world. In addition to this, however, is the fact that China's financial system is not robust. The ability of China's financial sector to draw in funds is far greater than its ability to use those funds in an efficient manner. Objectively speaking, it is simply necessary to have a relatively more efficient overseas financial sector distributing China's savings resources, so that China can turn those domestic savings into investment. Under the joint influence of a variety of factors, capital and financial accounts, as primarily represented by international direct investment, help maintain China's surplus. Since 1999, for over one decade, China's balance of payments has seen a surplus in both the current and the capital account. This has fueled the ongoing expectation that the RMB will appreciate.

The international exchange-rate trends also influence the multilateral RMB exchange rate

Whether the dollar is strong or weak, its condition is transmitted onto the 'effective exchange rate' of the RMB, and thereby also influences expectations of the RMB rate. At the start of the global financial crisis, the US dollar first weakened but then rose sharply as other countries became embroiled in the crisis as well. These included most European countries, Japan, and the newly emerging markets. A phenomenon of de-leveraging then began in the financial industry and continued throughout the crisis. Financial institutions that had pursued highly leveraged instruments began to redeem them in a process known as short covering. Short covering resulted in a decline in the prices of most assets, as well as low liquidity in the financial markets. As demand for liquidity increased, however, risk spreads and liquidity spreads widened. This resulted in a sharp rise in the US dollar exchange rate as de-leveraging continued.

Meanwhile, the de-leveraging led to a freezing of credit in the financial markets, as banks cut back on loans. Short positions on US dollars could only be covered by other market-oriented means. This resulted in a rush for 'corner solutions' of the US dollar, which in turn pushed up the dollar. Within only four months after July, 2008, the dollar had appreciated by over 20 percent relative to other major currencies. This had the effect of pushing up the real effective exchange-rate index of the RMB, which rose by 11.89 percent in 2008.

The international environment brought pressure to bear on the exchange rate of the RMB

By affecting the current-account surplus, the economic and financial situation around the world impacted the RMB exchange rate as well. As the subprime crisis in the United States gradually became a global crisis, and then a global recession, de-stocking and de-leveraging reduced demand. Overseas markets for Chinese goods declined. The Chinese foreign trade situation went into reverse. In November of 2008, for the first time since October, 2001, China's overall figure for monthly imports and exports experienced negative growth. Meanwhile, the monthly rate of increase for imports and exports experienced a 'double decline' for the first time since October of 1998. By January, 2009, imports had declined by 43.1 percent and exports had declined by 17.5 percent over the previous month. The global financial crisis had created a precipitous drop in overseas demand. Export volumes decreased, leading to a negative balance of trade in China. All of these factors resulted in a turnaround in the unilateral appreciation of the RMB.

Global trade protectionism generally brings the RMB exchange rate into play as a point of international friction. In October of 2008, the International Monetary Fund predicted that global economic growth would contract by 0.5 percent in 2009 which was 1.7 percentage points lower than the previous prediction. Within this figure, the IMF estimated that economies of developed countries would decline by 2 percent on average. For the first time since the Second World War, this meant that developed countries would be sliding into recession while developing countries and emerging markets would see lower growth rates, down by 3.3 percent. To combat the effects of the global financial crisis, it was natural for all countries to try to stimulate their own economies. This made it all the more likely that a trade war would be sparked by various kinds of protectionist measures.

At the time of writing, the political reality is that the White House and both houses of Congress are controlled by the more protectionist-minded Democratic Party, which adds to the anxieties. Upon assuming office, Obama passed a stimulus package which forced the inclusion of 'Buy America' provisions as a way to stand up to free trade sentiment both inside and outside the United States. Before leaving his position as Secretary of the Treasury, Henry Paulson put part of the blame for the international financial crisis on China's high savings. The new Secretary of the Treasury, Peter Geithner, has reiterated the comment that China 'manipulates its exchange rate.' Meanwhile, the International Monetary Fund, in order to ensure that it is in coordination with the new administration in the United States, has repeatedly delayed negotiations with China on exchange-rate misalignment. As the country with the largest trade surplus in the world, China has generally become the target for claims that it is responsible for the crisis and that it is endangering national security. It has become the primary victim of trade protectionism. Developing countries, mired in the financial crisis and trade competitors to China, have joined the ranks of such trading blocs as the United States, Japan, and Europe in a collective effort by launching an attack on China's RMB exchange-rate policies as well as a trade war. According to World Bank statistics, in the first quarter of 2010, 47 percent of newly initiated trade investigations and 82 percent of those concluded were either aimed at China or involved China.

The RMB exchange rate cannot help but be influenced by stereotyped thinking. The global economic crisis has inflicted heavy losses on emerging-market countries, leaving many in the midst of recession. For example, at the end of December, 2008, South Korea's foreign exchange reserves declined from USD 268 billion to USD 201.2 billion, while at the same time its foreign debt soared to USD 400 billion. Meanwhile, in Russia, the ruble declined precipitously after July of 2008 and within half a year had depreciated by 12.15 percent. One-quarter of the country's foreign-exchange reserves were used up in the space of three months, falling to a level of USD 450 billion, while Russia's foreign debt rose to USD 430 billion. Foreign investors include China among the emerging-market countries known as BRICs. In 2007, prior to the crisis, China's trade dependency was already at the high rate of 70 percent, higher than the great majority of emerging market economies. Once the crisis began, increased turbulence in global financial markets and general economic decline created international concern about the prospects for China's economic growth. This was transmitted via markets to the expectation for a devaluation of the RMB, which in turn affected the RMB spot exchange rate and the value of China's foreign exchange reserves. In contrast, once the crisis had begun to calm down, the inclination to assume greater risk again rose in international markets. After March of 2009, capital again began moving out of developed countries and toward emerging markets, whose currencies began to appreciate. As a method of quoting prices for the RMB, NDFs again went from a 'premium' to a 'discount,' which means that expectations moved from anticipating depreciation to anticipating appreciation of the RMB. (NDF = non-deliverable forwards.)

The impact of RMB exchange-rate movements on cross-border capital flows

Attempting to evaluate the impact of exchange-rate changes on cross-border capital flows is, in fact, equivalent to evaluating the effectiveness of capital controls. As Dooley (1986) has noted, if capital controls are to be effective, they must be able to maintain disparities between macroeconomic policy systems over a long period of time. Generally speaking, the effectiveness of capital controls should be measured by the extent to which they impact capital flows and enable policy objectives. If they have a notably positive impact on economic variables that can in fact be measured, then they are effective. In judging the effectiveness of capital controls, the two main methods adopted both inside and outside China are a price index and a flow index.

First, we discuss the price index. This judges the degree to which international capital is free to flow by evaluating the sustainability of domestic-overseas price differentials of given financial instruments. The price index measures the long-term consistency of the spread between markets. The most commonly used price index is that of interest-rate spreads. Under normal circumstances, a small spread indicates free flow of capital across borders, whereas a large spread shows that capital flows are restricted. A large spread also can be interpreted to mean that a country maintains a degree of independence in its monetary policies and that its domestic interest rates are not greatly affected by international interest-rate markets. Cheung and his fellow researchers[2] have used models to verify the interest-rate spreads between China and the United States. They believe that restrictions on short-term arbitraging activity are leading to pronounced interest-rate spreads and that these are also long-standing. When an offshore market exists, it is particularly possible to compare interest-rate spreads between offshore and onshore markets. If the spread is higher than zero and indeed quite evident, then this is an argument for the effectiveness of capital controls. Ma Guonan and his research team[3] have compared the yield curves of RMB markets inside and outside China, and have concluded that China's capital controls are still effective. They are continuing to block the convergence of yields at home and abroad. Jin Luo and Li Zinai[4] have studied the US dollar interest rates offered within China and outside China, and have also concluded that China's capital controls are basically effective.

Second, we look at the flow index. This method of analyzing the effectiveness of capital controls evaluates the relationship among a number of influencing factors, including capital flows as related to domestic and overseas interest rates, market expectations, the yields on stocks, and so on. In the absence of capital controls, capital flows rely closely on the above factors. Indeed, there is a certain cause and effect relationship. In addition, Yu Yang and a team of researchers[5] have analyzed the relationship between China's investment and savings. In a situation in which capital is completely liquid, it is not necessary for a country's investment to be derived from funding out of that country's savings. The relationship between investments and savings should be 0. In contrast, the less capital can flow freely in a country, the higher the correlation between that country's savings and investment. Their conclusion was that China's capital controls are effective over the short term but weaker over the longer term.

The impact of RMB exchange-rate movements on the overall situation of capital flows

Based on the two main methods of determining the effectiveness of capital controls, as described above, we conducted empirical analyses with respect to China's specific situation.

The influence of exchange rates on the spread between domestic and foreign interest rates

We selected Chibor as the indicator of RMB interest rates. (We did not choose Shibor since it has a much shorter time sequence and since it has insufficient ability to complete transactions.) Over the period between December of 1996 and August of 2010, we compared the daily data of US versus China interest rates (we used the three-month Chibor rate and the three-month Libor rate, see Figure 6.1). We discovered that the two rates were not synchronized and indeed the coefficient of correlation was only 0.44. However, the spread between the two was demonstrably smaller than it had been in the late 1990s. We then proceeded to conduct a 'Granger causality test,' and concluded that interest rates on the US dollar are a causal factor and an explaining factor for RMB interest rates. At the same time, it should be noted that this could be explained by the fact that China's degree of openness increased after it began Reform and Opening Up, which led to the convergence of the economic cycles of the two countries. The most important thing, however, is that a pronounced spread was maintained between the two sets of interest rates.

When one analyzes the data on RMB interest rates within China and outside China, the conclusion is even more apparent. We looked at the yields on RMB within China (using the one-month Chibor rate), and the yields implied in one-month RMB in offshore NDF markets, and compared the spread. In what follows, we simplify this to the term, the 'interest-rate spread.' The historical data is presented in Figure 6.2. It can be seen that both the spread itself and the volatility of the two rates is fairly large. The quantitative method used in Table 6.1 confirms

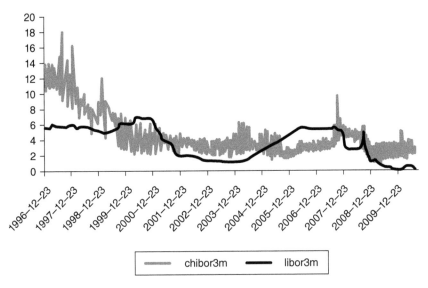

Figure 6.1 Historical data on the spread between Chinese and US interest rates.
Unit: percentage

Source: Reuters, CEIC.

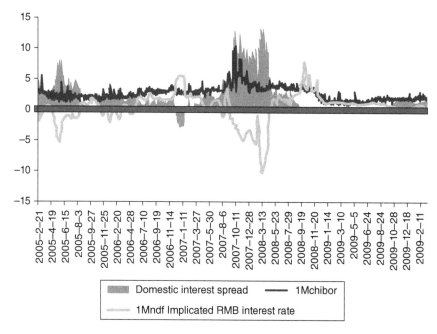

Figure 6.2 Domestic yields of RMB and implied yields of RMB on offshore NDF markets.
Units: percentage

Source: Reuters, CEIC.

that the interest-rate spread is decidedly not 0. In other words, China's capital controls are clearly still effective in maintaining a decisive spread between yields.

The above two analyses support the conclusion that China's capital controls are still effective. It is worth pointing out, however, that China's domestic rates and overseas rates are gradually approaching each other. Since this is an undeniable fact, in order to further verify our point, we analyzed trade flow data as follows.

The relationship between China's surplus in trade-settlement foreign exchange, and the spreads between interest rates, stock yields, and exchange rate expectations inside and outside China

We used the following ways to represent interest rates, stock yields, and expectations in our analysis. We used the difference between purchase and sale of foreign

Table 6.1 Regression analysis of the spread between US and Chinese interest rates

(1)	Spread = 2.95 − 0.004 T (18.35) (−6.87)	Adj −R^2 = 0.10 ; DW = 0.12
(2)	Spread = 3.64D_1 −16.49D_2 −0.009T1 + 0.049T_2 (25.87) (− 15.32) (−11.39) (16.69)	Adj −R^2 = 0.51 ; DW = 0.22

exchange for trade purposes to represent net foreign exchange inflows. (This includes imports and exports, services trade, and also capital accounts.) We used the interest rate of one-year central bank bills (China's central bank) versus the one-year Libor of the US dollar to represent the interest-rate spread between China and the United States. We used the spread in stock yields to represent the spread between asset yields (or return on assets) inside and outside China. We used the spread in one-year foreign and domestic forward discounts to represent the expectation that the RMB will appreciate (foreign NDF discount minus domestic forward discount).

In theory, there should be a positive correlation between net foreign-exchange inflows into China and the spread between US and Chinese interest rates, and there should also be a positive correlation between the spread between domestic and foreign return on assets and the expectation of the RMB to appreciate. In other words, the greater the expectation that the RMB will appreciate, the larger the spread between domestic and foreign return on assets, the greater the spread between Chinese and US interest rates, and the greater the net foreign-exchange inflow into China. We excluded the extra-ordinary effects of the financial crisis. We then selected the interest rates on one-year central bank bills (China's central bank) and the one-year Libor of the US dollar. We looked at data from January of 2000 to the second half of 2008. Table 6.2 illustrates the results. There is no notable correlation among the variables as described above, the China–US interest-rate spread, the spread on stock yields, and the expectations for an appreciating RMB as compared to the difference between purchase and sale of foreign exchange.

To go further in verifying the results as indicated above, in terms of a cause-and-effect relationship among these variables, we then applied a Granger causality test (see Table 6.3). We used the China–US interest-rate spread, the expectations of RMB appreciation,[6] the different between purchase and sale of foreign exchange (after having applied a smoothing test). The results show that there is no clear cause-and-effect correlation among these variables.

The impact of exchange-rate changes (the impact of an appreciating RMB) on speculative capital flows

Despite the results of the empirical analyses as described above, one must admit that speculative capital does seek to arbitrage rates in the context of a globalizing

Table 6.2 Correlation and regression analysis of several variables, namely China–US interest-rate spread, spread on stock yields, and expectation of RMB appreciation

Analytical method	*China–US interest rate spread*	*Stock yield spread*	*Expectation of RMB appreciation*
Correlation analysis	Correlation coefficient = 0.01	Correlation coefficient = 0.14	Correlation coefficient = 0.004
Regression analysis	Goodness of Fit (R^2) = 0	Goodness of Fit (R^2) = 0.014	Goodness of Fit (R^2) = 0

Table 6.3 Results of six different Granger causality tests

No.	Hypothesis	F-statistics	P value
1	China–US interest rate spread is not the explanation or cause of difference of foreign exchange purchase and sale.	0.5594	0.5736
2	Difference of foreign exchange purchase and sale is not the explanation or cause of China–US interest rate spread.	0.0728	0.9298
3	The expectation of RMB appreciation is not the explanation or cause of difference of foreign exchange purchase and sale.	0.7715	0.4654
4	Difference of foreign exchange purchase and sale is not the explanation or cause of the expectation of RMB appreciation.	0.5021	0.6070
5	Stock yield spread is not the explanation or cause of difference of foreign exchange purchase and sale.	1.4356	0.2435
6	Difference of foreign exchange purchase and sale is not the explanation or cause of stock yield spread.	1.7345	0.1825

Note:

a The data are from monthly statistics during January 2000 and June 2008.

b The empirical analyses as described above indicate that the causes for the net inflow of foreign exchange into China cannot be attributed to the tested variables. No clear causality exists between net foreign-exchange inflows and China–US interest-rate spreads, or the spread between domestic and foreign return on assets, or the expectations of an appreciating RMB. It may be that economic fundaments such as China's trade surplus may be more important as causes for the inflow of foreign exchange.

economic system, particularly as China's reform and opening up continues to integrate China and the rest of the world. In the analysis that follows, therefore, we look at short-term cross-border capital flows. We use the spread between the amount of foreign exchange coming in and the amount of China's trade surplus to evaluate these flows, that is the spread of the difference between foreign-exchange receipts and payments for trade in goods and the difference in imports versus exports (for short, we call this the 'foreign-exchange to trade-surplus spread.' We make the necessary quarterly adjustments to the figures. To a certain degree, this indicator can show us how well enterprises are achieving cross-border short-term inflow of foreign exchange through advancing foreign-exchange receipts and delaying foreign-exchange payments in the conduct of foreign trade.

The impact of RMB exchange rates on foreign direct investment

China's Ministry of Commerce currently releases public data on foreign direct investment in China with a high rate of frequency. In order to look at any causal relationship between such foreign direct investment and the RMB exchange rate, we applied a Granger causality test to the monthly data as released by the Ministry, which gives the 'actually utilized' amount of foreign capital. We tested that against the RMB exchange rate (see Table 6.4). The results show a pronounced cause-and-effect relationship between the two. That is to say, RMB exchange rates are indeed an explanatory cause of foreign direct investment

Table 6.4 Results of the Granger causality tests

No.	Null hypothesis	F-statistics	Prob. value
1	RMB exchange rate is not the explanation or cause of changes in FDI	3. 97	0. 03
2	FDI is not the explanation or cause of fluctuations of RMB exchange rate	1.54	0. 23

Note: Monthly data during January 2006 and July 2010.

movements. The opposite does not hold true – that is, foreign direct investment is not an explanatory cause of exchange-rate movements.

The influence on cross-border capital flows of NDF prices,
the spread between Chinese and US interest rates, and the spread
between stock-market yields

We used three variables in looking at the primary impacts on cross-border capital flows, flows that we defined as the differential between foreign-exchange earnings and China's trade surplus. Those three things were the spread between Chinese and US interest rates, the spread between stock-market yields, and the expectations for an appreciating RMB. The interest-rate spread was represented by the difference between Chibor for the RMB and Libor for the US dollar ('China–US interest-rate spread' for short). The stock-market spread was represented by the yield spread between the Hong Kong market and the Chinese mainland stock markets ('stock yield spread' for short). The RMB appreciation was represented by the one-year NDF forward premium (or discount) of the exchange rate of the RMB against the USD ('NDF premium or discount' for short).

We used monthly data, since that is the interval at which data is made public on such economic indicators as the differential between China's imports and China's exports. We selected a time period of seven years for the analysis, which had to do with the accessibility of data and the resulting accuracy of our analysis. This period, from 2000 to 2006, started at a point when China's foreign-exchange receipts and payments were basically even with each other before turning into a surplus in favor of China. The period also described the change from a positive to a negative spread on interest rates, and it went from a time when people expected the RMB to devalue to a period in which people expected it to appreciate. Our regression analysis used the following model:

Difference of foreign exchange earnings and trade surplus = 27.5 + 6.5 × NDF premium/discount + 4.3 × China–US interest rate spread – 0.1 × stock yield spread (1)

The unit for data used in this equation is USD 100 million. The unit for the NDF premium/discount is 1,000 base points, whilethe unit for the spread in China–US interest rates is 1 percentage point. The results of using the model demonstrated that there is a clear correlation between the differential in China's foreign-exchange earnings and its trade surplus and the China–US interest rate spread as well as the NDF premium/discount. The correlation with respect to the stock yield spread is not very apparent.

To further verify the above causality, we applied a Granger causality test to the China–US interest rate spread, NDF premium/discount, stock yield spread and the difference between foreign exchange earnings and trade surplus (see Table 6.5). The results indicated that the China–US interest rate spread and NDF premium/discount are indeed the causes of the difference between foreign exchange earnings and trade surplus. The opposite is not true: the differential between 'foreign-exchange earnings and China's trade surplus' is not the cause of changes in the spread between Chinese and US interest rates, nor the NDF premium/discount. Meanwhile, no causal relationship can be seen with respect to the differential between 'foreign-exchange earnings and China's trade surplus' and the stock yield spread.

From empirical results, we can see that the impact of the differential between stock market yields in Hong Kong and within the Mainland is minimal in terms of how that differential affects capital flows. This says even more clearly that China's controls on capital are effective in limiting the way international capital flows into the markets in question. Capital controls prevent the free investment choices that would otherwise be made on the basis of comparing the yields in these markets.

Table 6.5 Results of applying the Granger causality test to the effectiveness of China's capital controls

No.	Null hypothesis	F-statistics	Prob. value
1	China–US interest rate spread is not the explanation or cause for difference between foreign exchange earnings and trade surplus.	3.6068	0.0318
2	Difference between foreign exchange earnings is not the explanation or cause for China–US interest-rate spread.	2.6797	0.0750
3	NDF discount is not the explanation or cause for difference between foreign exchange earnings and trade surplus.	4.6940	0.0119
4	Difference between foreign exchange earnings and trade surplus is not the explanation or cause for NDF discount.	0.2592	0.7723
5	Stock yield spread is not the explanation or cause for difference between foreign exchange earnings and trade surplus.	0.0287	0.9718
6	Difference between foreign exchange earnings and trade surplus is not the explanation or cause for stock yield spread.	2.0276	0.1386

According to the results of Model (1) on page 196, if one removes the variable that has to do with a differential in stock-market yields, and instead sets up a dual regression model, the results are as follows:

Difference between foreign exchange earnings and trade surplus = 27.6 + 6.5 × NDF discount + 4.4 x China – US interest rate spread   (2)

According to this model, every percentage point increase in the spread between Chinese and US interest rates may increase capital inflows into China by USD 440 million. Such short-term cross-border capital flows are represented by the differential between China's foreign exchange earnings and China's trade surplus on a monthly basis. In annual terms, the increase therefore comes to USD 440 × 12 = USD 5.28 billion.

Meanwhile, for every increase of 1,000 basis points in the RMB to US dollar exchange rate as measured by NDF forward discount (which means the RMB is appreciating) may lead to an increase in short-term cross-border capital inflows into China of USD 650 million on a monthly basis. In annual terms, this variable would therefore increase capital inflows on an annual basis by USD 650 × 12 = USD 7.8 billion.

Analyzing the impact of exchange rates on capital flows
from the perspective of external debt

External debt can also be used as a clue in tracing the effect of exchange rates on capital flows. The definition of China's external debt is broad enough to include both registered external debt and trade credit. Registered external debt is relatively stable, due to strict regulatory controls (see Figure 6.3). Trade credit varies enormously, however. Its increase has been somewhat related to the financial crisis and the declining trend of foreign trade, but one cannot exclude the possibility that trade credit also is mixed up in the whole business of speculative capital.

To summarize the above, given the pronounced spread in interest rates between inside and outside China, the inflow of foreign capital is not clearly correlated with either expectations of RMB appreciation or the spread between interest rates for China's currency and foreign currencies. In overall terms, therefore, post-exchange-rate reform capital flows have been effectively controlled. Nevertheless, as China's economy continues to expand, and as both interest-rate differentials and expectations of a stronger RMB provide the impetus for speculative arbitrage, speculative capital flows will always find a way to enter. For example, the China–US interest-rate differential and the rising NDF discount may lead to massive increases in the 'foreign-exchange to trade-surplus spread.' In overall terms, nevertheless, the scale of these inflows remains modest.

Over the longer term, as China's economy becomes ever more integrated with the global economy, as China's investment environment improves and opens up, and as expectations for the RMB to appreciate continue, foreign exchange may well find a myriad of channels by which to enter the country. We must be highly

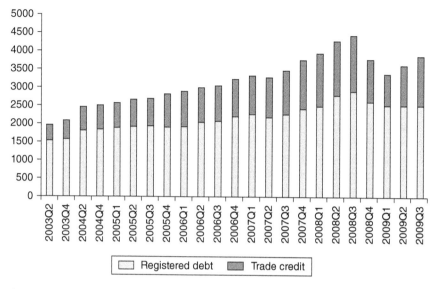

Figure 6.3 Changes in the amount of China's external debt.

objective, therefore, in how we evaluate the real effectiveness of our capital controls. From a long-term perspective, we must resolve these issues through a process of further deepening reform and opening up our economy. In a sequenced manner, we should push forward the convertibility of the capital account, expand the elasticity of the RMB exchange rate, and promote a greater balance in our international balance of payments.

Changes in the RMB exchange-rate formation mechanisms since the reform of 2005, and the impact of those changes on China's (ability to use) macroeconomic measures in controlling its economy

Changes in the RMB exchange-rate formation mechanisms since 2005

The initial stage of reform

Starting on July 21, 2005, China's reform of its exchange rate 'regime' took a major step forward. In terms of how it formulates the exchange rate of its currency, China began to implement a system described as a 'managing float, that is based on market supply and demand, and that is managed with respect to a basket of currencies.' The over-riding aim of this reform was to set up a sound exchange-rate system, based on market supply and demand and using a managed float, that maintained the RMB at a rate that was reasonable and basically stable at an equilibrium level.

Reform of China's exchange-rate mechanisms during this round of reform included the following three components.

First, it involved implementing a system that was a managed float, based on market supply and demand, and handled with respect to a basket of currencies. No longer would the RMB be pegged solely to the US dollar. Instead, it would float, as required by market supply and demand and as referenced to a basket of currencies. This so-called 'basket of currencies' would be modified depending on specific circumstances, including China's external trade conditions. The basket would be selected from among major currencies, each of which would be weighted according to its importance. At the same time, the RMB exchange rate would be adjusted and controlled in order to keep it at a reasonable and basically stable level around equilibrium. This management would be applied depending on the domestic and foreign economic and financial situation. It would be using market supply and demand as the 'foundation' while making adjustments with reference to a basket of currencies in calculating a multi-lateral exchange-rate index for the RMB.

In determining the currency composition of the basket, China takes into overall consideration major countries, regions, and currencies with a relatively large share of China's foreign trade activity, large amounts of foreign debt (interest costs), foreign direct investment (dividends), and so on. There are four main principles that come to bear on this decision. The amount of trade conducted in any given currency is the basis for selecting that currency and for determining its weighting. Appropriate consideration is given to the currency composition of the source of foreign debt. Appropriate consideration is given to factors affecting foreign direct investment of overseas businesses in China. Another consideration included in the mix is current account remittances that are of an uncompensated nature. Using a basket of currencies means that exchange-rate fluctuations of the various currencies vis-à-vis one another also affect the RMB. 'With reference to' does not, however, mean 'pegged to.' The RMB rate also depends on market supply and demand as an important consideration in forming the 'managed float.' This is beneficial to the future path of increasing the elasticity of the rate and to restraining the effect of unilateral speculation. It helps to preserve the multilateral stability of the RMB rate and also to protect the competitiveness of China's exports.

The second component of the exchange-rate reform of 2005 involved a staged approach to reforming the benchmark rate, the way trading prices are handled, management of the quoted rates, and to loosening of pricing limits. After the close of the markets every day, the People's Bank of China publicly announces the closing prices of the RMB against the US dollar and other traded currencies. These closing prices then become the 'intermediary prices' of the start of trading the next day. This signifies that the system has shifted from relying on the weighted average of the exchange rate to relying on the intermediary price as defined by the publicly announced closing price of the previous day. This allows China's central bank to intervene in the market in ways that are more independent and more flexible.

After July 21, 2005, the band within which the RMB traded against the US dollar on the interbank market every day still remained within an upper and lower limit of 0.3 percent of the intermediary price. The band within which non-US-dollar currencies were allowed to float was increased from 1 percent above and below the intermediary price to 1.5 percent. A symmetrical system was similarly applied to the quoted prices for spot rates on exchange and for cash, with the band for spot rates being 0.2 percent above and below the intermediary price and that for cash being 1 percent above and below the intermediary price. The system adopted for exchange of non-US dollar currencies was slightly different. In that case, a management system was adopted that looked at the spread between the buying and selling of a given currency. Since buying and selling prices are not necessarily symmetrical around an intermediary price, the posted rates of non-dollar currencies went from being 'one rate per day' to being 'several rates per day.'

After September 23, 2005, the daily floating band for the non-dollar currencies was further expanded, from 1.5 percent to 3 percent. In addition, the system for US dollars was also changed at this time. Instead of a symmetrical system, the 'spread system' was adopted and the bands were also further expanded for cash sales and spot-exchange. Spot exchange went from 0.2 percent to 1 percent above and below the intermediary rate, while cash could now be exchanged in a 4 percent band above and below the intermediary rate as opposed to the former 1 percent. Concurrent with these changes, banks were no longer restricted in the buy-and-sell price spreads of their posted rates for conversion of non-dollar currencies.

The third component of the reform of 2005 involved a single-event, small-scale revaluation of the RMB by 2 percent. This occurred on July 21, 2005, starting at 7 pm. The RMB rate was adjusted to become RMB 8.11 to USD 1. This rate then became the intermediary price for the start of trading the next day. 'Designated banks,' those allowed to deal in foreign exchange, then adjusted the rates that they posted for customers.

The emphasis of the RMB exchange-rate reform of 2005 was on exchange-rate formation mechanisms rather than on either raising or lowering the level of the RMB exchange rate in quantitative terms. The degree of the adjustment made in the RMB rate in July, 2005, relied on the degree of China's trade surplus at that time as well as its structure. At the same time, the revaluation took into consideration the ability of China's domestic enterprises to accommodate the change.

After the exchange-rate reform of 2005, the elasticity of the RMB–US dollar rate gradually increased. Between July 22 and December 30, 2005, the dollar fluctuated moderately against the RMB, with movements in both directions and change that was at a very stable level. By the end of 2005, the dollar had gone from RMB 8.11 to RMB 8.0702, according to the publicly disclosed prices announced at the end of each day by the People's Bank of China. Over the entire year, the RMB had therefore appreciated by 2.56 percent. At its lowest, the close-of-day intermediary price of the dollar was RMB 8.0702 (on December 30), and the highest was RMB 8.1128 (on July 27). These two figures differed by 426 basis points.

On January 4, 2006, another adjustment was made in the way the daily intermediary price was formed. An 'inquiry-based' trading method was introduced to foreign-exchange markets. Traders in the interbank foreign-exchange markets could now decide on their own whether they wanted to use the 'inquiry method' or the 'competitive method' to place trades. This increased the flexibility of trading. In order to increase liquidity, the system also officially adopted a method whereby foreign-exchange markets could 'make a market.' On a continuous basis, 'market makers' within the interbank market were obliged to quote both buying and selling prices in order to give liquidity to the market. By regulation, prior to the close of business each day, the China Foreign Exchange Trading Center asks market-makers for these prices. It then uses the prices in how it calculates the intermediary price of the RMB on the following day. In deriving that intermediary price, it excludes the highest and lowest of market-makers prices and creates a weighted average of the rest. The weighting is done by evaluating the quantity of trades performed by a given market-maker in the interbank market, and the circumstances of how it priced its quotations. The resulting intermediary price becomes the basis on which foreign-exchange designated banks determine their buying and selling prices for both cash and spot-exchange for various currencies, while staying within the floating range as prescribed by the People's Bank of China.

Once reform of the intermediary-price mechanism was complete, the RMB began to appreciate at a greater speed, amidst ongoing fluctuations up and down. In the first half of 2006, the quoted intermediary price was RMB 7.9956 to one US dollar, which represented an appreciation of 0.93percent. At the end of 2006, the price was RMB 7.8087 to one US dollar, which meant an appreciation of the RMB vis-à-vis the dollar of 2.39 percent. On June 29, 2007, the intermediary price was RMB 7.6155 to one US dollar, indicating an appreciation of 2.54 percent (see Table 6.6).

The second stage of reform: May, 2007, expanding the band
within which the RMB could trade against the US dollar

This stage not only increased the daily price range within which the RMB could be traded but also increased the degree to which the RMB exchange rate was set by the market. Starting on May 21, 2007, the band within which spot trading of the RMB against the dollar could be carried out in the interbank market was increased from three to five basis points. That is, the trading could float by plus or minus five basis points relative to the central parity rate that was announced every day by China's Foreign Exchange Trading Center.

Starting in the second half of 2007, the RMB began to appreciate notably against the dollar and at an accelerating pace. The central parity rate was RMB 7.3046 to the dollar at the end of 2007, which meant that the RMB had appreciated by 4.26 percent. In the first half of 2008, the central parity rate closed at 6.8594, representing an appreciation of 6.5 percent. The central parity rate at which the trading started every day was also moving in a much broader band. At the end of

Table 6.6 Appreciation of the RMB, between July 2005 and end-2008

	Period-end price	Appreciation against USD (%)
July 21, 2005	8.11	
The second half of 2005	8.0702	0.49
The first half of 2006	7.9956	0.93
The second half of 2006	7.8087	2.39
The first half of 2007	7.6155	2.54
The second half of 2007	7.3046	4.26
The first half of 2008	6.8591	6.50
The second half of 2008	6.8346	0.36

2005, after the exchange-rate reform, its degree of movement from one day to the next was a mere 0.021 percent. In the first half of 2006, the degree of movement increased to 0.043 percent, and in the second half of 2006, it increased to 0.056 percent. Although volatility gradually increased during this period, the market still felt that the speed of appreciation of the RMB after 2006 could not be compared to the extent to which the US dollar was depreciating. The exchange-rate system of the International Monetary Fund still adhered to the 'crawling peg' system. In the first half of 2007, the band within which the central parity rate floated reached 0.066 percent, then 0.094 percent in the second half of 2007 and 1.06 percent in the first half of 2008.

The third stage of reform: July 2008, narrowing the band

From July of 2008 until June of 2010, the RMB exchange rate retreated to a narrower band of fluctuations and returned to a de facto peg. Just as the overseas NDF market was anticipating the RMB would appreciate by 12 percent within one year, the subprime crisis in the United States evolved into a global financial crisis. After July of 2008, RMB appreciation against the dollar was cut off. In the second half of 2008, the closing price went to 6.8346, representing an appreciation of a mere 0.36 percent. The range within the central parity rate moved on a daily basis dropped back to 0.5 percent. From a situation in which the RMB appreciated in a unilateral direction, trading returned to two-way fluctuations and the exchange rate showed greater elasticity. In the second half of 2008, out of a total of 126 trading days, those in which the RMB depreciated against the dollar increased in number by 17 percent over the first half of the year. The RMB depreciated against the dollar for 55 percent of trading days in the second half of 2008. Expectations that the RMB would continue rising now shifted to an expectation of RMB depreciation, both inside and outside China.

Since the end of March, 2008, the NDF discount of overseas US dollars began to decline. As the subprime crisis gradually evolved into an international financial crisis, it drew global economies into an economic recession. By mid to late September, the US dollar went from a discount to a premium, with trading occurring in an increasingly broad band. This indicated that the expectation regarding RMB exchange rates abroad was reversing. Since mid-October, the forward RMB vis-à-vis US dollar exchanges rates in the domestic interbank market also shifted from discount status to a premium. With expectations for the RMB reversing, in the first week of December, 2008, the RMB–US dollar rate either fell nearly to the low end of the allowable band, or closed at the floor price for several consecutive days in the interbank foreign exchange market. Between 2009 and June, 2010, the rate fluctuated only within the narrow band of 6.82 to 6.84. This was interpreted as a return to a *de facto* peg, as set by the International Monetary Fund.

In retrospect, after the second quarter of 2009, the Chinese government went about very methodically implementing an economic stimulus plan that came to RMB 4trillion. The worst stage of the global financial crisis was already past. The overseas NDF markets showed that the RMB had already gone from expectations of 3 percent depreciation to a gradual trend towards zero depreciation. This was, therefore, an opportune time to restore the elasticity of the RMB exchange rate (see Figure 6.4).

In conclusion, the central bank of China can stabilize the two-way trading of the RMB vis-à-vis the US dollar, but it does not have the ability to stabilize the RMB exchange rate against multiple currencies. According to data from the Bank for International Settlements, in June of 2010, the nominal effective exchange-rate index of the RMB was 117.42. This showed a cumulative appreciation of

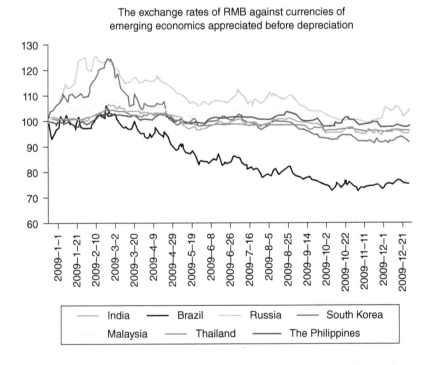

Figure 6.4 RMB exchange rates versus currency trends of newly emerging market economies.

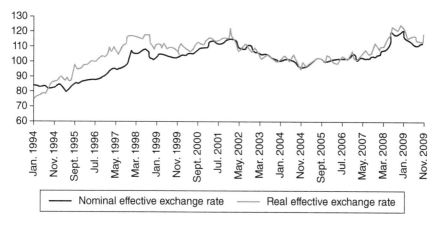

Figure 6.5 Trends of RMB effective exchange rates from January 1994 to June 2009.

18.5 percent since July, 2005, just after the exchange-rate reform. It showed a cumulative appreciation of 8.6 percent compared to just before the international financial crisis erupted. The real effective exchange-rate index of the RMB fluctuated in only minor increments, showing an overall tendency to appreciate. In June of 2010, the RMB's nominal effective exchange-rate index stood at 119.04, which meant a cumulative appreciation of 21.7 percent over the rate just prior to the reform of July, 2005. Relative to the rate in June of 2008, just prior to the eruption of the international financial crisis, this marked a cumulative appreciation of 8.2 percent (see Figure 6.5).

The fourth stage of reform: restarting the reform process in June 2010

On June 19, 2010, the People's Bank of China announced that it would now be resuming reform of the RMB exchange-rate formation mechanisms and would be strengthening the elasticity of the RMB rate. After reinitiating reform, the market went through a brief and temporary period of turbulence after which trading showed two-way transactions, with broad fluctuations, and a gradual weakening of the expectation for RMB appreciation. The degree to which market supply and demand were out of balance gradually calmed down. From June 20 until July 19 of 2010, the central parity rate of the RMB on the interbank market displayed two-way fluctuations and an overall attitude of stability. The RMB appreciated for thirteen trading days, it depreciated for eight days, and on one day it remained level. This was quite similar to the pattern one month after the 2005 reform. In twenty-two trading days in the first month after that reform, the RMB lost value for eight days and gained value for fourteen days.

The interbank market displayed even greater two-direction trading of the RMB vis-à-vis the US dollar, and a broad range of fluctuations, on average 104 basis points. On only two trading days did the trading price fluctuate in the 'zone' of appreciation, and on only four days did it move in the zone of depreciation. On sixteen days, it fluctuated in both directions. In contrast, in the one month following the reform of 2005, trading showed much more tendency to move only in the direction of appreciation. The RMB trading price fluctuated in the appreciating 'zone' for eight trading days, in the depreciating zone for four trading days, and in a two-way trading pattern for ten trading days.

When the government reinitiated exchange-rate reform, all sectors expressed approval. People felt that, from a long-term perspective, exchange-rate reform would be helpful in accelerating the process of industrial upgrading, that it would stimulate enterprises to shift their operations inland, and that it would promote more balanced regional development. That the central bank was now pushing forward exchange-rate reform did not mean that exchange rates would change to any great degree in the short term. It did mean that the rate would be set more in reference to a basket of currencies, somewhat on the order of setting up automatic adjustment mechanisms. Moreover, since markets for forward contracts, swaps, and currency swaps have developed quickly, enterprises have become much more adept at risk avoidance.

By mid-2010, the supply and demand situation in forward currency contracts was generally in balance and the expectation for an appreciating RMB was much less than it had been at the time of the 2005 exchange-rate reform. By July 20, 2010, this expectation was not even 1 percent on a domestic one-year forward contract for RMB. The overseas NDF market for one-year forward contracts for the RMB put the rate at 1.8 percent, basically in line with the 1.6 percent of June 18. To give a comparison, one month after the 2005 reform, the overseas NDF market for one-year forward contracts was showing an expectation of 4.1 percent appreciation of the RMB. Although this was slightly less than the six-month average (5 percent), it still was notably higher than during this current round of reform (see Table 6.7).

The impact of RMB exchange-rate formation mechanisms on China's ability to use macroeconomic measures in managing the economy

Over the long run, reform of China's RMB exchange-rate formation mechanisms will strengthen the autonomy of the country's monetary policies

The 'Impossible Trinity' concept says that, in the context of an open economy, it is not possible for three different policy objectives to coexist. These are 'maintaining free flow of capital,' 'maintaining an independent monetary policy,' and 'maintaining a fixed exchange rate.' Control over capital flows declines as an economy opens to the outside world. Given that fact, maintaining fixed exchange rates signifies that a government must sacrifice the independent sovereignty of its monetary policies. This then means that those policies are less effective.

The way in which China's exchange-rate regime is handled is also highly significant in terms of communicating monetary policy to the public. In addition to the

Table 6.7 Comparison of the context of the two periods in which RMB exchange-rate formation mechanisms were reformed

RMB–USD exchange rate		One month following the reform in 2010 (2010.6.20–2010.7.19)	One month following the reform in 2005 (2005.7.23.–2005.8.22)
Middle rates	Middle rate	6.7812	8.1047
	Middle rates appreciated after the reform	+ 0.7%	+ 2.1%
	The tertian floating band of middle rates	Between – –0.2% and +0.5%	Between –2.1% and +0. 06%
	Days when middle rates appreciated	13	14
	Days when middle rates leveled off	1	0
	Days when middle rates depreciated	8	8
Market trading rates	Daily fluctuation of trading rates	30 to 329 base points	—
	Average daily fluctuation of trading rates	104 base points	—
	Days when trading rates fluctuated upward	2	8
	Days when trading rates fluctuated downward	4	4
	Days when trading rates fluctuated around middle rates	16	10
NDF	Expected appreciation of 1-year RMB forward in the overseas NDF market.	1.8% (Before the reform in 2010: 1.6%)	4.1% (Before the reform in 2005: 5%)

positive contributions to monetary policy as noted above, a flexible exchange-rate system also helps curb the potential for inflation and asset bubbles. For example, when inflationary pressures are building, an appropriate degree of appreciation of the currency makes imports cheaper. Since China is resource-deprived and must import much of its primary goods, such exchange-rate adjustments alleviate the degree to which the country suffers from 'imported' inflationary pressure. A flexible exchange rate also improves the communication mechanisms by which China's monetary policies are transmitted to the public. Enterprises, commercial banks, and other microeconomic entities become more attuned to making their own self-initiated responses to a floating rate. This improves their nimbleness in dealing with market changes. Monetary and foreign-exchange markets develop further as a result, leading to much broader and deeper markets for all financial instruments. Meanwhile, financial institutions improve their risk management abilities as they seek to accommodate a flexible exchange-rate regime. They enhance their financial services and speed up product innovation. To a degree, all of these then provide a more secure microeconomic foundation and market foundation for the transmittal of monetary policy.

In the initial period of reform, insufficiently flexible exchange
rates and the lack of accompanying macroeconomic measures
lowered the effectiveness of macroeconomic policies. Moreover,
such policies mainly relied on quantitative measures

Since reform of China's exchange-rate mechanisms began, but particularly since 2006, the RMB has appreciated against the US dollar. Nevertheless, that appreciation was relatively slow-paced for the first two years. We conducted a country-by-country comparison using the real effective exchange rate as compiled by the Bank for International Settlements. From July, 2005, to October, 2006, the real effective exchange rate of the RMB appreciated by 4.4 percent. In contrast, the real effective exchange rate of the Korean won appreciated by 7.2 percent, that of the Thai baht appreciated by 11.5 percent, and that of the Indonesian rupiah by 27.8 percent. As compared to other currencies, therefore, the appreciation of the real effective exchange rate of the RMB was fairly sedate. Although this had a certain effect on moderating the speed at which China imported and exported goods, China's positive balance of trade continued to grow as usual because of its large base. At the same time, expectations were that the RMB would continue to appreciate, given the way expectations adapted to changes and given the bearish sentiment on the US dollar. These two factors meant that both China's international balance of payments surplus and its capital account surplus grew.

In response to an increasing amount of foreign exchange flowing into the country, China's central bank increased its foreign-exchange purchases and also its ability to hedge. It constantly employed new hedging methods. These included the ongoing measure of issuing and repurchasing (repo) central bank notes and adjusting upwards the reserve requirement on funds held in commercial banks. In 2005, the central bank initiated a foreign-exchange swap business. In 2007, it required banks to keep their reserve requirements available in the form of foreign currencies. In order to hold down inflation, in 2007 the central bank also began to get rid of the constraint of interest-rate parity and to adopt measures that allowed for raising interest rates. When domestic interest rates were higher than foreign interest rates, however, this also could lead to a vicious circle by attracting even more capital into the country. Since 2005, inflation as measured by the consumer price index (CPI) has stayed at a fairly low level in China other than import-type inflation in 2007. As measured in broader ways, however, such as the producer price index (PPI), or by the price of housing and other assets, inflation in China has risen to a considerable degree.

Having an inelastic RMB exchange rate hampered (and hampers) the autonomy of central bank policies to a very large degree. Issuing central bank notes, for example, as a way to draw in basic money supply gradually increased the hedging costs of the central bank. Since 2003, over the course of seven years, China's foreign-exchange reserves have already increased by USD 2 trillion. The amount of money supply put into the system by China's central bank (in order to buy up foreign exchange) has increased prodigiously, which has led to excessive liquidity. Right now in China, an excess of industrial capacity is already becoming apparent. Asset prices are already rising rapidly, and the overall economic system is already transitioning from overly fast to 'over-heating.' The cost of interest on notes that the central bank has issued added to the loss on foreign-exchange transactions, as a result of the appreciating RMB, equals an unrealized financial loss when the sum exceeds the returns to the central bank of managing foreign-exchange reserves. Naturally, the value of reserves should be measured in terms of purchasing power abroad, but even so, and even without considering these costs, the central bank is gradually losing its ability to hedge as China's foreign-exchange reserves mount up with increasing ferocity. The central bank is increasingly using newly issued bills to replace bills that have matured, while the amount that can be hedged against is limited. This is another reason for the over-abundance of base money supply, and the overly fast pace at which money supply is increasing. It is the source of the problem of excessive liquidity in the market (see Figure 6.6).

One cannot expect exchange rates to resolve the problem of a surplus in current accounts, and in the end trying to address the problem through exchange rates leads to use of 'administrative controls' as opposed to 'macroeconomic measures'

The slight amount of gradual appreciation of the RMB did indeed have a certain effect on moderating the pace at which China's foreign trade was growing, but by now that effect is declining. Before the exchange-rate reform, China's exports were increasing at a rate of 32 percent. On a month-to-month comparison, this fell to around 25 percent after the reform. In contrast, imports increased at a faster pace after the reform. From 14 percent growth prior to reform, they went to 23 percent growth after the reform. By the end of October, 2006, the RMB had appreciated 5.1 percent against the US dollar yet exports were still growing at a rate of around 25 percent. The reasons can be traced to the processing industry and the way the business is handled by companies with 'both ends outside China.' These have the ability to cope with fluctuations in the RMB exchange rate. They adopted such cost-saving means as increasing production efficiencies and lowering intermediary costs. Enterprises also raised their prices in order to transfer on the cost of a more expensive RMB. The People's Bank of China conducted a random sample survey of 1,000 enterprises in 19 different regions, and the results showed that enterprises of all sizes had the leeway to raise prices by a certain amount. In November of 2005, 84.8 percent of those enterprises surveyed had raised export prices over previous periods, or were at least holding them steady (even with an appreciating RMB). Some 12.1 percent of these enterprises exported 3 percent or more of their production. For nearly 70 percent of all enterprises, the primary

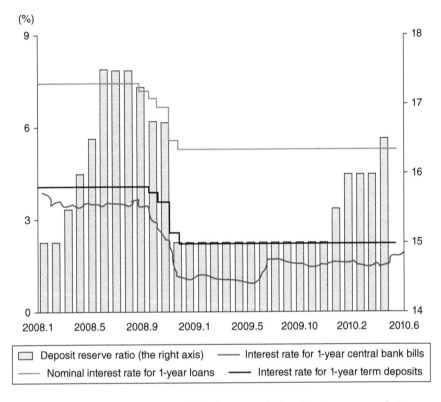

Figure 6.6 The reserve requirement for banks, as graphed against interest rates, between January 2008 and June 2010.

option for dealing with an appreciating RMB was to 'upgrade products, technological content, and value-added.' China's surplus in the current account went from a level equal to 3 percent of GDP in 2004 to 11 percent of GDP in 2007.

The extent of China's 'double surplus' in both the current and capital account in its international balance of payments can be likened to an ongoing flood, year after year. Meanwhile, the central bank's efforts to deal with this through hedging have not been effective. Issuing and repurchasing central bank notes cannot directly reduce money supply. All it does is influence the amount of 'loanable' funds that can be used by financial institutions. When reserve requirements are kept at over 2 percent of banks' excess reserves, the amount of money supply in public hands actually depends more on such 'window guidance measures' as limits on the size of bank loans. As liquidity in the banking system has increased, the frequent readjustments in reserve requirements and massive issues of central-bank notes have had an impact on the functioning of commercial banks. Indeed, these things have begun to affect the behavior and efficiency of the entire financial system. Meanwhile, the hedging costs of the central bank have been constantly increasing.

The stable exchange rate of the RMB vis-à-vis the US dollar in
the period between the second half of 2008 and the second half
of 2010 has been concerning and has brought on its own problems

After the global financial crisis of 2008, the RMB exchange rate vis-à-vis the US dollar was maintained at a stable intermediary rate. This also then meant that the real effective exchange rate of the RMB moved in sync with the dollar and, instead of declining, the RMB rate against all currencies appreciated. Combined with a contraction in overseas demand, this impacted the export sector in China and added to the problems of exporting enterprises. Since the fourth quarter of 2008, China has put out an intensive series of macroeconomic measures aimed at stimulating the economy, including stimulus measures and an appropriate broadening of money supply. The government has explicitly declared policy aims of maintaining stable growth, expanding domestic demand, and adjusting economic structure. It has swiftly implemented measures that invest in basic infrastructure, it has allowed banks to be more aggressive in extending credit, it has raised the rebates given to exporters by a large amount and in a comprehensive way, and it has relaxed the restrictions on doing business that is 'highly polluting, highly energy consuming, and resource intensive.' While this undoubtedly helps the immediate situation of dealing with an international financial crisis, at the same time it brings with it grave concerns. It adds to the financial burden of both central and local governments. It lowers the quality of bank credit. It increases the difficulty of conserving energy in the future and of reducing polluting emissions. One can say that if, at the time, China had been able to adopt other effective means of stabilizing its exchange rates, the negative side effects might have been less apparent.

Short-term and medium-term strategies for RMB exchange-rate adjustments, and supportive policy measures

We recommend taking advantage of the current situation, which is characterized by lower expectations of an appreciating RMB and greater balance in receipts and payments of foreign exchange. In line with the market-based orientation of reform, we recommend strengthening the use of exchange rates as a tool as opposed to using rate levels as a policy objective. We recommend using a more flexible exchange-rate regime in order to mitigate the impact of internal and external economic volatility. In more specific terms, we feel that the following policy measures could be adopted.

First, constantly improve the ability of the central bank to effect exchange-rate adjustments. That means utilizing the role of the interbank market as a 'market maker,' and gradually diminishing the direct interference of the central bank in exchange-rate levels. It means strengthening the ability of the market itself to be the sovereign force governing exchange rates. Move gradually away from a concentration on the bilateral relationship between the RMB and the US dollar, and instead focus on the stability of a multilateral 'real effective exchange rate' in order to preserve the overall competitiveness of China's export products. Not only can this further the process of having the market determine the formation of exchange rates, but it can serve our goal of maintaining economic growth. At the same time, it can help keep China from being in a passive or vulnerable position in any foreign-relations discussions on exchange rates.

Second, progressively broaden the range within which the RMB is allowed to trade. Make full use of the existing range of fluctuation in the interbank market prices for RMB–US dollar exchange; allow rates to reflect underlying economic fundamentals and market factors in a timely way and allow them to accommodate normal market volatility. Broaden out the range within which the RMB can fluctuate against the US dollar and further strengthen the independent ability of the interbank market to set prices and maintain price flexibility.

Third, put major effort into cultivating and developing a foreign-exchange market. Allow more types of entities to be engaged in the interbank market trading, and expand a more diversified base of market supply and demand. Inject more vigor into the existing markets for spot trades, forwards, foreign-exchange swaps, and currency swaps, as examples of various types of traded products involving the RMB and other currencies. Using pilot projects, incorporate new products into the market, including such derivative products as currency futures and options. Enable more currency brokers to join the market and participate in quoting prices as a way to enrich the trading platform of the interbank foreign-exchange market.

Short-term and medium-term policy measures that should accompany RMB exchange-rate reform

China's macroeconomic policy objectives should place strong emphasis on greater balance in the country's international balance of payments. The current account surplus should be set up as one of the targets that define macroeconomic policy objectives

The target for the current account surplus should be lowered to a level that is 4 percent to 5 percent of the country's GDP. (Since 2003, the average level has been 3.75 percent.) This should become a key 'guiding objective' in the 12th Five-Year Plan. As the world economy recovers and China's domestic economy gradually operates on a more normal basis, the country should gradually lower the amount of export rebates granted to exporters. It should again restrict the amount of product that can be exported by highly polluting and energy-consuming industries, as well as by resource-intensive industries. The country should aim for sustainable development. In a stable fashion, China should promote a transformation and upgrading of its processing-trade businesses, and should attempt to diversify its international trade. It should adjust the categories of quota-restricted and prohibited items in the processing trade, and should encourage businesses involved in the trade to move inland, toward central and western parts of China. We should vigorously expand trade with Africa, the Middle East, and newly emerging markets. At the same time, we should expand the importation of products for which there is demand within China. We should aim to reduce both tariff barriers and non-tariff barriers to trade, and should promote trade facilitation. We should increase the importation of high-tech items, particularly key equipment that China is not yet able to produce domestically, and we should increase imports of strategic energy resources. With an eye on opportune timing and the condition of international markets, we should import and enhance our strategic reserves of key materials and certain nonferrous metals. In terms of investing abroad, we should be proactive but also prudent as we implement our strategy of 'going global,' or 'striding out into the world.' At the same time, we should improve the financial services relating to imports and exports by increasing credit to foreign trade enterprises. We should provide more support to exporters by lowering the amount of collateral that must be put up for loans or credit, while at the same time we should improve risk prevention mechanisms that pertain to export credits.

China should reduce the number of initial public offerings
(IPOs) being carried out abroad that do not have any need for
foreign exchange

In the immediate and near future, China is in a position of having greater reserves of savings than it has the ability to invest those savings. Our policy should therefore stem from an understanding that we need to reduce this disparity. We must no longer continue the old way of thinking that blindly sought to import ever more foreign capital. According to incomplete statistics, since 2003, China has amassed some USD 300 billion through overseas IPOs. These were conducted in the form of issuing 'H-shares,' 'red chips,' and 'accompanying share allotments.' This has aggravated the imbalance in China's international balance of payments and has put pressure on the RMB to appreciate. In 2010 alone, the amount of foreign exchange flowing into China exceeded USD 40 billion, through the mechanism of 'issuing and allocating' shares by such financial institutions as the Agricultural Bank of China. Because of this, we must now adopt effective measures to limit the number of overseas listings that have no need for foreign exchange.

China should ensure that wages increase in step with increases in
GDP. It should realize a mode of economic growth that enables all to
benefit. To do that, it should guide the country in the direction of
industrial upgrading and transformation

We recommend that China develop a policy that incorporates a minimum wage and a plan for average wages to double every five years. (That would call for wage increases of 14 percent per year.) Moreover, we recommend that this become a key component in evaluating the performance of local (provincial) government officials. In this way, we should be able to kill three birds with one stone. First, through real appreciation (of the RMB) we will reduce upward pressure of nominal appreciation. Second, we will reduce the long-term gap between wage increases and GDP growth, resulting in the problem of ever-widening income disparities in the country. Third, this should also help alleviate greater pressures on the RMB to appreciate, while encouraging the restructuring and transformation of industries.

China should conduct research into establishing a new 'framework' for monetary policy altogether. As part of this, it should carry out a comprehensive evaluation of the degree to which the country's monetary and exchange-rate policies are 'tight' or 'loose'

After the exchange-rate reform of 2005, China's monetary policies no longer pegged the RMB to the US dollar. While this gave more independence to monetary policy, it also meant that China now faces the problem of losing its monetary 'peg.' The degree to which China's economy is 'open' now exceeds 70 percent. After the financial crisis, this meant that the turbulent international financial situation brought on volatile exchange rates and ever-greater external influences on China. Given this, China should now conduct a study of the experience of such countries as Canada, Sweden, and New Zealand, in creating a framework for monetary policies that are pegged to inflation. The target that determines government operations is an index of the monetary situation in the country, enabling a comprehensive judgment of the degree to which the country's monetary and exchange-rate policies are tight or loose.

China should improve controls over the inflow of foreign exchange, and should curb the short-term speculative inflow of capital

At this particular stage, strengthening controls over the inflow of foreign exchange will be beneficial in scaring and suppressing the illicit movement of foreign exchange. It will give the country some breathing room to enable domestic policy adjustments and exchange-rate reform to take effect. A system that categorizes enterprises by type can be set up for the immediate and near-term controls. Tighter investigations can be applied to foreign-exchange settlements that are declared as foreign-trade related, to ensure their validity. Such controls can be applied at both the 'application and approval' stage and after the fact. This will help curb the amount of foreign-exchange capital that is flowing into the country under false pretenses. China should also strengthen the effectiveness of its controls over credit denominated in foreign currencies, particularly trade credit. We should conduct research into the external debt management of foreign-funded enterprises, including how to reform and strengthen data collection on foreign trade credit. We should improve our understanding of how foreign-funded enterprises handle retained earnings, so as to contain the risks involved in hiding the amount of their external debt. We should curb the amount of speculative capital flowing into the country by employing such means as reserve requirements that are not charged interest, or the Tobin tax.

China should expand the channels through which capital can flow
out of the country, and it should promote management that involves
a balance in foreign-exchange receipts and payments

Capital controls will inevitably tend to be less effective as an economy opens up and as it becomes more market oriented. Because of this fact, China should move toward convertibility of RMB capital accounts in a prudent and orderly way. It should first go further in opening up channels through which capital can be exported, then promote two-way reasonable flows of capital. In specific terms, such measures would include relaxing policy restrictions on the ability of individuals to make direct investments overseas; continuing to support broadening of overseas financial investments that are made through the channel of 'qualified domestic institutional investors (QDII), as a means to meeting foreign-exchange demand from increased personal income of Chinese individuals and their need for more diversified investments. Measures would include expanding the scope of entities that can engage in such services, increasing the allowed investment amounts, and broadening the scope of allowed investments. They would include going further in opening up China's domestic securities markets to the outside world. They would include going further in broadening the rules on qualifications for Chinese multinationals to place funds abroad, and restrictions regarding the scale of those funds. They would include relaxing restrictions preventing foreign institutions from issuing RMB-denominated bonds, among other financing restrictions, and furthermore they would allow the external remittance of funds derived from such financing. They would include encouraging qualified overseas enterprises to list inside China on Chinese markets, on the one hand in order to develop China's stock and bond markets, and on the other hand in order to enable China's savings to be converted into investments.

Medium-term and long-term RMB exchange-rate policy options, and complementary policies necessary to support those options

As a kind of 'relative price,' exchange rates do play a certain role in regulating international balance of payments. At the same time, regulation of balance in payments cannot rely exclusively on the appreciation or depreciation of a country's currency. With respect to large countries, priority is given to domestic balance and to domestic policy while exchange-rate policy is secondary. China, therefore, should focus on restoring balance to its domestic economy while regarding foreign economic policy as supplementary. It should adopt a 'basket' of policy measures, under the assumption of first ensuring domestic balance.

A strategy for medium-term and long-term RMB exchange-rate policies

In 2010, China leapt to the position of being the second-largest economy in the world. The theory of the 'Impossible Trilogy' confirms that China cannot, and should not, abandon its own monetary policy objectives and instead be ruled by the economic policies of other countries. No one single exchange-rate regime is appropriate for all countries in the world, whether the options for exchange-rate systems are viewed from a theoretical or a practical perspective. Moreover, no single unchanging regime is appropriate for any one country, since conditions change. As a country evaluates its options, decisions must be made to choose among the three goals of price stability, exchange-rate stability, and the mobility of capital, irrespective of which exchange-rate regime is adopted. Having said that, the general trend is to adopt exchange-rate systems that are more flexible as a country's economy and financial systems open to the outside world.

Whether a system is pegged to one currency, or to a basket of currencies (that is, a multilateral exchange rate or an 'effective' exchange rate), the system is still that of a 'peg.' Over the medium term and long term, China's RMB exchange rate system should adopt a system that is a genuine 'managed float.' It should broaden the band within which the rate fluctuates, which means that any interference by the central bank should become the exception and not the general rule. The market itself should play the fundamental role in formulating exchange-rate prices. Meanwhile, the quantity of China's foreign-exchange reserves should change in small increments rather than violent fluctuations, which should enable the country's macroeconomic policies to be more effective.

Policy options as described above are based mainly on the following considerations. First, the fundamentals for a high degree of economic growth still exist within the Chinese economy. At the same time, China's economic structure is undergoing violent adjustments during this period of 'switching from one track to another.' Increasing the flexibility of the exchange rate will help accommodate changes in the equilibrium level of the exchange rate that derive from this restructuring of the economy. It will help avoid market distortions and misallocation of resources that derive from a misalignment of exchange rates. Second, as China's economy opens to the outside world, and in particular as its financial system opens, a more flexible exchange rate will help in dealing with external impacts, it will increase the autonomy of China's monetary policy, and reduce the country's reliance on capital controls. Third, following the international financial crisis, the pace of restructuring an international monetary system that has been dominated by the US dollar is picking up. Increasing the flexibility of the RMB exchange rate will help distance the RMB from excessive reliance on one currency and will help preserve the legitimate rights and interests of China in its international trade and economic relations.

Recommendation on policy measures that should accompany reform of the RMB exchange-rate formation mechanisms

In 1994, China unified its dual-currency mode of exchange rates. It adopted a basket of reforms that related to foreign trade, taxation, and the foreign-exchange system while, at the same time, instituting appropriately tight fiscal and monetary policies so as to contain excessive demand for foreign exchange. In one stroke, the country thereby turned around a longstanding shortage of foreign exchange and deflated a deeply entrenched expectation that the RMB would be devalued. In contrast to that set of reforms, in 2005, the country's reform of exchange-rate formation mechanisms was not accompanied by a set of supporting policy measures. This made policymakers rely excessively on exchange-rate adjustments as the means for dealing with the imbalance in China's international balance of payments. To a certain degree, this sped up appreciation of the RMB and created a self-fulfilling cycle of higher expectations. In order to realize the recommendations as presented above for short-term and medium-term reform of the RMB exchange-rate system, therefore, it will also be necessary to implement the following set of supportive measures.

1   China must accelerate the transformation of its mode of economic development and strengthen the role of domestic demand in 'pulling forward' economic growth. An imbalance in international payments is a reflection of domestic economic disequilibrium. Taking the need for domestic balance as a given, policy makers should move from restoring domestic balance toward promoting external economic balance. They should reform China's income-distribution system and increase the percentage of national income that goes to individual citizens. While stabilizing external demand, they should expand domestic demand and in particular consumer demand. Policies should open up market access in the fields of healthcare, education, energy, finance, IT, media, and culture. They should improve the market environment for fair competition, and they should expand service industries in particular. They should accelerate the strategic restructuring of China's domestic economy, improve systems that promote independent innovation, and promote the optimization of industrial structure and technology upgrading.

2   China must improve upon reforms that relate to factor pricing, and must emphasize the basic function of prices in regulating the economy. Priority should be given to pushing forward price reform of resources and taxes on resources. China must change the way it under-prices resources as a disguised way to subsidize exports. It must change the way it calculates taxes on resources on the basis of units or quantity, and should instead tax on the basis of value (ad valorem). In staged steps, the country should progressively begin to tax public utilities. It should lower personal income taxes, and it should declare a five-year target for doubling the average level of work-force wages in manufacturing industries. In a stable process, it should ensure that land, energy, electric power, and transport are all subject to market forces, that is, ensure that the prices of basic goods and public services are increasingly market oriented. It should continue to improve such social security systems as pensions, unemployment, and health insurance. China should genuinely implement its principle of 'national treatment' by creating a better investment climate for foreign business. This includes gradually reducing the excessively preferential treatment that favors domestic enterprises with respect to land, environmental protection requirements, labor force requirements, and so on.

3   China must be proactive in vigorously developing its financial markets, in order to turn savings more effectively into investment. It should erect a modern financial system that incorporates diverse forms of entities, a rational structure, excellent functionality, and highly secure and efficient operations. The country should constantly strive to improve the competitiveness and levels of service of its banking, insurance, and securities industries. It should develop financial markets and financing platforms that are multi-tiered and diversified so as to reduce the excessive reliance on foreign capital. It should continue to deepen reform of its own financial institutions, including improvements in financial regulatory systems. China should promote the formation of a yield curve that is reasonable and RMB-based. It should strengthen the operating capabilities and risk-management functions of financial institutions so as to improve the ability of the entire financial system to withstand risk.

4   China should push forward convertibility of the capital account so as to improve its ability to regulate and manage foreign economic relations. It should continue to push for greater facilitation of trade and investment. It should expand the import of advanced technologies and critical equipment, as well as the import of necessary resources and raw materials. Taking the necessity of adequate risk control as a given, the country should gradually realize the convertibility of RMB capital accounts. It should support those Chinese enterprises with sufficient qualifications in taking advantage of opportunities to merge with and acquire overseas assets that have fallen tremendously in price but still have stable earnings and carry a low risk. In an orderly procedure, the country should loosen restrictions on buying overseas securities and investments by both domestic institutions and private individuals. It should constantly seek to enable institutions and individuals to hold and to utilize foreign exchange. China should expand its pilot programs in allowing cross-border trade settlement in RMB. In a stable fashion, it should promote the 'opening up' of its currency and capital markets to the outside world. It should open up the various ways in which the RMB can serve the functions of foreign price valuation, settlement, payment, and storage of value.

5   China should strengthen its regulatory controls that govern risk. It should strengthen the ability of the markets to deal with exchange-rate volatility. It should continue to deepen reform of State-Owned Enterprises, and to set up legally defined corporate governance structures. It should rationalize its incentive mechanisms in terms of both incentives and constraints, and should strengthen the ability of enterprises themselves to control risk. China should constantly strive to upgrade the composition of its exports and should seek to improve the non-price-dependent aspects of competitiveness. It should speed up the process of instituting and improving upon monitoring systems and control mechanisms that handle two-way cross-border capital flows, within the understanding that there should be a balanced approach to such controls. It should accelerate the establishment of early-warning systems for international receipts and payments in order to improve the country's ability to

monitor and predict risk as related to the balance of payments. China should gradually transition from having financial products and innovations that are 'regulatory driven' to having such products be the result of market forces. It should vigorously support financial institutions as they develop RMB-based and foreign-currency based financial derivatives as the result of market demand. China should actively participate in international cooperative efforts with respect to crisis management and interventions. It should seek to expand the 'right to speak' of developing countries in all international financial and economic public endeavors. It should move further in promoting regional economic and monetary cooperation. It should use regional economic and financial unification as a counterforce against the dominant position of the US dollar. China should promote the development of a multi-polar international monetary system.

6   China should steadily promote the internationalization of the RMB. It should push for cooperation among all departments (economic sectors) in order to form a synergistic approach to valuation and settlement of the RMB, so as to provide a solid foundation of unified policy that underlies cross-border capital flows. The country should actively push for expansion of the use of the RMB in foreign economic and trade relations, and should expand the scope of using the RMB for both national and business purposes. China should gradually promote the convertibility of the capital account. It should increase the degree to which domestic financial markets are open to the outside world, and the depth of their offerings and business. China should promote the RMB as a currency that can be used for international settlement, on a global basis, in trade in goods, trade in services, and in capital receipts and payments.

Notes

1 Wen Jiandong: School of Banking and Finance, University of International Business and Economics, and the State Administration of Foreign Exchange.
2 Cheung, Yin-Wong, Menzie D. Chinn, and EijiFujii: The Chinese economy in global context: the integration process and its determinants, NBER Working Papers No. 10047, October, 2003.
3 Guonan Ma, Robert N. McCauley: Do China's capital controls still bind? Implications for monetary autonomy and capital liberalization, BIS Working Papers No. 233, August 2007.
4 Jin Luo and Li Zinai: Analysis of the effectiveness of China's capital controls, *World Economics*, 2005, Volume 8.
5 Yu Yang, Yang Haizhen: Empirical analysis of the effectiveness of China's capital controls, *Journal of Management*, 2005, Volume 5.
6 Since China launched a market in foreign-exchange forward contracts only recently, statistics for 2000 are not available. We therefore express the expectation of appreciation of the RMB through use of the NDF (non-deliverable forwards) and degree to which it is discounted.

7   An international comparison of exchange-rate policies in countries that have undergone economic transition

Zhang Bin[1]

'Increased productivity,' an 'appreciating currency,' and 'economic restructuring' are three expressions of the process of economic growth. After three decades of high-speed growth, China's economy is now confronting the challenges of economic restructuring and the need to adjust its exchange rates. Indeed, the challenges grow tougher by the day. In the near term, employment and economic growth will inevitably be affected. Policy adjustments will challenge the old mindset with respect to 'development.' They will require modification of existing systems and policy arrangements. The outstanding issue confronting policy makers is that of ensuring that China's existing systems and policy arrangements do not obstruct the functioning of relative pricing and economic restructuring in the course of development. Relative pricing and economic restructuring are intrinsic to enabling the country's ongoing economic growth.

The following study uses international experience as a reference point in evaluating the following questions. First, what are the causes of currency appreciation, as viewed from theory and international practice? Second, how have economic policy makers in other countries dealt with pressure on their currencies to appreciate? Third, what have the consequences been of measures to deal with currency appreciation, particularly with respect to foreign trade, the balance of trade, the terms of trade, commodity prices, economic growth, and economic structure? Fourth, in considering reform of the RMB exchange rate system, what lessons can be derived from the experience of other countries?

Pressure for a currency to appreciate: theory and international experience

Theoretical explanations

The main reason the currency of a fast-growing economy appreciates against another currency is greater productivity sustained over a long-term period. The simple and intuitive explanation is as follows. If one country's productivity grows faster than others, the goods that it trades on the international market will be more competitive. It will enjoy a greater ability to export and to employ import substitution. Each of these will lower its need for foreign currency and will therefore increase supply for such currency, such that the price of foreign currency will decrease. The forces of supply and demand in the market for currencies will mean that its own currency will appreciate in value. If advances in productivity are sustained, with respect to one country's traded goods versus those of others, the country's currency will continue to appreciate.

A systematic theoretical explanation was proposed for this in the 1960s and is known as the Balassa-Samuelson Effect (Balassa 1964; Samuelson 1964). It looked at the impact of changes in productivity of two countries on the relative prices of both traded goods and non-traded goods. In this model, both labor and capital could move freely. The basic conclusion of Balassa and Samuelson was that if one country's traded goods enjoyed a higher productivity relative to another country, the prices of its traded goods would go down and the real price of its currency would go up. The underlying logic of this was that the level of wages in sectors that produced traded goods would rise, as a result of rapid productivity increases.

If labor markets were perfectly competitive, then wages of non-traded sectors would increase correspondingly, leading prices of non-traded goods to increase as well. Suppose that international prices are not affected: then prices of traded goods will be determined by the international market and will not be influenced by changes in productivity or wages. Eventually, prices of non-traded goods will rise as well and the real exchange rate of the economy's currency will appreciate.

Under a system in which exchange rates are fixed, the primary channel through which the 'real exchange rate' can be expressed is through domestic prices, which will rise. Under a system in which the exchange rate is flexible, the way the 'real exchange rate' will be expressed is through appreciation of the currency. This may also be accompanied by the requisite amount of inflation.

If government does not intervene in the currency markets, the exchange rate will adjust on its own, responding to productivity increases. So-called 'pressure to appreciate' will not exist. Another factor, therefore, leading to a currency's 'pressure to appreciate' is government intervention – whether that is through the adoption of a fixed exchange-rate system or the adoption of other 'non-clean' systems that prevent spontaneous adjustments in supply and demand relationships of the exchange-rate market.

Pressure on a currency to appreciate has both internal and external aspects. Theoretical analysis has focused mainly on internal aspects. Very little systematic analysis has been done that looks at such 'external' aspects as political issues.

Internal pressure on a currency to appreciate is manifested mainly in the 'release' or increase in basic money supply, and the resulting risk of inflation and an asset bubble. Under most circumstances, pressures on currency to appreciate are the result of inventions by monetary authorities in their foreign exchange markets. Another common result of the intervention of monetary authorities in foreign exchange markets is the release of large quantities of one's own currency in the market in the course of purchasing foreign currencies. If the speed of currency intervention is too great, that is, too much of one's own currency is released too quickly, inflation and an asset-price bubble may result.

'Sterilization' measures have been regarded as one acceptable measure in dealing with the oversupply of currency caused by market interventions. Academic circles have raised doubts about their effectiveness and their sustainability, however. The effectiveness of such measures depends upon such conditions as effective policy controls over capital, and a situation in which domestic and foreign assets are not fully interchangeable. Even though such measures might be workable in the short run, in the long run, they are unsustainable. Ongoing large-scale sterilization measures lead to financial losses that the monetary authority finds too large to bear.

In the end, dissolving pressure on a currency to appreciate, while still maintaining the benefits of rising productivity, requires two things. One is adjustments to the nominal exchange rate. The other is inflation. Both of these result in an appreciation of the real exchange rate. In so doing, they reflect the necessary adjustment in relative prices as required by the rise in productivity.

Traditionally, research on currency appreciation has concentrated on macroeconomic stability. In addition to this, however, attention should be paid to the fact that currency pressures can result in imbalances of resource allocation and distortions of economic structure. The model presented by Zhang Bin and He Fang in 2005 emphasizes the problems that can arise when monetary authorities fail to allow the real exchange rate to adjust in line with changes in productivity. These problems include irrational resource allocation and structural problems in the economy. They include income distribution that is detrimental to workers but favorable to the owners of capital, a slowing of the movement of China's labor force from rural to urban areas, an excessive reliance on demand from overseas markets, and more of the economy engaged in manufacturing than in service industries.

The case of Germany

The text below focuses on two countries that experienced sustained and rapid economic growth, combined with pressures to appreciate their currencies. It looks as the measures each country adopted to deal with the pressures, and the consequences of those measures. In its period of rapid economic growth, the Deutschmark (DEM) appreciated by 1.8 times, going from DEM 4.17 to the US dollar in 1960 to DEM 1.49 to the US dollar in 1990. Germany's monetary authorities were under no great pressure from internal or external sources, for two reasons. First, the government had no intention of maintaining a fixed exchange rate system, and second, the government did not intend to risk inflation by intervening in currency markets.

Between 1960 and 1990, the DEM exchange rate and pressures on the currency to appreciate went through two main stages. The first was prior to the dissolution of the Bretton Woods system. The DEM was revalued against the dollar several times during this period. Pressures on Germany's monetary authorities, however, and the international debate on currency in general, focused mainly on how to preserve the Bretton Woods system. This was in contrast to the bilateral pressure that China is currently facing.

During the 1950s and 1960s, the United States was able to maintain a positive balance of trade but its massive numbers of armed forces stationed abroad and its foreign aid meant a depleted balance of international payments. During most of the Bretton Woods period, the US balance of payments was negative. In 1960, official gold deposits held by the government still totaled 5.08 million ounces. These had declined to less than 3 million by the time Bretton Woods was being dismantled. In 1962, US foreign debt began to exceed foreign assets and the disparity between the two then continued to grow. The US dollar was linked to gold, and the price of other currencies was linked to the dollar. The market now began to doubt this 'double link' system. Speculation in the dollar rose as a result.

As a major economic entity at the time, Germany had a responsibility to help the United States maintain the stability of the international currency system. The country revalued the DEM several times, intervening in the currency and gold markets to the extent of closing them down altogether. It increased its loans to the IMF and took other such measures. Generally speaking, however, pressures on Germany came mainly from the United States. In addition, topics under debate in the international community were not just about the exchange rate of any given country. They included such things as lowering US spending on foreign military activities, intervention in the gold market and currency markets, restraints on the movement of capital, amendments to the General Arrangements to Borrow of the IMF, and even abandoning the fixed ratio of the US dollar against gold. All of these were viewed as possible solutions to the problems at the time.

Germany's economy was growing strongly and the country's positive balance of trade was continuing to increase. The problem that Germany's monetary authorities confronted, however, was not just that their own country was facing pressure to appreciate but that all major currencies at the time were revaluing against the price of gold. This then required bilateral currency adjustments among all currencies.

In December of 1971, a number of countries signed the Smithsonian Agreement and simultaneously revalued their currencies against the US dollar. These countries included Germany, Japan, the United Kingdom, France, Italy, the Netherlands, and Sweden. At the same time, the United States ceased to sell gold at the price of USD 38 per ounce.

After the collapse of the Bretton Woods system, Germany adopted a floating exchange-rate system for the DEM (see Figure 7.1). Given the country's strongly positive balance of trade, expectations in the market for an appreciation of the currency were high. German intervention in the markets made it extremely difficult to control money supply on the domestic market, which exacerbated the inflation precipitated by the oil crisis.

On March 1, 1973, German monetary authorities bought in the record-breaking figure of USD 2.7 billion within the space of one day. The country closed foreign exchange markets on March 2 due to market pressure. Since then, Germany has adopted a floating exchange-rate regime, letting market supply and demand play

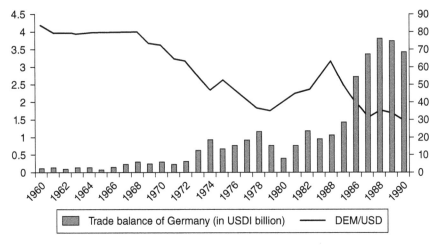

Figure 7.1 Germany's trade balance and its exchange rate.

Source: IFS.

a bigger role in determining exchange rates. Since the market has been able to release most intrinsic pressures on the currency, the DEM has been quite stable in terms of appreciation and depreciation. The country has not had to make dramatic adjustments in the course of the various joint international interventions that have followed, such as the Plaza Agreement.

The case of Japan

The Japanese yen also appreciated during a period when Japan's economy sustained rapid growth. Between 1960 and 1990, the Japanese yen (JPY) appreciated by 1.5 times relative to the US dollar, from 360 to one US dollar in 1960 to 144 to one US dollar in 1990 (see Figure 7.2). In contrast to Germany, however, Japan faced much greater internal and external pressure to appreciate its currency. The country adopted a number of measures to delay the pace of this. In the end, this only aggravated the pressure brought to bear on monetary policies and the appreciation was accomplished through stringent controls. Compared to the drawn-out process in Germany, Japan's currency appreciation was concentrated in several fairly short periods.

The overall process of JPY appreciation, between 1960 and 1990, can be divided into two stages. The first was from 1960 until the Nixon Shock in 1971. During this period, Japan gradually shifted to a positive trade account, while the fixed JPY–USD exchange rate stayed at 360. Before 1970, both policymakers in Japan and the public at large lacked confidence in the stability of the Japanese economy. They felt that the underlying foundation for a positive balance of trade was still not firm. All sides supported the existing monetary system, which

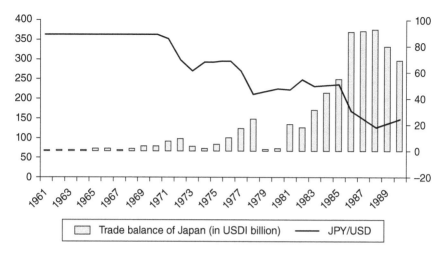

Figure 7.2 Japan's positive balance of trade, as graphed against its exchange rate.
Source: IFS

included a fixed exchange rate at 360 JPY to one US dollar. Instead of changing the exchange rate, all felt that the key to reducing the trade surplus would instead be to increase government spending and to increase imports. Appreciating the currency might lead the Japanese economy into a recession.

In mid-August, 1971, after Nixon gave his speech, markets began selling off the US dollar. With the exception of France, all major European countries temporarily shut down their currency markets. Japan, instead, continued to buy in foreign currency at the rate of 360 yen to the dollar. Within the space of two short weeks, Japan had purchased 4 billion US dollars. This was roughly equivalent to one-half of Japan's foreign exchange reserves at the time. To purchase that amount of dollars, the government released roughly 1.5 trillion yen into the market. At the time, Japan's total M1 money supply was only around 24 trillion. Monetary authorities were then faced with the choice between two evils: accept inflation, or revalue the currency. At the same time, the country began to confront international pressure (to appreciate) coming from the direction of the United States. At the end of 1971, Japan agreed to revalue its currency by 16.9 percent as stipulated in the Smithsonian Agreement. At the time, the extent of this appreciation was greater than that undertaken by any other currency.

After 1973, Japan adopted a floating exchange-rate system. For a period, the international market was highly distrustful of the currency, given its appreciation and also given the impact of the oil crisis, yet Japan's economy was the first to emerge from the oil crisis. Its trade surplus began to rebound, and its currency again began to feel the pressure to appreciate. After 1975, Japan's floating exchange-rate system made very frequent use of currency interventions. Most of these were in the form of buying in US dollars, so as to reduce the amount of pressure on the yen. Despite its appreciating currency, Japan still faced censure from the international community for its huge trade surplus and its many currency interventions. Trade sanctions imposed by the United States were increasingly severe.

The second oil crisis erupted in 1979. From that year until 1984, due to the high-interest policy of the United States and the fact that Japan's insurance companies and pension funds purchased millions of dollars worth of US government bonds, Japan faced little specific pressure to further appreciate its currency. The international community still regarded the US dollar as overvalued, however, which meant that all major currencies, including the mark and the yen, were under pressure to revalue. In August of 1985, the group that became known as the 'G5,' namely the USA, the UK, Germany, Japan, and France, signed the Plaza Agreement. Its aim was to prevent the US dollar from appreciating further. At the same time, delegates to the meeting pointed out that they were not seeking a rapid devaluation of the dollar either. Japan's Finance Minister at the time, Takeshita Noboru, declared in no uncertain terms that Japan could accept an appreciation of its own currency by ten to twenty percent. This was beyond the expectations of the United States. Japan was making this large concession in order to ameliorate trade sanctions imposed by the US Congress. The Plaza Agreement was implemented in very successful fashion, with the US dollar depreciating modestly, as desired. With the need to intervene much less than expected, the G5 was able to depreciate the US dollar by ten to twenty percent. After this, however, the Japanese yen kept on appreciating for several years, arousing criticism and displeasure from parties within the country. During this period, monetary authorities attempted a number of interventions, but with only modest results. Japan's Prime Minister and Finance Minister jointly sent a letter to the United States, requesting assistance in preventing further appreciation of the yen. Assistance was denied, and the reason given was that protectionist sentiment in the US Congress was very strong. Until real improvement could be shown in the country's trade surplus, the United States was unwilling to modify its exchange-rate policy. Japan then began to adopt a low interest-rate policy, partly in order to stimulate its domestic economy and partly in order to lessen pressure on the yen to appreciate following the Plaza Agreement.

Measures aimed at dealing with pressure to appreciate one's currency

Disparities in labor productivity between countries are the ultimate source of pressures to appreciate a country's currency. Such disparities are reflected in the international balance of payments. Through the mechanism of foreign-exchange markets, such disparities bring pressure to bear on the price of currencies, such that exchange rates are adjusted. There are two main categories of measures aimed at dealing with such pressure. The first is directed at exchange rates themselves, both through market forces and through external political pressure. The second is directed at the domestic economy and includes such things as low interest-rate policies, expansionist fiscal policies, trade policies, financial market regulations, and foreign investment policies. The purpose of these is to reduce trade surpluses and lessen pressure on the currency to appreciate.

Measures undertaken by Germany

Taking the dissolution of the Bretton Woods system as the line of demarcation, German measures to deal with an appreciating currency can be divided into two phases. During the time of the Bretton Woods system, Germany was the major party negotiating with the United States. The core issue was maintaining an international monetary system that involved a gold standard, a US dollar pegged to gold, and other currencies all pegged to the US dollar. The relevant measures that Germany adopted during this time were as follows:

In 1961, the DEM was appreciated against the USD by 5 percent.

In 1962, Germany put up USD 1 billion in capital to the part of the IMF called the General Arrangements to Borrow (GAB). Its main concern was that the US would need to borrow from the IMF.

In 1967, the President of the Deutsche Bundesbank, Karl Blessing, stated in a letter to the Chairman of the Federal Reserve of the United States that the Federal Republic of Germany officially agreed not to buy gold from the United States.

In April of 1969, the Finance Minister of Germany agreed that the country would re-evaluate its currency as part of a new multilateral currency arrangement. In the following two days, the Deutsche Bank purchased USD 4 billion as part of an effort to stabilize currency markets.

In May of 1969, the German Cabinet announced that it would refuse to revalue the mark 'forever.'

In May of 1969, Germany adopted new regulatory methods that controlled the influx of capital from abroad. The country reduced government expenditures, and implemented a mandatory fee that was equivalent to an export tax and an import subsidy, called a 'border-crossing (or transit) fee.' It temporarily implemented a 100 percent required reserve on foreign exchange deposits.

In September of 1969, Germany allowed the mark to float freely.

In October of 1969, the mark was revalued by 9.3 percent following an election. Germany loosened controls over the inflow of speculative capital.

In 1971, Carl Wilhelm Scheele, Minster of Economic Affairs of Germany, proposed the idea of havingall European currencies float, at a meeting of finance ministers of European countries. In August 1971, impacted by the speech given by Nixon, Germany closed its foreign exchange markets.

In December of 1971, Germany agreed to revalue the mark by 13.6 percent against the dollar as stipulated in the G10's Smithsonian Agreement.

In June of 1972, in order to maintain the exchange-rate levels specified by the Smithsonian Agreement, Germany and other countries intervened in foreign exchange markets.

On June 29, 1972, the German government stopped selling German treasury bonds to foreigners with the aim of relieving pressure on appreciating the mark.

Once Germany adopted a system of floating exchange rates, monetary authorities were less active in interventions. From 1973 to 1979, the currency appreciated steadily. From 1979 to 1984, it then depreciated in value. After the Plaza Agreement, signed in 1984, it again appreciated. Germany is more concerned with the stability of its domestic money supply, so has undertaken only limited interventions in the foreign exchange market. Most interventions before and after the Plaza Agreement were conducted in conjunction with a number of other countries.

Measures undertaken by Japan

In the latter part of the 1960s, on the eve of the demise of the Bretton Woods system, Japan began to face pressure in terms of the exchange rate of its currency. Initially, the pressure came from the United States, which felt that Japan had a responsibility to help the US improve the international payments situation. Nevertheless, the main issues and negotiating points at the time had to do with Europe, not with Japan. Japan adopted the following measures with respect to countering pressure to appreciate its own currency:

In June 1971, the Japanese government declared an 'Eight-Point Plan' to reduce its surplus of international payments and relieve pressure on appreciating the yen. The 'Eight-Point Plan' referred to: liberalizing imports, granting preferential tariffs to underdeveloped countries, cutting tariffs, boosting domestic and outbound capital investments, lowering non-tariff barriers, strengthening economic aid to foreign countries, evaluating the stimulus effect of export duties, and instituting a more 'orderly market.'

In December of 1971, Japan agreed to allow the yen to appreciate by 16.9 percent against the US dollar, as stipulated in the Smithsonian Agreement reached by the G10.

After the dissolution of the Bretton Woods system, pressure on the yen to appreciate lessened during the second oil crisis and the period of high interest rates in the United States. The rest of the time, pressure to appreciate continued, in tandem with the expansion of Japan's trade surplus. Japanese government measures to deal with this pressure included the following:

In 1977, Takeo Fukuda, Prime Minister of Japan, reshuffled his cabinet, absorbing in several 'expansionists' in the process, and established a ministerial position that was exclusively concerned with foreign economic affairs.

He appointed Ushiba Nobuhiko as Minister of Foreign Economic Affairs, with the aim of seeking compromise with the United States.

In 1978, Japan accepted the adoption of a plan to drive forward the world's economy through expansive fiscal measures, as put forward at the Bonn Summit.

In 1982, Japanese institutions were permitted to make foreign direct investments in other countries.

In 1984, the committee charged with evaluating the 'Japanese yenand the US dollar' submitted a report that recommended the opening up of Japanese financial markets, and particularly the development of a Japanese-yen currency market in Europe. At the time, economists belonging to the monetary school of thought believed that, given the huge trade surplus of Japan, the ongoing weakness of its currency related to the barriers and distortions of Japanese financial markets. These prevented the foreign exchange markets from coming up with a valid exchange rate.

In 1985, Takeshita Noboru, Finance Minister of Japan, signed the Plaza Agreement, agreeing to appreciate the yen by 10 to 20 percent.

In 1986, Nakasone Yasuhiro and Takeshita Noboru, Prime Minister and Finance Minister of Japan, jointly wrote a letter to President Reagan and Treasury Secretary Baker, asking for help in stopping the yen from appreciating further. This was rejected.

In 1986, Kiichi Miyazawa assumed the post of Finance Minister, after Takeshita Noboru. He held secret meetings with Treasury Secretary James Baker and reached an agreement on how to reduce US deficits while at the same time relieving pressures on currency appreciation in Japan. The main substance of the agreement said that Japan was to expand its fiscal stimulus program, including tax reductions, and was to cut the discount rate from 3.5 percent to 3 percent. The United States agreed to stop depreciating the dollar and it issued yen-denominated treasury bills to support this.

In 1987, Japan signed the Louvre Agreement and adopted measures to stimulate domestic demand and stabilize its exchange rate.

In 1988, Japan again lowered its interest rate from 3 percent to 2.5 percent. This was intended to stimulate the domestic economy and relieve the pressure on an appreciating yen.

Evaluation of the effectiveness of measures to deal with the pressure of an appreciating currency

Currency appreciation and measures adopted to relieve the pressure on currency appreciation inflict not only short-term, but also long-term, impacts on the real economy. In what follows, we look at the trajectory of major economic variables relevant to the exchange rate during a period of currency appreciation. We evaluate the relationships among them from the perspectives of foreign trade and terms of trade, macroeconomic stability, labor productivity, and economic structure.

Germany

Foreign trade and terms of trade

More than ten years of an appreciating currency did not prevent Germany from growing both its imports and its exports. In order to look at the real impact of currency fluctuations on real foreign trade, Figure 7.3 uses actual quantities rather than nominal values for imports and exports. This leaves out prices. These two variables have a much closer relationship with other real domestic economic variables such as employment and economic growth. From Figure 7.3, we can see that the exchange rate between the mark and the dollar fluctuated constantly after the 1970s, but both over the medium and long term, Germany's imports and exports continued on a steadily upward-rising trend line. During this same period, we can see that interventions in the mark–dollar exchange rate had a distinct impact on quantities imported and exported in the short term. After the mark started depreciating in 1980, real imports declined dramatically. Real exports were relatively stable. The real trade surplus increased. In 1985, after the mark appreciated substantially, the growth in real exports leveled off for a while, but real imports increased quickly and the real trade surplus contracted.

The appreciation of the mark was distinctly favorable to Germany's terms of trade. We were not able to find adequate data for the period prior to the 1980s, but the period from 1980 to 1995 shows the relationship between the mark–dollar exchange rate and Germany's terms of trade. Figure 7.4 demonstrates how terms of trade were not greatly impacted by a depreciated mark in the early part of the 1980s, but it also demonstrates that the appreciation of the mark after that was

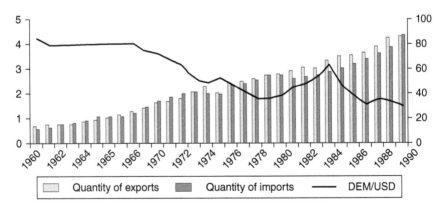

Figure 7.3 Germany's exports, imports, and the DEM to USD exchange rate.

Source: WDI.

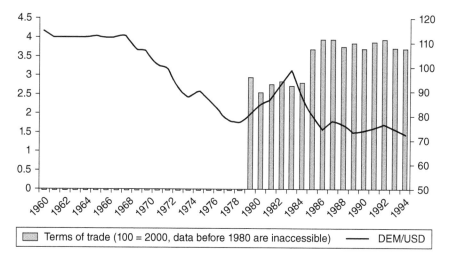

Figure 7.4 Terms of trade and the DEM to USD exchange rate.
Source: WDI.

tremendously beneficial to the terms of trade. Between 1985 and 1995, the mark appreciated from 2.46 to the dollar to 1.43 to the dollar. During the same period, the terms of trade rose from 93.3 to 107.4.

Macroeconomic stability

Two key indicators of macroeconomic stability are inflation and economic growth, specifically, the inflation rate and the degree to which it varies, and the deviation of real economic growth from potential economic growth. Prior to 1972, Germany pegged its exchange rate to the US dollar. Appreciation of the currency and its volatility were limited. Once Germany instituted policies that allowed the mark to float against the dollar, the country's currency began a period of distinct appreciation. In what follows, we compare Germany's macroeconomic conditions prior to and after this change in 1972.

During the period prior to 1972, when the mark was relatively stable, the inflation rate in Germany was an average of 2.8 percent between the years 1961 and 1972, with a standard deviation of 1.07. The deviation of real economic growth from potential economic growth in these years was 2.11. After 1972, the mark began to appreciate. Between 1973 and 1990, Germany's inflation rate averaged 3.78 with a standard deviation of 2.13. The deviation of real from potential economic growth was 2.01.

Generally speaking, Germany's inflation rate and the volatility of that rate were not greatly affected by the appreciation of its currency. Both stayed at a reasonable level. In the latter period, the somewhat higher average inflation rate and volatility were clearly impacted by the two oil crises. Nevertheless, the standard

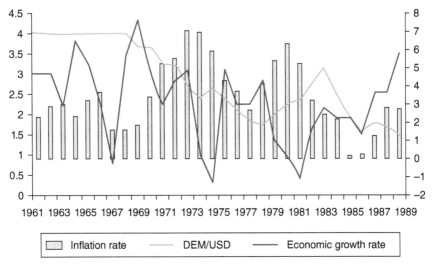

Figure 7.5 Economic volatility, inflation, and the DEM to USD exchange rate.
Source: WDI.

deviation of economic growth was essentially the same as the earlier period, which shows that Germany did not experience great economic volatility simply due to the appreciation of its currency. Germany did face intense economic shocks from the oil crises during the latter period, yet its real economy was able to remain relatively stable. To a certain degree, this may well have been due to the fact that it had adopted a floating exchange-rate system (see Figure 7.5).

Labor productivity and economic structure

From the perspective of economic growth and economic welfare, the key things that we are concerned with here are the impact of an appreciating currency and measures taken to deal with an appreciating currency on such things as labor productivity, industrial structure, and economic structure. Data on industrial structure was hard to come by in our research, but changes in labor productivity are fairly closely aligned with industrial structure. Figure 7.6 shows the fluctuations in the exchange rate of the mark as compared to the real GDP per working hour in Germany in the period from 1970 to 1995. Despite considerable appreciation of the currency, labor productivity as expressed by real GDP per working hour hardly changed. It fluctuated only slightly around the trend line.

With respect to changes in economic structure during a period of currency appreciation, we undertook the following evaluation. We looked at the ratio between service industries and GDP on the supply-side structure, and at the ratio between consumption and GDP on the demand-side structure. A nominal appreciation of the currency should suppress the price of tradable goods denominated

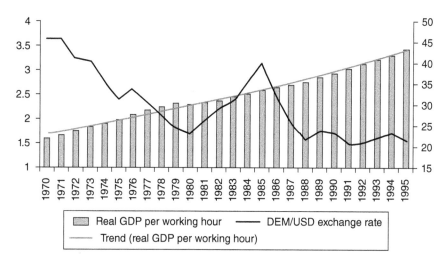

Figure 7.6 Labor productivity and the DEM to USD exchange rate.

Source: WDI. The real GDP per unit of working hour data came from Penn World Table 6.3.

in the domestic currency, and increase the relative prices of non-tradable products as represented by products of the service industry. This should drive capital and labor into service sectors, thereby improving the added-value of those sectors and increasing the 'service industries to GDP' ratio. At the same time, it should increase the added-value of 'service industries to GDP' ratio. Meanwhile, the 'industrial added-value to GDP' ratio should fall. In Germany, we observed that changes in the 'service industries added-value to GDP' ratio conformed perfectly to the theoretical expectation during periods of a fluctuating exchange rate.

Between 1970 and 1980, as the mark was appreciating, the 'service industries added-value to GDP' ratio climbed steadily from 48.2 percent in 1970, to 56.5 percent in 1980, at an average annual rate of 0.75 percent. In the early and mid-1980s, as the mark was depreciating, the growth of the 'service industries added-value to GDP' ratio fell, showing an average annual growth rate of only 0.29 percent between 1981 and 1985. After the Plaza Agreement in 1985, as the mark started a new round of appreciation, Germany's 'service industries added-value to GDP' ratio grew at an average annual rate of 0.76 percent between 1986 and 1995.

In the two decades between 1970 and 1990, Germany's 'service industries added-value to GDP' ratio grew consistently. During that same period, the exchange rate of the country's currency appreciated overall, with modest depreciation at times.

On the one hand, what this shows is that the exchange rate is only one of a number of factors influencing the ratios studied as above. Other key economic variables supported the upward trend of the 'service industries added-value to GDP' ratio in Germany (see Figure 7.7). On the other hand, the close link between the exchange rate and the ratio also indicates that exchange rates are of vital importance to the ratio.

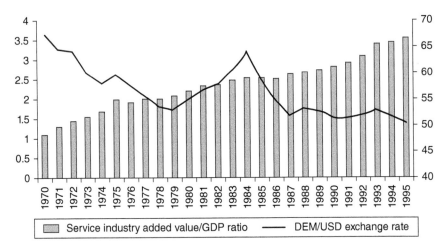

Figure 7.7 'Service industries added-value to GDP ratio,' and the DEM–USD exchange rate.

Source: WDI.

In order to counter pressures to appreciate their currency, economic policymakers in Germany were inclined to adopt a strategy of expanding domestic demand, to try to make up for the loss of economic stimulus caused by declining exports. Nevertheless, the experience of Germany indicates at the very least that the relationship between fluctuations in the exchange rate and the 'consumption-to-GDP' ratio is quite indeterminate (see Figure 7.8). Sometimes there was a positive correlation;

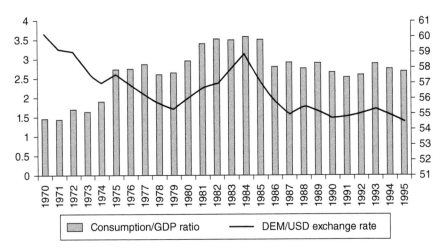

Figure 7.8 The consumption-to-GDP ratio, and the DEM–USD exchange rate.

Source: WDI.

at other times the correlation was negative. Over the entire period of the study, the consumption-to-GDP ratio in Germany was quite stable. It remained between 54.5 percent and 60 percent. It climbed twice in the decade between the mid-1970s and the mid-1980s, but this was not due to a sudden increase in consumption. Rather it was due to the sudden lowering of GDP growth due to both oil crises and the high interest-rate policy of the United States. If one omits these anomalies, the consumption-to-GDP ratio in Germany would have been stable.

Japan

Foreign trade and terms of trade

In overall terms, the appreciation of Japan's currency after the 1970s did not curtail a steady and constant growth in Japan's real exports and imports (see Figure 7.9). In the short term, however, imports and exports were impacted by exchange rates. In the period between 1980 and 1985, when the yen stopped appreciating relative to the dollar, Japan's real exports increased sharply while real imports stagnated. Japan's trade surplus grew dramatically.

In 1985 and 1986, after the yen appreciated sharply, real exports declined somewhat for a time while imports rose greatly and the real trade surplus fell to a degree. What this indicates is that, over a short period, the appreciating yen did play a role in reducing Japan's real trade surplus.

Appreciation of the yen has played a distinct role in improving Japan's terms of trade. We were unable to get data on this prior to the 1980s. From 1980 to 1995, however, we used the yen to dollar exchange rates and changes in the country's

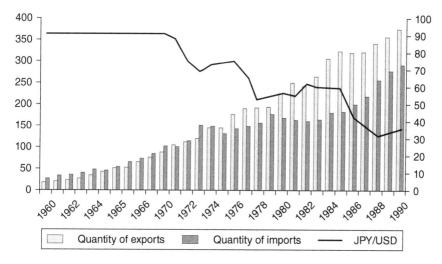

Figure 7.9 Japan's imports and exports, and the yen to US dollar exchange rate.

Source: WDI.

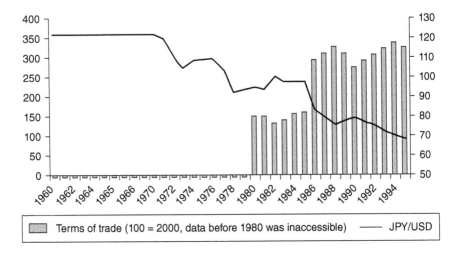

Figure 7.10 Japan's terms of trade, and the yen to US dollar exchange rate.

Source: WDI.

terms of trade for analysis. Figure 7.10 indicates that the appreciation of the yen brought with it a sustained improvement in Japan's terms of trade. Between 1980 and 1995, the yen appreciated from 226 to 94 to the dollar, while Japan's terms of trade rose from 79.7 to 114.9. Japanese economists believe that it was after the yen started appreciating substantially, in the aftermath of the Plaza Agreement in 1985, that the Japanese people came to realize the benefits of a stronger currency. The lower prices of imported goods were a particularly important contribution to the wellbeing of the Japanese people (Paul Volcker, ToyooGyohten, 1997).

Macroeconomic stability

Prior to 1972, the yen to dollar exchange rate remained relatively stable. After 1972, the yen consistently appreciated. Between 1961 and 1972, inflation was 5.8 percent on average, with a standard deviation of 1.3. The standard deviation of economic growth, regarded as the disparity between real economic growth and potential growth, was 2.82 in this period.

After 1972, while the yen appreciated, the average inflation rate was 5.54 (between 1973 and 1990) with a standard deviation of 5.55. The standard deviation of economic growth during this period was 2.24. Relatively speaking, there was no great difference between inflation and economic growth before and after the yen appreciated. There was, however, a great difference in volatility. The volatility of inflation went from a standard deviation of 1.3 to one of 5.5.

Germany and Japan both adopted a floating exchange rate in 1973, which makes it possible to compare the two. Between 1973 and 1990, the average inflation rate in Germany was 3.78 percent, with a standard deviation of 2.13. Both the inflation rate itself, and the volatility of the rate, were therefore far below those of Japan. Volatility in Japan may be attributed in large part to the operational errors of the country's monetary policy. The severe inflation after 1972 was closely related to the Japanese government's intervention in currency markets, during which a large amount of yen was put on the market (see Figure 7.11).

The asset price bubble that occurred in Japan was closely related to the country's exchange-rate policies. After 1985, Japanese authorities felt that the yen should not continue to appreciate. Under great pressure to intervene, the government indicated that it intended to do so. Government intervention alone was not sufficient to change the direction of market sentiment, however, which assumed an appreciating currency. As a result, yen-denominated prices of assets continued to rise, as per expectations. To exacerbate things, Japanese monetary authorities then constantly lowered the discount rate in order to try to relieve pressure on the currency appreciation. They did this despite the fact that the real economy was performing well, and this led to excessive liquidity in the market. The mainstream thinking among Japanese economists is that loose monetary policies were the primary cause of the country's asset price bubble (Koruda, 2003).

The worsening of Japan's fiscal situation was also closely related to the country's exchange-rate policy. The government believed that expansionary economic policies would contribute to reducing the trade surplus and bring down pressure on the currency to appreciate. In the latter part of the 1970s, the government adopted strongly expansionist fiscal policies, in part to appease the international community, which was registering complaints about Japan's trade surplus and its strong currency. As

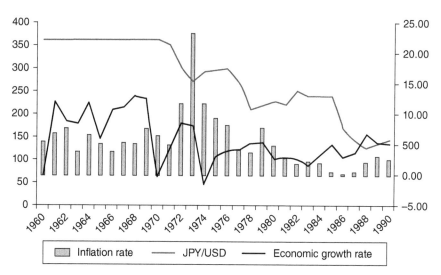

Figure 7.11 Economic volatility and inflation in Japan, and the yen to US dollar exchange rate.

Source: WDI.

a result, Japan's fiscal situation deteriorated. By 1985, the country's deficit was 22 percent of its budget. Outstanding public debt amounted to 42 percent of GNP, the highest percentage among all developed countries at the time. Moreover, throughout the mid-1980s, the Japanese government repeatedly promised the international community that it would increase domestic expenditures and cut taxes, with the same aim of reducing the trade surplus and the pressure on the yen to appreciate.

Labor productivity and economic structure

As described by Figure 7.12 below, we evaluated the fluctuations in the yen's exchange rate between 1970 and 1995 in terms of the 'real GDP per unit of working hour' in Japan. The real GDP per working hour fluctuated slightly around the trend line. In the 1970s, when the yen was appreciating greatly, labor productivity was above the trend line. It was below the trend line, however, in the early 1980s during a period when the yen was generally stable. It was also below the trend line in the mid- and late 1980s, when the yen was appreciating. We therefore cannot find any apparent correlation between labor productivity and the yen's exchange rate.

As the yen appreciated, the 'service industries value-added to GDP ratio' maintained a consistently rising trend. This is in line with theoretical expectations and also in line with the experience in Germany. The yen's exchange rate in the period between 1970 and 1995 can basically be viewed in three stages. The first saw appreciation from the early 1970s to the end of the decade. The second saw a leveling off until the mid-1980s. The third saw steady appreciation after that, until 1995. In the first period, when appreciation of the yen was occurring, the 'service industries value-added to GDP ratio' grew at an average annual rate of 0.65 percent. From 1981 to 1985, that rate remained stable, still growing, but at the

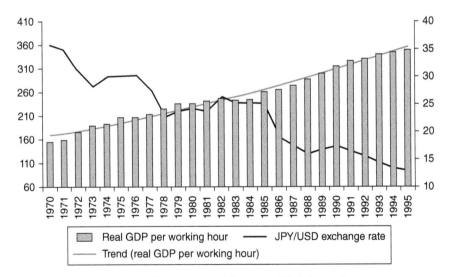

Figure 7.12 Labor productivity in Japan and the yen to US dollar exchange rate.

Source: WDI; the data for the real GDP per working hour came from Penn World Table 6.3.

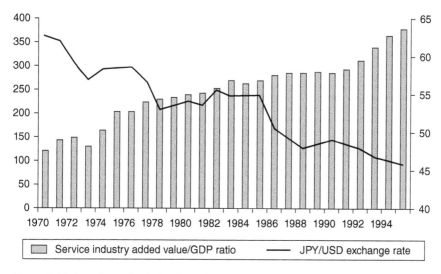

Figure 7.13 Japan's service industries value-added to GDP ratio, and the yen to US dollar exchange rate.

Source: WDI.

diminished rate of 0.38 percent. From 1986 to 1995, as the yen's value increased the ratio also grew, climbing to an annual rate of 0.67 percent.

Japan's experience once again makes it clear that, although a currency's exchange rate is not the only determinant on the 'service industries value-added to GDP ratio,' it has a major influence (see Figure 7.13).

Like labor productivity, it is hard to discern any relationship between exchange rate fluctuations and the 'consumption-to-GDP ratio.' In the 1960s, during a period when the yen to dollar exchange rate was relatively stable, the consumption-to-GDP ratio in Japan was also stable until the middle of the decade. It stayed at around 53 percent. After that, in the middle and latter part of the decade, it began to decline. In 1969 and 1970, it even dropped below 50 percent before starting to climb again. During more than two decades in which the yen steadily appreciated, the consumption-to-GDP ratio experienced both ups and downs – the exchange rate and the ratio did not appear to be closely linked. Overall, the consumption-to-GDP ratio in Japan has been quite stable, mostly staying between 50 percent to 54 percent (see Figure 7.14).

Lessons to be derived from the international experience with respect to reform of the RMB exchange-rate system in China

A summary of the international experience

By looking back at the experience of Japan and Germany over the past three decades, we have been able to recognize some underlying laws governing what

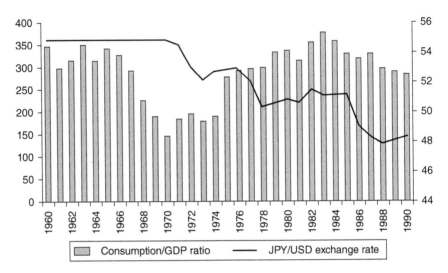

Figure 7.14 The consumption-to-GDP ratio in Japan, and the yen to US dollar exchange rate.

Source: WDI.

happened. As a result, we are now able to sum up some lessons about how to deal with the pressures of an appreciating currency.

First, in the face of massive changes in relative economic strength, measures taken merely to ameliorate the pressure of currency appreciation will have little effect. Real adjustments to the exchange rate are inevitable. Both Japan and Germany witnessed substantial currency appreciation for two decades. Although the early and mid-1980s saw some downturns, in the end the currency appreciation in both countries was considerable. The most direct pressure to appreciate came from the trade surplus of both countries, or, one could say, the trade deficit of the United States. Both Germany and Japan have highly competitive manufacturing sectors. Although a trade surplus, as a determining factor, is highly complex, in these cases the driving force behind the trade surplus was a rise in the productivity of the traded-goods sectors. This improved the competitiveness of exports and enabled import substitution. In Germany and Japan, an increase in labor productivity in the manufacturing sectors was what supported economic growth. As a result, the appreciation of their currencies was inevitable. Both countries adopted a range of measures to slow the rise. These included intervention in foreign-exchange markets, restrictions on the short-term inflow of foreign capital, export incentives, expansion of foreign direct investment, an increase in fiscal spending, and lowering the discount rate. In the end, the impact of these measures on imports, exports, and the trade surplus, was highly limited.

Second, not only is intervention unable to stop a currency from appreciating, but the price paid for trying to do so can be extremely high. Both Germany and Japan made several attempts in this regard. Not only did they pay a heavy price for it, but they did not accomplish stabilization of their currencies as a result. The experience of Japan has been particularly acute. In the early 1970s, the government of Japan placed over-reliance on the commitment made by the President and Treasury Secretary of the United States not to depreciate the dollar. Japan bought in US dollars from the market at the price of 360 yen to one dollar. The quantity of base-money yen that went into the market resulted in the severe inflation of 1973–1974. In the mid- and late 1980s, the Japanese government attempted to moderate the degree to which the yen was appreciating by increasing domestic government spending and repeatedly reducing the discount rate. The result was that low interest rates sparked an asset-price bubble and an ensuing economic crisis. The Japanese economy learned a tragic lesson from this experience: not only will rash, emergency government spending lead to enormous waste, but it will leave behind a deficit that lasts for years. To this day, the enormous deficit caused by the crisis is an ongoing hidden risk to Japan's economy. Japan's interventions failed to stop the yen from appreciating. They failed to solve the problems of a trade surplus in any fundamental way. In contrast with Germany, which intervened less in its currency markets, Japan's economy experienced greater inflationary volatility.

Third, the sustained appreciation of a currency will have a marked influence on real imports and exports in the short term, but will not change the trajectory of their growth in the medium to long term. Nor will an appreciating currency change the long-term trend of an increasing trade surplus. After the 1970s, both Japan and Germany saw dramatic appreciation of their currencies, and a correction to trade volume and trade balances occurred within one to two years following each rise in the currency. Imports and exports then returned to the long-term upward trend. Germany's trade surplus was maintained at a relatively lower level, while that of Japan was quite high and remained hard to bring under control.

Fourth, substantial and sustained currency appreciation can result in notably improved terms of trade and improved national welfare. The attitude of the public at large gradually shifts from initial opposition to understanding and support. The improvement of national welfare mainly derives from two considerations. The first is an improvement in labor productivity, which is to say, a rise in the productive capacity of the country overall. The second is an improvement in the country's terms of trade, which is to say, improvement in the country's ability to 'get a better deal.' With the same amount of domestically produced goods, the country can get more foreign-produced goods. In the case of Germany and Japan, improved terms of trade, driven by appreciating currencies, enabled an increase in national welfare. This provided the critical underpinning for acceptance by the public of a stronger currency.

Fifth, relatively large changes in the exchange rate had no marked effect on labor productivity. The examples of both Germany and Japan demonstrate that labor productivity basically stays on a trend line with only minor fluctuations despite large fluctuations in exchange rates. Labor productivity and exchange rates show little correlation, which also means that exchange rates are not a determining factor when it comes to labor productivity. Given the close relationship between economic structure and labor productivity, this would tend to mean that changing exchange rates will not impact the intrinsic processes of a restructuring economy.

Sixth, relatively large exchange-rate fluctuations do have a notable impact on industrial structure. Currency appreciation stimulates an increase in the 'service industries added-value to GDP ratio,' while currency depreciation slows it down. Both Japan and Germany had similar experiences in this regard. Currency appreciation was accompanied by an increase in contribution of service industries to the overall economy. In the early and mid-1980s, as the mark was depreciating and the yen was basically stable, the growth rate in this ratio fell by half, as compared to when both currencies were appreciating.

Lessons to be gained from the international experience as China reforms its RMB exchange-rate regime

First, given that China's relative economic power is growing rapidly, it will be hard to sustain an exchange-rate system that pegs the RMB to the dollar. China needs to shift toward a floating exchange-rate system that is guided by market supply and demand as soon as possible. The rise in productivity of China's manufacturing industries after the 1990s utterly changed China's situation with respect to foreign trade. Exports became more competitive. Import-substitution became more possible. These both played a role in increasing China's trade surplus. Looking at the experience of Japan and Germany under similar circumstances, if China were to continue in an attempt to peg the RMB to the dollar, not only would this not achieve a balance in supply and demand in currency markets, but it would bring tremendous pressure to bear on monetary supply within the country and on asset prices. If China continues with the peg, this will, moreover, lead to growing pressure from the international community, particularly those countries experiencing trade deficits. If these pressures are not mitigated, China's economy will be facing tremendous volatility. The country will be facing an asset-price bubble and the risk of a trade war. Meanwhile, it will be hard to maintain the current general level of the exchange rate in any event. Shifting as fast as possible to a floating exchange-rate system guided by market supply and demand is the best course to take in order to relieve pressure on the currency.

Second, excessively loose domestic monetary policies should not be adopted in order to lessen pressure on the currency to appreciate. The objective of having a stable exchange rate should be subservient to the goals of stabilizing inflation and asset prices. Germany and Japan provide an extremely clear contrast. Germany regarded 'stabilizing inflation' as the primary goal of monetary policy. Exchange rates were left up to the market. In contrast, Japan attempted to maintain exchange rate stability, or at least to moderate the degree of appreciation of the yen. To do this, it undertook major interventions in foreign exchange markets and even lowered the discount rate. The price the country paid for this was an inflation rate of over 10 percent in the 1970s, and a severe asset-price bubble in the mid- and late 1980s. Meanwhile, the yen simply continued to appreciate. During the same period, Germany's level of inflation and price volatility was far lower than that of

Japan. The mark rose but it also fell. Its depreciation in the early and mid-1980s was a major stimulus to Germany's economic growth at the time.

Third, temporary measures should be adopted to moderate the temporarily negative influence on the export sector of an appreciating currency. At the same time, the self-correcting capacities of the sector should be recognized. The experience of both Germany and Japan demonstrates that a major rise in the currency does have a short-term impact on real exports, exports, and the trade surplus, but that this moderates over a period of one to two years, with exports again rising to the general trend line. Temporary measures should be taken to relieve short-term problems brought on by challenges to exports, in order to prevent excessive volatility in the economy. At the same time, it is necessary not to underestimate the self-correcting abilities of the export sector.

Fourth, such fundamental supply-side factors as technological and systemic conditions help determine the trends of both exports and labor productivity. The role of exchange rates is much less apparent. Large currency appreciation will therefore not negatively affect exports and labor productivity in any noticeable way.

Fifth, exchange rate 'prices' are an important means by which resources are re-allocated. They help adjust economic structure. Currency appreciation is conducive to the development of service industries in particular. Once an economy has developed to a certain degree, service industries begin to occupy a larger percentage of the national economy and exchange rates play an extremely important role in making this happen. An appreciating currency increases the prices of non-traded goods, which helps attract resources into service industries. Not only is this concept supported in theory, but the experience of Germany and Japan shows it to be true. These countries have demonstrated the close relationship between the 'service industries-to-GDP ratio' and the extent of currency adjustments.

Sixth, over time, currency appreciation can bring about noticeably improved terms of trade and national welfare. Because of this, reform of the price-forming mechanisms of the RMB will increasingly gain domestic support. Certain exports that have a low value-added component will indeed face a problem of survival when the RMB appreciates. The great majority of people, however, will find that their purchasing power is enhanced. It will be easy for exporting sectors to blame their problems on an appreciating currency. At the same time, it will be hard for the vast majority of people to understand that their improved standard of living is due to the correlation between purchasing power and an appreciating currency. The case of Japan demonstrates that an appreciating currency initially faces domestic political opposition and criticism. Later, however, as national wellbeing improves, an appreciating currency is gradually understood and accepted.

Note

1 Zhang Bin: Director and Researcher of the Global Macroeconomic Research Laboratory of the Institute of World Economics and Politics of the Chinese Academy of Social Sciences.

Bibliography

Balassa, B. (1964) 'The Purchasing Power Parity Doctrine: A Reappraisal', *Journal of Political Economy* 72 (6): 584–596

Koruda, H. (2003) 'The Nixon Shocks and the Plaza Agreement: Lessons from Two Seemingly Failed Cases of Japan Exchange Rate Policy'. Speech paper submitted to the Institute of World Economics and Politics, Chinese Academy of Social Sciences

Samuelson, P.A. (1964) 'Theoretical Notes on Trade Problems', *Review of Economics and Statistics* 46 (2): 145–154

Volcker, P. and Gyohtenm, T. (1996) *Changing Fortunes*. Beijing: China Financial Publishing House

Index

For Product Safety Concerns and Information please contact our EU
representative GPSR@taylorandfrancis.com
Taylor & Francis Verlag GmbH, Kaufingerstraße 24, 80331 München, Germany

www.ingramcontent.com/pod-product-compliance
Ingram Content Group UK Ltd.
Pitfield, Milton Keynes, MK11 3LW, UK
UKHW021621240425
457818UK00018B/668